Praise for previous editions:

'Duncan Pritchard's *What is this thing called Knowled*
first introduction to epistemology. The summaries, up-to-date reading suggestions
and largely independent chapters make it very easy and flexible to use for instruc-
tors and students alike. The new chapters on applied epistemology are a great idea:
they show the relevance of epistemology to some of the most important problems
in modern-day life and society'.

Markus Lammenranta, *University of Helsinki, Finland*

'Pritchard's fourth edition of *What is this thing called Knowledge?* improves on an
already outstanding introductory text. With new chapters covering the relationship
between theory of knowledge and technology, law, politics and education this is a
highly accessible, but never condescending book. Thoroughly engaging, consistently
thought-provoking, exceptionally lucid, with attention to both classic debates and
contemporary developments, *What is this thing called Knowledge?* offers students a
superlative introduction to epistemology'.

Jill Rusin, *Wilfrid Laurier University, Canada*

'Pritchard's updated edition is a superior resource for students and scholars alike.
It expertly traverses the terrain surrounding familiar debates over the sources and
structure of knowledge, and then guides the reader through newer epistemic terri-
tories and applied domains'.

Robert Barnard, *University of Mississippi, USA*

what is this thing called knowledge?

- What is knowledge? Where does it come from? What kinds of knowledge are there? Can we know anything at all? What is the practical relevance of learning about epistemology?

This lucid and engaging introduction grapples with these central questions in the theory of knowledge, offering a clear, non-partisan view of the main themes of epistemology. Both traditional issues and contemporary ideas are discussed in 22 easily digestible chapters, each of which concludes with a useful summary of the main ideas discussed, study questions, annotated further reading, and a guide to internet resources.

Each chapter also features text boxes providing bite-sized summaries of key concepts and major philosophers, and clear and interesting examples are used throughout. This book concludes with an annotated guide to general introductions to epistemology, a glossary of key terms, and a summary of the main examples used in epistemology. This is an ideal first textbook in the theory of knowledge for undergraduates coming to philosophy for the first time.

This fifth edition has been revised throughout and features a new part devoted to social epistemology. In addition, the text as a whole has been refreshed to keep it up to date with current developments.

Duncan Pritchard FRSE is UC Distinguished Professor of Philosophy and Director of the *Center for Knowledge, Technology & Society* at the University of California Irvine, USA. His main research area is epistemology, and he has published widely in this field. His books include: *Epistemic Luck* (2005), *The Nature and Value of Knowledge* (with A. Millar and A. Haddock, 2010), *Epistemological Disjunctivism* (2012), *Epistemic Angst* (2016), *Scepticism: A Very Short Introduction* (2019), and *Skepticism* (with A. Coliva, Routledge, 2021).

What is this thing called?

The Routledge Philosophy *What is this thing called?* series of concise textbooks have been designed for use by students coming to a core area of the discipline for the first time. Each volume explores the relevant central questions with clear explanation of complex ideas and engaging contemporary examples. Features to aid study include text boxes, chapter summaries, study questions, further reading and glossaries.

Available:

What is this thing called Ethics? Second edition
Christopher Bennett

What is this thing called Metaethics?
Matthew Chrisman

What is this thing called Metaphysics? Third edition
Brian Garrett

What is this thing called Philosophy of Religion?
Elizabeth Burns

What is this thing called Philosophy of Language? Second edition
Gary Kemp

What is this thing called The Meaning of Life?
Stewart Goetz and Joshua W. Seachris

What is this thing called Global Justice? Second edition
Kok-Chor Tan

What is this thing called Knowledge? Fifth edition
Duncan Pritchard

For more information about this series, please visit:
https://www.routledge.com/What-is-this-thing-called/book-series/WITTC

BY DUNCAN PRITCHARD

what is this thing called knowledge?

Fifth edition

 Routledge
Taylor & Francis Group

LONDON AND NEW YORK

Cover image: © Marco Bottigelli/Getty Images

Fifth edition published 2023
by Routledge
4 Park Square, Milton Park, Abingdon, Oxon OX14 4RN

and by Routledge
605 Third Avenue, New York, NY 10158

Routledge is an imprint of the Taylor & Francis Group, an informa business

First edition published by Routledge, 2006
Fourth edition published by Routledge, 2018

British Library Cataloguing-in-Publication Data
A catalogue record for this book is available from the British Library

ISBN: 978-1-032-41071-5 (hbk)
ISBN: 978-1-032-41069-2 (pbk)
ISBN: 978-1-003-35611-0 (ebk)

DOI: 10.4324/9781003356110

Typeset in Berling and Arial Rounded
by codeMantra

MIX
Paper | Supporting
responsible forestry
FSC
www.fsc.org   FSC™ C013985

Printed in the United Kingdom
by Henry Ling Limited

For Mandi, Ethan, Alexander, and Grace

CONTENTS

preface to the fifth edition

One of the main things that I wanted to achieve with *What is this thing called Knowledge?* was to offer a genuinely introductory textbook that nonetheless covered the very latest developments in contemporary epistemology. Given the fast-moving nature of the debate in epistemology, this meant that one couldn't wait too long before producing a revised edition, for fear that this virtue of the book would be lost. This process has now led us to this fifth edition of the book. A good example of the importance of keeping the book fresh is the tremendous growth in recent years in the range of materials available in epistemology, including free online resources. Those working their way through this fifth edition are thus far better served when it comes to finding additional readings and research resources.

The fifth edition also sees an important structural change, in that a new part of the book has been added which deals with the social dynamics of knowledge. This covers central issues in social epistemology, such as disagreement, vice epistemology, and ignorance, and also offers an expanded discussion of epistemic injustice. All of the other chapters have been revised and updated too, with new material added on such topics as fake news.

Let me close by offering a particular thanks to all the students who have taken introductory courses in epistemology with me over the years. They have helped me to refine my ideas about what a good introductory text on this topic should cover, and how it should cover it (many of them appear in the text in terms of the names I have chosen for protagonists in certain examples). In a very real sense, they have helped to make – and, as the book goes from edition to edition, *continue* to make – this book what it is.

how to use this book

This book has been designed to make it as user-friendly as possible, so that it can guide you through the theory of knowledge with the minimum fuss. It is composed of 22 short chapters, which fall into 5 main sections.

The first part (Chapters 1–6) explores general topics in the theory of knowledge, particularly concerning the nature and value of knowledge. In this part, we look at such issues as the Gettier problem, the nature of rationality, and the relevance of epistemic virtues to knowledge. The second part (Chapters 7–10) looks at where our knowledge comes from, and considers the role of, for instance, perception and memory in helping us to acquire, and retain, knowledge. The third part (Chapters 11–13) asks what kinds of knowledge there are, and considers in this regard moral, religious, and scientific knowledge. The fourth part (Chapters 14 and 15), new to this volume, explores the social dynamics of knowledge. It covers such core topics of social epistemology as disagreement, vice epistemology, ignorance, and epistemic injustice. The fifth part (Chapters 16–19) examines how we can apply what we have learnt from the theory of knowledge to the specific domains of technology, education, law, and politics. The sixth and final part (Chapters 20–22) examines the scope of our knowledge, and to that end considers sceptical arguments that purport to show that the possession of knowledge – or at least the possession of certain kinds of knowledge at any rate – is impossible.

Each chapter closes with a summary of the main points made in that chapter and some questions for discussion. For those who wish to explore the topic discussed in that chapter further, there is also a section recommending additional introductory and advanced reading. A further section identifies free internet resources that are relevant to that chapter. (If you want some general further reading on the theory of knowledge as a whole, there is a section towards the back of the book with bibliographic details.) Within each chapter, you'll find text boxes that give further information relevant to what is being discussed in the main text, such as more information about a historical figure who has been mentioned.

Although terminology is avoided where possible, you don't need to worry if you come across a technical word that you don't understand, since all terminology is explained at the back of the book in a glossary. (Technical words that have corresponding entries in the glossary are identified in the text by being in **bold** at first mention.) Finally, at the very end of the book, there is an index.

Part I

what is knowledge?

1
some preliminaries

- Types of knowledge
- Two basic requirements of knowledge: truth and belief
- Knowing versus merely 'getting it right'
- A brief remark on truth

TYPES OF KNOWLEDGE

Think of all the things that you know, or at least *think* you know, right now. You know, for example, that the earth is round and that Paris is the capital of France. You know that you can speak (or at least read) English, and that two plus two is equal to four. You know, presumably, that all bachelors are unmarried men, that it is wrong to hurt people just for fun, that *The Godfather* is a wonderful film, that water has the chemical structure H_2O, and so on.

But what is it that all these cases of knowledge have in common? Think again of the examples just given, which include geographical, linguistic, mathematical, aesthetic, ethical, and scientific knowledge. Given these myriad types of knowledge, what, if anything, ties them all together? It is this sort of question that is asked by those who study **epistemology**, which is the theory of knowledge. The goal of this book is to introduce you to this exciting field of philosophy. By the end of this book, you should be able to count yourself as an epistemologist.

In all the examples of knowledge just given, the type of knowledge in question is what is called **propositional knowledge**, in that it is knowledge of a **proposition**. A proposition is what is asserted by a sentence which says that something is the case – for example, that the earth is flat, that bachelors are unmarried men, that two plus two is four, and so on. Propositional knowledge will be the focus of this book, but we should also recognise that it is not the only sort of knowledge that we possess.

There is, for example, **ability knowledge**, or *know-how*. Ability knowledge is clearly different from propositional knowledge; I know how to swim, for example, but I do not thereby know a set of propositions about how to swim. Indeed, I'm not

DOI: 10.4324/9781003356110-2

altogether sure that I could tell you how to swim, but I do know how to swim nonetheless (and I could prove it by manifesting this ability – by jumping into a swimming pool and doing the breaststroke, say).

Ability knowledge is certainly an important type of knowledge to have. We want lots of know-how, such as to know how to ride a bicycle, to fly a plane, to programme a computer, and so on. Notice, however, that, while only relatively sophisticated creatures like humans possess propositional knowledge, ability knowledge is far more common. An ant might plausibly be said to know how to navigate its terrain, but would we want to say that an ant has propositional knowledge, that there are facts which the ant knows? Could the ant know, for example, that the terrain it is presently crossing is someone's porch? Intuitively not, and this marks out the importance of propositional knowledge over other types of knowledge like ability knowledge, which is that such knowledge presupposes the sort of relatively sophisticated intellectual abilities possessed by humans.

TWO BASIC REQUIREMENTS OF KNOWLEDGE: TRUTH AND BELIEF

Henceforth, when we talk about knowledge, we will have propositional knowledge in mind, unless explicitly stated otherwise. Two things that just about every epistemologist agrees on are that a prerequisite for possessing knowledge is that one has a belief in the relevant proposition, and that that belief must be true. So if you know that Paris is the capital of France, then you must believe that this is the case, and your belief must also be true.

Take the truth requirement first. In order to assess this claim, consider what would follow if we dropped this requirement. In particular, is it plausible to suppose that one could know a false proposition? Of course, we often *think* that we know something and then it turns out that we were wrong, but that's just to say that we didn't really know it in the first place. Could we genuinely know a false proposition? Could I know, for example, that the moon is made of cheese, even though it manifestly isn't? I take it that when we talk of someone having knowledge, we mean to exclude such a possibility. This is because to ascribe knowledge to someone is to credit that person with having got things right, and that means that what we regard that person as knowing had better not be false, but true.

Next, consider the belief requirement. It is sometimes the case that we explicitly *contrast* belief and knowledge, as when we say things like, 'I don't merely believe that he was innocent, I *know* it', which might on the face of it be thought to imply that knowledge does not require belief after all. If you think about these sorts of assertions in a little more detail, however, then it becomes clear that the contrast between belief and knowledge is being used here simply to emphasise the fact that one *not only* believes the proposition in question but *also* knows it. In this way, these assertions actually lend support to the claim that knowledge requires belief, rather than undermining it.

As with the truth requirement, we will assess the plausibility of the belief requirement for knowledge by imagining for a moment that it doesn't hold, which would mean that one could have knowledge of a proposition which one did not even believe. Suppose, for example, that someone claimed to have known a quiz answer, even though it was clear from that person's behaviour at the time that she didn't believe the proposition in question (perhaps she put forward a different answer to the question, or no answer at all). Clearly, we would not agree that this person did have knowledge in this case. Again, the reason for this relates to the fact that to say that someone has knowledge is to credit that person with a certain kind of success. But for it to be *your* success, then belief in the proposition in question is essential, since otherwise this success is not creditable to *you* at all.

• KNOWING VERSUS MERELY 'GETTING IT RIGHT'

It is often noted that belief *aims* at the truth, in the sense that when we believe a proposition, we believe it to be the case (i.e. to be true). When what we believe *is* true, then there is a match between what we think is the case and what is the case. We have got things right. If mere true belief suffices for 'getting things right', however, then one might wonder why epistemologists do not end their quest for an account of knowledge right there and simply hold that knowledge is nothing more than true belief (i.e. 'getting things right').

There is in fact a very good reason why epistemologists do not rest content with mere true belief as an account of knowledge, and that is that one can gain true belief entirely by *accident*, in which case it would be of no credit to you at all that you got things right. Consider Harry, who forms his belief that the horse Lucky Lass will win the next race purely on the basis of the fact that the name of the horse appeals to him. Clearly this is not a good basis on which to form one's belief about the winner of the next horse race, since whether or not a horse's name appeals to you has no bearing on its performance.

Suppose, however, that Harry's belief turns out to be true, in that Lucky Lass *does* win the next race. Is this knowledge? Intuitively not, since it is just a matter of *luck* that his belief was true in this case. Remember that knowledge involves a kind of success that is creditable to the agent. Crucially, however, successes that are merely down to luck are never credited to the agent.

In order to emphasise this point, think for a moment about successes in another realm, such as archery. Notice that if one genuinely is a skilled archer, then if one tries to hit the bullseye, and the conditions are right (e.g. the wind is not gusting), then one *usually* will hit the bullseye. That's just what it means to be a skilled archer. The word 'usually' is important here, since someone who isn't a skilled archer might, as it happens, hit the bullseye on a particular occasion, but she wouldn't *usually* hit the bullseye in these conditions. Perhaps, for example, she aims her arrow and, by luck, it hits the centre of the target. Does the mere fact that she is successful on this one occasion mean that she is a skilled archer? No, and the reason is that she would not be able to repeat this success. If she tried again, for example, her arrow would in all likelihood sail off into the heavens.

Having knowledge is just like this. Imagine that one's belief is an arrow, which is aimed at the centre of the target, truth. Hitting the bullseye and forming a true belief suffices for getting things right, since all this means is that one was successful on that occasion. It does not suffice, however, for having knowledge any more than hitting the bullseye purely by chance indicates that one is skilled in archery. To have knowledge, one's success must genuinely be the result of one's efforts, rather than merely being by chance. Only then is that success creditable to one. And this means that forming one's belief in the way that one does ought usually, in those circumstances, to lead to a true belief.

Harry, who forms his true belief that Lucky Lass will win the race simply because he likes the name, is like the person who happens to hit the bullseye, but who is not a skilled archer. Usually, forming one's belief about whether a horse will win a race simply by considering whether the name of the horse appeals to you will lead you to form a false belief.

Contrast Harry with someone who genuinely knows that the race will be won by Lucky Lass. Perhaps, for example, this person is a 'Mr Big', a gangster who has fixed the race by drugging the other animals so that his horse, Lucky Lass, will win. He knows that the race will be won by Lucky Lass because the way he has formed his belief, by basing it on the special grounds he has for thinking that Lucky Lass cannot lose, would normally lead him to have a true belief. It is not a matter of luck that Mr Big hits the target of truth.

The challenge for epistemologists is thus to explain what needs to be added to mere true belief in order to get knowledge. In particular, epistemologists need to explain what needs to be added to true belief to capture this idea that knowledge, unlike mere true belief, involves a success that is creditable to the agent, where this means, for example, that the agent's true belief was not simply a matter of luck.

As we will see, it is in fact surprisingly difficult to give an unproblematic account of knowledge which meets this requirement. This has led some commentators to be doubtful about the whole project of defining knowledge. Perhaps there just is nothing that ties all cases of knowledge together, or perhaps there is such an essence to knowledge, but it is so complex that it is a futile task to seek an account of it.

In this book, however, we will proceed with optimism on this score. Even if an unproblematic definition of knowledge is unavailable, there are a number of plausible accounts on offer, even though none of them is entirely uncontentious. Moreover, the very practice of evaluating these different views about knowledge itself casts light upon what knowledge is, even if it does not result in a neat definition of this notion.

In any case, while the project of elucidating knowledge is central to epistemology (it is the principal focus of Chapters 1–6), it is important not to overstate its importance. As this book testifies, there is more to epistemology than the quest to define knowledge. One can examine the different ways in which knowledge is acquired and retained, for example, such as via our perceptual faculty of sight and our faculty of memory (see Chapters 7–10). Or one can examine the different kinds of knowledge there are, such as religious, scientific, or moral knowledge (see Chapters 11–13). Or one can consider the social dynamics of knowledge, such as how we should respond to disagreements or the social mechanisms that prevent testimony from being given its due weight (see Chapters 14 and 15). Or one can consider how the theory of knowledge applies to specific practical domains, like technology, education, law, and politics (see Chapters 16–19). Finally, there are sceptical challenges to be engaged with, challenges which purport to show that knowledge is impossible to possess; however, we define it (Chapters 20–22 deal with sceptical challenges and related issues).

● A BRIEF REMARK ON TRUTH

I want to end this chapter by commenting a little more on truth (note that I'll be saying more about truth at the end of the book). After all, the reader might be tempted to observe that it is odd that we have taken our understanding of truth as given and gone straight ahead to examine knowledge. Do we really have a better grip on what truth is than on what knowledge is?

It is true (if you'll forgive the pun) that I'm taking a certain common-sense conception of truth for granted here. In particular, I'm going to assume that truth is *objective* in the following sense: at least for most propositions, your thinking that they are true does not make them true. Whether or not the earth is round, for example, has nothing to do with whether or not we think that it is, but simply depends upon the shape of the earth.

Most of us uncritically take this conception of truth as obvious, but there are some philosophers who think that this view of truth is unsustainable. I think that their reasons for rejecting this account of truth rest on a number of interrelated mistakes, and when I return to this issue at the end of the book I will explain what some of the core mistakes are. For now, however, it is enough that this conception of truth is intuitive. If you also think that it is intuitive, then that is all to the good. If, on the other hand, you don't, then I urge you to set this matter to one side until later on.

● CHAPTER SUMMARY

- Epistemology is the theory of knowledge. One of the characteristic questions of epistemology concerns what all the myriad kinds of knowledge we ascribe to ourselves have in common: *What is knowledge?*
- We can distinguish between knowledge of propositions, or propositional knowledge, and know-how, or ability knowledge. Intuitively, the former demands a greater degree of intellectual sophistication on the part of the knower than the latter. Our focus in this book will be on propositional knowledge.
- In order to have knowledge of a proposition, that proposition must be true and one must believe it.

- Mere true belief does not suffice for knowledge, however, since one can gain mere true belief purely by luck, and yet you cannot gain knowledge purely by luck.
- In this book, I will be assuming a common-sense objective view of truth which holds that (for the most part at least) merely thinking that something is true does not make it true.

STUDY QUESTIONS

1 Give examples of your own of the following types of knowledge:

- scientific knowledge;
- geographical knowledge;
- historical knowledge;
- religious knowledge.

2 Explain, in your own words, what the difference between ability knowledge and propositional knowledge is, and give two examples of each.
3 Why is mere true belief not sufficient for knowledge? Give an example of your own of a case in which an agent truly believes something, but does not know it.
4 Think about the 'objective' and 'common-sense' view of truth that I described at the end of this chapter. Is this view of truth a matter of common sense to you? If so, then try to formulate some reasons that someone might offer in order to call it into question. If, on the other hand, it is not a matter of common sense as far as you are concerned, then try to explain what you think is wrong with this view of truth.

INTRODUCTORY FURTHER READING

Blackburn, Simon (2005) *Truth: A Guide for the Perplexed* (Harmondsworth: Allen Lane). A very readable introduction to the issues as regards the philosophy of truth. This is a good place to start if you want to learn more about this topic.
Lynch, Michael (2010) 'Truth', *Routledge Companion to Epistemology*, S. Bernecker & D. H. Pritchard (eds), Ch. 1, pp. 3–13 (London: Routledge). An accessible and completely up-to-date survey of the main issues as regards the philosophy of truth.
Shope, Robert K. (2002) 'Conditions and Analyses of Knowing', *The Oxford Handbook to Epistemology*, P. K. Moser (ed.), pp. 25–70 (Oxford: Oxford University Press). See pp. 25–30 for a good clear discussion of the need for the truth and belief conditions in a theory of knowledge, and of why knowledge isn't just mere true belief.

ADVANCED FURTHER READING

Lynch, Michael (2005) *True to Life: Why Truth Matters* (Cambridge, MA: MIT Press). A very readable introduction to the issues as regards the philosophy of truth.

Pritchard, Duncan (2005) *Epistemic Luck* (Oxford: Oxford University Press). An in-depth discussion of the idea that knowledge is incompatible with luck.

Ryle, Gilbert (1949/2002) *The Concept of Mind* (Chicago, IL: University of Chicago Press). This is the classic discussion of ability knowledge, in contrast to propositional knowledge (see especially §2).

Williamson, Timothy (2001) *Knowledge and Its Limits* (Oxford: Oxford University Press). An influential defence of the 'knowledge-first' program in epistemology, whereby we should resist attempts to analyse knowledge and instead treat it as a primitive notion that we should analyse other notions in terms of. Note that this book is demanding for a novice.

• FREE INTERNET RESOURCES

Dowden, Bradley & Shwartz, Norman (2006) 'Truth', *Internet Encyclopedia of Philosophy*, www.iep.utm.edu/t/truth.htm. A neat and comprehensive overview of the philosophical discussions regarding truth. Note that it can be a little demanding for the beginner in some places.

Glanzberg, Michael (2018) 'Truth', *Stanford Encyclopedia of Philosophy*, http://plato.stanford.edu/entries/truth/. A sophisticated overview of the literature on the philosophy of truth. Not for the beginner.

Ichikawa, Jonathan Jenkins & Steup, Matthias (2017) 'The Analysis of Knowledge', *Stanford Encyclopedia of Philosophy*, http://plato.stanford.edu/entries/knowledge-analysis/. An excellent overview of the recent work on the theory of knowledge.

Truncellito, David (2007) 'Epistemology', *Internet Encyclopedia of Philosophy*, www.iep.utm.edu/e/epistemo.htm. Read up to the end of §2.b for more on the basic requirements for knowledge.

2

the value of knowledge

- Why care about knowledge?
- The instrumental value of true belief
- The value of knowledge
- The statues of Daedalus
- Is some knowledge non-instrumentally valuable?

WHY CARE ABOUT KNOWLEDGE?

One question in epistemology concerns what is perhaps the most central issue for this area of philosophy. It is this: why should we care about whether or not we have knowledge? Put another way: is knowledge valuable and, if so, why? The importance of this question resides in the fact that knowledge is the primary focus of epistemological theorising. Hence, if knowledge is not valuable, then that should give us cause to wonder whether we should rethink our understanding of the epistemological enterprise.

In this chapter, we will examine this issue in more detail and discover, perhaps surprisingly, that the value of knowledge is far from obvious.

THE INSTRUMENTAL VALUE OF TRUE BELIEF

One way of approaching the topic of the value of knowledge is to note that one can only know what is true, and truth in one's beliefs does seem to be valuable. If truth in one's beliefs is valuable, and knowledge demands truth, then we may be at least halfway towards answering our question of why knowledge is valuable.

Truth in one's beliefs is at least minimally valuable in the sense that, *all other things being equal*, true beliefs are better than false ones because having true beliefs enables us to fulfil our goals. This sort of value – a value which accrues to something in virtue of some further valuable purpose that it serves – is known as **instrumental value**.

DOI: 10.4324/9781003356110-3

Think, for example, of the value of a thermometer. Its value consists in the fact that it enables us to find out something of importance to us (i.e. what the temperature is). This is why a working thermometer is valuable to us, but a broken thermometer isn't (unless, of course, it serves some other purpose, such as by being a handy paperweight).

In contrast, some things seem to be of **non-instrumental value**, in that they are valuable for their own sake, and not simply in terms of some further useful purpose that they serve (like thermometers). Friendship, for example, is valuable in this way. For while friendship is undoubtedly useful, and therefore of instrumental value, one would be missing out on something important if one didn't appreciate the fact that having friends is good for its own sake. Indeed, someone who only values their friends because it serves their wider interests arguably doesn't have any real friends.

In order to see the instrumental value of true belief, think about any subject matter that is of consequence to you, such as the time of your crucial job interview. It's clearly preferable to have a true belief in this respect rather than a false belief, since without a true belief you'll have difficulty making this important meeting. That is, your goal of making this meeting is best served by having a true belief about when it takes place rather than a false one.

The problem, however, lies with the 'all other things being equal' clause which we put on the instrumental value of true belief. We have to impose this qualification because sometimes having a true belief could be unhelpful and actually impede one's goals, and in such cases, true belief would lack instrumental value. For example, if one's life depended upon it, could one really summon the courage to jump a ravine and thereby get to safety if one knew (or at least truly believed) that there was a serious possibility that one would fail to reach the other side? Here, it seems, a false belief in one's abilities would be better than a true belief if the goal in question (jumping the ravine) is to be achieved. So while true belief might *generally* be instrumentally valuable, it isn't *always* instrumentally valuable.

Moreover, some true beliefs are beliefs in trivial matters, and in this case, it isn't at all clear why we should value such beliefs at all. Imagine someone who, for no good reason, concerns herself with measuring each grain of sand on a beach, or someone who, even while being unable to operate a telephone, concerns herself with remembering every entry in a foreign phonebook. In each case, such a person would thereby gain lots of true beliefs but, crucially, one would regard such truth-gaining activity as rather pointless. After all, these true beliefs do not obviously serve any valuable purpose, and so do not seem to have any instrumental value (or, at the very least, what instrumental value these beliefs have is vanishingly small). It would, perhaps, be better – and thus of more value – to have fewer true beliefs, and possibly more false ones, if this meant that the true beliefs that one had were regarding matters of real consequence.

At most, then, we only seem able to marshal the conclusion that *some* true beliefs have instrumental value, not all of them. As a result, if we are to show that knowledge is valuable, then we need to do more than merely note that knowledge entails truth and that true belief is instrumentally valuable. Nevertheless, this conclusion need not be that dispiriting once we remember that while knowledge requires truth, not every instance of a true belief is an instance of knowledge (as we saw in the previous chapter, for example, some true beliefs are just lucky guesses, and so not knowledge at all). Accordingly, it could just be that those true beliefs that are clearly of instrumental value are the ones that are also instances of knowledge.

The problem with this line of thought ought to be obvious, since didn't our 'sand-measuring' agent *know* what the measurements of the sand were? Moreover, didn't our agent who was unable to jump the ravine because she was paralysed by fear fail to meet her goals because of what she *knew*? The problems that afflict the claim that all true beliefs are instrumentally valuable therefore similarly undermine the idea that all knowledge is instrumentally valuable. There is thus no easy way of defending the thesis that *all* knowledge must be valuable.

There is also a second difficulty lurking in the background here, which is that even if this project of understanding the value of knowledge in terms of the value of true belief were to be successful, it would still be problematic because it would entail that knowledge is no more valuable than mere true belief. But if that's right, then why do we value knowledge more than mere true belief?

● THE VALUE OF KNOWLEDGE

So we cannot straightforwardly argue from the instrumental value of true belief that *all* knowledge must therefore be instrumentally valuable. That said, we can perhaps say something about the specific value of knowledge that is a little less ambitious and which simply accounts for why, in general and all other things being equal, we desire to be knowers as opposed to being agents who have mostly true beliefs but lack knowledge (or, worse, have mostly false beliefs). After all, if we want to achieve our goals in life, then it would be preferable if we had knowledge which was relevant to these goals since knowledge is very useful in this respect. The idea is, therefore, that while not all knowledge is instrumentally valuable, in general it is instrumentally valuable and, what is more, it is of *greater* instrumental value, typically at least, than mere true belief alone (thus explaining our intuition that knowledge is of more value than mere true belief).

Consider the following case. Suppose I want to find my way to the nearest restaurant in an unfamiliar city. Having mostly false beliefs about the locale will almost certainly lead to this goal being frustrated. If I think, for example, that all the restaurants are in the east of the city, when in fact they are in the west, then I'm going to spend a rather dispiriting evening trudging around this town without success.

True beliefs are better than false beliefs (i.e. are of more instrumental value), but not as good as knowledge. Imagine, for instance, that you found out where the nearest restaurant was by reading a map of the town which is, without your realising it, entirely fake and designed to mislead those unfamiliar with the area. Suppose further, however, that, as it happens, this map inadvertently shows you the right route to the nearest restaurant. You therefore have a true belief about where the nearest restaurant is, but you clearly lack knowledge of this fact. After all, your belief is only luckily true, and as we saw in Chapter 1, you can't gain knowledge by luck in this way.

Now one might think that it is neither here nor there to the value of your true belief whether it is also an instance of knowledge. So long as you find the nearest restaurant, what does it matter that you don't know where it is but merely have a true belief about where it is? The problem with mere true belief, however, is that, unlike knowledge, it is very *unstable*. Suppose, for example, that as you were walking to this restaurant, you noticed that none of the landmarks corresponded to where they ought to be on the fake map in front you. You pass the town hall, for instance, and yet according to the map, this building is on the other side of town. You'd quickly realise that the map you're using is unreliable, and in all likelihood you'd abandon your belief about where the nearest restaurant was, thereby preventing you from getting there.

In contrast, imagine that you form your belief about where the nearest restaurant is by looking at a reliable map, and thereby *know* where the nearest restaurant is. Since this is genuine knowledge, it would not be undermined in the way that the mere true belief was undermined, and thus you'd retain your true belief. This would mean that you would make it to the restaurant after all, and thereby achieve your goal. Having knowledge can thus be of greater instrumental value than mere true belief since having knowledge rather than mere true belief can make it more likely that one achieves one's goals.

Plato (*c.*427–*c.*347 BC)

Bodily exercise, when compulsory, does no harm to the body; but knowledge which is acquired under compulsion obtains no hold on the mind.

Plato, *The Republic*

Plato is one of the most influential philosophers who ever lived. He resided for most of his life in the city of Athens, in Greece, which is where he came under the influence of Socrates (470–399 BC) and where he in turn influenced the philosophical development of Aristotle (384–322 BC). After Socrates' death – an account of which is offered in Plato's book, *The Apology* – Plato founded 'The Academy', a kind of early university in which a range of topics were taught, but principally philosophy.

Plato's writing was often in the style of a dialogue between Socrates, the mouthpiece of Plato, and an imagined adversary (or adversaries) on topics of vital philosophical importance. In *The Republic*, for example (perhaps his most famous work), he examines the question, central to political philosophy, of what the ideal political state is. Of more interest for our purposes, however, is his book *The Theaetetus*, in which he discusses the nature of knowledge.

● THE STATUES OF DAEDALUS

The previous point picks up on a famous claim made by the ancient Greek philosopher Plato (*c*.427–*c*.347 BC), regarding knowledge. In his book, *The Meno* (see §§96d–100b), Plato compares knowledge to the statues of the ancient Greek sculptor Daedalus which, it is said, were so realistic that if one did not tether them to the ground, they would run away. Plato's point is that mere true belief is like one of the untethered statues of Daedalus, in that one could very easily lose it. Knowledge, in contrast, is akin to a tethered statue, one that is therefore not easily lost.

The analogy to our previous discussion should be obvious. Mere true belief, like an untethered statue of Daedalus, is more likely to be lost (i.e. run away) than knowledge, which is far more stable. Put another way, the true belief one holds when one has knowledge is far more likely to remain fast in response to changes in circumstances (e.g. new information that comes to light) than mere true belief, as we saw in the case just described of the person who finds out where the nearest restaurant is by looking at a reliable map, as opposed to one who finds out where it is by looking at a fake map.

Of course, knowledge isn't *completely* stable either, since one could always acquire a false, but plausible piece of information that seems to call one's previous true information into question; but this is less likely to happen when it comes to knowledge than when it comes to true belief. In the example given earlier, suppose that the map is indeed reliable, and thus that you do know where the nearest restaurant is. Nevertheless, there might still be further misleading counter-evidence that you could come across which would undermine this knowledge, such as the testimony of a friend you bump into who tells you (out of mischief) that the map is a fake. In the light of this new information, you'll probably change your belief and so fail to get to the restaurant after all.

Even so, however, the fact remains that knowledge is more stable than mere true belief. In the case just described, for example, the fact that the map had been working so far would give you good grounds to continue trusting it, and so you might naturally be suspicious of any testimony you receive to the contrary. Suppose a perfect stranger told you that the map was a complete fake. Would that lead you to change your belief given that it has been reliable so far? Probably not. A friend's testimony carries more weight than a stranger's, but even this testimony might be ignored if you had reason to think your friend might be playing a trick on you.

If you merely had a true belief about where the nearest restaurant was, in contrast, and had no good reason in support of that true belief, then all kinds of conflicting information would undermine that belief. As we saw, as soon as you start walking on your journey and you notice that none of the landmarks correspond to their locations on the map, then you would be liable to tear the map up in despair, even though the map is, in the one respect that is important to you (how to get to the nearest restaurant), entirely reliable.

There is a good reason why knowledge is more stable than mere true belief, and this is because knowledge, unlike mere true belief, could not easily be mistaken. Imagine, for instance, a doctor diagnoses a patient by (secretly) tossing a coin, thus leading the patient to form a particular belief about what is wrong with her. Suppose further that this diagnosis is, as it happens, correct. Clearly the doctor does not know what is wrong with the patient, even though she happened to get it right on this occasion, and neither does the patient know what is wrong with her given that she acquired her belief by listening to the doctor. The problem here is that it was just a matter of luck that the doctor chanced upon the right answer, and thus it is also a matter of luck that the patient formed a true belief about what was wrong with her. In both cases, they could so easily have been wrong.

Compare this scenario, however, with that in which a doctor forms her diagnosis of the patient's illness in a diligent fashion by using the appropriate medical procedures. This doctor will (in most cases at least) end up with the same correct diagnosis as our irresponsible doctor, and thus the patient will again acquire a true belief about the nature of her condition. This time, though, the doctor and the patient will *know* what the correct diagnosis is. Moreover, there is no worry in this case that this verdict could so easily have been mistaken; given that the doctor followed the correct procedures, it is in fact very *unlikely* that this diagnosis is wrong. Here we clearly have a case in which our goal of correctly determining the source of someone's illness is better served by the possession of knowledge rather than the possession of mere true belief because of the instability of mere true belief relative to knowledge (i.e. the fact that mere true belief, unlike knowledge, could so easily be wrong). In this sense, then, knowledge is more valuable to us than true belief alone.

For the most part, then, if one wishes to achieve one's goals, it is essential that one has, at the bare minimum, true beliefs about the subject matter concerned. True belief is thus mostly of instrumental value, even if it is not always of instrumental value. Ideally, however, it is better to have knowledge, since mere true belief has an instability that is not always conducive to success in one's projects. Since knowledge entails true belief, we can therefore draw two conclusions. First, that most knowledge, like most mere true belief, is of instrumental value. Second, and crucially, that knowledge is of greater instrumental value than mere true belief.

• IS SOME KNOWLEDGE NON-INSTRUMENTALLY VALUABLE?

At this point, we might wonder whether the value of knowledge is only ever instrumental. That is, we might wonder whether the value of knowledge is *always* dependent upon what further goods knowledge helps you attain (as when knowledge of the correct diagnosis of your illness helps you in your recovery). Are there kinds of knowledge which have non-instrumental value (i.e. the kind of value that we saw friendship as having above)?

In order to see how knowledge could be non-instrumentally valuable, think of those types of knowledge which are very refined, such as *wisdom* – the sort of knowledge that wise people have. Wisdom is clearly at least instrumentally valuable since it can enable one to lead a productive and fulfilled life. Crucially, however, it seems that knowledge of this sort would still be valuable even if, as it happens, it *didn't* lead to a life that was good in this way. Suppose, for instance, that nature conspires against you at every turn so that, like the biblical character Job, you are subject to just about every dismal fate that can befall a person. In such a case, one's knowledge of most matters may well have no instrumental value at all because one's goals will be frustrated by forces beyond your control regardless of what you know.

Nevertheless, it would surely be preferable to confront this misfortune as a wise person, and not because such wisdom would necessarily make you feel any better or enable you to avoid these disasters (whether wise or not, your life is still wretched). Instead, it seems, being wise is just a good thing, regardless of what further goods it might lead to. That is, it is something that is good *for its own sake*; something which has non-instrumental value. And notice that this claim marks a further difference between knowledge and mere true belief, since it is hard to see how mere true belief could ever be of non-instrumental value.

There may be stronger claims that we can make about the value of knowledge, but the minimal claims advanced here suffice to make the study of knowledge important. Recall that we have seen that knowledge is at least for the most part instrumentally valuable in that it enables us to achieve our goals, and that it is more instrumentally valuable in this respect than true belief alone. Moreover, we have also noted that some varieties of knowledge, such as wisdom, seem to be non-instrumentally valuable. Clearly, then, knowledge is something that we should care about. Given that this is so, it is incumbent upon us as philosophers to be able to say more about what knowledge is and the various ways in which we might acquire it. These are the goals of epistemology.

● CHAPTER SUMMARY

- One of the central tasks of epistemology is to explain the value of knowledge. But while it is obvious that we do value knowledge, it is not obvious why this is the case, nor what the nature of this value is.
- One way of accounting for the value of knowledge is to note that if you know a proposition, then you have a true belief in that proposition, and true beliefs are clearly useful, and therefore valuable. In particular, true belief has instrumental value in that it enables you to achieve your goals.
- One problem with this proposal is that it is not obvious that *all* true beliefs are instrumentally valuable. For one thing, some true beliefs are so trivial that it seems that they have no value at all. For another, sometimes it is more useful to have a false belief than a true belief.
- Moreover, even if one could evade this problem, another difficulty would remain, which is that, intuitively, knowledge is *more* valuable than mere true belief. If this

intuition is right, then we need to say more than simply that knowledge entails true belief and that true belief is instrumentally valuable.

- One option is to say that knowledge is of greater instrumental value than mere true belief, since it is more useful to us (it enables us to achieve more of our goals than mere true belief alone). Part of the explanation one might offer for this could be that there is a 'stability' to knowledge which is lacking in mere true belief in that in knowing that something is the case one couldn't have easily been wrong.

- We also explored another suggestion, which was that *some* knowledge is of non-instrumental value (i.e. is valuable for its own sake). The example we gave here was that of *wisdom*. The idea, then, is that while knowledge is generally of greater instrumental value than mere true belief, some knowledge is also, in addition, non-instrumentally valuable (unlike mere true belief, which is never non-instrumentally valuable).

• STUDY QUESTIONS

1 What does it mean to say that something has instrumental value? Explain your answer by offering two examples of your own of something that is instrumentally valuable.

2 Is true belief always instrumentally valuable? Evaluate the arguments for and against this claim, paying attention to such issues as the fact that sometimes false beliefs can be useful (as in the case of the person trying to jump a ravine), and that true beliefs can sometimes be entirely trivial (as in the case of the person who measures grains of sand).

3 Is knowledge of *greater* instrumental value than mere true belief, insofar as the latter is indeed generally instrumentally valuable? Consider some cases in which one person has a mere true belief while someone else in a relevantly similar situation has knowledge. Is it true to say that the latter person's knowledge is of more instrumental value than the former person's mere true belief?

4 What does it mean to say that something has non-instrumental value? Explain your answer by offering two examples of your own of things that might be non-instrumentally valuable.

5 Is knowledge *ever* non-instrumentally valuable? Evaluate this question by considering some plausible candidates for non-instrumentally valuable knowledge, such as the knowledge possessed by the wise person.

• INTRODUCTORY FURTHER READING

Annas, Julia (2003) *Plato: A Very Short Introduction* (Oxford: Oxford University Press). This is a succinct and very readable introduction to Plato's philosophy.

Greco, John (2010) 'The Value Problem', *Routledge Companion to Epistemology*, S. Bernecker & D. H. Pritchard (eds), Ch. 21, pp. 219–31 (London: Routledge). An accessible survey of the main issues as regards epistemic value.

● ADVANCED FURTHER READING

Kvanvig, Jonathan (2003) *The Value of Knowledge and Pursuit of Understanding* (Cambridge: Cambridge University Press). A highly influential contemporary discussion of the value of knowledge.

Pritchard, Duncan, Millar, Alan & Haddock, Adrian (2010) *The Nature and Value of Knowledge: Three Investigations* (Oxford: Oxford University Press). A three-pronged contribution to the debate about the value of knowledge. Note that it is quite demanding.

Zagzebski, Linda (1996) *Virtues of the Mind: An Inquiry into the Nature of Virtue and the Ethical Foundations of Knowledge* (Cambridge: Cambridge University Press). A clear, challenging, and historically-oriented account of knowledge which pays particular attention to the issue of the value of knowledge, including those types of knowledge, like wisdom, that might plausibly be regarded as non-instrumentally valuable.

● FREE INTERNET RESOURCES

Bradley, Ben & Zimmerman, Michael J. (2019) 'Intrinsic Versus Extrinsic Value', *Stanford Encyclopedia of Philosophy*, http://plato.stanford.edu/entries/value-intrinsic-extrinsic/. A great survey of the literature on intrinsic and non-intrinsic (e.g. non-instrumental) value.

Carter, Adam, Pritchard, Duncan & Turri, John (2022) 'The Value of Knowledge', *Stanford Encyclopedia of Philosophy*, http://plato.stanford.edu/entries/knowledge-value/. A very up-to-date and thorough overview of the debate regarding the value of knowledge.

Chappell, Tim (2019) 'Plato on Knowledge in the *Theaetetus*', *Stanford Encyclopedia of Philosophy*, http://plato.stanford.edu/entries/plato-theaetetus/. An excellent overview of Plato's view of knowledge, as expressed in his book, *The Theaetetus*.

Kraut, Richard (2022) 'Plato', *Stanford Encyclopedia of Philosophy*, http://plato.stanford.edu/entries/plato/. A very good overview of the life and works of Plato.

Perseus Archive, Tufts University, www.perseus.tufts.edu/hopper. An open-access archive of ancient Greek and Roman texts, including the works of Plato.

Schroeder, Mark (2021) 'Value Theory', *Stanford Encyclopedia of Philosophy*, http://plato.stanford.edu/entries/value-theory/. A comprehensive and completely up-to-date survey of the main philosophical issues as regards value.

3
defining knowledge

- The problem of the criterion
- Methodism and particularism
- Knowledge as justified true belief
- Gettier cases
- Responding to the Gettier cases
- Back to the problem of the criterion

THE PROBLEM OF THE CRITERION

Anyone who wishes to offer a definition of knowledge – who wishes to say what knowledge *is* – faces an immediate problem, which is how to begin. Now it might seem as if the answer here is obvious, in that one should start simply by looking at the cases in which one has knowledge and considering what is common to each case. So, for example, one might think of such paradigm cases of knowledge acquisition as the scientist who, upon conducting her experiments, correctly determines the chemical structure of the substance before her, or the 'star' witness in the murder trial who knows that the defendant is guilty of the murder because she saw him do it in clear daylight. The thought is that all one needs to do is determine what is common to each of these paradigm cases and one will be well on one's way to discerning what knowledge is.

The problem with this suggestion, however, is that if one doesn't already know what knowledge is (i.e. what the defining characteristics, or *criteria*, of knowledge are), how can one correctly identify cases of knowledge in the first place? After all, one cannot simply assume that one knows what the criteria for knowledge are without thereby taking a definition of knowledge for granted from the outset. But, equally, neither is it plausible to suppose that we can correctly identify instances of knowledge without assuming knowledge of such criteria, since without a prior grasp of these criteria how are we supposed to tell what is a genuine case of knowledge and what isn't?

DOI: 10.4324/9781003356110-4

Roderick Chisholm (1916–99)

> We start with particular cases of knowledge and then from those we generalise and formulate criteria [*which tell*] us what it is for a belief to be epistemologically respectable.
>
> Chisholm, *The Foundations of Knowing*

The American philosopher Roderick Chisholm was without doubt the most influential epistemologist of the second half of the twentieth century. A good deal of his influence is due to his best-selling textbook on epistemology, *Theory of Knowledge*, which was first published in 1966 (a third edition came out in 1989) and which quickly became a standard text in this area throughout the world. His influence is also felt through his students – such as Keith Lehrer and Ernest Sosa – who have gone on to become very prominent philosophers in their own right.

Central to Chisholm's contribution to epistemology is a commitment to epistemic internalism and a version of classical foundationalism. In addition, he published important work in epistemology on such areas as the problem of the criterion and the epistemology of perception. Chisholm also made significant contributions to other areas of philosophy, such as metaphysics and ethics.

This difficulty regarding defining knowledge is known as the **problem of the criterion**, and it dates right back to antiquity. We can roughly summarise the problem in terms of the following two claims:

1 I can only identify instances of knowledge provided I already know what the criteria for knowledge are.
2 I can only know what the criteria for knowledge are provided I am already able to identify instances of knowledge.

We thus seem to be faced with a dilemma. We must either assume that we can independently know what the criteria for knowledge are in order to identify instances of knowledge, or else we must assume that we can identify instances of knowledge in order to determine what the criteria for knowledge are. Either way, the dubious nature of the assumption in question appears to call the legitimacy of the epistemological project of defining knowledge into dispute.

● METHODISM AND PARTICULARISM

Although the problem of the criterion dates right back to antiquity, the contemporary focus on it is due almost entirely to the work done on this problem by the

American philosopher **Roderick Chisholm** (1916–99). As he noted, historically, philosophers have tended to begin by assuming that they already know – or at least are able to identify through philosophical reflection alone – what the criteria for knowledge are, and have proceeded on this basis to examine the issue of whether or not we have any knowledge. Chisholm calls such a stance **methodism**, and cites as a famous example of a methodist the French philosopher **René Descartes** (1596–1650), whom we will hear more about in the next chapter.

In contrast to methodism, Chisholm argues that we should grip the other horn of the dilemma and adopt a position that he calls **particularism**. According to particularism, rather than assuming that one can identify the criteria for knowledge independently of examining any particular instances of knowledge, one should instead assume that one can correctly identify particular instances of knowledge and proceed on this basis to determine what the criteria for knowledge are.

There is much to be said both for and against these two positions. One of the main advantages of methodism is that it doesn't begin by assuming the falsity of **scepticism** (i.e. the worry that we might not know anything much at all), since it leaves it an open question whether there is anything that meets the criteria for knowledge. (We will be considering the problem of scepticism in its own right at the end of the book.) The big problem facing the view, however, is that it just seems plain mysterious how we are to get a grip on the criteria for knowledge without appealing to particular instances of knowledge.

Persuaded by this sort of objection to methodism, most epistemologists have followed Chisholm in opting for particularism instead. In favour of particularism is the thought that if one has to assume anything in this regard (as seemingly we must, given the problem of the criterion), it is far less extravagant to suppose that we can correctly identify particular cases of knowledge independently of any prior awareness of what the criteria for knowledge are than to suppose that we can identify what the criteria for knowledge are without prior appeal to cases of knowledge. Unsurprisingly, those sympathetic to scepticism will baulk at the particularist methodology since they will argue that the claim that we do indeed possess knowledge is something that has to be *shown*, not assumed.

Notice that the problem of the criterion might not be so pressing if the criteria for knowledge were entirely obvious, since if they were, then the assumption – key to methodism – that we can know what the criteria for knowledge are independently of examining any particular instances of knowledge (by simply reflecting on the concept of knowledge, say) would not be nearly so implausible. The difficulty, however, is that reflection itself indicates that there is no simple account of the criteria for knowledge available.

For example, we saw in Chapter 1 that it is certainly the case that if one is to know a proposition, then one had better have a true belief in that proposition. If knowledge required only true belief, then we might be entitled to think that so obvious a set of criteria for knowledge could be determined without making use of any putative instances of knowledge (though note that we have already begun to illicitly bring examples into our discussion, so this claim is far from uncontentious). In this way, we might be able to weaken the force of the problem of the criterion.

The difficulty, however, as we also saw in Chapter 1, is that knowledge demands much more than mere true belief. Moreover, as we will now see, specifying just what it demands in this regard is notoriously difficult. Accordingly, even if this strategy of claiming that the criteria for knowledge are manifest could work in principle (which is far from obvious), it won't work in practice for the simple reason that the criteria for knowledge are manifestly *not* manifest at all.

● KNOWLEDGE AS JUSTIFIED TRUE BELIEF

We noted in Chapter 1 that knowledge cannot just be true belief since one can, for example, gain a true belief in all manner of bizarre and inappropriate ways, and in such cases one would not think that one had knowledge. Think again about our gambler from Chapter 1, Harry, who forms his belief about which horse will win the race by considering which horse's name most appeals to him. Even if the horse does go on to win the race, so that Harry's belief is true, he clearly did not know that this would happen.

So it seems that there must be more to knowledge than just true belief. But what could this additional component be? The natural answer to this question, one that is often ascribed to Plato, is that what is needed is a *justification* for one's belief, where this is understood as being in possession of good reasons for thinking that what one believes is true. This proposal is known as the **classical account of knowledge**. It is also sometimes referred to as the 'tripartite' (i.e. three-part) account of knowledge.

Back in Chapter 1, we contrasted Harry with a 'Mr Big' who bases his belief that Lucky Lass will win on excellent grounds, for he has fixed the race by drugging the other horses. That justification is the missing ingredient in our account of knowledge certainly seems to accord with the cases of Harry and Mr Big, since what the former lacks, but the latter possesses, is the ability to offer good reasons in favour of his belief, and this is just what being justified intuitively involves. It is thus plausible to contend that knowledge is simply justified true belief and, while this isn't as straightforward an analysis as one which held that knowledge is merely true belief, it is fairly simple. Perhaps we could determine that these were the criteria for knowledge by reflection alone without difficulty.

● GETTIER CASES

Unfortunately, matters are not nearly so straightforward. The reason for this is that this classical theory of knowledge has itself been shown to be completely untenable. The person who illustrated this was a philosopher named Edmund Gettier (1927–2021) who, in a three-page article, offered a devastating set of counter-examples to the classical account: what are now known as **Gettier cases**. In essence,

Gettier's amazing article

The tale behind Edmund Gettier's famous article on why the classical three-part, or *tripartite*, account of knowledge is unsustainable is now part of philosophical folklore. So the story goes, Edmund Gettier was a young American philosopher who knew that he needed to get some publications under his belt if he was to get tenure in his job (in the USA, junior academic appointments are usually provisional on the person publishing their research in suitably high-profile journals). Spurred on by this consideration, he looked around for something to write about, something which was interesting, publishable, and, most of all, something which could be written up very quickly.

While it is said that he had no real interest in epistemology at that time (and, as we will see, he has shown little interest since), he was struck by the prevalence of the justified-true-belief account of knowledge in the literature, and believed it to be fatally defective. In a quick spurt of activity, he wrote a short three-page article outlining his objection to the view, and sent it to the highly regarded philosophy journal *Analysis*, which specialises in short papers of this sort. It was duly published in 1963 and created quite a storm.

Initially, there were responses from philosophers who felt that the problem that Gettier had highlighted for the classical account of knowledge could be easily resolved with a mere tweak of the view. Very soon, however, it became apparent that such easy 'fixes' did not work, and quickly a whole industry of papers on the 'Gettier problem', as it was now known, came into being.

The most incredible part of this story, however, is that Gettier, having written one of the most famous articles in contemporary philosophy, never engaged at all with the vast literature that his short paper prompted. Indeed, he never published anything else in epistemology. The paper he'd written had gained him the tenure that he wanted, and that, it seems, was enough for him as far as publishing in epistemology was concerned.

In 2013, I helped organised an international conference at the University of Edinburgh in honour of the 50th anniversary of Gettier's famous article, with many of the world's leading epistemologists in attendance. Needless to say, it wasn't possible to persuade the man himself to participate in this event. Gettier sadly passed away in 2021.

what Gettier showed was that you could have a justified true belief and yet still lack knowledge of what you believe because your true belief was ultimately gained via luck in much the same way as Harry's true belief was gained by luck.

We will use a different example from the ones cited by Gettier, though one that has the same general structure. Imagine a man, let's call him John, who comes downstairs one morning and sees that the time on the grandfather clock in the hall says '8.20'. On this basis, John comes to believe that it is 8.20 a.m., and this belief is true, since it *is* 8.20 a.m. Moreover, John's belief is justified in that it is based on excellent grounds. For example, John usually comes downstairs in the morning about this time, so he knows that the time is about right. Moreover, this clock has been very reliable at telling the time for many years and John has no reason to think that it is faulty now. He thus has good reasons for thinking that the time on the clock is correct.

Suppose, however, that the clock had, unbeknownst to him, stopped 24 hours earlier, so that John is now forming his justified true belief by looking at a stopped clock. Intuitively, if this were so then John would lack knowledge even though he has met the conditions laid down by the classical account of knowledge. After all, that John has a true belief in this case is, ultimately, a matter of luck, just like Harry's belief that Lucky Lass would win the race.

If John had come downstairs a moment earlier or a moment later – or if the clock had stopped at a slightly different time – then he would have formed a false belief about the time by looking at this clock. Thus, we can conclude that knowledge is not simply justified true belief.

There is a general form to all Gettier cases, and once we know this, we can use it to construct an unlimited number of them. To begin with, we need to note that you can have a justified false belief, since this is crucial to the Gettier cases. For example, suppose you formed a false belief by looking at a clock that you had no reason for thinking wasn't working properly but which was, in fact, and unbeknownst to you, not working properly. This belief would clearly be justified, even though it is false. With this point in mind, there are three stages to constructing your own Gettier case.

First, you take an agent who forms her belief in a way that would usually lead her to have a false belief. In the example above, we took the case of someone looking at a stopped clock in order to find out the time. Clearly, using a stopped clock to find out the time would usually result in a false belief.

Second, you add some detail to the example to ensure that the agent's belief is justified nonetheless. In the example above, the detail we added was that the agent had no reason for thinking that the clock wasn't working properly (the clock is normally reliable, is showing what appears to be the right time, and so on), thus ensuring that her belief is entirely justified.

Finally, you make the case such that while the way in which the agent formed her belief would normally have resulted in a justified false belief, in this case, it so happened that the belief was true. In the stopped clock case, this is done by stipulating that the stopped clock just happens to be 'telling' the right time.

Putting all this together, we can construct an entirely new Gettier case from scratch. As an example of someone forming a belief in a way that would normally result in a false belief, let's take someone who forms her belief that Madonna is across the street by looking at a life-sized cardboard cut-out of Madonna which is advertising her forthcoming tour, and which is posted just across the street. Forming one's belief about whether someone is across the street by looking at a life-sized cut-out of that person wouldn't normally result in a true belief. Next, we add some detail to the example to ensure that the belief is justified. In this case, we can just stipulate that the cut-out is very authentic-looking, and that there is nothing about it which would obviously give away the fact that it is a cardboard cut-out – it does not depict Madonna in an outrageous costume that she wouldn't plausibly wear on a normal street, for example. The agent's belief is thus justified. Finally, we make the scenario such that the belief is true. In this case, for instance, all we need to do is stipulate that, as it happens, Madonna *is* across the street, doing some window shopping out of view of our agent. Voila, we have constructed our very own Gettier case!

• RESPONDING TO THE GETTIER CASES

There is no easy way to respond to the Gettier cases, and since Gettier's article back in 1963, a plethora of different theories of knowledge have been developed in order to offer account of knowledge that is Gettier-proof. Initially, it was thought that all one needed to do to deal with these cases is simply tweak the classical account of knowledge. For instance, one proposal was that in order to have knowledge, one's true belief must be justified and also not in any way based on false presuppositions, such as, in the case of John just described, the false presupposition that the clock is working and not stopped. There is a pretty devastating problem with this sort of proposal, however, which is that it is difficult to spell out this idea of a 'presupposition' such that it is strong enough to deal with Gettier cases and yet not so strong that it prevents us from having most of the knowledge that we think we have.

For example, suppose that John has a sister across town – let's call her Sally – who is in fact at this moment finding out what the time is by looking at a working clock. Intuitively, Sally *does* gain knowledge of what the time is by looking at the time on the clock. Notice, however, that Sally may believe all sorts of other related propositions, some of which may be false – for example, she may believe that the clock is regularly maintained, when in fact no one is taking care of it. Is this belief a presupposition of her belief in what the time is? If it is (i.e. if we understand the notion of a 'presupposition' liberally), then this false presupposition will prevent her from having knowledge of the time, even though we would normally think that looking at a reliable working clock is a great way of coming to know what the time is.

Alternatively, suppose we understand the notion of a 'presupposition' in a more restrictive way such that this belief isn't a presupposition of Sally's belief in the time. The problem now is to explain why John's false belief that he's looking at a working clock counts as a presupposition of his belief in the time (and so prevents him from counting as knowing what the time is) if Sally's false belief that the clock is regularly maintained is not also treated as a presupposition. Why don't they *both* lack knowledge of what the time is?

If this problem weren't bad enough, there is also a second objection to this line of response to the Gettier cases, which is that it is not clear that the agent in a Gettier case need presuppose *anything* at all. Consider a different Gettier case in this regard, due to Chisholm. In this example, we have a farmer – let's call her Gayle – who forms her belief that there is a sheep in the field by looking at a shaggy dog which happens to look just like a sheep. As it turns out, however, there *is* a sheep in the field (standing behind the dog), and hence Gayle's belief is true. Moreover, her belief is also justified because she has great evidence for thinking that there is a sheep in the field (she can see what looks to be a sheep in the field, for example).

Given the immediacy of Gayle's belief in this case, however, it is hard to see that it really presupposes any further beliefs at all, at least unless we are to understand the notion of a presupposition *very* liberally. Gayle simply sees what looks like a sheep and directly forms her belief on that basis. And notice that if we do understand the notion of a presupposition so liberally that Gayle counts as illicitly making a pre-supposition, the problem then re-emerges of how to account for apparently genuine cases of knowledge, such as that intuitively possessed by Sally.

The dilemma for proponents of this sort of response to the Gettier cases is thus to explain how we should understand the notion of a presupposition broadly enough so that it applies to the Gettier cases while at the same time understanding it nar-rowly enough so that it doesn't apply to other non-Gettier cases in which, intui-tively, we would regard the agent concerned as having knowledge. In short, we want a response to the problem which explains why John lacks knowledge in such a way that it doesn't thereby deprive Sally of knowledge.

Once it was recognised that there was no easy answer to the problem posed to the classical account of knowledge by the Gettier cases, the race was on to find a radically new way of analysing knowledge which was Gettier-proof. We will con-sider some of these proposals below. One feature that they all share is that they understand the conditions for knowledge such that they demand more in the way of co-operation from the world than simply that the belief in question is true. That is, on the classical account of knowledge, there is one condition which relates to the world – the truth condition – and two conditions that relate to us as agents – the belief and justification conditions. These last two conditions, at least as they are usually understood in any case, don't demand anything from the world in the sense that they could obtain regardless of how the world is. If I were the victim of a hallucination, for example, then I might have a whole range of wholly deceptive experiences, experiences which, nonetheless, lead me to believe something and, moreover, to justifiably believe it. (For example, if I seem to see that, say, there is a glass in front of me, then this is surely a good, and thus justifying, reason for believing that there is a glass in front of me, even if the appearance of the glass is an illusion.) The moral of the Gettier cases, however, is that you need to demand more from the world than simply that one's justified belief is true if you are to have knowledge.

In the stopped-clock Gettier case, for example, the problem came about because, although John had excellent grounds for believing what he did, it nevertheless remained that he did not know what he believed because of some oddity in the world – in this case that the normally reliable clock had not only stopped but also stopped in such a way that John still formed a true belief. It thus appears that we need an account of knowledge which imposes a further requirement on the world over and above the truth of the target belief – that, for example, the agent is, *in fact*, forming his belief in the right kind of way. We will return to this issue later on (see especially Chapter 6).

● BACK TO THE PROBLEM OF THE CRITERION

So where does this leave us as regards the problem of the criterion that we started with? One thing that is certain is that the criteria for knowledge are far from obvious, and this calls into question the idea that we could determine such criteria without making reference to actual cases of knowledge. This conclusion is, however, double-edged in that if it really is the case that knowledge is such a complicated notion, then how can it be that we are able to identify cases of knowledge correctly even while lacking a prior grasp of what the criteria for knowledge are? Right from the start of the epistemological project, then, we are faced with a deep and seemingly intractable puzzle, one that appears to undermine our prospects for making any progress in this area.

● CHAPTER SUMMARY

- One of the central tasks in epistemology is to offer a definition of knowledge. The problem of the criterion, however, shows us that this task is in fact very difficult, if not impossible.
- Here, in a nutshell, is the problem of the criterion. Suppose we begin the task of defining knowledge by pointing to cases in which we have knowledge and trying to identify what is common to each case. The problem with this suggestion is that it assumes that we can already identify cases of knowledge, and thus that we already know what the marks, or *criteria*, of knowledge are. Alternatively, we might begin the task of defining knowledge by simply reflecting on the nature of knowledge and determine its essence that way. That is, through reflection we might determine what the criteria for knowledge are. The problem with this suggestion, however, is that it is difficult to see how we could possibly identify the criteria for knowledge without first being able to identify particular cases of knowledge. It seems, then, that either one must assume that one has (at least some of) the knowledge that one thinks one has, or else one must assume that one knows, independently of considering any particular instance of knowledge, what the criteria for knowledge are. Neither assumption is particularly plausible.
- We next considered a very influential theory of knowledge known as the classical (or tripartite) account of knowledge. According to this proposal, knowledge is to be understood as justified true belief, where a justification for one's belief consists of good reasons for thinking that the belief in question is true.
- Despite the surface plausibility of the classical account of knowledge, we also saw that it was untenable. This was illustrated by appeal to Gettier cases, which are

cases in which one forms a true justified belief and yet lacks knowledge because the truth of one's belief is largely a matter of luck. (The example we gave of this was that of someone forming a true belief about what the time is by looking at a stopped clock which just so happens to be displaying the right time.)

• There is no easy answer to the Gettier cases; no simple way of supplementing the tripartite account of knowledge so that it can deal with these cases. Instead, a radically new way of understanding knowledge is required, one that demands greater co-operation on the part of the world than simply that the belief in question be true.

• STUDY QUESTIONS

1 Check that you understand the problem of the criterion. In order to get clear in your own mind exactly what the problem is, try to formulate this problem in your own words – have a go at offering a definition of knowledge without appealing either to instances of knowledge or to the presupposition that you already know what the criteria for knowledge are.
2 Explain in your own words the distinction between methodism and particularism. For each position, offer one reason in favour of the view and one against.
3 What is the classical account of knowledge? How does the classical account of knowledge explain why a lucky true belief doesn't count as knowledge?
4 What is a Gettier case, and what do such cases show? Try to formulate a Gettier case of your own.
5 In what way might it be said that the problem with Gettier cases is that they involve a justified true belief which is based on a false presupposition? Explain, with an example, why one cannot straightforwardly deal with the Gettier cases by advancing a theory of knowledge which demands justified true belief that does not rest on any false presuppositions.

• INTRODUCTORY FURTHER READING

Hetherington, Stephen (2010) 'The Gettier Problem', *Routledge Companion to Epistemology*, S. Bernecker & D. H. Pritchard (eds), Ch. 12, pp. 119–30 (London: Routledge). A very useful survey of the main issues raised by Gettier-style examples.

Shope, Robert K. (2002) 'Conditions and Analyses of Knowing', *Oxford Handbook to Epistemology*, P. K. Moser (ed.), pp. 25–70 (Oxford: Oxford University Press). A comprehensive treatment of the problem posed by Gettier cases and the various contemporary responses to that problem in the literature. The discussion that starts on p. 29 is most relevant to this chapter. Note that as this chapter develops, it becomes increasingly more demanding.

• ADVANCED FURTHER READING

Chisholm, Roderick (1973) *The Problem of the Criterion* (Milwaukee, WI: Marquette University Press). This is the classic discussion of the problem of the criterion of (relatively) recent times.

Shope, Robert K. (1983) *The Analysis of Knowing a Decade of Research* (Princeton, NJ: Princeton University Press). A comprehensive survey of the initial wave of responses that were offered to the Gettier cases. Not for beginners.

Steup, Mathias, Turri, John & Sosa, Ernest (eds) (2013) *Contemporary Debates in Epistemology* (2nd edn, Oxford: Wiley). This edited collection contains a useful debate (§7) between Duncan Pritchard and Stephen Hetherington on whether knowledge is incompatible with luckily true belief.

Zagzebski, Linda (1999) 'What Is Knowledge?', *Blackwell Companion to Epistemology*, J. Greco & E. Sosa (eds), pp. 92–116 (Oxford: Blackwell). A very thorough overview of the issues surrounding the project of defining knowledge, especially in the light of the Gettier cases.

• FREE INTERNET RESOURCES

Feldman, Fred & Feldman, Richard (2019) 'Roderick Chisholm', *Stanford Encyclopedia of Philosophy*, http://plato.stanford.edu/entries/chisholm/. A well-written overview of the work of this important twentieth-century epistemologist. See especially §§3–4.

Gettier, Edmund L. (1963) 'Is Justified True Belief Knowledge?', *Analysis*, 23, 121–23 [freely available online here: www.ditext.com/gettier/gettier.html]. The article which started the contemporary debate about how best to define knowledge and which contains, by definition, the first official Gettier cases.

Hetherington, Stephen (2005) 'Gettier Problems', *Internet Encyclopedia of Philosophy*, www.iep.utm.edu/g/gettier.htm. An overview of the Gettier problem, and the main responses to it, by a leading epistemologist.

Ichikawa, Jonathan Jenkins & Steup, Matthias (2017) 'The Analysis of Knowledge', *Stanford Encyclopedia of Philosophy*, http://plato.stanford.edu/entries/knowledge-analysis/. An excellent and comprehensive overview of the issues regarding the project of defining knowledge.

Truncellito, David (2007) 'Epistemology', *Internet Encyclopedia of Philosophy*, www.iep.utm.edu/e/epistemo.htm. Read up to the end of §2.b for more on the basic requirements for knowledge.

4

the structure of knowledge

- Knowledge and justification
- The enigmatic nature of justification
- Agrippa's trilemma
- Infinitism
- Coherentism
- Foundationalism

KNOWLEDGE AND JUSTIFICATION

Pick a belief that you hold, a belief the truth of which you are about as certain of as anything else you believe. Take, for example, your belief that the earth orbits the sun, rather than vice versa. If you are certain about this matter then, intuitively, you must regard this belief as being rightly held, as being *justified*. Now ask yourself the following question: what is it that justifies this belief?

This question is vital to the theory of knowledge since, as we saw in Chapter 3, even though Gettier cases show that justification is not sufficient (with true belief) for knowledge, it is at least plausible to suppose that justification is *necessary* for knowledge. Accordingly, understanding what constitutes justification is essential to understanding what constitutes knowledge. As we will see, however, it is very hard to specify the nature of justification.

THE ENIGMATIC NATURE OF JUSTIFICATION

One possible answer to this question of what justifies your belief that the earth orbits the sun could be that *nothing* justifies it; that this belief does not need further support in order to be rightly held. However, as far as most beliefs are concerned (if not all of them), this possibility is not very plausible.

Think of one's belief as being like a house. If a house lacks foundations, then it falls down. The same applies to a belief. If it lacks a solid foundation – if there is nothing

DOI: 10.4324/9781003356110-5

that is justifying this belief – then the belief is not properly held, and so 'falls down'. After all, if one can rightly hold a belief without that belief being supported by good grounds of any sort, then that seems to preclude us from making any epistemic distinction between the beliefs of rational and irrational agents.

For example, one could imagine a child forming a belief that the moon is a balloon on no particular basis whatsoever. If we are to regard our belief that the earth orbits the sun as unsupported by further grounds, then this puts it on par with this child's belief about the moon. Surely, however, our belief is justified in a way that the child's belief is not. And note that the difference here cannot be simply that our belief that the earth orbits the sun is true since, as we noted in Chapter 3, a belief does not have to be true to be justified. Those living a thousand years ago, before it was widely known that the earth went around the sun, were surely justified in believing that the sun orbited the earth.

So it seems that, at least in the vast majority of cases, there must be some sort of support that can be offered in favour of one's belief; some sort of supporting ground or reason. In the case of one's belief that the earth goes around the sun, one possible supporting reason that might be offered in favour of this belief could be that one read that this is so in a science textbook, one that was written by an expert in the field. In effect, what one is doing here is supporting one's belief that the earth goes around the sun by offering one's further belief that this claim can be found in a reliable textbook.

The problem with supporting one's beliefs by offering further beliefs, however, is that it invites the question of what grounds these 'supporting' beliefs. Since we have already rejected the possibility that our beliefs can, in the main at least, be justified while being groundless, this means that we must offer further support for the supporting beliefs. Moreover, insofar as we grant that it is these supporting beliefs that are in some way justifying the original belief, then if we are unable to offer adequate grounds to back up the supporting beliefs then neither the supporting beliefs *nor* the original belief are justified. If I believe that the earth goes around the sun because that's what science textbooks tell me, but I have no good reason for believing what science textbooks tell me, then I can hardly consider my belief that the earth goes around the sun to be adequately supported. The trouble is, of course, whatever grounds I offer in favour of my belief that I can trust what science textbooks tell me will be itself a further belief that stands in need of support, and so a regress looms. Once one starts offering grounds in favour of one's belief, one seems doomed to continue offering further grounds endlessly on pain of failing to offer any adequate support for the original belief.

In order to see this point more clearly, think again of the analogy with the house. We noted above that a house that lacks any foundations will fall down. But a house that has a foundation which is supported by a further foundation, and a further foundation, and a further foundation, and so on indefinitely, will be no better off. Unless there is something holding the whole structure up, then having a limitless series of foundations will do nothing to stop the building tumbling to the floor.

In real life, of course, we will be unable to offer new grounds in favour of our beliefs beyond a certain point. Instead, we will start to return to claims that have already been entered. What justifies you in believing that the earth orbits the sun? Because that's what science textbooks tell you. What justifies you in believing what science textbooks tell you? Because, back in school, your science teacher assured you that they were good sources of information of this sort. What justifies you in trusting what your science teacher told you? Because what she said tallied with what is printed in science textbooks. Here we have a chain of justification that has eventually come full circle in that a supporting reason – regarding what's written in science textbooks – offered earlier is reappearing further down the chain of justification. But a circular justification is hardly much of a justification.

Think again of the analogy with the house. If the foundations for that house rest on further foundations which ultimately rest in turn on the original foundations, then the house won't have a chance of standing for long. *Something* needs to be holding everything up, and as matters stand nothing is doing this job at all!

● AGRIPPA'S TRILEMMA

We thus seem to be faced with three unpalatable alternatives regarding how we answer the question of what justifies our beliefs. These alternatives are as follows:

1 our beliefs are unsupported;
2 our beliefs are supported by an infinite chain of justification (i.e. one in which no supporting ground appears more than once); or
3 our beliefs are supported by a circular chain of justification (i.e. one in which a supporting ground appears more than once).

All of these alternatives are unpalatable since they all seem to imply that we aren't really justified in holding our original belief. Just as a house with no foundations, or with an unending chain of foundations, or with circular foundations, would not be well supported – it would simply fall down – so a belief with no foundations (i.e. Option 1), or with an unending chain of foundations (i.e. Option 2), or with circular foundations (i.e. Option 3) would not be well supported, and thus, intuitively, would not be justified.

This problem regarding the structure of justification is known as **Agrippa's trilemma**, named after the ancient Greek philosopher **Agrippa**. A *trilemma* is like a dilemma except that it forces you to choose from *three* unpalatable options rather than just two. What's useful about this puzzle is that it enables us to focus our attentions on the different ways in which knowledge might be structured if it is to avoid the trilemma. Three particular kinds of epistemological theory suggest themselves.

● INFINITISM

The least plausible (and thus historically less popular) response to Agrippa's trilemma involves embracing Option 2 and holding that an infinite chain of justification

> ## Agrippa (*c.* AD 100)
>
> The [Pyrrhonian] sceptic, being a lover of his kind, desires to cure by speech, as best he can, the self-conceit and rashness of the dogmatists.
>
> Sextus Empiricus, *Outlines of Pyrrhonism*
>
> Agrippa belongs to a group of ancient Greek philosophers who are known as Pyrrhonian sceptics. Very little is known about him because, in common with other Pyrrhonian sceptics, he doesn't seem to have written anything himself. In essence, the reason for this is that such philosophers don't think that you should ever assert anything, and so they certainly don't think that you should write down what your philosophical views are for posterity. Indeed, all we really know about Agrippa relates to the trilemma that was attributed to him by the ancient Greek historian Diogenes Laertius (*c.* AD 250) in his history of Greek philosophy. In this work, as in the other main source for our knowledge of the Pyrrhonian sceptics – *Outlines of Pyrrhonism*, by Sextus Empiricus (*c.* AD 200) – the Agrippan sceptical strategy was actually expressed in terms of *five* sceptical strategies which are designed to induce doubt. Since it is three of these strategies which pose the main sceptical threat, however, Agrippa's sceptical challenge was soon understood in terms of them alone, and thus we get Agrippa's trilemma as it is described here.

can justify a belief. This position is known as **infinitism**. On the face of it, the view is unsustainable because it is unclear how an infinite chain of grounds could ever justify a belief any more than an infinite series of foundations could ever support a house. Nevertheless, this view does have some defenders, and those who advance this thesis argue that aside from brute counter-intuition, it isn't obvious why an infinite chain of grounds can't justify.

For reasons of space, we won't dwell on this view here, however, but focus instead on the two theories about the structure of justification, and thus knowledge, which have been historically more popular (see the further readings at the end of this chapter for a recent defence of infinitism).

• COHERENTISM

A more plausible (and more popular) response to Agrippa's trilemma takes on Option 3 and holds that a circular chain of supporting grounds *can* justify a belief. This view, known as **coherentism**, is usually supplemented with the proviso that the circle of justification needs to be sufficiently large if it is to play this supporting role, so the position accepts that small circles of justification won't do. Still, it is hard to reconcile coherentism with the simple-minded thought that a circular chain of justification, no matter how large, offers no support to a belief at all.

W. V. O. Quine (1908–2000)

No statement is immune to revision.

Quine, 'Two Dogmas of Empiricism'

The American philosopher **Willard Van Orman Quine** was without doubt one of the towering figures of twentieth-century philosophy. One of the guiding themes of Quine's work was a rejection of what is known as 'first' philosophy (see the box on **René Descartes**), where this is understood as a standpoint which is prior to, and completely independent of, scientific investigation and from which science can be evaluated. In this spirit, Quine argued against there being claims – such as philosophical claims – which cannot be, even in principle, revised by future science.

Such a view naturally goes hand in hand with coherentism, where the epistemic standing of any belief depends on one's network of beliefs as a whole, with no one belief standing apart, epistemically, from the others.

Aside from his coherentism, Quine also made significant contributions to such areas of philosophy as logic, the philosophy of language, metaphysics, and the philosophy of truth.

Part of the motivation for coherentism tends to be somewhat practical in that coherentists claim that we do in fact justify our beliefs in the way that they describe, in that our grounds for believing any particular proposition often implicitly involve a general network, or 'web', of other beliefs that we hold. One way of expressing this idea is by saying that the particular beliefs that we hold reflect a general world view that we have. That I experience the world in the way that I do – such that I spontaneously form beliefs about that world – is a product of this world view.

Consider, for example, the difference between myself and someone who lived several hundred years ago and who still thinks that the sun orbits the earth rather than vice versa. Given his world view, his seeing the sun rising in the morning lends support to his belief that the earth is the centre of the sun's orbit. In contrast, someone like myself who lives in the present day, and who therefore knows that the earth in fact orbits the sun, treats the sun's 'rising' in the morning as indicating nothing of the sort. We each have different world views which inform the beliefs that we spontaneously form. Notice, however, that while the person who lives prior to the Copernican revolution is wrong in his beliefs, it is plausible to suppose that his belief is justified by virtue of the background of beliefs that he holds. Given the way his belief is supported by the general world view that he holds, and the mesh of beliefs that make up this world view, it is entirely reasonable for him to believe that the sun's rising in the morning is further confirmation of his belief that the sun orbits the earth.

Still, even if this is in fact the way in which we ordinarily form our beliefs – by implicit appeal to a network of beliefs which make up our general world view – that fact by itself doesn't ensure that we are right to do so. Perhaps we are just not careful enough in how we form our beliefs, and this lack of care is reflected in how we simply take a certain world view for granted. After all, it took quite some time before people abandoned the old pre-Copernican picture of how the earth and the sun interacted, which prompts the question of whether if people had been more critical of their world view and the beliefs that make up this world view, then this would have resulted in this false picture of how the earth relates to the sun being overturned far quicker. In short, the point is that the mere fact that we all have a tendency to form beliefs in a certain way does not by itself show that we *ought* to form our beliefs in this way.

The motivation for coherentism isn't just practical, however, since part of the story involves pointing out that given the implausibility of alternative theories, it is essential that we understand justification in this way. We have already looked at infinitism, which is clearly an unintuitive view (though note that this is not to say that it is false), so it remains to consider the third option – and certainly the most popular option, historically – that is available.

● FOUNDATIONALISM

This option is known as **foundationalism**, and it responds to Agrippa's trilemma by accepting, in line with Option 1, that sometimes a belief can be justified without being supported by any further beliefs. On the face of it, this view might seem problematic for the reason mentioned above regarding how beliefs that are not properly grounded – such as the child's belief that the moon is a balloon – do not appear to be likely candidates to be counted as justified. What the dominant form of foundationalism argues, however, is that some beliefs do not require further justification because they are, in a sense, *self-justifying*. This type of foundationalism is known as **classical foundationalism** and it argues that knowledge is structured in such a way that chains of justification end with special self-justifying foundational beliefs which do not stand in need of any further support.

René Descartes (1596–1650)

I think, therefore I am. (*Cogito ergo sum.*)

Descartes, *Discourse on Method*

The French philosopher and mathematician René Descartes is one of the founding fathers of modern philosophy. His most famous work is his *Meditations on First Philosophy* in which, among other things, he offers a radically new way of approaching epistemology.

(continued)

(continued)

Descartes' idea is that in order to put our knowledge on a secure foundation, it is necessary to first subject it to what he called the 'method of doubt'. This involves doubting as much as can be doubted among one's beliefs until one finds the indubitable, and thus epistemologically secure, foundation on which one's knowledge can be built. In the service of this end, Descartes put forward a number of radical **sceptical hypotheses** – scenarios which are indistinguishable from normal experience, but in which one is radically in error, such as that one's experiences are a product of a dream – in order to discover which of his beliefs were immune to doubt. By applying the method of doubt, Descartes was led to the conclusion that the indubitable foundation of our knowledge is our belief in our own existence, since in doubting our existence, we thereby prove that we exist (since how else could we be able to doubt?). Hence the famous claim, 'I think, therefore I am'.

Ironically, the powerful sceptical arguments that Descartes invented have held more sway than his subsequent anti-sceptical arguments. Accordingly, although it was not his aim to make us sceptical about the possibility of knowledge, this is in fact what his epistemological investigations seem to have achieved.

Aside from his work in epistemology, Descartes made important contributions to just about every other area of philosophy as well. In addition, he also conducted research on scientific and mathematical questions, making a longstanding contribution to, for example, geometry.

Perhaps the most famous exponent of classical foundationalism is Descartes, whom we first saw in Chapter 3. Descartes argued that the foundations for our knowledge were those beliefs that were immune to doubt and which were therefore certain and self-evidently true. The example he gave of such a belief was one's belief in one's own existence. As Descartes argued, such a belief is indubitable because in doubting it one proves that one is alive to doubt it, and therefore proves that it is true. Such a belief is therefore by its nature self-justifying, and so does not stand in need of further grounds in order to be justifiably held. In a sense, one's belief in this proposition is, plausibly, infallible, in that one could not possibly be in error in this regard. If this is right, then any chain of justification which ended with this belief could thus properly stop at this juncture.

The main problem facing classical foundationalism has always been to identify those self-justifying beliefs that can serve as foundations; or at least offer an account of the foundational beliefs that is not unduly restrictive. The difficulty is that it seems there must be some fairly strict constraint put on foundational beliefs if we are to allow them to serve as the basis for our non-foundational beliefs. But if the constraints on foundational beliefs are too strict, then we risk having a set of foundational beliefs which is problematically small.

For example, suppose one argues, plausibly, that the foundational beliefs had better be those beliefs that one is infallible about – that is, beliefs which just could not be wrong – since only an immunity to error of this sort would ensure that these beliefs could be justified without reliance on any further beliefs. The idea would thus be that the epistemic status of one's everyday **fallible** beliefs which could be in error is traced back to infallible foundational beliefs where the regress of justification comes to an end.

The problem, however, is that there are very few (if any) beliefs that we are infallible about, and the candidate beliefs in this regard do not seem to be able to perform the function of supporting most of our everyday beliefs. Take my belief that two plus two makes four, for example, something which I might plausibly take myself to be infallible about, since it is far from obvious how I could be wrong about this (though with a little ingenuity we can think of cases in which even this belief might be rationally in doubt). Even if this is right, it is far from clear how this belief is supposed to support the numerous beliefs about the world that I currently hold – such as that I am currently sitting at my desk – since this mathematical belief bears no obvious relation to my beliefs about the world.

The same goes for the belief in one's existence that we looked at above in our discussion of Descartes' classical foundationalism. How could the great mass of beliefs that I have about the world be dependent upon a very narrow and specific belief of this sort? The only way to deal with this problem is, it seems, to weaken the requirements one sets on foundational beliefs, perhaps allowing that they could be fallible beliefs after all. For example, maybe one's beliefs about one's immediate experience – about how the world seems to you, for instance – should be regarded as foundational beliefs. The problem with this approach, however, is that it faces the problem of explaining why such beliefs deserve to be treated as foundational in the first place (such beliefs are not obviously infallible). That is, we are stuck between two unpalatable options here. Either we set the requirements on foundational beliefs quite high so that they are plausible, but then face the problem of explaining how such a narrow set of foundational beliefs can serve as a foundation for all the non-foundational beliefs; or else we set the requirements on foundational beliefs quite low, but then face the problem of explaining just why such beliefs should be treated as foundational at all.

It is thus not clear that we get any more comfort from the threat posed by Agrippa's trilemma by appealing to a form of foundationalism than we do by appealing to one of the other standard responses to this problem, such as coherentism or infinitism.

● CHAPTER SUMMARY

- We began by noting that, intuitively, if we are to have knowledge, then we must be justified in what we believe. We therefore asked the question of what justification is.
- According to Agrippa's trilemma, there are only three alternatives in this regard, and none of them are particularly appealing on the face of it. The first alternative is to regard one's belief as being justified by nothing at all; no further grounds. The

problem with this option is obvious, since if there is nothing supporting the belief, then in what sense can it be justified? (We used the analogy with a house to illustrate this. A house with no foundations will not stand.) The second alternative is to regard one's belief as justified by a further ground which, presumably, will be itself another belief. The problem with this suggestion is that this further belief will also need to be justified, since if the original belief is based on an unjustified second belief, then it is hard to see how the second belief can offer any support to the first belief. But if the second belief needs to be justified, then that belief will itself need to be supported by a further belief, and so on indefinitely. We thus have an infinite regress looming. (Consider the analogy with the house again. A house with an unending series of foundations will not stand.) Finally, there is the third option of allowing the supporting beliefs, at some point in the chain of justification, to be beliefs that have appeared elsewhere in the chain. This option thus allows circular justifications. This third option is not appealing either, however, since a circular chain of justification seems little better than no justification at all. (To return to the analogy, a house with a circular set of foundations, with no foundations holding all the other foundations up, will not stand.) It thus seems hard to fathom how any belief could be justified.

- We considered three responses to Agrippa's trilemma, where each of them took one of the unpalatable options just mentioned. The first option was infinitism, which holds that an infinite chain of grounds *can* justify a belief.
- The second response was coherentism, as defended by Quine, which holds that a circular chain of grounds, so long as it has the right sort of properties at any rate (e.g. being large enough), *can* justify a belief.
- Finally, we looked at foundationalism, and classical foundationalism in particular – as defended by Descartes – which holds that there are some grounds which do not require any further support, and which can thus act as foundations for the beliefs that rest upon them. We noted that what is specific to classical foundationalism is that it regards these 'foundational' beliefs as having properties which ensure that they are self-justifying – such as the property of being indubitable or infallibly held. The problem facing this view, however, is that it is difficult to find an account of these foundational beliefs that is plausible while at the same time counting a sufficient number of our beliefs as foundational so that they can support the other beliefs we hold.

• STUDY QUESTIONS

1 Describe, in your own words, Agrippa's trilemma. Consider a belief that you hold and then try to use Agrippa's trilemma to call into question this belief (you may find it helpful to try this with a friend).

2 What is infinitism, and how does it respond to Agrippa's trilemma? What, if anything, is wrong with it?

3 What is coherentism, and how does it respond to Agrippa's trilemma? What do you think of the claim made by some defenders of coherentism that it offers the best description of how we in fact go about justifying our beliefs? Do you agree?

Assuming that it is true, do you think this fact is relevant to whether or not coherentism is true?

4 What is foundationalism, and how does it respond to Agrippa's trilemma? Explain, in your own words, what properties foundational beliefs must have according to classical foundationalism, and give three examples of your own beliefs which might be said to have these properties.

5 Why did Descartes think that his belief in his own existence was a foundational belief? Could foundational beliefs of this sort provide support for your beliefs about the world? If so, then explain how. If not, then say why.

● INTRODUCTORY FURTHER READING

Bett, Richard (2010) 'Pyrrhonian Skepticism', *Routledge Companion to Epistemology*, S. Bernecker & D. H. Pritchard (eds), Ch. 37, pp. 403–13 (London: Routledge). A helpful overview of Pyrrhonian scepticism, and its import for the contemporary epistemological debate.

Chisholm, Roderick (1989) *The Theory of Knowledge* (Englewood Cliffs, NJ: Prentice-Hall). A classic textbook in epistemology which also contains an influential defence of a version of classical foundationalism.

Williams, Bernard (1978) *Descartes: The Project of Pure Inquiry* (Harmondsworth: Penguin). A classic introduction to the philosophy of Descartes, paying particular attention to his epistemology.

Williams, Michael (2001) *Problems of Knowledge* (Oxford: Oxford University Press). See Chapter 5 for an excellent introduction to Agrippa's trilemma, and some of the issues that it raises.

● ADVANCED FURTHER READING

Bailey, Alan (2002) *Sextus Empiricus and Pyrrhonian Scepticism* (Oxford: Oxford University Press). A lively treatment of Pyrrhonian scepticism.

Bonjour, Laurence (1985) *The Structure of Empirical Knowledge* (Cambridge, MA: Harvard University Press). Perhaps the most comprehensive defence of coherentism in recent times. Note, however, that Bonjour has since recanted and now advances a form of foundationalism.

Hookway, Christopher (1988) *Quine: Language, Experience and Reality* (Oxford: Polity Press). A classic book introducing the philosophy of W. V. O. Quine.

Steup, Mathias, Turri, John & Sosa, Ernest (eds) (2013) *Contemporary Debates in Epistemology* (2nd edn, Oxford: Wiley). This edited collection contains three useful debates relevant to this section: (1) a discussion (§9) between Jim Pryor and Richard Fumerton on foundationalism (via the topic of 'immediate justification'); (2) a debate (§10) between Catherine Elgin and James van Cleve on coherentism; and (3) a discussion (§11) between Peter Klein and Carl Ginet on the merits of infinitism (Klein is the foremost contemporary advocate of infinitism).

• FREE INTERNET RESOURCES

Comesaña, Juan & Klein, Peter (2019) 'Skepticism', *Stanford Encyclopedia of Philosophy*, http://plato.stanford.edu/entries/skepticism/. See §5 for an overview of Pyrrhonian scepticism – and of Agrippa's trilemma in particular – and some of the main responses.

Newman, Lex (2019) 'Descartes' Epistemology', *Stanford Encyclopedia of Philosophy*, http://plato.stanford.edu/entries/descartes-epistemology/. A helpful introduction to the epistemological ramifications of Descartes' epistemology.

Thorsrud, Harold (2004) 'Ancient Greek Skepticism', *Internet Encyclopedia of Philosophy*, www.iep.utm.edu/s/skepanci.htm. An overview of ancient scepticism, including discussion of the style of scepticism, known as Pyrrhonian scepticism, which was advocated by Agrippa, and discussion of Agrippa's trilemma. See especially §3.

Vogt, Katya (2018) 'Ancient Skepticism', *Stanford Encyclopedia of Philosophy*, http://plato.stanford.edu/entries/skepticism-ancient/. An excellent overview of ancient scepticism, including discussion of the style of scepticism, known as Pyrrhonian scepticism, which was advocated by Agrippa, and discussion of Agrippa's trilemma.

5

rationality

- Rationality, justification, and knowledge
- Epistemic rationality and the goal of truth
- The goal(s) of epistemic rationality
- The (un)importance of epistemic rationality
- Rationality and responsibility
- Epistemic internalism/externalism

RATIONALITY, JUSTIFICATION, AND KNOWLEDGE

We often praise people for their rationality and, conversely, criticise others for their irrationality. For example, a judge who is clear-headed and conscientious in her reasoning when forming a judgement in the light of the evidence put before her might well be commended for her rationality. In contrast, we would no doubt chastise a judge who reached her verdict simply by tossing a coin on the grounds that such activity is irrational. A crucial question for epistemologists, however, has been how to explain the distinction that is being made here.

The importance of this question for those who wish to theorise about knowledge is that intuitively, it is only rational beliefs that are candidates for knowledge, with irrational beliefs by their nature not being instances of knowledge. Think again of the rational judge, for example, and one of the beliefs that she forms in reaching a verdict, such as regarding the defendant's guilt. Such a well-founded belief, if true, seems an obvious candidate for knowledge. If the belief had been formed irrationally, however – such as if it had been formed as part of a judgement that was reached in the light of prejudice against the defendant's race or religion, rather than in terms of the facts of the case – then intuitively, it wouldn't count as a case of knowledge. If you believe that a defendant is guilty because of the colour of her skin, rather than because of the evidence, then even if this belief is true, it won't count as a case of knowledge, and one natural explanation for this is that the belief in question is irrational and irrational beliefs don't count as knowledge.

Another reason for those who theorise about knowledge to be interested in rationality is that there seems to be a close connection between rationality and justification. In particular, it is plausible to suppose that, in most cases at least, a justified belief

DOI: 10.4324/9781003356110-6

is a rational one, and vice versa. Think again of the rational judge's belief in the defendant's guilt. Wouldn't we also say that it was justified? In contrast, consider the irrational judge's belief in the defendant's guilt based on prejudice. Wouldn't we say that it was unjustified? Moreover, given that (as we noted in Chapter 4) justification is plausibly necessary for knowledge, this close connection between justification and rationality would explain why we also tend to regard rationality as necessary for knowledge as well. For now, we will focus on rationality independently of justification, but there are prima facie grounds for thinking that the two notions are closely associated, and we will return at the end of the chapter to look at the relation between these two notions in more detail.

• EPISTEMIC RATIONALITY AND THE GOAL OF TRUTH

Before we begin our examination of rationality we need to notice that as theorists of knowledge we are interested in a specific sort of rationality, what is known as **epistemic rationality**, since it is only this sort of rationality that is relevant to the theory of knowledge. Very simply, epistemic rationality is a form of rationality which is aimed at the goal of true belief.

In order to see this distinction between types of rationality that are epistemic and those that aren't, consider the following case (one that we have seen before, as it happens, in Chapter 2). Suppose that you need to jump a ravine in order to save your life (you are being pursued by an angry mob, perhaps, and this is the only escape route). Knowing what you do about your psychology, you may be entirely aware that if you reflect on the dangers involved in this jump, then you won't be able to summon the necessary commitment and concentration to make the required leap. In such circumstances, where your aim is to save your skin, the best course of action is to ignore the dangers as best as you can – to set them from your mind – and focus solely on the leap. Moreover, insofar as one can 'manufacture' one's beliefs, it would also be wise to do what you can to convince yourself that you can indeed make this jump, since it is only if one is convinced that one will succeed (and failure doesn't bear thinking about).

In a sense, what you are doing here is entirely rational, since the course of action that you are undertaking is indeed the best way to achieve your goals. The kind of rationality here, however, is not epistemic rationality, since it is not a rationality that is aimed at truth at all. Indeed, if anything, this sort of rationality is aimed at a sort of self-deception. If, in contrast, one were focused solely on gaining true beliefs, then that would actually *mitigate* against you attaining the goal in question since it would lead you to recognise the dangers involved in the jump and so undermine your attempt to successfully make that jump.

Because the rationality in this case is not aimed at the truth, even if the belief that resulted from this course of action was indeed true (i.e. you could make this jump), it wouldn't be a case of knowledge since you can't come to know that you can make a leap by reflecting on how you must make the leap in order to survive. Compare this case with that of the belief formed by the rational judge, who forms her belief by judiciously weighing up the evidence involved. Clearly this belief, if true, can count as an instance of knowledge, thus again indicating that the rationality in question is epistemic rationality.

Moreover, notice that although the non-epistemic form of rationality in play in the 'self-deception' case does result in you holding a belief as a result of undertaking a course of action, we could just as well talk about the rationality of your *action* as your belief. It is rational, for example, for you to confidently make that leap given that your goal is to save your life. As epistemologists, however, we are primarily interested in belief rather than action, since it is only beliefs that can amount to knowledge, as we saw in Chapter 1.

Pascal's wager

> If God does not exist, one will lose nothing by believing in him, while if he does exist, one will lose everything by not believing.
>
> Blaise Pascal, *Pensées*

A good way of highlighting the distinction between a rational belief and a specifically epistemically rational belief is by considering **Pascal's wager**, named after the French philosopher, scientist, and mathematician Blaise Pascal (1623–62). The devoutly religious Pascal wanted to show that belief in God is rational. To this end, he offered the argument that one has nothing to lose and everything to gain by believing in God, and thus that belief in God is the rational thing to do.

After all, if one believes in God and this belief is false, then one has lost very little, while if the belief is true, then the reward of eternal life in Heaven will more than compensate for whatever potential inconvenience belief in God's existence brought you during your life. In contrast, if you don't believe in God, then you run the risk of spending an eternity in Hell, which is clearly a heavy price to pay. Moreover, you have to do one or the other (believe or not believe), so there is no way of avoiding this choice.

Put another way, we can imagine the issue of whether we should believe in God as being like a bet (or *wager*) that we all must take. Either we bet on God's existence (and so believe in God), or we bet on God's non-existence (and so don't believe in God). Pascal is saying that given the fantastic possible benefits that can accrue from having a true belief in God (i.e. eternal life), the tremendous costs involved in failing to believe in God if God does exist (i.e. eternal damnation), and the absence of any substantial costs in falsely believing in God's existence, the best thing to do is bet on God's existence: it is rational to believe in God.

(continued)

(continued)

There has been much philosophical debate over the effectiveness of this argument, but note that even if the argument works, it does not show that belief in God is epistemically rational, as Pascal fully recognised. Pascal is not, for example, saying that this argument gives you a reason for thinking that God does in fact exist (i.e. for thinking that a belief in God's existence would be *true*), only that it is *prudent* (and thus in this sense rational) for you to believe in God, which is not the same thing. Pascal thus gives us a neat illustration of how a belief can be (in some sense) rational without thereby being epistemically rational.

The kind of rationality that we are particularly interested in as theorists of knowledge is thus epistemic rationality. Note that that's not to say that there aren't close connections between epistemic and non-epistemic forms of rationality – indeed, we would expect there to be many overlaps and similarities – it is just that our primary focus as theorists of knowledge is epistemic rationality. With this point in mind, we will proceed.

• THE GOAL(S) OF EPISTEMIC RATIONALITY

One problem facing the notion of epistemic rationality is that to say that this form of rationality is concerned with true belief doesn't tell us all that much since we still need to know exactly *how* it is concerned with true belief. As we will see, explaining how epistemic rationality is concerned with true belief is harder to do than it might initially appear.

Let's start with perhaps the most natural way of understanding epistemic rationality. If true belief is the goal of an epistemic rationality, then the obvious way of understanding this claim is to demand that one should *maximise* one's true beliefs (i.e. try to believe as many truths as possible). With this account of epistemic rationality in mind, we could explain the rationality of the non-coin-tossing judge in terms of the way in which she formed her judgement on the grounds that evaluating all the evidence in a careful and objective manner (i.e. without allowing oneself to be swayed by the emotion of the case) is a good way of getting to the truth in this regard. In contrast, while the coin-tossing judge may well end up delivering the same verdict as our rational judge, we would not count her as rational because the method she is using to form her belief is not likely to lead to the truth.

There are problems with the *maximising* conception of epistemic rationality, however. For example, if this account of epistemic rationality just means that we should try to have as many true beliefs as possible, then it is open to some fairly straightforward counter-examples. After all, memorising names and addresses from the phone book may well lead one to have thousands of true beliefs, but the beliefs in question wouldn't be of any consequence. Indeed, we would usually regard this sort of truth-seeking behaviour as very *irrational*. Even setting this problem to one side, however, there remains the fundamental difficulty that the best way to maximise the number of one's true beliefs might well be to believe just about anything, since this would ensure that one has the most chance of believing the truth. Crucially, of course, this sort of truth-seeking strategy would lead one to form lots of *false* beliefs as well, and that is hardly desirable.

One way of dealing with this latter problem (we will come back to the former problem in a moment) might be to modify our conception of epistemic rationality so that it demands not that one maximises truth in one's beliefs, but rather that one *minimises* falsehood. That way we would be able to treat any agent who simply believes as many things as possible as irrational on the grounds that this will not be the best way of minimising falsehood. The problem with this suggestion, however, is that the best way of minimising falsehood in one's beliefs is surely not to believe anything (or at least believe as little as possible), but this would mean that one would have very few true beliefs either, if any.

What is needed then is some way of balancing the goal of maximising truth in one's beliefs with the related goal of minimising falsehood. We want agents to take some risks regarding the falsity of their beliefs, and so we don't want them to be overly cautious and not believe anything; but equally neither do we want agents to go 'all out' for the truth at the expense of widespread falsity in their beliefs. Specifying just how we should understand this 'balanced' conception of rationality is, however, quite hard to do.

THE (UN)IMPORTANCE OF EPISTEMIC RATIONALITY

Moreover, don't forget that we still have the outstanding problem of specifying epistemic rationality such that it doesn't count someone who merely aims to believe lots of trivial truths (such as names in a phone book) as epistemically rational.

One way of responding to this problem is to deny that there is any challenge here to respond to. That is, one could argue that such beliefs are entirely epistemically rational, and that's the end of the matter. Proponents of this line of thought will concede, of course, that there is *something* irrational about this way of forming one's beliefs, but will claim that the irrationality in question is not epistemic (recall that we noted above that there may be other types of rationality besides epistemic rationality). That is, they will argue that this person has rather trivial goals, and that this is to be deplored, but that, from a purely epistemic point of view, there is nothing wrong with forming one's beliefs in this way.

The problem with this line of thought is that it has the unfortunate consequence of trivialising epistemic rationality, since the specifically epistemic rationality that we are interested in as epistemologists does not turn out to be all that rational, generally speaking. That said, one might respond by pointing out that there is a lot more to life than gaining true beliefs and that this way of dealing with the problem in hand simply recognises this fact. Put another way, we are interested in gaining knowledge, and thus true beliefs, because we have all sorts of other goals that this knowledge can be utilised in the service of, such as furthering our relationships, our career, and our interests. A life purely devoted to gaining true beliefs might not be a life that we are interested in leading. In short, one should be rational in all the many ways that one can be rational, and not just be concerned with being epistemically rational.

There is another way of responding to problem posed by trivial truths, which is to claim that, contrary to first appearances, the agent in the 'phone book' case, and others like her, are not epistemically rational after all. This way of responding to the problem is not nearly as hopeless as it might at first sound. After all, the thing about important truths is that they beget lots of other truths. If I come to have true beliefs about the ultimate physics of the universe, for example, then I will thereby acquire many other true beliefs about related matters. Learning names from the phone book is not like that, since these truths are pretty much self-standing – in acquiring these true beliefs you are unlikely to acquire many others. Thus, if your goal is to maximise true belief, while minimising false beliefs, then you would be wise to aim at those true beliefs of substance and set such trivial goals as memorising names in a phone book to one side. If this is right, then epistemic rationality is rescued from the grip of this objection.

There is thus some room for manoeuvre when it comes to this objection to epistemic rationality. On the one hand, one can accept the objection while maintaining that its importance can be easily overestimated, in that there is more to being rational than being epistemically rational. On the other hand, one can resist it and claim that the cases offered for thinking that being epistemically rational means that one should pursue trivial true beliefs are based on a mistake.

• RATIONALITY AND RESPONSIBILITY

Even if we have a suitable conception of what the goals of epistemic rationality are, problems still remain. In the examples given above of the rational and irrational judges, we implicitly took it for granted that the agents were in some sense responsible for the truth-seeking procedures that they were employing. There is a good reason for this, since, typically at least, we only praise or blame agents for doing things where they can reasonably be thought to be responsible for their actions. The rational judge is thus epistemically responsible, and so praiseworthy, for her conscientious behaviour because she could have been biased or careless in passing her judgement if she'd been so inclined. Equally, the irrational coin-tossing judge is epistemically irresponsible, and so blameworthy, for her epistemically reckless behaviour because she could have used proper procedures if she'd wanted to.

It isn't always obvious, however, that agents can be held responsible for the way in which they form their beliefs. One consideration in this respect is that some beliefs, such as basic perceptual beliefs, are both *spontaneous* and *involuntary*, and so just don't seem to be the sort of thing that agents can have any control over. If, in good lighting conditions and so forth, I see my father come into the hallway, then I will *immediately* form a belief that he is in the hallway – there is no room here for a prior rational deliberation. In this regard, beliefs are very unlike actions (most actions at any rate), since the latter do tend to be in our control.

Even setting this issue to one side, there remains the problem that sometimes agents are simply taught the wrong **epistemic norms** to follow, where an epistemic norm is a rule which one follows in order to gain true beliefs. That one should take care when weighing up evidence, and be as impartial as possible as one does so, is an example of an epistemic norm, since it enables one to have a better chance of getting to the truth. We are usually taught these kinds of norms – often tacitly – as we grow up (our teacher might, for example, criticise us for guessing an answer to a question rather than working it out properly).

Imagine, however, someone who has been raised by being taught all the *wrong* epistemic norms (she has been isolated from the world at large, say, and has been systematically misled by all those that she has come into contact with in her secluded community). Suppose, for example, that she has been taught that one ought to find out the truth about certain subject matters (such as whether or not a defendant is guilty) by simply tossing a coin. Is this person forming her beliefs in an epistemically rational way?

One possibility here is that we might regard this agent as being entirely epistemically rational, at least in one sense of that notion, since, *by her lights* at least, she is forming her beliefs in the right kind of way. There is, one might argue, a very big difference between someone who forms her belief by tossing a coin who *should know better* – who has, that is, been taught the correct epistemic norms – and someone who forms her belief by tossing a coin and who, *to the best of her knowledge*, believes that this is the right way to proceed. In the former case, the agent is responsible for the way in which she is forming her belief, and so blameworthy, in a way that is not applicable in the latter case.

The kind of epistemic rationality that is at issue here is called a **deontic epistemic rationality**. It holds that an agent's belief is epistemically rational just so long as the agent does not contravene any epistemic norm in coming to form that belief *by her own lights*. That is, an agent can be epistemically rational *and* employ the wrong epistemic norms, just so long as she is not to blame for her employment of the wrong epistemic norms. Since even those who form their beliefs by tossing a coin can sometimes count as epistemically rational on this view, deontic epistemic rationality is a very weak conception of what epistemic rationality demands.

In contrast, a stronger, *non-deontic* conception of epistemic rationality would demand that agents not only do not blamelessly contravene any epistemic norm but also that the epistemic norms in question should be, as a matter of fact, the *right* ones (i.e. the truth-conducive ones). In this non-deontic view, even the agent who blamelessly forms her belief by tossing a coin does not count as epistemically rational, and this might be thought to be an advantage of the thesis. The problem with this stance, however, is that it appears to break the very intuitive connection between epistemic rationality and epistemic responsibility. We don't blame the hapless agent who forms her belief by tossing a coin for her epistemic failings since it isn't her fault that she was taught the wrong epistemic norms – by her lights at least, she is being epistemically responsible. And yet on this view, we should count her as not being epistemically rational nonetheless. In short, on this proposal epistemic responsibility and epistemic rationality can come apart.

● EPISTEMIC INTERNALISM/EXTERNALISM

It thus seems that we are caught between two opposing conceptions of epistemic rationality. The first has the advantage of directly connecting the notion of epistemic rationality with that of epistemic responsibility, but has the drawback that the demands it imposes are very weak. The second imposes a stronger constraint on epistemic rationality, but does so at the expense of breaking the link between epistemic rationality and epistemic responsibility. We might call the former deontic notion of epistemic rationality an **epistemic internalist** conception of epistemic rationality in that it ties epistemic rationality to what the agent can be held accountable for. In contrast, we might call the latter notion of epistemic rationality an **epistemic externalist** conception of epistemic rationality in that it breaks the connection between epistemic rationality and what the agent can be held accountable for. Roughly speaking, epistemic internalism makes one's epistemic standing something that one has control over; while epistemic externalism allows that one's epistemic standing can sometimes depend on factors outside one's control (e.g. whether one has been taught the right epistemic norms).

There is a general philosophical issue here which has ramifications for epistemology as a whole. The problem is that the best way in which to get to the truth (i.e. the most reliable way) need not be discernible to the agent herself. The question we therefore need to ask is whether our epistemology should be *egocentric*, and therefore focused on what the agent is able to discern (i.e. what the agent has good reason to believe are the correct epistemic norms, whether or not they really are the correct epistemic norms); or whether it should be *non-egocentric* in the sense that it allows that other considerations can play a role in determining whether or not an agent's belief is epistemically rationally held (e.g. whether the epistemic norms that the agent is using are, in fact, the right ones).

In order to see how this issue relates to epistemology as a whole, it is worthwhile considering how the notion of epistemic rationality relates to concepts like justification and knowledge, which are central to epistemological theorising. On the face of it, there ought to be a close connection between justification and epistemic rationality, since we often use terms like 'rational' and 'justified' as if they were roughly synonymous. With this in mind, we might argue that justification is just epistemic rationality. Accordingly, if one held that epistemic rationality is just deontic epistemic rationality, then one would end up with an *epistemic internalist egocentric* conception of justification. The problem with this proposal is that it would have the consequence that justified true belief and knowledge could come *radically* apart. After all, our coin-tossing agent, who is only deontically epistemically rational, could hardly be said to *know* anything on this basis, since even if she does end up with a true belief by employing the wrong epistemic norm, it would merely be a matter of luck that her belief is true, and we don't normally treat agents who get to the truth via luck as knowers. In this view of the relationship between justification and epistemic rationality, however, the agent concerned would be entirely justified in forming her belief this way.

On the face of it, this might look like just another Gettier case in which one has a justified true belief which is not thereby knowledge, and so one might think that the problem at hand here is just a variant on the familiar problem posed by Gettier cases more generally. Notice, however, that the case just described is in fact importantly different from a normal Gettier case. This is because in Gettier cases, the agent typically forms her belief via the correct epistemic norm; it is just that the truth of the belief is nevertheless lucky. In this case, in contrast, the agent is employing the wrong epistemic norm, albeit blamelessly. Given this difference between the two sorts of cases, the divorce between justified true belief and knowledge opened up by this conception of the relationship between deontic epistemic rationality and justification may remain even if we found a way to deal with the Gettier cases – the two problems are thus importantly different.

Another reason to think that a conception of justification in terms of deontic epistemic rationality pulls justification apart from knowledge is that we often ascribe knowledge to agents even when they don't form their beliefs responsibly, just so long as they form their beliefs in the right kind of way (i.e. they don't contravene the right epistemic norms). Accordingly, it seems that deontic epistemic rationality cannot be necessary for knowledge, since this form of rationality entails that the belief in question was responsibly formed, and yet knowledge, it seems, does not require this.

For example, consider the way that a small child may go about forming a perceptual belief by simply believing what she seems to see (e.g. she sees a toy in front of her, and so believes that there's a toy in front of her). Suppose that circumstances are otherwise normal and there is nothing specific to indicate that her senses should be doubted in this case (e.g. there aren't any very effective holograms in the vicinity that look just like actual toys). Wouldn't we say that such a belief is an instance of knowledge – that the child *knows* that there is a toy in front of her? The problem is, of course, that we would hardly regard the child as believing responsibly, since she isn't in fact paying any attention to how she forms her belief at all – she's simply doing what comes naturally to her, entirely unreflectively (notice that this is not necessarily to say that she's being *irresponsible* in her believing). Nevertheless, forming your beliefs in this way (i.e. in response to what your senses tell you in normal circumstances and where there are no specific reasons for doubt) is a generally reliable way to form one's beliefs about the world, and, indeed, a good way of gaining knowledge in this regard. Moreover, it doesn't seem to contravene any epistemic norms. So even while not believing responsibly, one can, intuitively, gain knowledge, and this seems to suggest that knowing does not require deontic epistemic rationality.

If we want to have a conception of justification which is understood in terms of epistemic rationality but which also bears a more direct relationship to knowledge, then we might therefore be attracted to the idea of characterising justification in terms of non-deontic epistemic rationality. The difficulty facing this proposal, however, is that our everyday notion of epistemic rationality does seem to be closely associated with epistemic responsibility, and thus with the deontic conception of epistemic rationality. After all, we *would* normally regard an agent as epistemically rational if she responsibly formed her belief via the blameless use of the wrong epistemic norms. Moreover, consider those cases – like that of the child's perceptual belief just outlined – in which the agent concerned does not form her beliefs in a responsible manner. Would we really say that such a belief, even while being (let's agree) a case of knowledge, is epistemically rational? (Of course, we wouldn't say that it was epistemically *irrational*, but that's not the same thing.)

There is thus no straightforward way of reconciling these conflicting intuitions about the relationship between such notions as epistemic rationality, epistemic responsibility, justification, and knowledge, and much of contemporary epistemological theorising has been concerned with offering different pictures of how these concepts relate to one another. Indeed, this conflict of intuitions has prompted some to argue that perhaps we should treat epistemic rationality and knowledge as very different types of notions. The thought is that perhaps justification is, essentially, epistemic rationality, and that epistemic rationality is just deontic epistemic rationality, and thus that we should simply accept that there is no direct connection between knowledge and justification. On this proposal, we replace the traditional conception of epistemology which seeks an integrated account of these three notions with one that regards epistemology as concerned with *two* distinct projects. The first is to analyse those epistemic concepts that are closely tied to epistemic responsibility: epistemic rationality and justification. The second is to analyse knowledge. At the very least, the problems that we have explored here should give us pause to take this suggestion very seriously indeed.

● CHAPTER SUMMARY

- Rationality is important to epistemologists since there seems to be a close connection between having a rational belief and having knowledge (and, conversely, between having an irrational belief and lacking knowledge). Moreover, as we have seen in a previous chapter, knowledge is closely connected with justification, and there seems to be a tight connection between rationally held beliefs and justified beliefs. Understanding rationality could thus cast light on the theory of knowledge, whether indirectly (via the light it casts on justification) or directly.
- The type of rationality that we are interested in as epistemologists is epistemic rationality. Epistemic rationality is specifically aimed at true belief.

- One way of understanding epistemic rationality is that it demands that one should try to maximise one's true beliefs (i.e. have as many true beliefs as possible).
- We noted two problems with the proposal. The first was that one could achieve this goal by acquiring lots of trivial true beliefs (e.g. by learning all the names in a phone directory). Intuitively, however, this is not a very rational thing to do at all. The second problem was that one could maximise one's true beliefs by believing as much as possible, but this would also result in lots of false beliefs. Intuitively, however, having truth as a goal means not just having lots of true beliefs, but also avoiding having false beliefs.
- Reflection on the second problem led us to consider a different conception of epistemic rationality, one that demanded not that we maximise true beliefs but that we minimise false ones. The key problem with this proposal, however, is that the best way to go about meeting this requirement is by believing *nothing*, and this is hardly what we would regard as epistemically rational behaviour.
- We thus concluded that what was required of epistemic rationality was to achieve a balance between the two goals of maximising true beliefs and minimising false beliefs.
- There still remained the problem of apparently epistemically rational agents who devote themselves to gaining trivial true beliefs (e.g. by learning all the names in a phone book). We saw two ways of responding to this problem. The first response embraced the problem and argued that all that it showed is that there is nothing irrational, from a purely epistemic point of view, with such behaviour. The second response argued that the problem was illusory because such cases do not stand up to close scrutiny: the agent in these cases is not, in fact, epistemically rational after all.
- We then distinguished between two conceptions of epistemic rationality: deontic and non-deontic conceptions. According to a deontic epistemic rationality, one is epistemically rational just so long as one forms one's beliefs responsibly. On this proposal, one can form one's beliefs by using the wrong epistemic norms just so long as one does so blamelessly. In contrast, a non-deontic epistemic rationality demands that one employs the right epistemic norms.
- The deontic conception of epistemic rationality is a form of epistemic internalism in that it draws a close connection between epistemic standing and what the agent can be held epistemically responsible for. In contrast, the non-deontic conception of epistemic rationality is a form of epistemic externalism in that it allows that one can responsibly form one's beliefs and yet, because one blamelessly employs the wrong epistemic norms, one's belief is not epistemically rational. Roughly speaking, epistemic internalism makes one's epistemic standing something the agent has control over; while epistemic externalism allows that one's epistemic standing can sometimes depend on factors outside one's control (e.g. whether one has been taught the right epistemic norms).
- We noted that the deontic conception of epistemic rationality seems closest to our ordinary use of the term 'rational' and our ordinary understanding of 'justification'. Nevertheless, this type of epistemic rationality does not seem to bear such a close relation to knowledge; or at least not as close as a non-deontic conception

of epistemic rationality. We thus considered the possibility that there are two distinct epistemological projects: one which examines knowledge, and another which examines justification and deontic epistemic rationality. In this picture, while there may be important connections between the two projects, they are not as closely related as we might at first suppose.

● STUDY QUESTIONS

1 What is epistemic rationality? Try to give a description of it in your own words and offer one example of each of the following:

- an epistemically rational belief;
- a belief which is not epistemically rational but which might plausibly be considered rational in some other respect; and
- a belief which is not rational in *any* sense, epistemic or otherwise.

2 Make sure to explain your examples fully and also explain why they fit the relevant description.

3 Why can't we simply understand epistemic rationality as demanding that we *maximise* the number of our true beliefs?

4 Why can't we understand epistemic rationality as demanding that we *minimise* the number of our false beliefs?

5 Explain, in your own words, why the fact that many true beliefs are entirely trivial might be thought to pose a problem for epistemic rationality. How should one respond to this problem, do you think?

6 What is an epistemic norm? Give an example of your own of a possible epistemic norm.

7 What does it mean to call a conception of epistemic rationality *deontic*? In what sense is a deontic conception of epistemic rationality a form of epistemic internalism? Give examples to illustrate your answers.

8 Is it essential for possessing knowledge that one forms one's belief in an epistemically rational way? Why might it be thought problematic to think that it is essential? Is justification and epistemic rationality the same thing, do you think? As best as you can, try to answer these questions with the distinction between a deontic and non-deontic conception of epistemic rationality explicitly in mind.

● INTRODUCTORY FURTHER READING

Foley, Richard (2010) 'Epistemic Rationality', *Routledge Companion to Epistemology*, S. Bernecker & D. H. Pritchard (eds), Ch. 4, pp. 37–46 (London: Routledge). An excellent overview of the topic of epistemic rationality, written by one of the leading figures in the field.

Steup, Mathias, Turri, John & Sosa, Ernest (eds) (2013) *Contemporary Debates in Epistemology* (2nd edn, Oxford: Wiley). This edited collection contains a useful debate (§14) between Jonathan Kvanvig and Marian David on whether truth is the primary epistemic goal.

• ADVANCED FURTHER READING

Foley, Richard (1987) *The Theory of Epistemic Rationality* (Cambridge, MA: Harvard University Press). An influential account of epistemic rationality in the contemporary epistemological literature.

Kornblith, Hilary (ed.) (2001) *Epistemology: Internalism and Externalism* (Oxford: Blackwell). Collects many of the classic papers on the epistemic externalism/internalism distinction together in one place. Note that some of these papers are not for beginners.

Lehrer, Keith (1999) 'Rationality', *Blackwell Guide to Epistemology*, J. Greco & E. Sosa (eds), pp. 206–19 (Oxford: Blackwell). This is a rather involved discussion of the topic by one of the main experts in the field, but certainly worth reading.

Pritchard, Duncan (2021) 'Intellectual Virtues and the Epistemic Value of Truth', *Synthese*, 198, 5515–28. A recent articulation, and defence, of the idea that the epistemic good is truth that tries to avoid some of the difficulties discussed here (such as the problem posed by trivial truths).

• FREE INTERNET RESOURCES

Hájek, Alan (2017) 'Pascal's Wager', *Stanford Encyclopedia of Philosophy*. A concise overview of Pascal's wager and some of the issues that it raises.

Pappas, George (2014) 'Internalist vs. Externalist Conceptions of Epistemic Justification', *Stanford Encyclopedia of Philosophy*, https://plato.stanford.edu/entries/justep-intext/. A comprehensive overview of the externalism/internalism distinction as it applies to epistemic justification.

Poston, Ted (2008) 'Internalism and Externalism in Epistemology', *Internet Encyclopedia of Philosophy*, www.iep.utm.edu/i/int-ext.htm. An excellent discussion of the externalism/internalism debate in epistemology.

Saka, Paul (2005) 'Pascal's Wager about God', *Internet Encyclopedia of Philosophy*, www.iep.utm.edu/pasc-wag/. A helpful discussion of the issues surrounding Pascal's wager.

6
virtues and faculties

- Reliabilism
- A 'Gettier' problem for reliabilism
- Virtue epistemology
- Virtue epistemology and the externalism/internalism distinction

RELIABILISM

Whatever else we might want to say about knowledge, one thing that is clear is that knowledge involves a cognitive success that is creditable to the agent. This is why (or at least part of the reason why) we don't count someone as having knowledge if she merely gets to the truth by luck. For example, if I form my belief about what the weather will be like tomorrow simply by tossing a coin, then, even if this belief happens to turn out to be true, I won't count as a knower since I gained this true belief only by luck. After all, it wasn't a cognitive success of mine that I gained this true belief, but it was instead just due to serendipity. What we want from an epistemological theory is thus some account of knowledge which accommodates this intuition that knowledge involves creditable cognitive success, where this means that if one knows what one truly believes then one has gained this true belief in a non-lucky fashion.

As so often in philosophy, the devil lies in the detail, since there are a number of different and incompatible ways in which we can spell out this idea of knowledge as creditable non-lucky true belief. As we saw in Chapter 3, one obvious way of doing this – by defining knowledge as justified true belief – was found to be susceptible to devastating counter-examples (the Gettier cases), and so unsustainable. We therefore need to look elsewhere for an account of knowledge. One thought that one might have in this regard is that knowledge must be true belief that is gained in a reliable way, where 'reliable' here means that, at the very least, the method used is more likely to get you to the truth than not. This sort of view is known as **reliabilism**.

One can see the attractions of the position. After all, the problem with my belief in the 'coin-tossing' case is simply that coin-tossing is not a very reliable way of

DOI: 10.4324/9781003356110-7

finding out the truth about what the weather will be tomorrow (indeed, it is not a very reliable way of finding out the truth about *anything*), since more often than not this method will lead me to form false beliefs about tomorrow's weather. Compare coin-tossing in this respect with consulting an authoritative weather news source. This way of finding out what the weather will be like tomorrow *is* reliable (though, note, not infallible, as it is sometimes wrong). Relatedly, were you to gain a true belief via this method, then we would be unlikely to regard you as lucky. Instead, we would treat you as a knower since you found out the truth in the right kind of way. This case thus lends support to the thesis that knowledge requires reliability, in that it supports the idea that a reliably formed true belief will be a cognitive success that is creditable to the agent rather than to luck.

• A 'GETTIER' PROBLEM FOR RELIABILISM

So there does seem to be a certain plausibility in the reliabilist idea that knowledge is basically true belief that is reliably formed. The problem with this proposal, however, is that if it is understood simply as the thesis that knowledge is reliable true belief, then it is susceptible to a number of rather serious problems. In particular, it seems that sometimes one can form a true belief in a reliable fashion and yet it still be a matter of luck that one's belief is true. If this is right, then reliability does not exclude knowledge-undermining luck and so cannot serve to demarcate bona fide knowledge, which involves a cognitive success that is creditable to the agent, from mere lucky cognitive success, which does not.

Recall the Gettier-style counter-example that we considered in Chapter 3, which was originally due to Roderick Chisholm. In this example, we have a farmer called Gayle who forms her belief that there is a sheep in the field by looking at a shaggy dog which happens to look just like a sheep. As it turns out, however, there *is* a sheep in the field (standing behind the dog), and hence Gayle's belief is true. Moreover, her belief is also justified because she has great evidence for thinking that there is a sheep in the field, given that she can see what looks to be a sheep in the field. Gayle thus has a justified true belief. Nonetheless, she lacks knowledge because it's just a matter of luck that her belief is true, given that what she is looking at is a shaggy dog and not a sheep.

In this rendering of the example, the focus is on Gayle's justification for her true belief. Notice, however, that her belief is also formed in a reliable fashion. Gayle is, after all, a farmer, and so is someone who we can reasonably suppose is very good at spotting sheep in a field. Moreover, what she is looking at does look just like a sheep. Accordingly, she is forming her belief in a way that would ordinarily lead to true beliefs, it's just that it happens to result in a false belief in this case. (Remember that a reliable belief-forming process just needs to generally result in true beliefs; it doesn't need to be infallible. Indeed, if knowledge demanded an infallible notion of reliability, then we wouldn't know very much, if anything, as most, if not all, of our belief-forming processes are fallible.) This means that this example is not just a case of a justified true belief that fails to amount to knowledge due to the presence of knowledge-undermining luck but also a case of a reliable true belief that fails to amount to knowledge due to the presence of knowledge-undermining luck. This is why a simple form of reliabilism, such that knowledge is just reliable true belief, is susceptible to Gettier-style counter-examples.

• VIRTUE EPISTEMOLOGY

Nevertheless, there is *something* right about the reliabilist idea that knowledge must be gained by a process which tends towards the truth. After all, the feature of the standard construal of justification that Gettier cases trade upon is that one could form one's justified true belief in ways that in no way tend towards the truth (e.g. by looking at a stopped clock). As we saw in Chapter 1, however, gaining knowledge is like having a skill at getting at the truth. Think again of the example of a skilled archer hitting the bullseye that we gave there. Insofar as this archer genuinely is skilled, then it is not a matter of happenstance that she hits the target this time. Instead, we would expect her to hit the target across a range of relevantly similar conditions (such as if she were standing two inches to her left, or if the light was oh so slightly darker, or the wind oh so slightly stronger, and so on); this is just what it means to hit the target because of one's skill, rather than just because one got lucky.

The same goes for the knower. This ought not to be someone who just happened to form a true belief, but rather someone who would have got a true belief in a range of relevantly similar circumstances. In the 'stopped clock' Gettier case, for example, the problem is that the agent only happened to have a true belief, since if she'd have looked at the clock a minute later or earlier, then she would have formed a false belief. Contrast this with someone looking at a working – and thus *reliable* – clock. This person will tend to have true beliefs across a range of relevantly similar scenarios, such as if the time were slightly different, and so the way in which she is forming her belief is more akin to the skill of the archer in hitting the bullseye.

So although we cannot understand knowledge as simply reliable true belief, we ought to be careful about completely dismissing the reliabilist proposal. Perhaps, for example, there is some way of modifying the view so that it can evade the Gettier-style problem that we have raised?

One way in which one might modify the position could be to demand that knowledge is true belief that is gained as a result of the operation of reliable *epistemic virtues* or *cognitive faculties*.

An **epistemic virtue** (sometimes called an *intellectual virtue*) is a kind of cognitive skill that enables one to gain true beliefs. Crucially, however, it is unlike many other cognitive skills in that it constitutes an admirable character trait, one that specifically concerns one's intellectual character, and hence incorporates a desire for the truth. An example of such a trait is *conscientiousness*. An agent who is conscientious in the way in which she forms her beliefs (i.e. she is careful to avoid error and takes all available evidence into account) will be more likely to form true beliefs than someone who is unconscientious. This is the sense in which being conscientious is a cognitive skill, since it helps one form true beliefs in relevant situations. Relatedly, like other cognitive skills, it has reliability built into it, as being conscientious helps one to reliably form true beliefs (unlike being *un*conscientious, which wouldn't help one reliably form true beliefs).

Note that it is part of what it means to be conscientious that one is motivated to get to the truth. If one is simply acting like someone who is conscientious, without actually caring about the truth, then one wouldn't in fact be exhibiting this character trait at all. As we will see in a moment, most cognitive skills do not require one to care about the truth. This is part of why an epistemic virtue like conscientiousness is an admirable intellectual character trait, in that we consider it to be an element of character in this sense that one cares about the truth.

Another reason why we think of epistemic virtues as admirable character traits is that one must acquire and then cultivate them – they are not cognitive skills that one gains by default. It is thus a reflection of one's character that one is the kind of person who has acquired an epistemic virtue like conscientiousness. In order to see why we would care about these admirable intellectual character traits, think about the kind of intellectual character that we would want someone who occupies an important social role to have, such as a judge. We would surely want them to have acquired the relevant intellectual skills and for these skills to be motivated by a desire for the truth (and not, for example, by a desire for personal gain). In short, we would want them to have the admirable intellectual character of someone who has the epistemic virtues, such as the epistemic virtue of conscientiousness.

A **cognitive faculty** is also a cognitive skill, and hence also has reliability built into it, though it is importantly different from an epistemic virtue. In particular, one's cognitive faculties are natural and innate, in the sense that they are part of our normal cognitive endowment as human beings. For example, one's perceptual faculties, such as one's eyesight, are cognitive faculties, in that, when working properly in an environment for which they are suited at least, they are cognitive skills that enable you to reliably gain true beliefs, in this case about the world around you. Other cognitive faculties include one's memory and one's capacity for reasoning.

Unlike the epistemic virtues, one's cognitive faculties don't require one to be motivated by the truth. When I open my eyes in the morning, I gain lots of true beliefs about my environment regardless of whether I care about the truth. Since they are part of one's natural cognitive endowment, one also doesn't need to do anything in order to acquire one's cognitive faculties; one simply has them. This marks another important difference between one's cognitive faculties and one's epistemic virtues. These differences between the cognitive faculties and the epistemic virtues explain why the former are not regarded as admirable character traits, since it is no reflection of one's character that one has them. This is the sense in which one's cognitive faculties are epistemically lower-grade cognitive skills than one's epistemic virtues. Even so, however, one's cognitive faculties are very important to gaining knowledge. Indeed, a great deal of our knowledge, especially our knowledge of our immediate environments, is gained via our cognitive faculties.

With the epistemic virtues and the cognitive faculties in mind, consider the proposal that knowledge is the result of true beliefs that are formed via these kinds of cognitive skills. The idea behind this adaptation to the general reliabilist thesis is that what is important when we talk about reliability is not the reliability of the process by which the belief was formed *simpliciter*, but rather the specific reliability of the *agent* (and thus the agent's cognitive traits, such as her epistemic virtues and cognitive faculties) in gaining beliefs of this sort. Because this type of proposal essentially defines knowledge in terms of the epistemic virtues and cognitive faculties, it is known as **virtue epistemology**. Virtue epistemology is one of the oldest views in the theory of knowledge – a version of virtue epistemology was advanced by the ancient Greek philosopher, **Aristotle** (384–22 BC).

In order to see what this reliabilist version of virtue epistemology involves, consider an example originally proposed by the American philosopher **Alvin Plantinga** (1932–). Imagine someone who has a brain lesion that has an extraordinary side-effect, in that it leads the subject to form the true belief that they have a brain lesion. This would thus be a case in which one is forming one's true belief via a belief-forming process that is highly reliable. Nonetheless, I take it that there is no temptation here to suppose that our agent's reliable true belief amounts to knowledge. Note that the problem is not that the true belief is due to luck, as given how the belief is formed the subject is effectively guaranteed to have a true belief in this case. Instead, the more natural explanation of why this true belief doesn't amount to knowledge is that it isn't in any way reflective of the agent's cognitive abilities. Indeed, given that this true belief is effectively a cognitive *malfunction* on the part of the agent, albeit one that happens to result in a true belief, it is obviously not attributable to the agent's cognitive abilities.

Compare, in this regard, our subject's belief that he has a brain lesion, caused by the brain lesion, and the belief of his brain surgeon that he has a brain lesion, gained by looking at X-rays of his brain. The brain surgeon's true belief is also reliably formed, but there's a crucial difference, in that the reliability of his true belief *does* reflect his cognitive abilities, such as his cognitive ability to accurately interpret brain X-rays. This is why the brain surgeon's reliable true belief amounts to knowledge but our hapless agent with the brain lesion's reliable true belief does not.

Virtue epistemology is able to explain what is going on here, since it will claim that what such cases show is that the mere reliability of one's belief-forming processes is not enough for knowledge. This is because there can be reliable belief-forming processes that have nothing to do with one's cognitive abilities, as the brain lesion case illustrates. Instead, what is required for knowledge is that one's true belief is the result of those specific reliable belief-forming processes constitute one's cognitive abilities, such as one's epistemic virtues and cognitive faculties. In this way, reliabilism, understood as a kind of virtue epistemology, can capture the idea that knowledge involves a cognitive success that is creditable to the agent. The point behind this version of reliabilism is that when one has knowledge one has reliably got to the truth because of one's cognitive abilities, rather than merely because one formed one's belief in a reliable fashion (where the reliability may have nothing to do with one's cognitive abilities, as happens in the brain lesion case).

Aristotle (384–22 BC)

All men by nature desire to know.

Aristotle, *Metaphysics*

Aristotle is, with Plato (*c.*427–*c.*347 BC), one of the two towering figures of ancient Greek philosophy. Many of the philosophical disputes engaged in today were discussed by Aristotle, and the views that he presented all those years ago are still common currency in the contemporary debate.

Aristotle spent most of his life in Athens. He studied under Plato at Plato's Academy, and then went on to teach there. Later, he founded his own school of philosophy, The Lyceum. One of the many interesting events of Aristotle's life – and perhaps the most significant in terms of world history – was his tutelage of Alexander the Great, over whom he exercised a considerable degree of influence (perhaps as much influence as one can exercise over a strong-headed military leader). Aside from contributing to just about every area of philosophy (indeed, he could rightly be said to have single-handedly created certain sub-branches of philosophy), he also did work in areas that we would today classify as biology, anthropology, psychology, physics, cosmology, chemistry, and literary criticism.

The range of Aristotle's work is such that to attempt a brief summary of it would be pointless. One general feature of his work that does stand out, however, is the plainness of his rhetorical style and the direct way in which he approached philosophical problems. Aristotle was clearly a practical man who wished in his philosophy to offer words that could help others more usefully live their lives. For him, philosophy was not an abstract affair at all, but an essential part of a good life.

● VIRTUE EPISTEMOLOGY AND THE EXTERNALISM/INTERNALISM DISTINCTION

While construing reliabilism as a kind of virtue epistemology is certainly an improvement, there are some serious problems that remain for the view. To begin with, notice that even the revised version of reliabilism seems to struggle with Gettier-style cases. Recall the case of the farmer that we considered above. As we noted, this Gettier-style case seems to apply to reliabilism just as it did to the traditional proposal that knowledge is justified true belief, in that the farmer's luckily true belief that there is a sheep in the field is formed via a reliable belief-forming process. Changing our focus from a simple form of reliabilism to one that is cast along virtue epistemology lines doesn't seem to make any difference here. The farmer's reliable true belief is the product of his cognitive abilities after all, in this case his cognitive faculties involved in perception. The modified form of reliabilism thus still faces the Gettier problem, as even reliable true belief that is the result of one's cognitive faculties and epistemic virtues can nonetheless be subject to knowledge-undermining luck.

There is also a second type of problem that faces reliabilism, even on the virtue epistemic reading, which is that on this proposal, it is sometimes very easy to have knowledge. Consider the following example that is often discussed in epistemology, that of the **chicken-sexer**. A chicken-sexer is, so the story goes at any rate, someone who, by being raised around chickens, has acquired a highly reliable trait that enables them to distinguish between male and female chicks. Crucially, however, chicken-sexers tend to have false beliefs about how they are doing what they do because they tend to suppose that they are distinguishing the chicks on the basis of what they can see and touch. Tests have shown, however, that there is nothing distinctive for them to see and touch in this regard, and that they are actually discriminating between the chicks on the basis of their smell. Furthermore, imagine a chicken-sexer who not only has false beliefs about how she is distinguishing between the chicks but also hasn't yet determined whether she is reliable in this respect (e.g. she hasn't sought an independent verification of this fact). Would we really say that such a person *knows* that the two chicks before her are of a different sex?

If one is persuaded by the general reliabilist thesis, at least in its modified guise as a type of virtue epistemology, then one will be inclined to answer 'yes' to this question. After all, the agent is gaining a true belief in this regard by employing her reliable cognitive faculties – in this case her reliable 'chicken-sexing' faculty. Moreover, her cognitive success does seem to be creditable to her, in that she is gaining a true belief by properly employing one of her own reliable cognitive abilities. It is not, for example, a matter of luck that her belief is true.

Nevertheless, some epistemologists feel uneasy about allowing ascriptions of knowledge to chicken-sexers. Imagine, for example, that the chicken-sexer claimed to know that the chicks before her were of a different sex. Wouldn't this sound like an improper assertion to make? After all, from her point of view, she has no good reason at all for thinking that this belief is true.

The strange case of the chicken-sexer

Philosophers often use rather strange examples in order to illustrate their points, and epistemologists are no exception. One of the stranger cases epistemologists discuss is that of the chicken-sexer. As we have seen, the idea is that there are agents who can reliably determine the sex of a chick via their sense of smell, but who tend to think that they are doing this not via their sense of smell at all but via their other senses, such as sight and touch. Typically, the chicken-sexer case is also supplemented with the additional piece of information that the agent concerned doesn't know that her ability works.

What is interesting about the chicken-sexer case is that it tests some of our intuitions about the importance of reliability in gaining knowledge. If reliability is all important, as reliabilism (a form of epistemic externalism) claims, then the mere fact that these agents don't know how they are doing what they are doing (or even how reliable they are) ought not to bar them from gaining knowledge. In contrast, one might think that in order to know it is not enough that one is reliable, as one must also have good reason to think that one is reliable. This is the standard line taken by epistemic internalists.

You might be surprised to learn that there is actually some debate as to whether there really are chicken-sexers as we have just described them. Some claim, for example, that chicken-sexers are not reliable, or that they are indeed reliable but gain their beliefs in exactly the way that they think they are gaining their beliefs (i.e. via their sense of touch and sight). Given that there is this controversy about chicken-sexers, one might naturally hold that epistemologists should abstain from using the example until the matter is settled.

This way of thinking is based on a mistake, however, since it really doesn't matter whether the chicken-sexer example is true in the way it is usually described. What is important is only that it *could* very well be true, where its possible truth highlights an important difference between those theories that hold that reliability is all-important, and those which maintain that mere reliability by itself can never suffice for knowledge (i.e. unless it is supplemented with adequate grounds for thinking that one is reliable).

The conflict of intuitions in play here relates to whether you think that it is always essential that 'internal' factors are involved in the acquisition of bona fide knowledge, such as the agent being in the possession of good reasons for believing what she does. In this case, for instance, if the agent is credited with knowledge, then this will be because purely 'external' factors have obtained, such as the true belief being formed via a reliable cognitive ability. This factor is 'external' because the agent has no good reason for believing that she is reliable in this respect, and so the fact that she is reliable is in this sense 'external' to her. Those who are inclined towards the view that 'internal' factors are essential to knowledge are called *epistemic internalists*, while those who think that 'external' factors alone can at least sometimes suffice for knowledge are called *epistemic externalists*.

We saw this distinction for the first time at the end of Chapter 5 when we were discussing epistemic rationality. The issue then was whether there was a close link between being epistemically rational and being epistemically responsible for one's beliefs (i.e. making sure one had adequate supporting evidence for thinking that one's beliefs were true), and we noted that epistemic internalists tended to demand a closer connection between epistemic rationality and epistemic responsibility than epistemic externalists.

We can see this point re-emerging here with our discussion of chicken-sexers. After all, the epistemic externalist (of a reliabilist stripe at any rate) would count such a person as having knowledge, and yet we would hardly regard her beliefs as being responsibly formed. She has not, for example, acquired any evidence in support of her chicken-sexing beliefs but simply formed them 'blindly' from a rational point of view, even though her true belief is the result of a reliable cognitive ability. In contrast, the epistemic internalist would be inclined to deny knowledge to this agent because she lacks adequate evidence in favour of her beliefs. For the epistemic internalist, it is not enough to be reliable, one must also have good grounds for thinking that one is reliable. In doing so, though, one will tend to be epistemically responsible for one's beliefs; hence the close tie between epistemic responsibility and epistemic internalism.

Typically, the epistemic virtues like conscientiousness are understood in such a way that to be virtuous in this sense demands of the agent that she always has good grounds available to her in support of what she believes. To be conscientious is, after all, to reflect on one's evidence and how it supports one's beliefs. Accordingly, one way of staying within the epistemic internalist model while still offering a virtue epistemology is to hold that in order to know, it is not enough merely to form one's belief via a reliable cognitive faculty, such as a chicken-sexing faculty. Instead, one must also have formed one's belief in a way that is epistemically virtuous (i.e. via an epistemic virtue), and thus in a way that is supported by adequate grounds. On this view, the chicken-sexer lacks knowledge because, although she is forming her belief via one of her reliable cognitive faculties, she is not exercising her epistemic virtues – she is not, for example, being conscientious in the way that she forms her belief, since she has no good reason at all for believing what she does.

We thus have a distinction emerging between epistemic externalist (and, usually at least, reliabilist) versions of virtue epistemology and epistemic internalist versions of virtue epistemology. While the former claim that sometimes one can have knowledge merely by exercising one's reliable cognitive faculties, as the chicken-sexer does, the latter demand that one can only gain knowledge by employing one's epistemic virtues, and thereby gaining adequate supporting grounds in favour of one's beliefs.

This is an important difference, but it is also important not to exaggerate it. After all, while these two sorts of views take a very different stance when it comes to cases like the chicken-sexer, when it comes to most instances of knowledge, where both cognitive faculties and epistemic virtues are involved, they will tend to produce the same verdict. That said, the practical differences between a theory of knowledge that insists on the epistemic virtues and one that doesn't can be significant, as we will see in later chapters of this book.

• CHAPTER SUMMARY

- We began by looking at a view known as reliabilism, which, in its simplest form, holds that knowledge is reliably formed true belief. The idea behind such a position was to use the reliability requirement to capture the intuition that when one has knowledge one does not merely happen upon the truth, but rather one gets to the truth in a way that would normally ensure that one has a true belief (i.e. one uses a *reliable* process).

- We saw, however, that there was a Gettier-style problem for this view in its simplest form, in that one could reliably form true beliefs in a way that the true beliefs formed are still essentially due to luck, and hence not genuine cases of knowledge at all.
- One way of developing reliabilism is to restrict the kinds of reliable processes that are relevant to whether or not an agent has knowledge. In particular, the suggestion we looked at held that to gain knowledge one must gain one's true belief via one's epistemic virtues or cognitive faculties, where these are understood so that they by their nature are reliable. Proposals of this kind are called *virtue epistemology*.
- This modification of reliabilism enables it to deal with one kind of problem that reliabilism faces, which concerns cases where one's reliable true belief has nothing to do with one's cognitive abilities, and hence doesn't amount to knowledge. We gave the 'brain lesion' case to illustrate this point. Even this modified version of reliabilism still faces the Gettier problem, however.
- A different problem facing reliabilism, even in this modified form, is that it allows knowledge in some controversial cases. The case we looked at was that of the chicken-sexer, an agent who is reliably forming her beliefs about the sex of chicks, but who is doing so even though she has false beliefs about how she is doing what she's doing, and even though she has no good reason for thinking that she is reliable in this regard. Reliabilists tend to allow knowledge in such cases, but some think that one cannot gain knowledge simply by being reliable, even when the reliability is the result of a cognitive ability. Instead, these critics hold that one must further have grounds for thinking that one is reliable.
- This dispute over the chicken-sexer example is a manifestation of the debate between *epistemic externalists* and *epistemic internalists*. While epistemic internalists insist that knowers must always be in possession of supporting grounds for their beliefs, epistemic externalists allow that sometimes one might have knowledge even while lacking such grounds – just so long as one meets other relevant conditions, such as a reliability condition. Reliabilists, and those virtue epistemologists who regard their view as a variant on reliabilism, thus tend to be epistemic externalists. Since employing an epistemic virtue, unlike employing a cognitive faculty, tends to always result in an agent having supporting grounds for her beliefs, one way of advancing a virtue epistemology which is allied to epistemic internalism is to insist that the employment of an epistemic virtue is essential to gaining knowledge.

● STUDY QUESTIONS

1 What does it mean to say that one has formed one's belief in a *reliable* way? Could a belief so formed be false, do you think? Give an example of a reliable and

an unreliable way of forming a belief about the following subject matters (try to avoid repetition in your answers):

- the time;
- the capital of France; and
- the solution to a crossword puzzle clue.

2 In your own words, try to say how the 'brain lesion' example creates problems for a simple form of reliabilism. Try to formulate your own counter-example to simple reliabilism that is structured in the same way as the brain lesion case.

3 What is an epistemic virtue? What is a cognitive faculty? How are they different? Give two examples of each.

4 What is a virtue epistemology? As best as you can, try to explain what it means to cast reliabilism as a form of virtue epistemology, and how understanding reliabilism in this way enables it to evade the brain lesion case.

5 Why does virtue epistemology still seem to face the Gettier problem?

6 What is the chicken-sexer case? How does this example highlight the differences between epistemic externalism and epistemic internalism? In answering the latter question, try to state, in your own words, what the epistemic externalism/internalism distinction is.

● INTRODUCTORY FURTHER READING

Barnes, Jonathan (2000) *Aristotle: A Very Short Introduction* (Oxford: Oxford University Press). A readable and (as the title suggests) short book on Aristotle's work by an international expert on ancient philosophy.

Battaly, Heather (2008) 'Virtue Epistemology', *Philosophy Compass*, 3, 639–63 (Oxford: Wiley). An excellent and very up-to-date survey of the recent literature on virtue epistemology.

Bonjour, Laurence & Sosa, Ernest (2003) *Epistemic Justification: Internalism vs. Externalism, Foundations vs. Virtues* (Oxford: Blackwell). See especially part two, which offers an accessible defence of virtue epistemology by one of its most famous proponents.

● ADVANCED FURTHER READING

Greco, John (2010) *Achieving Knowledge: A Virtue-Theoretic Account of Epistemic Normativity* (Cambridge: Cambridge University Press). Greco offers an influential version of virtue epistemology that is explicitly cast as a form of reliabilism. (Note, in particular, the response he offers to the Gettier problem.)

Kornblith, Hilary (ed.) (2001) *Epistemology: Internalism and Externalism* (Oxford: Blackwell). A great collection of classic and recent papers on the epistemic externalism/internalism distinction, including specific papers devoted to reliabilism. (Note that some of the papers are not for beginners.)

Pritchard, Duncan (2022) 'Intellectual Virtue and Its Role in Epistemology', *Asian Journal of Philosophy*, 1, [DOI: 10.1007/s44204-022-00024-4]. In this article, I offer a comprehensive account of what role the notion of epistemic, or intellectual, virtue might play in epistemology. (Note that at the time of writing at least this article is open-access.)

Sosa, Ernest (2011) *Knowing Full Well* (Princeton, NJ: Princeton University Press). Sosa's version of virtue epistemology is by far the most influential in the contemporary epistemological literature. This text provides a helpful overview of the main contours of his position.

Steup, Mathias, Turri, John & Sosa, Ernest (eds) (2013) *Contemporary Debates in Epistemology* (2nd edn, Oxford: Wiley). This edited collection contains a useful debate (§6) between Jason Baehr and Linda Zagzebski on the merits of virtue epistemology.

Zagzebski, Linda (1996) *Virtues of the Mind: An Inquiry into the Nature of Virtue and the Ethical Foundations of Knowledge* (Cambridge: Cambridge University Press). A very readable, and influential, statement of an epistemically internalist version of virtue epistemology.

● FREE INTERNET RESOURCES

Baehr, Jason (2004) 'Virtue Epistemology', *Internet Encyclopedia of Philosophy*, https://iep.utm.edu/virtue-epistemology/. A first-rate, if a little dated now, survey of the main issues regarding virtue epistemology.

Shields, Christopher (2020) 'Aristotle', *Stanford Encyclopedia of Philosophy*, https://plato.stanford.edu/entries/aristotle/. A helpful and reasonably accessible overview of the main themes in Aristotle's thought.

Turri, John, Alfano, Mark & Greco, John (2021) 'Virtue Epistemology', *Stanford Encyclopedia of Philosophy*, https://plato.stanford.edu/entries/epistemology-virtue/. An excellent and up-to-date overview of the topic.

Part II

where does knowledge come from?

7

perception

- The problem of perceptual knowledge
- Indirect realism
- Idealism
- Transcendental idealism
- Direct realism

● THE PROBLEM OF PERCEPTUAL KNOWLEDGE

A great deal of our knowledge of the world is gained via perception – that is, via our sensory faculties, such as our sense of sight, hearing, touch, and so forth. My knowledge, if that's what it is, that I am presently at my desk writing these words is itself largely perceptually gained. I can see the computer before me, and I can feel the hard touch of the computer keyboard on my fingers as I type. If we know much of what we think we know, then we must have a great deal of perceptual knowledge. As we will see, however, it is far from obvious that we do have widespread perceptual knowledge of the world around us, at least as that knowledge is usually understood.

Part of the problem is that the way things look isn't always the way things are; appearances can be deceptive. There are familiar examples of this sort of deception, such as the way a straight stick will look bent when placed underwater, or the mirages that result from wandering dehydrated through a barren desert. In these cases, if one were not suitably refining one's responses to one's sensory experiences, then one would be led into forming a false belief. If one did not know about light refraction, for example, then one would think that the stick really is bending as it enters the water; if one did not know that one was experiencing a mirage, then one would really believe that there was an unexpected oasis on the horizon.

There are also less mundane cases of perceptual error where the misleading nature of perceptual experience is more widespread. One could imagine, for example, an environment in which one's sensory experiences are a completely unreliable guide as to the nature of the environment. This could be achieved by hiding the real colours of the objects in the environment by employing fluorescent lights, or by using visual tricks to distort one's sense of perspective in order to give the impression that objects are closer or farther away than they really are. The existence of perceptual

DOI: 10.4324/9781003356110-9

error of this sort reminds us that, while we must depend upon our perceptual faculties for much of our knowledge of the world, the possibility always remains that these faculties can lead us into forming false beliefs if left unchecked.

Given that we can usually correct for misleading perceptual impressions when they occur – as when we make use of our knowledge of light refraction to account for why straight sticks appear bent when placed in water – the mere possibility of perceptual error is not that worrying. The problem posed by perception is not, then, that it is a fallible way of gaining knowledge of the world; instead, it is its apparent *indirectness*.

Consider the visual impression caused by a genuine sighting of an oasis on the horizon, and contrast it with the corresponding visual impression of an oasis on the horizon formed by one who is hallucinating. Here is the crux: *these two visual impressions could be exactly the same*. The problem, however, is that it seems that if this is the case then what we experience in perception is not the world itself, but something that falls short of the world, something that is common to both the 'good' case in which one's senses are not being deceived (and one is actually looking at an oasis) and the 'bad' case in which one's senses are being deceived (and one is the victim of a hallucination). This line of reasoning, which makes use of undetectable error in perception in order to highlight the indirectness of perceptual experience, is known as the *argument from illusion*.

The **argument from illusion** suggests an 'indirect' model of perceptual knowledge, such that what we are immediately aware of when we gain such knowledge is a sensory impression – a *seeming* – on the basis of which we then make an inference regarding how the world is. That is, in both the deceived and non-deceived 'oasis' case just considered, what is common is a sensory impression of an oasis on the horizon which leads one to infer something about the world: that there really is an oasis on the horizon. The difference between the two cases is that while the inference generates a true belief in the non-deceived case, it generates a false belief in the deceived case. In the former case, one is thus in a position, all other things being equal at least, to have perceptual knowledge that there is an oasis before one; while in the latter case perceptual knowledge is out of the question because one's visual impressions are deceptive.

But why is the indirectness, in this sense, of perceptual knowledge a problem? Well, the worry is that on this model of our perceptual interactions with the world, it seems that we are never actually perceiving a world external to our senses at all, strictly speaking, since our experiences are forever falling short of the world and requiring supplementation from reason. But isn't this conclusion more than just a little odd? Think of your perceptual experiences just now as you read this book. Aren't you *directly* experiencing the book in your hands?

Moreover, notice that this picture of the way we perceive the world, and thus gain perceptual knowledge, seems to have the result that our perceptual knowledge is far less secure than we might have otherwise thought. We normally regard our perceptual knowledge as the most secure of all. We often say, for example, that seeing is believing, and if we do indeed see something in clear daylight with our own eyes, then this will tend to trump any counter-evidence we might have. For example, suppose that those around you assure you that your brother is out of town, and yet you see him walking towards you in the high street. Surely the testimony of your peers would be quickly disregarded and you would immediately believe that he is in town. According to our ordinary conception of perceptual knowledge, then, it is *privileged* relative to (at least some) other types of knowledge. But if perceptual experience does not put us in direct contact with the world, as the argument from illusion suggests – such that perceptual knowledge rests in part on an inference – then it appears that our perceptual knowledge is no more privileged than other 'indirect' knowledge that we have of the world. In short, our knowledge of the world when we see that things are so is no better than it is when, say, we are merely told that things are so. But why, then, are we so confident in our perception-based judgements about the world?

• INDIRECT REALISM

The way of understanding perceptual knowledge which embraces the apparent indirectness of perceptual experience that we just noted is known as **indirect realism**. It holds that we gain knowledge of an objective world indirectly by making inferences from our sense impressions. The main argument for indirect realism is, in essence, the *argument from illusion* just given. The general idea is that the phenomenon of perceptual illusion highlights that what is presented to us in perceptual experience is not the world itself but merely an impression of the world from which we must draw inferences about how the world really is.

There is also another type of consideration in favour of indirect realism. This concerns the distinction between *primary qualities* and *secondary qualities* that was drawn (in modern times) by the philosopher **John Locke** (1632–1704), himself a proponent of a version of indirect realism. A **primary quality** is a feature of an object that the object has independently of anyone perceiving the object. In contrast, a **secondary quality** of an object is dependent upon the perception of an agent.

A good example of a primary quality is shape, in that the shape of an object is not in any way dependent upon anyone perceiving that object. Compare shape in this respect with colour. The colour of an object is a secondary quality in that it depends upon a perceiver. If human beings were kitted out with different perceptual faculties, then colours would be discriminated very differently. Indeed, think of the animal kingdom in this respect, where there are creatures who can see colours that we can't see, and also creatures who are unable to see colours that we can see. Colour is very different to shape in this regard. The shape of an object doesn't vary depending on which creature is experiencing it, even if the creature in question has very different sensory capacities when compared to normal human beings.

Note that this is not to suggest that colour is in some way an unreal or illusory feature of an object, since it is certainly a stable fact about, say, the UK's Royal Mail postboxes that they will generate a visual impression of redness to any person with the standard visual faculties who is looking at the postbox in normal lighting

John Locke (1632–1704)

No man's knowledge . . . can go beyond his experience.

Locke, *An Essay Concerning Human Understanding*

The English philosopher John Locke is perhaps most noted for his work on political theory, especially regarding the limits of the power of the state. Indeed, Locke's broadly liberal conception of the role of the state was very influential on the establishment of the US constitution.

In his philosophy more generally, Locke belongs to a school of thought known as **empiricism**, which traces all knowledge of any substance back to sensory experience. Along with **George Berkeley** (1685–1753) and **David Hume** (1711–76), Locke is often referred to as one of the British empiricists. This commitment to empiricism is reflected in his famous claim that the mind at birth is like a *tabula rasa* – that is, like a 'blank slate' on which nothing is written. What Locke means by this is that there are no innate ideas. Instead, all our ideas, and thus our knowledge, are derived via experience of the world.

conditions. It is thus a real feature of the world that there are objects that generate visual impressions in this way. The point is rather that the colour of an object is not intrinsic to the object in the way that its shape is, but instead depends upon there being perceivers who respond to the object with the appropriate visual impressions.

The indirect realist is clearly in a good position to accommodate the primary/secondary quality distinction. After all, there is, on this view, a distinction between the world as it is perceived and the world as it really is, independently of it being perceived. This distinction maps neatly onto the primary/secondary quality distinction, with the secondary qualities of an object belonging to the former realm, and the primary qualities of an object belonging to the latter realm.

The chief problem with indirect realism is that by making our perceptual knowledge of the world inferential, it threatens to dislocate us from the world altogether. Intuitively, what I am aware of when I open my eyes is the world itself, not a sensory impression of the world from which I infer specific beliefs about the world. Indeed, once one has departed down the road of indirect realism, it is not difficult to see the attraction of a widespread scepticism about our knowledge of the world (i.e. the view that it is impossible to know anything about the world). After all, if what I am immediately aware of when I perceive is only an impression of the world from which I must then make an inference about the way the world is that could be either right or wrong, then why should I think that I have *any* knowledge at all of how the world really is?

This point is exacerbated once one considers the possibility that the way the world appears and the way that it really is could be drastically different. Suppose, for example, that I am being radically deceived in my sensory impressions by some mischievous super-being who is 'feeding' me sensory impressions that are entirely misleading. If all that I am directly aware of in perceptual experience is the way the world appears, then it seems that I could never be in a position to detect that this deception was going on. If it were taking place, however, then the way the world appeared would be no guide at all to how the world is, and thus the inferences I would be making about the nature of the world on the basis of my visual impressions would be dubious at best. Given this problem, it seems that all that I am entitled to take myself to know according to indirect realism is how the world appears, not how it really is.

This difficulty is known as the **problem of the external world**. While this problem is one that must be dealt with, in some form, by all theories of perceptual knowledge, it does seem as if indirect realism aggravates this difficulty by offering an account of perceptual knowledge which makes our knowledge of the external world shakily inferential rather than direct. Indeed, some have responded to indirect realism by arguing that, if this is how we are to understand perceptual knowledge, then we lose any grounds for thinking that there is a world that is independent of our experience of it (i.e. a world which is 'external' in the relevant sense).

● IDEALISM

The view which denies that there is an external world in this sense – that is, which denies that there is a world that is independent of our experience of it – is known as **idealism**. Perhaps the most famous exponent of a version of this position is George Berkeley (1685–1753). Idealists respond to the problem of the external world by claiming that perceptual knowledge is not knowledge of a world that is independent of our perception of it, but rather knowledge of a world that is *constituted* by our perception of it. On this proposal, the world is, so to speak, 'constructed' out of appearances rather than being that which gives rise to such appearances, and thus it is not 'external' in the relevant sense at all. (Another way of putting the point is that for the idealist there are only secondary qualities.) As Berkeley famously put it in his book *A Treatise Concerning the Principles of Human Knowledge*, 'To be is to be perceived'. This is a very dramatic conclusion to draw, and appears to call much of our ordinary conception of the world and our relation to it into question.

If idealism is not qualified in some way, then it will end up maintaining that the world ceases to exist when no one is perceiving it. For example, one can't say that a tree fell in the forest if there was no one around to see or hear (or otherwise sense) it fall; if no one experienced the falling of the tree, then according to idealism the event didn't happen. This is clearly a very radical claim to make! Indeed, at first blush at least, it might be hard to distinguish a simple-minded idealism of this sort from plain scepticism about our perceptual knowledge. Note, however, that, unlike the sceptic, the idealist claims that we *do* know a great deal about the world. But the idealist does this by making what we mean by the 'world' so different from what we usually take it to mean that it feels as if the idealist is agreeing with the sceptic after all.

George Berkeley (1685–1753)

To be is to be perceived.

Berkeley, *A Treatise Concerning the Principles of Human Knowledge*

George Berkeley, otherwise known as Bishop Berkeley (he was the Bishop of Cloyne in what is now the Republic of Ireland), was, like John Locke (1632–1704) and David Hume (1711–76), an empiricist. An empiricist is someone who believes that all knowledge of substance is ultimately derivable from experience. (Locke, Berkeley, and Hume are collectively known as the British empiricists.) Unlike Locke and Hume, however, Berkeley famously saw in empiricism a motivation for idealism – the view that there is no mind-independent world.

Berkeley led a very interesting life, including a spell living in Bermuda. He also has the unusual distinction of having a city (and a university) named after him, the city of Berkeley in California.

Berkeley's way of lessening some of the more outlandish consequences of a simple idealism was to introduce the idea of an ever-present God. With God in the picture, we now no longer need to worry about what to make of unobserved events, since all events will be observed by an all-seeing God. Accordingly, we aren't forced to say that events which aren't observed by us mere mortals therefore don't happen. Berkeley was a Christian – a bishop, in fact – so this appeal to God is unsurprising. This sort of refinement to idealism would clearly offer little comfort to an idealist who was also an atheist, though!

• TRANSCENDENTAL IDEALISM

Others have tried to lessen the more counter-intuitive aspects of idealism while retaining the guiding thought behind it in different ways. One prominent version of idealism which is modified to make it more appealing is the **transcendental idealism** proposed by **Immanuel Kant** (1724–1804).

Kant agrees with the simple idealist that what we are immediately aware of in sensory experience is not the world itself. Nevertheless, unlike the idealist, he argues that we are required to suppose that there is an external world that gives rise to this sensory experience since, without this supposition, we would not be able to make any sense of such experience. Very roughly, the idea is that we can only make sense of our perceptual experiences as responses to an external world, even if we are not directly acquainted with this world in perceptual experience. Reason thus tells us that there must be an external world, even if it's impossible to directly perceive that world.

Immanuel Kant (1724–1804)

All our knowledge begins with the senses, proceeds then to the understanding, and ends with reason. There is nothing higher than reason.

Kant, *Critique of Pure Reason*

Immanuel Kant is quite possibly the most important and influential philosopher of the modern era. Although he contributed to just about every area of philosophy, he is generally known for his transcendental idealism and his contribution to ethics. As regards the former, the leading idea was that much of the structure that we ascribe to the world – such as the temporal or casual order – is in fact a product of our minds. In ethics, he is mostly known for arguing that the source of the moral good lies in the good will. A morally good action is thus one that is done with a good will (though note that Kant imposes some rather austere demands on what counts as a good will, so good acts are not as easy to come by as this short précis might suggest!).

Aside from philosophy, Kant also taught and wrote on such subjects as anthropology, physics, and mathematics. Famously, Kant spent his entire life in the city of Königsberg in what was then East Prussia (the city is now called Kaliningrad, and is part of Russia). It was said that he was such a creature of routine that the locals called him the 'Königsberg clock'. This was because they could reliably set their clocks by seeing him walk past their houses, as he would always pass at the same time every day.

On the face of it, such a view might look like a version of indirect realism, and hence not a type of idealism at all, since doesn't it just make our knowledge of the world indirect? What is key to the view, however, is that we cannot gain knowledge of a world that is independent of experience through experience at all, directly or otherwise. In this sense, then, transcendental idealism *is* a form of idealism. Unlike simple idealism, however, Kant claims that reason shows us that, given the nature of our experiences, there must be a mind-independent world beyond experience which gives rise to these experiences. So although we have no experiential knowledge of a world that is independent of experience, we do have knowledge of its existence through reason.

• DIRECT REALISM

All this talk of idealism can make one wonder whether something didn't simply go wrong in our reasoning right at the start of our thinking about this topic. How could it be that reflecting on the nature of our perceptual experience of the world has led us to think that perhaps there is no external world to have knowledge of in the first place (or at least no external world that we can know through experience)? With this in mind, it is worth considering the prospects for the simple-minded *direct realism*.

In its most straightforward form, **direct realism** takes our perceptual experiences at face value and argues that, at least in non-deceived cases, what we are aware of in perceptual experience is the external world itself. That is, if I am genuinely looking at an oasis on the horizon right now, then I am directly aware of the oasis itself, and thus I can have perceptual knowledge that there is an oasis before me without needing to make an inference from the way the world seems to how it is.

One obvious attraction of direct realism is that of all the accounts of perceptual knowledge it most accords with common sense. A further motivation for the proposal is that the other theories of perceptual knowledge, such as indirect realism and idealism, are far too quick to infer from the fact that our perceptual experience could be undetectably misleading that we are therefore only directly aware of the way the world seems to us rather than the way the world is. The idea is that although it is true that in deceived cases, such as the scenario in which I am visually presented with a mirage of an oasis, I am not directly aware of the world but only with the way the world appears, this should not be thought to entail that in non-deceived cases, such as where I am actually looking at an oasis in the distance, I am not directly acquainted with objects in the world. According to direct realism, the fact that I'm not always able to distinguish between deceived and non-deceived cases is neither here nor there, since it is not held to be a precondition of perceptual knowledge that one can tell the genuine cases of perceptual knowledge apart from the merely apparent cases.

Of course, the direct realist cannot leave matters there, since she needs to go on to explain how such a view is to function. For one thing, she needs to develop a theory of knowledge which can allow us to have perceptual knowledge directly via perceptual experience even in cases where one is unable to distinguish genuine from apparent perception. Moreover, she also needs to offer an explanation of the primary/secondary quality distinction. Nevertheless, given the unattractiveness of indirect realism and the versions of idealism that are suggested by the move to indirect realism, direct realism needs to be taken very seriously indeed.

• CHAPTER SUMMARY

- A great deal of our knowledge of the world is gained via perception (i.e. via our senses). Our senses are sometimes prone to deceive us, although, as we noted, this is not a problem in itself, since we can often tell when they are not to be trusted (as when we see a stick 'bend' as it enters water). What is problematic about perceptual experience is brought out via the argument from illusion. In essence, this states that since a situation in which we are deceived about the world could be one in which we have, it seems, exactly the same experiences as we would have in a corresponding undeceived case, we don't directly experience the world at all.
- The conception of perceptual knowledge suggested by the argument from illusion is that of indirect realism. This holds that there is an objective world out there, one that is independent of our experience of it – this is the 'realism' part

– but that we can only know this world indirectly through experience. In particular, what we directly experience is only how the world appears to us, and not how it is. On this basis, we can then make inferences to how the world really is.

- Indirect realism can also easily account for the primary/secondary quality distinction – the distinction between those (primary) properties or qualities of an object that are inherent in the object, such as its shape, and those (secondary) properties or qualities of an object that are dependent upon the perceiver, such as its colour.

- According to indirect realism, we don't have any direct experience of the external world, and this has prompted some to argue for a view known as idealism, which maintains that there is no external world. In particular, idealism maintains that the world is constructed out of appearances and does not extend beyond it – that is, there is no mind-independent world.

- We also looked at a more refined form of idealism, known as transcendental idealism. Transcendental idealism maintains that, while we are unable to have any experiential knowledge of the external world (i.e. a world that is independent of experience), nevertheless, given the nature of our experience, we can use reason to show that there must be an external world that gives rise to our experiences.

- Finally, we considered a common-sense view of perceptual experience called direct realism. This view holds that we can directly experience the world, and so rejects the conclusion usually derived from the argument from illusion that direct experience of the world is impossible.

• STUDY QUESTIONS

1 Describe two examples of when your experiences have been a misleading guide as to the way the world is.

2 What is the argument from illusion? What is indirect realism? Explain, in your own words, why the argument from illusion offers support for indirect realism.

3 Explain, in your own words, what the primary/secondary quality distinction is. Pick an object, and give an example of a primary quality that this object has and a secondary quality that this object has.

4 Explain, in your own words, what idealism is. Do you find this position plausible? If not, say why. If so, then try to think why others might find it implausible, and try to see if you can offer any considerations in defence of the view in light of these concerns.

5 What is transcendental idealism? How does it differ from idealism? How does it differ from indirect realism?

6 What is direct realism? Do you find this position plausible? If not, say why. If so, then try to think why others might find it implausible, and try to see if you can offer any considerations in defence of the view in light of these concerns.

INTRODUCTORY FURTHER READING

Dancy, Jonathan (1987) *Berkeley: An Introduction* (Oxford: Blackwell). A classic introduction to Berkeley's philosophy.

Dunn, John (2003) *Locke: A Very Short Introduction* (Oxford: Oxford University Press). An accessible introduction to Locke's philosophy.

Scruton, Roger (2001) *Kant: A Very Short Introduction* (Oxford: Oxford University Press). A very readable introduction to Kant's philosophy.

Sosa, David (2010) 'Perceptual Knowledge', *Routledge Companion to Epistemology*, S. Bernecker & D. H. Pritchard (eds), Ch. 27, pp. 294–304 (London: Routledge). A sophisticated, yet reasonably accessible, overview of the epistemological issues raised by perception.

ADVANCED FURTHER READING

Pritchard, Duncan (2012) *Epistemological Disjunctivism* (Oxford: Oxford University Press). A detailed defence of a contemporary epistemological proposal that is closely connected to an influential form of direct realism.

Robinson, Howard (1994) *Perception* (London: Routledge). A good discussion of the central issues in this area. Not for the beginner.

Shwartz, Robert (ed.) (2003) *Perception* (Oxford: Blackwell). A nice collection of articles on the philosophy of perception, including both historical texts and contemporary readings.

FREE INTERNET RESOURCES

Crane, Tim & French, Craig (2021) 'The Problem of Perception', *Stanford Encyclopedia of Philosophy*, https://plato.stanford.edu/entries/perception-problem/. A comprehensive discussion of the metaphysics of perception (as opposed to its epistemology).

Downing, Lisa (2011) 'George Berkeley', *Stanford Encyclopedia of Philosophy*, http://plato.stanford.edu/entries/berkeley/. A helpful introduction to the work of Berkeley.

Lyons, Jack (2016) 'Epistemological Problems of Perception', *Stanford Encyclopedia of Philosophy*, https://plato.stanford.edu/entries/perception-episprob/. An excellent overview of the central issues in the field.

Rohlf, Michael (2020) 'Immanuel Kant', *Stanford Encyclopedia of Philosophy*, https://plato.stanford.edu/entries/kant/. A helpful, and recently updated, overview of Kant's life and works.

Uzgalis, William (2022) 'Locke', *Stanford Encyclopedia of Philosophy*, https://plato.stanford.edu/entries/locke/. An excellent and recently updated overview of the life and works of Locke.

8

testimony and memory

- The problem of testimonial knowledge
- Reductionism
- Credulism
- The problem of memorial knowledge

THE PROBLEM OF TESTIMONIAL KNOWLEDGE

Think of all the things that you think you know right now – such as that the earth is round, or that the Nile flows through Egypt. Most of these beliefs will have been gained not by finding out the truth of the claim in question yourself, but by being *told* that this claim was true by others. Indeed, often we do not even remember exactly how we come by most of our beliefs. I don't recall who it was who first told me that the earth was shaped as it is (or whether I was 'told' it at all, as opposed to reading it in a book, or seeing the image on a TV screen), but I do know that this isn't the kind of claim that I could verify for myself with my own eyes, since this would involve an investigation that is well beyond my present means (e.g. a space mission). This might not seem particularly worrying, given that others have seen that this is the way things are and have passed this information on to the rest of the world (with pictures and so forth). Still, one might be troubled by the extent to which what we believe is dependent upon the word of others. What is our justification for forming our beliefs via the word of others?

The issue here is that of the status of **testimony**, where this means not only the formal verbal transmission of information that one finds taking place in a courtroom but also the intentional transmission of information in general, whether verbally or through books, pictures, videos, and so forth. A great deal of what you learn you learn via the testimony of others rather than by finding out the truths in question for yourself. It is actually quite important that you find out the truth of most of what you believe in this way since if what you believed was restricted to only those

DOI: 10.4324/9781003356110-10

claims that you could verify yourself (i.e. without any assistance from others), then you wouldn't be able to know all that much about the world. Someone like myself, who has never visited northern Africa, for example, would be unable to know which country the Nile flows through, and much else besides. Much of our knowledge is thus *social* in the sense that it involves a process of co-operation between lots of different people, including people in different parts of the world and even people who have long since passed away but who transmitted their knowledge on to subsequent generations.

Sometimes, of course, the testimony we receive is false or misleading. For example, someone with a political agenda might try to make us think that a certain problem, such as immigration, is much worse than it actually is in order to further their own political ends. In itself, this kind of testimonial deceit is not all that troubling since we have a number of checks and balances which we can use to evaluate the testimony of others. If, for example, we know that someone has something to gain by making us believe a certain claim (as in the political case just mentioned), then we instinctively put this claim under greater scrutiny than we would have done otherwise.

The same goes for testimony that, on the face of it, must be false (i.e. testimony that conflicts with other beliefs that we currently hold). If someone told me that the Nile does not flow through Egypt, I wouldn't simply accept this claim at face value but would rather test its credibility. Is the person making the assertion authoritative in this regard (is she, for example, a geography teacher)? Does this testimony accord with what is in my atlas and, if not, why not? This is not to say that we never accept testimony that conflicts with our other beliefs, since even our most ingrained beliefs can change over time; look at how human beings have adjusted their beliefs to accommodate the fact that the earth goes around the sun rather than vice versa. Rather, the point is that we are more suspicious when it comes to surprising testimony than when it comes to testimony that accords with what we already believe, and this helps us to avoid being radically misled.

These policies for dealing with problematic testimony do not, however, wholly justify our practice of relying on testimony. After all, we often check suspect testimony by comparing it with other testimony we have received. For example, I evaluate the politician's claim about immigration by considering it in the light of the newspaper articles I've read on the subject from reliable news sources, but these too are instances of testimony. One might wonder, then, whether there is any way of justifying our reliance on testimony as a whole.

Suppose, for example, that all, or nearly all, of the testimony that we receive is false or misleading. How would we tell? Perhaps everyone is out to trick us, as in the film *The Truman Show*. In this film, the protagonist, Truman, is, without being aware of it, the main character in a TV show – whose world is in fact nothing more than a TV production set. Just about everything that he has been told is false. If the majority of the testimony that we received were misleading in this way, how would we find out? Typically, one might try to detect deception by asking someone reliable, but clearly this option is of little use in this case!

> ## The Truman Show
>
> *The Truman Show* is a 1998 movie starring Jim Carrey as Truman Burbank. On the face of it, Truman is a normal man: married, working in insurance, and living in a small American town. In reality, however, Truman's life is being controlled by Christof (played by Ed Harris), a TV producer whom he has never met, who is broadcasting Truman's life live to the nation in a reality TV show called *The Truman Show*. Everyone around poor Truman is thus an actor, and a great deal of what he is told on a day-to-day basis is false. Slowly, though, Truman starts to realise that something fishy is going on, and he tries to escape.

In short, the problem of testimonial knowledge is that we are unable to offer any *independent* grounds for a wide range of the testimony-based beliefs that we hold (i.e. grounds which are not themselves simply other testimony-based beliefs). Unless we have some general entitlement to trust testimony, it seems to follow that much of our knowledge is on a rather insecure footing.

• REDUCTIONISM

If one is troubled by this sort of problem, then one solution could be to claim that the justification for a testimony-based belief will always ultimately rest on non-testimonial evidence. That is, if one's testimony-based belief is to be justified, then it is not enough that one's evidence for this belief is itself merely gained via testimony. Instead, one needs further non-testimonial grounds, such as personal experience of the fact that this informant is reliable (e.g. one might have observed on a number of occasions in the past that this person's testimony has turned out to be true).

This way of understanding testimony is often known as **reductionism**, since it tries to trace testimonial justification back to the non-testimonial evidence that we have, thereby 'reducing' testimonial justification to non-testimonial justification. Historically, this position is often associated with the Scottish Enlightenment philosopher David Hume (1711–76).

If we take the reductionist thesis entirely at face value, then it is susceptible to some fairly immediate problems. Think again of the protagonist in *The Truman Show*. In this model, Truman is justified in believing all those things which he can vouch for himself or which he has gained via a testimonial source which he knows is reliable because he has verified its reliability for himself in the past.

When it comes to Truman's 'local' beliefs about his immediate environment, such as whether the newspaper shop is presently open, this seems fine because he can independently verify what is being asserted. Moreover, where he can't verify these 'local' claims, he can at least usually be sure that the informant in question is generally reliable about 'local' matters like this. Furthermore, most of Truman's beliefs in this respect will be true, since although his world is in one sense make-believe, it is true that there are shops and buildings and people inhabiting this TV production set (i.e. it is not a dream or an illusion). Truman's 'local' beliefs thus appear, on the whole at least, to be entirely in order by reductionist lights, even though Truman is the victim of a widespread conspiracy to deceive him.

The problem with Truman's beliefs, however, does not reside in his 'local' beliefs about shop opening hours or which building is where on the town square, but rather concerns his 'non-local' beliefs, such as that the earth is round. After all, Truman has only vouched for the reliability of his informants when it comes to local matters about which he can verify, yet the problem here is their reliability about *non-local* matters. There is no inherent reason why reliability in the one case should extend to the other. My doctor is a reliable informant about medical conditions, but that doesn't mean that she is thereby a reliable informant regarding whether or not I need the electrics in my house rewired. The same goes for the people in Truman's world. That they are reliable informants when it comes to local matters, such as whether the shops are open on the high street, does not mean that they are going to be reliable informants when it comes to non-local matters, such as the shape of the earth.

David Hume (1711–76)

> Reason is, and ought to be, the slave of the passions, and can never pretend to any other office than to serve and obey them.
>
> Hume, *A Treatise on Human Nature*

David Hume is Scotland's most important philosopher and arguably the greatest ever philosopher to write in the English language. Born in Edinburgh, he led an interesting and varied life, writing a celebrated history of England as well as a number of central works in philosophy. Possibly his greatest work, *A Treatise on Human Nature*, was completed by the time he was 26. Hume's intellectual achievements made him a key figure in a period of history known as the *Age of Enlightenment*, a time of great intellectual ferment.

Hume's philosophy is characterised by his empiricism, which is the belief that all knowledge is ultimately traceable back to the senses. Hume's empiricism led him to be sceptical about a lot of things that his contemporaries took for granted, particularly when it came to religious belief. His scepticism about religious belief created lots of personal obstacles for him – for example, it was what prevented him from taking up a Chair in Philosophy at the University of Edinburgh, despite being by far the most deserving candidate – but he pressed on regardless. Because of his ardent empiricism, Hume is often described, along with George Berkeley (1685–1753) and John Locke (1632–1704), as one of the British empiricists.

The trouble is, of course, that Truman is unable to verify their reliability about non-local matters of this sort. So while lots of Truman's testimony-based beliefs are in order, there is an important class of testimony-based beliefs that he holds – those that concern non-local matters – that are problematic by reductionist lights since he has no independent grounds for them. Herein lies the rub, however; we are all in pretty much the same situation as Truman in this regard, since we are no more able to independently verify our non-local beliefs than Truman can. According to reductionism, it thus seems that we know a lot less than we thought we knew.

• CREDULISM

Some have reacted to this conclusion by rejecting reductionism altogether and arguing instead that we don't always need to have further grounds in favour of a testimony-based belief in order to justifiably hold it. Instead, there is, they claim, a default presumption in favour of testimony-based beliefs such that they are justifiably held unless there is a special reason for doubt. Accordingly, we don't need to worry about the problem of offering independent support for our ('non-local') testimony-based beliefs on this view, since such beliefs can be justified in the absence of *any* independent grounds.

According to this proposal, Truman was entirely justified in holding his non-local beliefs until counter-evidence that called these beliefs into question emerged. (In the film this consisted of lighting rigs falling onto the ground near where he stood, and people coming up to him in the street to tell him that he was part of a TV show.)

This position is often known, somewhat pejoratively, as **credulism**. (Another name for the position is *nonreductionism*.) Historically, this kind of thesis is usually associated with the work of another Scottish Enlightenment philosopher, and a contemporary of Hume, **Thomas Reid** (1710–96).

The credulist approach to the justification of testimonial belief may be more in accord with common sense, since it would allow us to have the widespread testimonial knowledge that we typically credit to ourselves. But this common-sense element to the view also highlights one of its least appealing features, which is that it appears to simply turn our naturally trusting nature into a virtue. The key point is this: perhaps we *should* be more suspicious about the information we receive, even though this would place a lot of restrictions on what we may justifiably believe.

Perhaps, however, there is a way of understanding the credulist thesis so that it is not quite so permissive. Recall the epistemic externalism/internalism distinction that we first drew in Chapter 5. In particular, recall that epistemic externalism allowed that one could be justified in believing a certain proposition – and hence potentially know that proposition – even though one lacked grounds in support of that belief, just so long as some further relevant facts about the belief were true (e.g. it was formed by a reliable process). One way of developing the credulist position could be along epistemic externalist lines. On this reading, while it is true that one's testimony-based beliefs can be justified, and hence possible cases of knowledge, even though one is unable to offer any independent grounds in their favour, it is not that the justification

Thomas Reid (1710–96)

It is evident that, in the matter of testimony, the balance of human judgement is by nature inclined to the side of belief.

Reid, An Inquiry into the Human Mind

Like his contemporary, David Hume (1711–76), Thomas Reid was one of the main figures in a period of Scottish history known as the Scottish Enlightenment, in which radical new ideas came to the fore. Unlike Hume, however, who was notoriously prone to take a sceptical attitude towards the beliefs held by most of those around him, Reid was a defender of what is known as a 'common-sense' philosophy, which put the claims of common sense above the conclusions of abstract philosophical reasoning.

Just as in his treatment of testimony, Reid favoured trusting our common-sense judgements, so in his treatment of perception he favoured a view known as direct realism, which maintains that we are able to experience the world directly.

for these beliefs isn't based on *anything*. Instead, the justification is in virtue of some further relevant fact about the belief. For example, it could be that trusting testimony is, as a matter of fact, a reliable way of forming belief. One could thus allow that the agent can be justified in forming a testimony-based belief even while lacking supporting grounds for that belief, while not at the same time conceding that the belief is not being epistemically supported by anything, since it *is* being epistemically supported, just not by grounds that the agent can offer in the belief's favour.

As we saw in Chapter 6, however, epistemic externalism is a controversial thesis, and it may seem particularly controversial when applied to this case. If we are not already persuaded by the credulist idea that a testimony-based belief could be justified even though the agent is unable to offer adequate supporting grounds, then it is not obvious why adding that the belief is, as it happens, reliably formed would make a difference. Remember that the agent has no reason for thinking that the belief is reliably formed. Still, if one finds epistemic externalism independently plausible, then modifying the credulist thesis along epistemic externalist lines might look like an attractive way of making the view more palatable.

● THE PROBLEM OF MEMORIAL KNOWLEDGE

So far in this chapter we have talked about the epistemology of testimony without saying anything about memory. Notice, however, that the same sort of problem faces the justification of our reliance on memory as we saw above facing our reliance on testimony. Just as we depend upon testimony in a great deal of the beliefs that we form, we also depend upon memory. Think, for example, of your belief about where you live or what your name is. Furthermore, just as there seems no obvious reason why testimony should necessarily be thought trustworthy, so there seems no obvious reason why memory should necessarily be thought trustworthy. If that's right, then whether or not we can trust our memory might be thought to depend on what independent grounds we can offer for thinking that memory is trustworthy (i.e. grounds which are not themselves dependent upon the use of one's memory).

It seems, then, that in common with a reductionist view about the epistemology of testimony, we similarly ought to advance a parallel reductionist view about the epistemology of memory. Such a proposal would contend that a memory-based belief is only justified, and thus a case of knowledge, if it can be given adequate *independent* (i.e. non-memorial) epistemic support.

The problem is, of course, that, just as with testimony-based beliefs, when one thinks of the grounds, one can offer in favour of one's memory-based beliefs, one will usually think of further memory-based beliefs, and so the required independent epistemic support is lacking. For example, suppose I think I recall being told by a geography teacher that the Arctic is not in fact a land mass at all, but merely a block of ice, and so believe on this basis that the Arctic is a block of ice. If this recollection is true, then I would have grounds to trust this belief, since geography teachers are good sources of information about matters such as this. But what further grounds can I cite in support of this memory-based belief? Note that the obvious grounds that would naturally spring to mind in such a case would tend to be themselves memory-based beliefs. For example, I might say in support of this memory-based belief that I recall putting this answer down in a class test and having the answer marked correct, which would indeed support the original memory that I was told by a geography teacher that the Arctic is a block of ice. But this further belief is itself gained by memory, so unless I am already presupposing the epistemic legitimacy of using memory to gain knowledge, then this further belief wouldn't obviously be of any use.

The reductionist demand as regards memorial justification and knowledge, just like the parallel demand as regards testimonial justification and knowledge, thus seems to lead to a kind of scepticism in that it turns out that we lack a lot of the knowledge that we would ordinarily attribute to ourselves. One way around this problem is to opt for a version of credulism as regards memorial justification and knowledge, and therefore argue that we should grant memory-based beliefs a default epistemic status, such that beliefs so formed are justified, and hence candidates for knowledge, just so long as we have no special grounds for doubt. As with the credulist position as regards testimony, however, the problem with the view is that it merely seems to make a virtue out of necessity. Absent a general ground for trusting memory, it is just not clear why we should be willing to grant such a default status to memory-based belief.

Just as we saw above that credulism as regards testimony can be understood along epistemic externalist lines, one could try running the same line here. Accordingly, one would hold that one's memory-based beliefs for which one lacks adequate grounds can still be justified, and hence potential cases of knowledge, just so long as further relevant facts about the beliefs obtain, such as that the beliefs were reliably formed (i.e. trusting one's memory is a reliable way to form one's beliefs). As with credulism about testimony that is cast along epistemic externalist lines, whether you find this sort of rendering of credulism about memory plausible will depend on whether you find epistemic externalism plausible (and even then you might not think that epistemic externalism is applicable in this case).

So just as there is no easy answer to the question of how one justifies one's reliance on testimony, it is equally difficult to say what justifies one's reliance on memory.

● CHAPTER SUMMARY

- Testimonial knowledge is knowledge that we gain via the testimony of others. In the usual case, this will simply involve someone telling us what they know, but we can also gain testimonial knowledge in other more indirect ways, such as by *reading* the testimony of others (in a textbook like this one, say).
- A lot of what we believe is dependent upon the testimony of others. Moreover, it is hard to see how we could independently verify for ourselves much of what we are told via testimony since such verification would itself involve making appeal to further testimony-based beliefs that we hold, and so would simply be circular.
- One response to this problem is *reductionism*, which claims that we need to be able to offer non-testimonial support for our testimony-based beliefs if they are to be rightly held. In doing so, we would offer non-circular justification for our testimony-based beliefs. The problem is, however, that for a large number of our testimony-based beliefs, this is practically impossible, and so reductionism seems to entail that we know very little of what we usually think we know.
- We also looked at a very different response to the problem of testimonial knowledge, which is known as *credulism*. This view maintains that we can rightly hold a testimony-based belief even if we are unable to offer independent support (non-testimonial or otherwise) for it, at least provided there are no special reasons for doubt. Thus, since we don't need to offer independent support for a testimony-based belief in order for it to be rightly held, we don't need to worry about whether such independent support would be circular. The chief worry about credulism, however, is that it might be thought simply to license gullibility.
- We did consider, however, the possibility that credulism could be understood as an epistemic externalist thesis, such that while one could have justified testimony-based beliefs even while being unable to offer adequate supporting grounds for those beliefs, nevertheless one's beliefs should meet a further relevant condition, such as that they were formed in a reliable way (i.e. that testimony should be in fact reliable, even if we lack good reason for thinking that it is). Such an epistemic externalist rendering of credulism inherits the problems of epistemic externalism more generally, however.
- Finally, we turned to the issue of the epistemology of memory, and found that it raises many of the same issues that testimony does. In particular, there seems no obvious reason to think that our memory is trustworthy by its nature. Absent such a reason, it seems that for a memory-based belief to be justified, and hence a case of knowledge, is for that belief to be given adequate epistemic support from

independent grounds (i.e. non-memorial grounds). We thus seem led to a form of reductionism about memorial justification and knowledge. The trouble is, as with testimony, such independent grounds are usually lacking. Accordingly, again as with testimony, there is a similar move in the debate concerning the epistemology of memory towards a kind of credulism about memory-based beliefs which accords them a default epistemic standing (with the credulist thesis possibly supplemented by an appeal to some version of epistemic externalism). Such a view (even in its epistemic externalist guise) faces the same kinds of problems that afflict the parallel credulist position regarding testimony.

● STUDY QUESTIONS

1 Try to briefly state in your own words what testimony is. Classify the following cases in terms of whether they are examples of testimony:

- someone telling you that your car has been stolen;
- seeing your car being stolen;
- reading a note from a friend telling you that your car has been stolen;
- remembering that your car has been stolen; and
- seeing that your car is no longer in front of your house and inferring that it has been stolen.

2 Try to briefly state in your own words what reductionism about testimony holds, and why someone might endorse this view. Think of *four* beliefs that you hold which you are certain of but which would not meet the requirements laid down by reductionism.

3 Try to briefly state in your own words what credulism about testimony holds, and why someone might endorse this view. Is this view preferable to reductionism?

4 Why might one supplement one's credulism by appealing to some form of epistemic externalism? Describe what such a rendering of credulism would look like, and critically evaluate it. (Along the way, try to state clearly what the epistemic externalism/internalist amounts to.)

5 Explain, in your own words, why the problem facing memorial knowledge and justification is broadly analogous to the problem we have seen facing testimonial knowledge and justification. State what a reductionist and a credulist view would be as regards memory, and specify, where applicable, which view you find to be most plausible. (If you find neither view plausible, say why.)

● INTRODUCTORY FURTHER READING

Bernecker, Sven (2010) 'Memory Knowledge', *Routledge Companion to Epistemology*, S. Bernecker & D. H. Pritchard (eds), Ch. 30, pp. 326–34 (London: Routledge). A comprehensive overview of the main epistemological issues as regards memory.

Lackey, Jennifer (2010) 'Testimonial Knowledge', *Routledge Companion to Epistemology*, S. Bernecker & D. H. Pritchard (eds), Ch. 29, pp. 316–25 (London: Routledge). A detailed survey of the main epistemological issues as regards testimony.

• ADVANCED FURTHER READING

Coady, C. A. J. (1992) *Testimony: A Philosophical Study* (Oxford: Clarendon Press). This is the classic text on the epistemology of testimony, which defends a credulist approach. Very readable, with sections that apply the account of testimony offered to specific domains, such as legal testimony.

Coady, David (2012) *What to Believe Now: Applying Epistemology to Contemporary Issues* (Oxford: Wiley-Blackwell). A provocative contemporary treatment of the epistemology of testimony, which focuses on the relevance of the epistemology of testimony to issues in contemporary debate (e.g. the debate about climate change).

Lackey, Jennifer & Sosa, Ernest (eds) (2005) *The Epistemology of Testimony* (Oxford: Oxford University Press). A contemporary collection of papers on the subject, containing articles from most of the leading figures in the field. Not for the novice, but essential reading if you want to develop your grasp of the epistemology of testimony and are already familiar with much of the background of the area.

Martin, Charles Burton & Deutscher, Max (1966) 'Remembering', *The Philosophical Review*, 75, 61–196. This is the classic article on the epistemology of memory, and can be found in many anthologies of epistemology articles. Note, however, that it is really quite difficult, and hence is not the sort of thing that you are likely to be able to follow on the first reading.

• FREE INTERNET RESOURCES

Leonard, Nick (2021) 'Testimony, Epistemological Problems of', *Stanford Encyclopedia of Philosophy*, http://plato.stanford.edu/entries/testimony-episprob/. This is an outstanding and state-of-the-art entry on the epistemology of testimony. It includes lots of detail about the debates in this area and a comprehensive list of references to other articles that might be of use.

Michaelian, Kourken & Sutton, John (2017), 'Memory', *Stanford Encyclopedia of Philosophy*, https://plato.stanford.edu/entries/memory/. Although perhaps of less use to those new to epistemology, this is a fine overview of recent work on memory.

Morris, William Edward & Brown, Charlotte R. (2019) 'David Hume', *Stanford Encyclopedia of Philosophy*, http://plato.stanford.edu/entries/hume/. An excellent, and recently updated, overview of the work of Hume.

Nichols, Ryan & Yaffe, Gideon (2014) 'Thomas Reid', *Stanford Encyclopedia of Philosophy*, https://plato.stanford.edu/entries/reid/. A very helpful overview of the work of Reid.

Senor, Thomas D. (2009) 'Epistemological Problems of Memory', *Stanford Encyclopedia of Philosophy*, http://plato.stanford.edu/entries/memory-episprob/. An excellent overview of the epistemological issues as regards memory by one of the leading figures working on this area.

9
a priority and inference

- A priori and empirical knowledge
- The interdependence of a priori and empirical knowledge
- Introspective knowledge
- Deduction
- Induction
- Abduction

A PRIORI AND EMPIRICAL KNOWLEDGE

A common distinction in philosophy is that between **a priori** and **empirical knowledge** (the latter is sometimes known as **a posteriori knowledge**). Very roughly, this distinction relates to whether the knowledge in question was gained independently of an investigation of the world through experience (what is known as an *empirical* inquiry). If it was, then it is a priori knowledge; if it wasn't, then it is empirical (or a posteriori) knowledge.

Suppose, for example, that I come to know that all bachelors are unmarried simply by reflecting on the meanings of the words involved (e.g. that 'bachelor' just means unmarried man, and thus it follows that all bachelors must be unmarried men). Given that I gained this knowledge simply by reflecting on the meanings of the words involved rather than by undertaking an investigation of the world, it is a priori knowledge.

Contrast my a priori knowledge in this respect with my knowledge that the tropic of Cancer is in the northern hemisphere, which is knowledge that I gained by looking in a reliable atlas. Since I acquired this knowledge by making an investigation of the world (i.e. by looking up the tropic of Cancer in an atlas), it is thus empirical knowledge.

Notice that the same distinction also applies to justification. A belief is a priori justified if that justification was gained independently of a worldly investigation (e.g. by reflecting on the meanings of the words involved). In contrast, a belief is empirically justified if that justification was gained via a worldly investigation (e.g. looking something up in an atlas).

DOI: 10.4324/9781003356110-11

One way in which this distinction is often made is to say that a priori knowledge (/justification) is knowledge (/justification) that one gains simply by sitting in one's armchair, while empirical knowledge (/justification) demands that one get out of one's armchair and make further (empirical) inquiries. In this way, we can see that it is not only truths of meaning (e.g. all bachelors are unmarried) that one can have a priori knowledge of, but also other claims, such as logical and mathematical truths. For example, we do not need to make empirical inquiries in order to discern that two plus two equals four, since we can discover this simply by reflecting on our mathematical concepts.

Notice that any proposition which one can have a priori knowledge of one can also have empirical knowledge of. For example, I could come to know that all bachelors are unmarried men not only by reflecting (in my armchair) on the meanings of the words involved but by looking up the meaning of the word 'bachelor' in a dictionary (i.e. by getting out of my armchair and making an empirical inquiry). The converse of this is not true, however, in that it doesn't follow that any proposition which one can have empirical knowledge of one can also have a priori knowledge of. The only way to find out which hemisphere the tropic of Cancer is in is by getting out of one's armchair and making an empirical investigation – this just isn't the sort of proposition that one can have a priori knowledge of.

• THE INTERDEPENDENCE OF A PRIORI AND EMPIRICAL KNOWLEDGE

A great deal of our knowledge, including our empirical knowledge, makes use of further knowledge which is both empirical and a priori. Imagine, for example, a detective who is trying to work out who committed a murder, and who discovers, via the reliable testimony of a witness, that one of the suspects – let's call him Professor Plum – was in the pantry at the time of the murder. Now the detective also knows that if someone is in one place at a certain time, then they can't be in another place at the same time, and thus he infers that Professor Plum was not in the hallway at the time of the murder, something that may well be very salient to the investigation as a whole. (It might be known, for example, that the murder was committed in the hallway, and thus that Professor Plum is off the hook.)

In this case, the detective is making the following sort of inference, where 1 and 2 are premises from which a conclusion, C, is drawn:

1 Professor Plum was in the pantry at the time of the murder.
2 If Professor Plum was in the pantry at the time of the murder, then he wasn't in the hallway.

Therefore:

C Professor Plum was not in the hallway at the time of the murder (and so is innocent).

Let's take it as given that both premises are known. The first premise of this inference, 1, is clearly empirical knowledge since it was gained by listening to the testimony of a witness. Premise 2, however, is not obviously empirical knowledge at all, since it seems to be something that you could discover without making any investigation of the world. That is, merely by reflecting on what it means to be located somewhere, you could realise that someone could not be in two places at once and thus that if Professor Plum is in one place (in this case the pantry), then he couldn't also simultaneously be in another place (in this case the hallway). Indeed, presumably, this is just how the detective came by this knowledge in this case, and so it is a priori knowledge. The conclusion is obviously empirical knowledge, however, since it was gained, in part, by making an empirical inquiry (i.e. listening to the testimony of a witness). So although the inference in this case leads to a conclusion that is empirical knowledge, it also makes use of a priori knowledge as well.

• INTROSPECTIVE KNOWLEDGE

An important variety of a priori knowledge is gained by **introspection**. This is where we try to discover something by examining our own psychological states.

Suppose, for example, that I sought to determine whether I really wanted to get involved in a certain relationship, and I recognised that I had conflicting thoughts in this regard. One way in which I might try to resolve this issue could be to examine how I really feel about this person. The kinds of questions I might ask myself could be as follows: Do I enjoy her company? Does being around her make me happy, or make me anxious? Am I getting further involved in this relationship simply because I feel pressured to do so? In asking questions of this sort, I will, with any luck, discover how best to proceed. Notice, however, that the kind of enquiry that I am conducting here is not an empirical enquiry, since I am not investigating the world at all. Rather I am 'looking into' myself and investigating what I find there. This is, after all, the kind of enquiry that one could undertake in one's armchair. This is introspection and when it yields knowledge – what is known as *introspective knowledge* – it is often the case that the knowledge it yields is a priori knowledge.

Introspection need not only be involved in settling affairs of the heart in the manner just described, since we use introspection all the time to settle more mundane issues. Suppose my partner, while fiddling with the gas fire, asks me whether I smell a gas leak. If I was unaware of smelling gas, I might reflect further on the nature of my experiences to see if there is anything unusual about them. In doing so, I am introspecting my experiences and thereby examining them in order to extract new information.

Notice that when introspection is used in this kind of way, the knowledge that it yields is empirical knowledge. After all, the original experience (i.e. being in the room which may or may not contain a gas leak) was gained via interaction with the world. Nevertheless, there is a non-empirical component to the introspective knowledge gained in this case, since one is examining one's experience independently of gaining any further empirical information. In this way, for example, one might come to believe that there is a smell of gas in the room, even though one did not recognise this at the time (perhaps one was not looking out for a gas leak, and so merely noted that something smelt strange without further wondering what the smell was of).

● DEDUCTION

Consider again the argument we gave previously:

1 Professor Plum was in the pantry at the time of the murder.
2 If Professor Plum was in the pantry at the time of the murder, then he wasn't in the hallway.

Therefore:

C Professor Plum was not in the hallway at the time of the murder (and so is innocent).

This is clearly a good argument for the conclusion, but what do we mean by 'good' here? Well, at the very least we mean that premises 1 and 2 support the conclusion, C, in the following sense: if the premises are true, then the conclusion must be true as well. In other words, it just isn't possible for the premises in this argument to be true and yet the conclusion be false, which is to say that the truth of the premises *entails* the truth of the conclusion. This is what is known as **validity**; this argument is valid.

This argument is more than just valid, however, since the premises are (we supposed above) also true. (Indeed, we claimed that they were known to be true.) For the sake of argument, however, suppose that Professor Plum had not been in the pantry at the time of the murder. One of the premises, 1, would then have been false. Nevertheless, it would still have been the case that *if* these premises had been true, *then* the conclusion would have been true as well. You can thus have a valid argument even if it has false premises. If the premises are false, the argument is still a good argument in the sense of being valid, even though it gives us no reason for thinking that the conclusion is true because of the falsity of the premises. Since the argument considered above is both valid and has true premises, then it has an additional virtue: it is an argument that is not only good in the sense of being valid but also gives us reason for thinking that the conclusion is true (since the premises are true). This virtuous property of arguments is known as **soundness**, and it applies when a valid argument has true premises. Our argument is thus not only valid but also sound.

When one reasons via a valid argument, we call this **deduction**. Deductive arguments are very important to the acquisition of knowledge since they enable one to expand one's knowledge. By having knowledge of the premises in the above argument one can thereby infer the conclusion and in doing so gain knowledge of a new proposition.

Moreover, valid arguments which lack true premises, and so are not sound, can still be epistemically useful. If I am justified in believing the premises of a valid argument, then, in most cases at least, I am justified in believing the conclusion of that argument. This is so even if, as it happens, one of the premises is, without my being aware of it, false, which would mean that the conclusion might be false also (and so not a candidate for knowledge). In order to see this, notice that even if premise 1 in the argument above is in fact false, it would still follow that if I am justified in believing it (e.g. if I was told that 1 was the case by a reliable witness) and I am also justified in believing premise 2, then I would be justified in believing the conclusion, C. Accordingly, even if deductive arguments do not always extend knowledge, it is plausible that they do always extend justified belief.

• INDUCTION

Not all acceptable types of argument are deductive, however. Consider the following inference:

1 Every observed emu has been flightless.

Therefore:

C All emus are flightless.

This argument is clearly not deductive, since it is entirely possible, even granted the truth of premise 1, that there is an unobserved emu around somewhere that is not flightless. That is, since the premise can be true and yet the conclusion simultaneously be false, this argument is not a valid argument. Nevertheless, given that we have observed lots of emus across a suitable length of time and in lots of different habitats, then it does seem that this is an entirely legitimate inference to make.

That is, the argument seems perfectly acceptable provided that we interpret 1 along the following lines:

1* Lots of emus have been observed over many years and in a wide range of environments, and they have always been flightless.

Therefore:

C All emus are flightless.

The point about adding this detail to 1 is that inferences of this sort are only legitimate, provided that the sample is sufficiently large and representative. If one had only seen a couple of emus, or only observed lots of emus in one very specific environment (e.g. at a particular lake), then the fact that they were flightless in this case need not be any indication at all that emus are, in general, flightless birds. In order for this style of reasoning to be acceptable, it thus seems required that the sample in question is large and representative enough. This sort of non-deductive reasoning is known as **induction**.

In the case of deduction, it is obvious why the reasoning is legitimate, since deductive inferences, being valid, preserve truth. If your premises are true, then you can be assured that your conclusion is true also. Accordingly, it ought to be uncontentious to suppose that one can go directly from knowledge of the premises to knowledge of the conclusion. In the case of induction, however, this defence does not work since one might know the premises and yet lack knowledge of the conclusion because the conclusion is false. For example, if there were an unobserved emu somewhere which was not flightless, then one might know the premise in the above argument, legitimately infer the conclusion, and yet lack knowledge of the conclusion because it wasn't true.

Nevertheless, it is plausibly the case that good inductive arguments (i.e. ones which make an inference from a large and representative sample), like deductive arguments, always extend justified belief. If I am justified in believing the premise, 1*, of the above inductive argument, then I am justified in believing the conclusion, even if, as it happens, the conclusion is false. The reason for this is that good inductive arguments, while they do not have premises which entail the conclusion, do have premises which make that conclusion likely. They are thus very useful, albeit fallible, ways of forming true beliefs and thereby extending one's justified belief (and, hopefully, knowledge too).

• ABDUCTION

Not all non-deductive arguments have the same form as that just considered. Rather than proceeding from a large and representative sample to an unrestricted conclusion, some non-deductive arguments instead proceed from a single observed phenomenon to an explanation of that phenomenon, usually via the implicit use of connecting premises of some sort. For example, consider the following inference:

1 There are feet exposed under the curtain in the hall.

Therefore:

C There is someone hiding behind the curtain.

This seems like a perfectly legitimate form of reasoning. Moreover, like the inductive inferences considered above, the premise clearly does not entail the conclusion, as happens in a deductive argument. Crucially, however, this type of reasoning is very unlike the inductive inference above in that it does not make appeal to a large and representative set of observations. Instead, this style of argument, often known as **abduction**, usually proceeds, as in the case just outlined, from a single observed phenomenon to the best explanation of that phenomenon. This is why this style of reasoning is sometimes called **inference to the best explanation**.

Before we can evaluate this type of reasoning, we need to fill in the gaps here. While it might seem that abductive inferences are as stark as the one just described, if one reflects on the example, one will quickly realise that there is much that is implicit. For example, we would only infer that there is someone behind the curtain because of what else we know about the likelihood of there being feet behind the curtain without there being someone there to whom the feet belong. If, for example, we were in the unfortunate (and rather gruesome) situation of being in a room in which there were dismembered feet to be found, then it is unlikely that we would have so quickly inferred C from the observation contained in 1.

Once one makes this element of abductive inference explicit, however, it starts to look like a shorthand way of expressing a normal inductive argument. That is, why do we infer from the fact that we can see feet under the curtain that there is a person there? Well, because we know, from previous experience, that there is an observed regularity between feet being under the curtain and a person behind the curtain to whom the feet belong. When abductive inferences are just abbreviated versions of normal inductive inferences in this way, they pose no special problems.

Not all abductive inferences can easily be reconstrued as normal inductive inferences in disguise, however. Imagine, for example, that one came across a wholly unusual phenomenon for the first time, such as a corn circle in a field. There are numerous possible explanations for this phenomenon – from the relatively mundane, such as that it was caused by freak atmospheric conditions, to the quite bizarre, such as

Sherlock Holmes

Sherlock Holmes, the famous fictional detective of London's Baker Street, often reached his conclusions by making abductive inferences, much to his colleague Dr Watson's amazement. Simply by observing someone's clothing and demeanour, for example, Holmes would draw quite startling (and usually true) conclusions about that person.

In the story *A Scandal in Bohemia*, for instance, Holmes deduces, simply from taking a good look at Watson, that he has got very wet recently and that his maid is careless. Holmes explains how he knows this by pointing out that the leather on the inside of Watson's left shoe is scored by six almost parallel cuts, as if caused by someone who has carelessly scraped round the edges of the sole in order to remove crusted mud from it. This suggests to Holmes that Watson has recently been out in very wet weather and that his maid has been careless in cleaning his shoes.

Holmes isn't obviously drawing on a series of observations of shoes in order to reach this conclusion, but rather regards the conclusion that he offers as being the best explanation of what he sees. It thus appears to be an abductive inference.

that Martians created the circles as a sign to humankind. Which explanation should one choose? Clearly, one cannot make appeal to any observed regularity in this case because, by hypothesis, this is the first time that this sort of phenomenon has been observed. On normal inductive grounds alone, then, one should hold one's fire and wait for further information before one forms a judgement.

That said, I think most people would regard the simplest and most conservative explanation of this phenomenon to be preferable to any explanation which would involve one making radical adjustments to one's beliefs. That is, it seems common sense to explain this phenomenon in terms of freak atmospheric conditions if one can, rather than by resorting to explaining it in terms of Martian activity. This reflects the fact that in ordinary life, we tend to treat the best explanation of a phenomenon as being that explanation which, all other things being equal, is the simplest one, in the conservative sense of being most in keeping with what we already believe.

The problem with this kind of regulative principle on abductive inference is that there seems no good reason for thinking that explanations which are simple and conservative in this way are more likely to be true than complex or unconservative explanations. In any case, the only grounds we could have for thinking that it is legitimate to use such regulative principles in abductive inference could be inductive grounds for thinking that simplicity and conservatism have helped us to get to the truth in the past. It seems then that if abductive inference is to be legitimate at all, it must reduce to an inductive inference at some point, however complicated the 'reduction' might be. That is, despite the apparent differences between abductive and normal inductive inferences, abductive inferences always seem to make implicit use of further information or regulative principles which, if properly employed at any rate, are inductively grounded.

If that's right, then abductive inferences will be acceptable just so long as the corresponding inductive inferences are acceptable; more generally, abduction is an acceptable form of inference if induction is. As we will see in Chapter 10, however, there is in fact cause to doubt whether induction is a legitimate way of drawing inferences, and so both induction and abduction are problematic.

• CHAPTER SUMMARY

- We began by noting a distinction between *a priori knowledge* and *empirical knowledge*. The former is knowledge that you have gained without having to investigate the world (i.e. armchair knowledge), while the latter is gained, at least in part, via a worldly investigation.
- An important kind of a priori knowledge is gained by introspection, which is where we 'look inwardly' and examine our own psychological states rather than 'look outwardly' and investigate the world. As we saw, however, not all introspective knowledge is a priori knowledge.
- We then looked at different kinds of inference. In particular, we made a distinction between inferences that are *deductive* and inferences that are *inductive*. The

former kind of inference is where the premise(s) *entail* the conclusion (i.e. given that the premise(s) are true, the conclusion must also be true).

- Inductive arguments, in contrast, are inferences from premise(s) which provide support for the truth of the conclusion without actually entailing it (i.e. the premise(s) could be true without the conclusion being true). We noted that good inductive arguments are ones that provide strong support for the truth of the conclusion, and this will usually mean that their premises appeal to a representative sample in providing this support for the conclusion.

- Finally, we noted that many non-deductive inferences do not seem to have the same form as normal inductive inferences, even though they involve premise(s) which do not entail the conclusion. Instead, these inferences involve making an inference regarding what is the best explanation of a certain phenomenon – what is known as an *abductive* inference. Nevertheless, despite their superficial differences, it seems that any legitimate form of abductive inference will be an abbreviated version of an inductive inference.

• STUDY QUESTIONS

1 Explain, in your own words, the distinction between a priori and empirical knowledge. Give two examples of each type of knowledge, and explain why they are of that type.

2 What is introspection? Give an example of your own of introspective knowledge, and say whether the knowledge in question is a priori or empirical.

3 What is a deductive argument? Give an example of your own of a deductive argument.

4 What is the difference between an argument which is merely valid and one that is, in addition, sound? Give an example of your own to illustrate this distinction.

5 What is an inductive argument, and how is it different from a deductive argument? Give an example of your own of an inductive argument which you think is a good argument. Say why you think this argument is a good argument.

6 What is an abductive argument, and how is it different from a normal inductive argument? Why might one think that abductive arguments, at least when cogent, are in fact normal inductive arguments in disguise?

• INTRODUCTORY FURTHER READING

Bonjour, Laurence (2010) 'A Priori Knowledge', *Routledge Companion to Epistemology*, S. Bernecker & D. H. Pritchard (eds), pp. 283–93 (London: Routledge). A helpful overview of the contemporary literature on a priori knowledge.

Jenkins, Carrie (2008) 'A Priori Knowledge: Debates and Developments', *Philosophy Compass*, https://doi.org/10.1111/j.1747-9991.2008.00136.x. (Oxford: Blackwell). A survey of contemporary work on a priori knowledge. It can be a little demanding in places, but overall is accessible enough to just about count as 'introductory' further reading.

● ADVANCED FURTHER READING

Casullo, Albert (2012) *Essays on A Priori Knowledge and Justification* (Oxford: Oxford University Press). This is an important contemporary book on a priori knowledge and justification from the recent literature. Not for beginners.

Lipton, Peter (1991) *Inference to the Best Explanation* (London: Routledge). A very readable overview of the issues. Well worth reading if you want to find out more about abductive arguments.

Steup, Mathias, Turri, John & Sosa, Ernest (eds) (2013) *Contemporary Debates in Epistemology* (2nd edn, Oxford: Wiley). This edited collection contains a useful debate (§8) between Laurence Bonjour and Michael Devitt on a priori knowledge.

● FREE INTERNET RESOURCES

Douven, Igor (2021) 'Abduction', *Stanford Encyclopedia of Philosophy*, https://plato. stanford.edu/entries/abduction/. A comprehensive, and recently updated, overview of the main issues concerning inference to the best explanation.

Russell, Bruce (2020) 'A Priori Justification and Knowledge', *Stanford Encyclopedia of Philosophy*, http://plato.stanford.edu/entries/apriori/. A systematic overview of the literature on a priori justification and knowledge. Recently updated.

Schwitzgebel, Eric (2019) 'Introspection', *Stanford Encyclopedia of Philosophy*, http://plato.stanford.edu/entries/introspection/. This entry doesn't just offer an excellent survey of the philosophical literature on introspection but also covers some of the relevant empirical work from psychology too.

10

the problem of induction

- The problem of induction
- Responding to the problem of induction
- Living with the problem of induction I: falsification
- Living with the problem of induction II: pragmatism

● THE PROBLEM OF INDUCTION

As we saw in Chapter 9, it is very important to be able to account for the legitimacy of inductive inferences because we use them all the time to acquire knowledge. Think of the activity of the scientist when she is conducting her experiments. Here the inferences involved are almost exclusively inductive, since they often move from a premise which concerns an observed, and often representative, sample, to an entirely general claim which goes beyond the restricted claim found in the premises. For example, a scientist might make a series of observations of penguins in a range of different conditions and on this basis draw general conclusions about penguin behaviour. This looks like a perfectly reasonable inductive inference to make, even if, in common with all inductive inferences, the conclusion is not entailed by the premises, but merely made reasonable.

Given the prevalence of inductive inferences in scientific practice, it would thus seem to follow that if induction is not a legitimate way of gaining knowledge, then this would preclude us from gaining a lot of what we regard as scientific knowledge. The problem isn't restricted to science either, as much of our day-to-day knowledge is also dependent upon inductive inferences (as when, for example, one draws conclusions about which postal service to use based on one's past interactions with them). Nonetheless, our dependence on inductive inferences has been shown to be problematic by a famous argument – due to David Hume (1711–76) – that appears to show that inductive reasoning is unjustified.

DOI: 10.4324/9781003356110-12

We noted in Chapter 9 that inductive inferences appear legitimate provided that the sample used is sufficiently large and representative. Recall the 'emu' example that we gave there, and what we said about it. Here's the basic inference again:

1 Every observed emu has been flightless.

Therefore:

C All emus are flightless.

As we noted, this inference seems acceptable just so long as the observations of emus are made in a representative range of cases (in lots of different environments and circumstances, say), and there is a sufficiently large number of observations (e.g. just a couple of observed emus would not do). That is, we need to read 1 as something like 1*:

1* Lots of emus have been observed over many years and in a wide range of environments, and they have always been flightless.

The inductive inference from 1* to C does seem to be a good inference because, given the sorts of observations in play in 1*, C seems very likely to be true.

The issue that Hume raised, however, was how we could be sure that the regularities that are observed within a representative sample (e.g. between being an emu and being a flightless bird) should increase the likelihood that the unrestricted generalisation (i.e. that all emus are flightless birds) is true. The problem is that it seems that our only defence for this claim is an inductive one (i.e. that representative samples have supported such unrestricted generalisations in the past). But if that's the case, then this means that inductive inferences are only justified provided they make use of the conclusions of further inductive inferences. Accordingly, there can be no non-circular way of justifying induction (i.e. no way of justifying it which does not itself make appeal to a further inductive inference).

Let's break this argument down into stages. Hume's first point is that the inference from 1* to C in the inductive argument above is problematic unless it is supplemented with a further premise that is effectively left unstated in the argument. We can express this tacit premise as follows:

2 A certain regularity has been observed across a sufficiently large and representative sample, which means that it is likely that the regularity applies in general.

With this additional premise in play, there is no mystery about why we can legitimately infer C from 1*, since the representativeness of the sample at issue in 1* will ensure, in line with 2, that the conclusion is likely to be true. But how, if at all, do we know 2? Intuitively, the only way one could know such a claim is via another inductive inference: by observing a correlation between observed regularities across sufficiently large and representative samples and the unrestricted regularity itself. But that means that an inductive inference is only legitimate, provided it makes use of a further claim which is itself gained via induction. Accordingly, concludes Hume, the epistemic support we have for inductive inferences is circular, since they only generate justified belief in the conclusion provided one already makes use of a further inductive inference. As a result, there could be no non-circular justification of induction. This is known as the **problem of induction**.

• RESPONDING TO THE PROBLEM OF INDUCTION

It is not altogether obvious how one should respond to the problem of induction. One line of response is to claim that such a fundamental epistemic practice as induction does not stand in need of justification, and thus that we can legitimately employ it without worrying about whether a non-circular justification is available. This does seem rather ad hoc, however, and is hardly an intellectually satisfying approach to the problem.

Another possibility is to claim that just so long as induction works, it does not matter whether we are in possession of non-circular reasons for thinking that it is a legitimate way of arguing. That is, the thought would be that just so long as a premise like 2 is true, then it can be legitimately employed in an inductive argument – it doesn't matter whether we have any good independent (i.e. non-inductive) reasons for thinking that it is true. Such a move might be made by one who endorses epistemic externalism (i.e. one who holds that one can be justified in holding a belief, and thus have knowledge, even while lacking supporting grounds, just so long as certain 'external' conditions obtain, such as that one forms one's belief in a reliable fashion). In this case, the epistemic externalist could hold that we can be justified in holding a belief in the conclusion of an inductive argument even though, granted the problem of induction, we lack any good reason for thinking that this belief is true, just so long as induction is in fact a reliable way of forming one's beliefs.

This type of move will not appeal to everyone. In particular, it will not appeal to epistemic internalists who think that in order to be justified in holding a belief, one must always be in possession of appropriate supporting grounds. The problem for the epistemic internalist, however, is to explain how our widespread induction-based beliefs are justified given that, as Hume seems to have shown, there are no non-circular grounds available in support of these beliefs. The choice between the two views is thus very stark indeed.

• LIVING WITH THE PROBLEM OF INDUCTION I: FALSIFICATION

Interestingly, not everyone thinks that it is vital that we respond to the problem of induction by finding a way of resolving it. Instead, some argue that this is a problem that we can live with.

Perhaps the most famous proponent of a view of this sort is **Karl Popper** (1902–94), who argued that the problem of induction was not nearly as pressing as it might at first seem because we don't in fact make use of inductive inferences all that often. In particular, he claimed that science, properly understood, does not make use of inductive inferences at all, but instead proceeds deductively.

In order to see what Popper means by this, consider again the inference that we looked at above concerning emus:

1* Lots of emus have been observed over many years and in a wide range of environments, and they have always been flightless.

Therefore:

C All emus are flightless.

This is clearly an inductive inference since the truth of the premise is compatible with the falsity of the conclusion (i.e. the premise makes the conclusion likely, but does not entail it). Moreover, it also seems to accurately represent the way in which a scientist might go about discovering that all emus are flightless – that is, observe lots of emus in lots of different conditions and then draw a general conclusion about whether or not they can fly.

Karl Popper (1902–94)

Good tests kill flawed theories; we remain alive to guess again.

Popper (attributed)

Karl Popper was born in Austria but spent most of his academic life working in Britain. His most famous philosophical contribution was the advocacy of the process of **falsification** as an alternative to induction when it came to understanding science. He claimed that the methodology of science was not to slowly and inductively build up a case for a generalisation, but rather to formulate bold generalisations and then seek to refute them by finding counter-examples to the generalisation.

Popper claimed that the mark of a scientific theory was that it was *falsifiable* – that is, that there was some observation or set of observations which would show that it was false. With this benchmark for what constitutes a scientific theory in mind, Popper argued against certain theories which purported to be scientific but which weren't, Popper claimed, falsifiable. The two theories that Popper focused upon in this regard were Marxism and psychoanalysis. In both cases, argued Popper, any apparent counter-evidence to the view is always explained away so that nothing is ever allowed to count decisively against the theory. But that just goes to show, claimed Popper, that such views are not falsifiable and hence not scientific theories at all.

Popper claims, however, that in fact science proceeds not in this inductive fashion at all but rather by making bold generalisations and then trying to *falsify* them (i.e. by trying to show that the bold generalisation is false). When successful, this process is what Popper calls *falsification*. For example, to take the emu case just described, the scientist who suspects that all emus are flightless will boldly put forward this hypothesis for testing. 'Testing' the hypothesis, however, does not mean looking for evidence in its favour, but rather looking for decisive evidence *against* it. In this case, for instance, it will mean looking for an emu which can fly.

Notice the form of the inference that would take place if one were to falsify a hypothesis in this way – that is, if one were to discover a flying emu. First, we have our bold hypothesis:

H All emus are flightless.

We also have our definitive counter-evidence to H, the observation of a flying emu:

1 There exists a flying emu.

From this observation we can conclude that the bold hypothesis, H, is false, since this states that all emus are flightless:

C Not all emus are flightless.

What is important about this inference from 1 to C, however, is that it is entirely *deductive*, not inductive. If there does indeed exist a flying emu, then it follows deductively that not all emus are flightless; this conclusion is not merely likely, given the premise, but *must* be the case.

Popper's idea is thus that by offering bold hypotheses which they then try to falsify, scientists are in effect proceeding deductively rather than inductively. That is, they do not try to find lots of evidence which supports, albeit inconclusively, the conclusion of an inductive inference; rather they make a bold generalisation which they then try to falsify conclusively, where if this falsification takes place, they can deductively conclude that the bold generalisation is false.

If Popper is right on this score, then it follows that we needn't be quite as troubled by the problem of induction as we might have thought we should be, since it is not as if as much of our knowledge of the world – gained through science – is dependent upon induction as we originally supposed. But does Popper's rather radical solution to the problem work?

There are a number of problems with Popper's proposal; we shall here consider the two main ones. The first problem arises because if we understand our scientific knowledge in the way that Popper suggests, then it's not clear that we have all that much scientific knowledge. As it happens, no one has ever observed a flying emu (as far as we know at any rate). Do we not know, then, that all emus are flightless? Not according to Popper. If we found a flying emu, then we could deductively come to know that *not all* emus are flightless, but knowing that *all* emus are flightless would require induction, and recall that by Popper's lights, we haven't legitimated our use of *that*. It seems, then, that we can never know the unfalsified generalisations that scientists make; we can only know the falsity of those generalisations that have been shown to be false. Accordingly, it appears that we lose a lot of our scientific knowledge on the Popperian view after all.

The second problem with Popper's proposal arises because it is not obvious that scientists are able to deduce the falsity of one of their bold generalisations simply by observing what seems to be a decisive counter-example to the generalisation. Consider again the case of the emus. Suppose that for many centuries, people had observed that emus were flightless, and so came to believe that all emus are flightless. Now suppose that one day a scientist comes into the room and claims that she's just seen a flying emu. How would you respond?

One certainly wouldn't abandon one's belief that all emus are flightless just on the basis of this single instance of testimony. After all, given the long history of observations of flightless emus, other explanations of what this scientist seems to have observed seem far more preferable. At the uncharitable end of the spectrum, one might suspect that the scientist was simply wrong in her observation, or perhaps even deceitful. Even if one trusts the scientist, however, there are still ways in which one could challenge the observation. One could note that there are birds in the area that can look a lot like emus in certain conditions. More radically, one might simply assert that whatever this creature was that was flying, it couldn't have been an emu, since it is characteristic of emus that they don't fly, and so it must have been a different creature entirely, perhaps a new type of bird not seen before, one that is just like an emu in every respect except that it flies.

The crux of the matter is that one isn't rationally obliged to take any observation at face value. In particular, there seems nothing essentially irrational about objecting to the observation in the sorts of ways just outlined, provided that the generalisation called into question by the observation is sufficiently well confirmed by other observations. The problem, however, is that if there is rational room for manoeuvre regarding whether one accepts an observation at face value, then it appears as if there is even less scientific knowledge on the Popperian view than we thought, since, unless one accepts the observation at face value, one can't make the relevant deductive inference to the denial of the bold generalisation and so come to know that the generalisation is false. That is, the upshot of this objection is that not only does this view prevent us from knowing that any generalisation about the world is true, it also doesn't follow on this view that we necessarily have much in the way of knowledge that many generalisations about the world are false either.

• LIVING WITH THE PROBLEM OF INDUCTION II: PRAGMATISM

A very different way of living with the problem of induction is offered by Hans Reichenbach (1891–1953). Reichenbach agrees with Hume that there is no justification for induction. However, Reichenbach argues that it is nevertheless rational, at least in one sense of that term, to make inductive inferences. In essence, Reichenbach's idea is that induction is rational because if we don't employ induction, then we are guaranteed to end up with very few true beliefs about the world, while if we do use induction then we at least have the chance to form lots of true beliefs about the world through our inductive inferences. That is, if anything is going to work, then it is going to be induction, so it is in this sense rational to use induction, even though we have no justification for thinking that it does work. Reichenbach therefore offers a practical – or *pragmatic* – response to the problem of induction, rather than an epistemic response.

In order to understand Reichenbach's point, consider one of the examples that he uses: the rationality of someone who is terminally ill, and with very little time left, choosing to try a new experimental operation even though there is not, at present, any reason to think it will save his life. The point is that in this case the choice is between certain death and the faint possibility of life. Given that the agent is faced with this choice, it is rational that he should opt for the operation even though he has no good grounds for thinking that it will be successful. If anything will save the agent's life, it will be this operation.

Touching the Void

Touching the Void is a famous documentary made in 2003. It is a dramatic retelling of a real-life incident involving two mountain climbers who face disaster after one of them has an accident on the mountain Siula Grande in the Peruvian Andes. One of the most spectacular scenes in the film concerns the moment when the main protagonist has to make a choice between certain death and the unknown. He has fallen deep into the heart of a glacier and is now hanging there in the darkness unable, due to his injuries, to climb out. The choice he is faced with is either to hang there in the darkness until he eventually passes out and dies, or else cut the rope and let himself fall deeper into the darkness of the glacier below him. For all he knows, the fall would kill him, but, equally, there is always the possibility that he might survive the fall. The gamble pays off in that the hero survives the fall and then miraculously finds a way out of the glacier.

According to Reichenbach, the choice made by this climber is essentially the same as that facing us as regards induction. Just as the climber has no reason to think that cutting the rope will benefit him, we have no reason to trust induction. Nevertheless, given the alternatives involved, cutting the rope is the most rational thing to do since it leaves open the *possibility* of survival. In the same way, trusting induction is the most rational thing to do given the choices facing us in light of the problem of induction, according to Reichenbach, since it is only by employing induction that we have any hope of systematically forming true beliefs about the world.

Likewise, according to Reichenbach, we face the choice between not using induction and losing all chance of gaining lots of true beliefs about the world through these inferences, or using it and potentially gaining lots of true beliefs about the world. With the choice so framed, using induction even though one lacks a justification for this style of inference seems perfectly rational.

With our discussion of epistemic rationality in mind from Chapter 5, notice that the kind of rationality in play here is not obviously an epistemic rationality. Reichenbach is quite clear that we have no good grounds for thinking that our trust in our inductive inferences will be rewarded with true beliefs. In this sense, then, Reichenbach's advice to us to trust induction should remind us of Pascal's wager. Recall that the point of this wager was, in essence, that since what one gains (i.e. infinite life) by believing in God if the belief is true is enormous relative to the losses (i.e. the inconvenience of having the belief) involved if the belief is false, hence it is rational to believe in God's existence. Like Reichenbach's defence of induction, then, Pascal's wager doesn't offer us a reason to think that a certain claim is true (e.g. that God exists), only that we have most to gain by groundlessly supposing that it is true.

There is a key difference, however, between Reichenbach's defence of induction and Pascal's wager, which is that while Pascal's wager is not aimed at all at the goal of gaining true beliefs about God's existence – it is just concerned to show us which belief in this regard is most in our interest to believe – Reichenbach's defence of induction *is* aimed at the goal of gaining true beliefs, albeit in a roundabout way. That is, Reichenbach is saying that if gaining lots of true beliefs is what you are interested in, then the best thing to do is trust induction, even though we lack a justification for induction. So while such a belief in induction is not directly epistemically rational (i.e. it is not supported by grounds in favour of the truth of that belief), it is *indirectly* epistemically rational in that belief in induction is, according to Reichenbach, the sort of thing that an epistemically rational person should believe. With this point in mind, it may be that Reichenbach's way of dealing with the problem of induction is not quite so merely pragmatic as many (including Reichenbach himself) have supposed.

• CHAPTER SUMMARY

- We began by looking at Hume's problem of induction. This problem arises because it seems impossible to gain a non-circular justification for induction. This is because inductive inferences are only legitimate, provided we are already entitled to suppose that observed regularities provide good grounds for the generalisations we inductively infer from those regularities. The trouble is that our grounds for this supposition themselves depend upon further inductive inferences (i.e. that we have found the connection between observed regularities and the relevant generalisations to hold in the past). But if this is right, then our justification for making any particular inductive inference will itself be at least partly inductive, and this means that there can be no non-circular justification for induction.

- One way in which commentators have responded to the problem of induction is by arguing that such a fundamental epistemic practice does not stand in need of justification, but we noted that this was not a very intellectually satisfying way of responding to the problem. A better approach, one that is in the same spirit, is to defend induction on epistemic externalist grounds. On this proposal, our lack of adequate grounds in support of induction need be no bar to gaining justified beliefs using induction just so long as induction is, as a matter of fact, reliable. We noted that those epistemologists who adhere to epistemic internalism will not find such an approach very plausible.
- We then considered one way of responding to the problem of induction, due to Popper. This held that the problem of induction does not undermine as much of our knowledge as we might think because most apparently inductive knowledge – in particular, most scientific knowledge – is in fact gained via deduction. Popper argues that rather than make tentative inferences from observed regularities, scientists in fact formulate bold hypotheses that they then try to decisively refute, or *falsify* – a process which is deductive rather than inductive. We noted two problems facing this view: that it seemed to undermine a great deal of our scientific knowledge after all; and that it wasn't clear that we could make sense of scientific methodology in terms of falsification anyway.
- Finally, we looked at Reichenbach's *pragmatic* way of living with the problem of induction. On this proposal, one concedes that one lacks a justification for induction, but argues that, nonetheless, employing induction is the most rational thing to do. This is because if any method of inference is going to get us true beliefs about the world, it will be induction. We can thus be assured that induction is the best method available, even if we have no justification for it, and thus, since we have to form beliefs about the world, it is rational to use induction.

STUDY QUESTIONS

1 Try to describe, in your own words, the problem of induction. Use a particular inductive inference that would otherwise seem legitimate as an illustration of the problem.

2 How might an epistemic externalist respond to the problem of induction? Do you find such an approach plausible? Explain and defend your answer.

3 What does Popper mean when he says that the methodology of science is one of falsification, rather than induction, and why is falsification a deductive process? Give an example to illustrate your points. Is Popper right, do you think? If he is right, does this help us live with the problem of induction? Explain and defend your answer.

4 What does Reichenbach mean when he says that employing induction is rational, even though we lack a justification for induction? How is Reichenbach's approach to the rationality of employing induction similar to Pascal's wager, and how is it different?

● INTRODUCTORY FURTHER READING

Bird, Alexander (2010) 'Inductive Knowledge', *Routledge Companion to Epistemology*, S. Bernecker & D. H. Pritchard (eds), Ch. 25, pp. 271–82 (London: Routledge). An admirably clear summary of the epistemological issues regarding induction. Ideally, to be read in conjunction with Morrison (2010).

Morrison, Joe (2010) 'Skepticism about Inductive Knowledge', *Routledge Companion to Epistemology*, S. Bernecker & D. H. Pritchard (eds), Ch. 41, pp. 445–53 (London: Routledge). An overview of the literature regarding the problem of induction. Ideally, to be read in conjunction with Bird (2010).

● ADVANCED FURTHER READING

Harris, James (2021) *Hume: A Very Short Introduction* (Oxford: Oxford University Press). An accessible overview of Hume's life and works, including his discussion of induction. (Note that there is also an earlier version of a book on Hume in Oxford University Press's 'very short introduction' series, written by A. J. Ayer, who was himself an important 20th Century philosopher. This earlier book is interesting in its own right, but it is not as accessible and authoritative as the book by Harris).

Howson, Colin (2001) *Hume's Problem: Induction and the Justification of Belief* (Oxford: Oxford University Press). An influential discussion of Hume's problem of induction.

Swinburne, Richard (ed.) (1974) *The Justification of Induction* (Oxford: Oxford University Press). This is a classic collection of important papers on the problem of induction. Note that some of these papers are not for beginners.

● FREE INTERNET RESOURCES

Henderson, Leah (2018) 'The Problem of Induction', *Stanford Encyclopedia of Philosophy*, http://plato.stanford.edu/entries/induction-problem/. An excellent and comprehensive survey of the literature on the problem of induction. Note that it is quite difficult in places.

Huber, Franz (2008) 'Confirmation and Induction', *Internet Encyclopedia of Philosophy*, http://www.iep.utm.edu/c/conf-ind.htm. This entry is only really suitable for more advanced readers, as it is quite formal in places, but if one is able to follow it, it does repay careful study.

Psillos, Stathis & Stergiou, Chrysovalantis (2010) 'The Problem of Induction', *Internet Encyclopedia of Philosophy*, https://iep.utm.edu/problem-of-induction/. A superb survey of the philosophical issues surrounding the problem of induction.

Thornton, Stephen (2021) 'Karl Popper', *Stanford Encyclopedia of Philosophy*, http://plato.stanford.edu/entries/popper/. A recently updated overview of the philosophy of Popper, including plenty of information about Popper's views on falsification and induction.

Part III

what kinds of knowledge are there?

11

scientific knowledge

- What is science?
- Science versus *pseudo*-science
- The structure of scientific revolutions
- Concluding remarks

WHAT IS SCIENCE?

In the previous part of this book, we looked at the different sources of knowledge. Our task in this part of the book is to examine some specific kinds of knowledge. Scientific inquiry is widely considered to be a paradigmatic way of acquiring knowledge about the world around us, and hence it is natural to begin by focusing on the nature of specifically scientific knowledge. In order to delineate a type of knowledge that is distinctively scientific, however, we first need to determine what science is. As we will see, this is far from obvious.

Here is one answer to this question: science is just what people who are professional scientists do (e.g. those active in university science departments, or in the scientific research wings of large corporations). So, for example, astrology, which is not practised by professional scientists (but by, e.g. newspaper columnists), is not a science, whereas astronomy, which is practised by professional scientists, is. A moment's reflection should reveal that this isn't a particularly helpful account of what science is.

For example, couldn't someone undertake a scientific inquiry and yet be an amateur, and so not be part of any professional scientific community? Moreover, do all the inquiries undertaken by professional scientists as part of their work count as scientific inquiries? After all, there will inevitably be some corruption within the professional scientific community, where individual scientists forge results in order to secure grants and promotion, and to get one over their more diligent colleagues. Do even these corrupted inquiries count as scientific simply in virtue of the protagonist in question belonging to the professional scientific community? Note that even the contrast between astronomers and astrologers isn't all that helpful in this regard

DOI: 10.4324/9781003356110-14

once we inspect it more closely. There are *professional* astrologers, after all, and such people may be regarded by themselves and those around them (e.g. their clients) as bona fide scientists. We clearly need to dig a little deeper.

In order to bring the question of what science is into sharper relief, consider the fact that in many Western countries (especially the USA), there is a vibrant public debate going on as to whether *creationism* (the view that the universe was created relatively recently by an act of God) should be taught alongside evolutionary theory in publicly funded schools as an alternative scientific theory. We are all familiar with the general idea that the universe was created by God, which is a view that many religious people hold (but which is not held by those who do not have religious belief). What is distinctive about creationism (sometimes known as *intelligent design*) is that it is not being proposed merely as a religious point of view, but rather as a bona fide scientific theory, one that is a genuine competitor to the widely accepted scientific proposal known as evolutionary theory.

It is important to emphasise that creationism, qua a putative scientific theory, is incompatible with evolutionary theory, in that these two proposals can't both be true. In particular, creationism is a more specific proposal than the general claim that the universe was created by God. In principle, one could endorse evolutionary theory and also believe that the universe was created by a divine being, but one could not endorse evolutionary theory and also believe the specific doctrine of creationism. This is because creationism adds to the general claim that the universe was created by God a number of further claims which are in conflict with evolutionary theory.

We have already noted one of these claims, which is that creationists believe that the universe was created relatively recently (i.e. in the last few thousand years) on the basis that this short time frame for the creation of the world is suggested in the Bible. It is, of course, vital to evolutionary theory that this is a process which has taken place over a very long time period, since evolutionary development is by its nature very slow. If the universe was created a few thousand years ago, then there is no way that evolution could have taken place.

Given that creationists hold that the universe was created relatively recently, it is obviously important to the view that it incorporates an alternative explanation of such things as the fossil record, and why, for example, these fossils are not as old as they appear to be. The standard answer in this regard is that when the universe was created, the signs of a more distant past, such as a fossil record, were also created. Again, we have a creationist claim which is inconsistent with evolutionary theory, in that the latter takes the age of the fossil record to be as it appears to be.

We will mention one more inconsistency between creationism and evolutionary theory. This is the creationist contention that evolutionary theory cannot account for the complexity found in nature. In particular, creationists have argued that, far from being the best available scientific account of the complexity found in nature, evolutionary theory, in fact, struggles to explain some key types of natural complexity, such as the adaptive immune system. The reason for this, they maintain, is that these types of complexity are irreducibly complex, and hence cannot have arisen via an incremental process from less complex entities as evolutionary theory claims.

This last claim made by creationists is hotly disputed by proponents of evolutionary theory, who argue that whatever problems the view faces, it nonetheless offers an excellent explanation of the complexity found in nature. In any case, while creationism has some support outside of the scientific community, it must be conceded that it is a minority view within this community, where evolutionary theory is the dominant position. Here, then, is the million-dollar question: is creationism a scientific proposal, albeit one not widely endorsed by the professional scientific community as evolutionary theory is, or is it merely a *pseudo*-scientific proposal masquerading as a bona fide scientific view?

● SCIENCE VERSUS PSEUDO-SCIENCE

In order to answer this question, we need to think a bit more deeply about what it is that divides genuine science from fake science (*pseudo*-science). There is a voluminous literature in the philosophy of science on just this topic, but for our purposes we can short-circuit this huge literature to a certain extent by considering the judgement passed down by one Judge William Overton in 1982, in a famous ruling known as *McLean versus the Arkansas Board of Education.*

The background to the case was that it had been decreed that creationism should be taught in publicly funded schools in Arkansas alongside evolutionary theory as an alternative scientific account of our origins. The court case was brought by those unhappy with this development, who argued that creationism is not a scientific proposal but merely the expression of a certain religious view, and hence had no place being taught in a US publicly funded school (since the US constitution forbids the advocacy of religion in publicly funded schools). After hearing the testimony of various parties, including the testimony of several influential philosophers of science, Judge Overton was called upon to give a ruling in this case. He decreed that creationism wasn't a genuine scientific proposal, and so it would not be constitutional for it to be taught in publicly funded schools. What is interesting for our purposes is that Judge Overton offered a very concise summary of the conditions which mark out genuine science (like evolutionary theory) from *pseudo*-science (like creationism). He summarised them as follows:

1 It is guided by natural law;
2 It has to be explanatory by reference to natural law;
3 It is testable against the empirical world;
4 Its conclusions are tentative (i.e. are not necessarily the final word); and
5 It is falsifiable.

All of these claims are plausible criteria for distinguishing genuine science from *pseudo*-science, but they are also individually contentious too. Let's look at each of them more closely.

We will begin with the first two. 'Natural law' here simply refers to the laws of nature, so the first claim is saying that a scientific theory appeals to laws of nature (and is consistent with those laws), and the second claim is saying that a scientific theory explains phenomena by appealing to laws of nature. Clearly, creationism doesn't satisfy either of these criteria since a key part of the view is an appeal to explicitly *supernatural* events, such as divine intervention in the world. Moreover, creationism is quite open about explaining phenomena by appealing to such super-natural events. Evolutionary theory, on the other hand, does not appeal to anything supernatural (i.e. it does not appeal to anything outside the natural law).

Next, consider points 3 and 5. To say that a theory is testable against an empirical world means that one can find evidence in nature which would count in its favour, and also evidence which, even by the lights of the proponents of the view, could count against it (i.e. counter-evidence). It's pretty clear what could constitute evidence in favour of evolutionary theory, such as finding new fossils that confirm a hypothesis of evolutionary theory as yet unconfirmed by the fossil record. It's also pretty clear what could count as counter-evidence against evolutionary theory. If, for example, we discovered something in nature which did seem to be irreducibly complex in the way that some creationists allege, then this would be very strong evidence against evolutionary theory.

But what would count as evidence for, or counter-evidence against, creationism? To focus our minds, let us attend specifically to the question of what could count as counter-evidence against this view. Given that evolutionary theory and creationism are incompatible views, the obvious place to start here is with the evidence for evolutionary theory, since this will tend to be counter-evidence against creationism. So, for example, consider the fossil record, which appears to suggest that the world has existed for a very long time. Creationism explains this putative counter-evidence away by appealing to a supernatural explanation (i.e. that God created the world replete with the traces of a distant ancestry, such as a fossil record). The trouble is that any putative evidence one would care to list against creationism can easily be explained away by the same technique. Thus, creationism doesn't appear to be empirically testable at all.

The demand made in claim 5 (i.e. that a scientific theory must be falsifiable) is stronger than that in claim 3, but of the same sort. (Note that we have met falsi-fication before, in Chapter 10, where it was presented as part of a view known as *falsificationism*, which purported to offer a way out of the problem of induction. But for our current purposes try to set this to one side and consider condition 5 in its own right. We will critique this condition in due course.) To say that a scientific theory must be falsifiable means not just that there could potentially be empirical evidence which counts against it, but also that there could be empirical evidence which decisively shows that the view must be wrong. Finding something in nature which seems irreducibly complex in the way described above would be counter-evidence against evolutionary theory, but given the tremendous success of the view, one would hardly think that this should suffice to reject the view out of hand. Per-haps the view just needs to be adapted in some peripheral way to account for this newly discovered phenomenon, or perhaps on closer inspection this phenomenon is not what it appears and so doesn't present the challenge to evolutionary theory that it seems to. Even so, one can certainly imagine how a wealth of counter-evidence against evolutionary theory could emerge over time to make the view simply untenable, such that it will have been falsified. Crucially, however, since creationism is immune to empirical counter-evidence, it follows, a fortiori, that it is thereby immune to falsification too, since no body of counter-evidence could ever emerge which sufficed to falsify it.

That leaves claim 4. In a sense, claim 4 follows from claim 3. As noted above, to say that a theory is testable against the empirical world is to say that there can potentially be counter-evidence to this theory in nature. If that's right, however, then any scientific proposal will inevitably be provisional, since who knows what counter-evidence might be around the corner? This is why even a well-confirmed scientific theory like evolutionary theory is nonetheless open to counter-evidence. This is not because it lacks adequate empirical support, since it enjoys a very high level of empirical support, but rather reflects the fact that even a very high level of empirical support is compatible with there being as-yet-unknown counter-evidence which counts against the view, perhaps fatally so. It is in the very nature of scientific theorising that it be tentative in this way, in the sense that scientific inquiries are by their nature entirely open. That is, there is always scope to learn more about the world, such as by developing new technologies that widen our empirical horizons (think, for example, of how the invention of the microscope or the telescope expanded the kinds of empirical evidence available to scientists), or by developing new perspectives on the scientific evidence we already have (such as when one discovers that a body of scientific data has been corrupted by a hitherto undetected bias). In short, there is no such thing as the 'final word' in science.

Crucially, creationism is not a tentative proposal in this sense. Indeed, the people who endorse creationism endorse it precisely because it accords with their previously held religious faith. Accordingly, since no matter what evidence they unearth they would retain their religious conviction (that's what makes it *faith*, after all), so their commitment to creationism isn't sensitive to future potential counter-evidence. In this sense, at least, it is very different to the sort of provisional endorsement of a theory that is the hallmark of scientific inquiry.

We can bring this point into sharp relief by noting that there is a very different direction of fit between theory and evidence when one compares the viewpoints of creationism and evolutionary theory. Proponents of evolutionary theory endorse this view *because* it is the view that the scientific evidence supports (i.e. they believe the theory because of the evidence in its favour). If sufficient counter-evidence came along which counted against this proposal, then – like other scientific proposals in the past that were once widely held but which are now widely rejected – it would be ultimately replaced by an alternative scientific proposal that could accommodate the data better.

Indeed, the history of science includes a number of high-profile cases where a well-entrenched scientific theory is cast aside in favour of a competing proposal on account of its inability to deal with a growing body of counter-evidence. For example, it was once widely held that there was an element known as 'phlogiston' that was contained in combustible substances and which was released during combustion. But over time, as the counter-evidence to this theory built and built, it was realised that there simply is no such element.

In contrast to the tentative way in which scientists endorse their theories, such that they would reject theories if the counter-evidence against them became strong enough, there is nothing tentative about the creationists' advancement of their view. Recall that proponents of creationism have already decided, on non-scientific grounds, that God created the universe, and so their endorsement of creationism is ultimately not because of the scientific evidence in its favour but because it accords with their already held religious conviction (i.e. they seek evidence in favour of the theory because it supports what they believe). For that reason, they are unlikely to alter their endorsement of creationism in response to scientific evidence, no matter how much this evidence might count against their theory. They endorse creationism not because it fits with the scientific evidence, but rather because it fits with what they already believe, and what they will continue to believe whatever scientific evidence comes their way.

Thus far evolutionary theory seems to have very much the upper hand over creationism, with the latter looking distinctively like *pseudo*-science rather than genuine science. But before we definitively draw this conclusion, we should pause to consider some further points that are relevant here. To begin with, we should note that the epistemic sin of dogmatism (i.e. sticking to one's view no matter what counter-evidence comes along) is not confined to creationism. Indeed, there are undoubtedly proponents of evolutionary theory who are so psychologically wedded to the view that they would no more be inclined to reject it than a creationist would be inclined to reject creationism in light of the counter-evidence. Do such people cease to be scientists on account of this fact?

Well, they certainly cease to be good scientists, since the eschewal of dogmatism is held to be an ideal of scientific endeavour, something that scientists should aspire towards. But is bad science thereby *pseudo*-science? This is a deep point, in that while there is clearly a difference to be drawn between bad science and *pseudo*-science, the distinction is far from sharp. Indeed, once we acknowledge that genuine science can be done badly, then this raises the question of why we should exclude creationism from the canon of genuine science at all. Why not instead regard it merely as genuine science done in a sub-optimal way (i.e. as bad science, rather than *pseudo*-science)?

We are thus faced with a three-way distinction between good science, bad science, and *pseudo*-science. The exemplars of normal scientific inquiry fall into the first camp, but it is unclear who falls into the other two camps. Here is one 'test' that we can run. While good science incorporates most if not all of the claims 1–5 listed previously, bad science falls down on at least two of these claims, and *pseudo*-science doesn't satisfy any of them. This would get us a broadly satisfying result. For example, it would make bad science at least an approximation of good science, unlike *pseudo*-science, which isn't even in the ballpark of being genuine science. Another advantage of this proposal is that the difference between the three categories wouldn't be at all sharp, in that it would be a matter of degree: good science shades into bad science, which ultimately shades into *pseudo*-science. This way of conceiving of these three categories seems borne out in our normal ways of thinking about inquiry, in that there doesn't seem to be a sharp distinction between good and bad science or between bad science and *pseudo*-science, even though there are intuitively three genuine categories in play here.

Note, however, that this way of characterising the nature of scientific endeavour takes for granted that Judge Overton's classification of science is broadly correct, and yet, as we will see in the next section, this is open to question.

The climate change debate

One of the most important scientific debates of modern times concerns climate change (i.e. global warming). What makes this scientific debate so significant is the danger that such climate change might pose, not just to particular regions of the world, but to human civilisation itself. Indeed, if climate change does pose such an existential threat, then it has profound implications for public policy, since obviously this will entail that a great deal of our resources should be redirected to offset such a calamity.

What is interesting about the climate change 'debate' is that in one sense, it isn't really a debate at all, in that most of the scientists concerned are broadly in agreement both about the fact that there is climate change and that this climate change is at least in large part due to human activity. Inevitably, as with all scientific debates, one would expect there to be competing views in play about particular claims. In this debate, for example, there are arguments within the scientific community about the precise extent of the global warming and, relatedly, about what is the best short- to medium-term prediction of further global warming in the future. But such local scientific disagreements belie a general scientific consensus regarding the main issues.

Of course, consensus is not the same thing as universal acceptance. In the climate change debate, as with most scientific views, there are some scientists who explore, and perhaps even advance, perspectives that are at odds with the prevailing consensus. But there is nothing inherently unusual about that; indeed, it is just what we would expect, as every scientific consensus incorporates some 'outliers' who don't accept the prevailing orthodoxy.

Interestingly, however, despite this prevailing scientific consensus about climate change, the media representation of the issue often presents the scientific community as being completely at odds, as if there is no consensus among climate change scientists about this topic. There are various possible reasons for this.

(continued)

(continued)

One possible explanation is that media outlets simply misunderstand that scientific debate, even when there is lots of agreement, also still involves disagreement and also some radical 'outlier' proposals that challenge the prevailing conventional wisdom. Thus, when journalists discover any disagreement within science – even when the disagreement concerns relatively minor matters, or where the dissenter is clearly taking a minority view within the discipline – they tend to represent this as being something more dramatic than it is, as if in this particular field there is an unusually high level of disagreement.

A second possible explanation is that the demands of the media are not the same as those of science. The media have a responsibility to give both sides of a debate a fair and even hearing, even when only one of the sides to the debate is scientifically respectable. Moreover, the media are concerned with a good story, and reporting on consensus isn't nearly as newsworthy in this regard as reporting on dissent.

A third possible explanation is that there are some actors within the public debate on climate change who simply aren't scientists, or at least aren't scientists who have expertise in the relevant fields. Dissent from these quarters looks very much like a scientific debate, and one can see why a media outlet might represent it as such (e.g. the person making the relevant editorial decision to include a particular dissenting voice might not be particularly scientifically informed about the debate at issue). And yet when scientific expertise comes up against dissent, we surely take into account where this dissent comes from and what its epistemic credentials are. Dissent from a scientist who does not work in the relevant field is prima facie questionable in a way that dissent from a scientist who is an expert in the relevant field is not.

A final possible explanation that we will consider here (this list is not meant to be exhaustive) is that given the enormous implications for public policy involved in the climate change debate, it is perhaps unsurprising that the scientific consensus might not be taken at face value. Dealing with climate change may be expensive, and may involve significant changes to our way of life, particularly in the developed world. Won't we be particularly suspicious of the evidence in favour of climate change given this fact? Moreover, we should also always remember that there are some powerful elements in society, such as some large multinational corporations, who may have a lot to gain by encouraging people to think that the scientific community is more divided on the climate change issue than it is.

● THE STRUCTURE OF SCIENTIFIC REVOLUTIONS

In a seminal book published in the early 1960s, entitled *The Structure of Scientific Revolutions*, the US philosopher of science Thomas Kuhn offered a highly influential,

Thomas Kuhn (1922–96)

> The historian of science may be tempted to exclaim that when paradigms change, the world itself changes with them.
>
> Kuhn, *The Structure of Scientific Revolutions*

The US philosopher of science Thomas Kuhn has the unusual distinction of being a philosopher whose influence extended well beyond philosophy, and indeed well beyond academia. His landmark book *The Structure of Scientific Revolutions*, which was originally published in 1962 (but which has been reprinted many times since), was widely seen as offering support for a kind of relativism about rationality. Scientific inquiry, after all, is often held to be a paradigm case of rationality, and so if the rationality of scientific beliefs is paradigm-relative, as Kuhn's book appears to suggest, then that implies that rationality is more generally a paradigm-relative notion. Such relativism about rationality was viewed by many as being in keeping with a wider cultural relativism, a view that was sweeping the intellectual world at the time and which accorded with the massive social change that occurred in many Western countries during the 1960s and 1970s.

Like many of the best philosophers of science, Kuhn had a strong scientific background (his undergraduate degree from Harvard was in physics), and he also had a solid knowledge of the history of scientific endeavour (tellingly, one of his specialities in this regard was the Copernican revolution, about which he wrote his first monograph). Kuhn never lost his interest in the actual practice of science, and notably interviewed the famous Danish physicist (and Nobel Prize laureate) Niels Bohr the day before Bohr died. Kuhn worked at a variety of US universities during his career, including Harvard, Berkeley, Princeton, and MIT. He worked on topics in the philosophy of science right up to his death, in 1996.

but also radical, new conception of the nature of scientific progress. We tend to think of scientific progress as a largely incremental affair. As scientific inquiry proceeds, so our 'bank' of scientific data increases and our scientific theories adapt to accommodate this growth of information, sometimes transforming themselves quite extensively along the way if the new scientific data is particularly significant. In this way, or so the standard thinking goes, we gradually acquire more and more scientific knowledge.

Kuhn was keen to undermine this 'incremental' view of scientific progress. In particular, he argued that rather than there being a neat incremental rational process by which one scientific proposal was replaced by a competing proposal, it is at least sometimes the case that such theory change involves a 'scientific revolution', one that embraces a complete 'paradigm shift'. During such periods of revolutionary scientific change, it is not that the new scientific theory is merely a peripheral adaption of the old; rather the new theory is fundamentally different. More specifically, the new scientific paradigm will question scientific commitments that were thought to be above serious question under the old scientific paradigm. Indeed, it will also (eventually) incorporate its own set of new scientific commitments which are above question.

It is for this reason that Kuhn argues for the **incommensurability** of the new revolutionary scientific theory and the old scientific theory it is replacing. That is, the former is not an adaption of the latter as the 'incremental' view of scientific progress suggests, but rather a radical new way of scientific theorising which has nothing that is clearly in common with the old view. As a result, it is difficult, if not impossible, to compare the two scientific paradigms side by side, since they each constitute radically different ways of scientific theorising, not only in terms of how they respond to the scientific evidence but also in terms of what they take the relevant scientific evidence to be in the first place.

In order to understand the radical nature of this proposal, we need to realise that it calls into question the very idea of scientific progress as the accumulation of scientific knowledge. Notice that if scientific revolutions incorporate such radical theoretical change, then the new scientific knowledge that accrues after the scientific revolution can hardly be thought to be incorporating the body of scientific knowledge constituted by the old scientific theory. This is because what was 'known' before is not supplemented with additional scientific knowledge, but rather replaced in its entirety with a completely new body of scientific knowledge.

Kuhn's conception of science also seems at odds with at least some of the components of genuine science according to Judge Overton's ruling. In particular, Judge Overton's account of genuine science treats scientific theories as being answerable to scientific evidence, where this means empirical evidence about the world (such as scientific observations). But Kuhn's account of science radically blurs the distinction between evidence and theory since, as we have seen, what counts as evidence, and what this evidence demonstrates, is in Kuhn's view itself a theory-dependent matter.

Condition 5 in Judge Overton's ruling, and possibly condition 3 as well, is thus problematic in a Kuhnian picture. Condition 5 suggests that when the old scientific theory is replaced by the new revolutionary scientific paradigm this is because empirical evidence came to light which demonstrated its falsity. But in the Kuhnian picture, the old scientific paradigm may well be very adept at accommodating the empirical evidence, and relative to this paradigm there may well be no definitive empirical counter-evidence which is fatal to the view. Of course, the new scientific paradigm may have a conception of the scientific evidence on which the old scientific paradigm is refuted, but a paradigm-relative falsification of a theory is quite different from the kind of falsification that Judge Overton had in mind, which was not meant to be relative to a particular scientific paradigm.

Condition 3 is potentially dubious by Kuhnian lights for the same reason. If the empirical evidence that a scientific theory is answerable to is itself theory-dependent, such that different theories will have different conceptions of what counts as the relevant empirical evidence, then it is that much harder to make sense of the idea of a scientific theory being 'tested' relative to empirical evidence. At most, it seems we can make sense of the idea that a scientific theory is being tested relative to the empirical evidence *by its own lights*. But that's a very different claim to the idea that there is a body of theory-neutral scientific evidence out there which scientific theories can be tested against, which is clearly what Judge Overton had in mind.

CONCLUDING REMARKS

It should be noted that Kuhn's views as expressed in *The Structure of Scientific Revolutions* are controversial, and many philosophers of science reject the radical picture of scientific change that he articulated. Indeed, in later life, Kuhn himself seemed to significantly moderate his position. Even so, the account of the structure of scientific revolutions that he offered constitutes a radical challenge to the traditional view of science and scientific progress, and thus helps us to refine our thinking about why, if at all, we should continue to endorse the traditional view.

CHAPTER SUMMARY

- We began by exploring the difficulty of explaining exactly what constitutes genuine scientific endeavour, as opposed to non-scientific endeavours. As we noted, certain kinds of theoretical proposals, such as the religiously informed view known as *creationism*, are at least superficially very much like scientific theories.
- Next, we considered a famous ruling by Judge William Overton, who was trying to decide whether creationism could be taught in publicly funded schools as an alternative to evolutionary theory. The key question at issue here was whether creationism is a genuine scientific theory, or merely a *pseudo*-scientific view. To settle this issue, we saw Judge Overton putting forward five conditions that genuine science had to satisfy. These were:

  1 It is guided by natural law;
  2 It has to be explanatory by reference to natural law;
  3 It is testable against the empirical world;
  4 Its conclusions are tentative (i.e. are not necessarily the final word); and
  5 It is falsifiable.

- As we saw, there is a strong prima facie case that creationism, unlike evolutionary theory, struggles to satisfy these conditions.
- In exploring Judge Overton's five conditions on genuine science, we noted a three-way distinction that can be drawn between good, bad, and *pseudo*-science, where the last two categories have a diminishing level of commonality with the first category.
- Finally, we considered a radically different way of thinking about scientific thinking, proposed by Thomas Kuhn. On this proposal the kind of scientific change that takes place when scientific revolutions occur is not to be thought of as an incremental, rational process from an old scientific theory to a new one. Instead,

the revolutionary scientific theory is held to be *incommensurable* with the old theory, in the sense that there is no significant commonality between the two. In particular, this means that the two theories will not only disagree about what the scientific evidence demonstrates, but will also disagree about what counts as scientific evidence in the first place. As we saw, this conception of scientific change challenges a traditional way of thinking about scientific knowledge as the accumulation of knowledge, and it is also potentially incompatible with some of Judge Overton's conditions for genuine science.

• STUDY QUESTIONS

1　In your own words, try to explain what it means for a scientific theory to be empirically testable. Why might someone claim that creationism is not an empirically testable theory? Would they be right to do so?

2　What is the difference between a theory being empirically testable and it being empirically falsifiable? Why might someone claim that no scientific theory is falsifiable?

3　Are the conclusions of good scientific inquiry in their nature provisional? Would it matter if they weren't?

4　If creationism isn't an empirically testable theory, then does that mean it can't be a genuine scientific theory? Is there any definitive criterion, or criteria, which could distinguish genuine science from *pseudo*-science?

5　Is *pseudo*-science really just bad science? Consider the arguments for and against this claim.

6　Try to explain in your own words Kuhn's account of the structure of scientific revolutions. Why might it be thought that this account is incompatible with a conception of scientific progress as the accumulation of scientific knowledge?

• INTRODUCTORY FURTHER READING

Achinstein, Peter (2010) 'Scientific Knowledge', *Routledge Companion to Epistemology*, S. Bernecker & D. H. Pritchard (eds), Ch. 32, pp. 346–57 (London: Routledge). A fairly comprehensive introductory overview of the main issues regarding scientific knowledge.

Chalmers, Alan F. (2013) *What Is This Thing Called Science?* (4th edn, Indianapolis, IN: Hackett Publishing Company). One of the most widely used contemporary introductions to the philosophy of science, and for good reason, as it is a superb overview of the main issues in this area: accessible, authoritative, and very readable.

Goldacre, Ben (2009) *Bad Science* (London: HarperCollins). I cannot recommend this book highly enough. Although it is not a text on the philosophy of science, reading this book will give you a fantastic introduction to the scientific method and why it is so important. In particular, the approach of the book is to highlight some examples of 'bad' (and, arguably anyway, '*pseudo-*') science, and in the process, it emphasises the virtue of 'good' science.

● ADVANCED FURTHER READING

Bird, Alexander (2022) *Knowing Science* (Oxford: Oxford University Press). A brand new book exploring the nature of scientific knowledge, written by one of the leading philosophers of science.

Gillies, Donald (1993) *Philosophy of Science in the Twentieth Century* (Oxford: Blackwell). An excellent, if intellectually demanding, account of contemporary themes in the philosophy of science.

● FREE INTERNET RESOURCES

Bird, Alexander (2018) 'Thomas Kuhn', *Stanford Encyclopedia of Philosophy*, http://plato.stanford.edu/entries/thomas-kuhn/. An excellent summary of Kuhn's work in the philosophy of science, written by an expert in the field.

Crasnow, Shannon (2020) 'Feminist Perspectives on Science', *Stanford Encyclopedia of Philosophy*, https://plato.stanford.edu/entries/feminist-science/. A lot of the issues we've explored in this chapter, especially concerning the putative objectivity of scientific knowledge, have been explored by feminist philosophy of science. This survey offers an excellent overview of the relevant literature.

De Cruz, Helen (2022) 'Religion and Science', *Stanford Encyclopedia of Philosophy*, http://plato.stanford.edu/entries/religion-science/. This is a detailed and nuanced account of how religion and science relate to one another. Recently updated.

Hansson, Sven Ove (2021) 'Science and Pseudo-Science', *Stanford Encyclopedia of Philosophy*, https://plato.stanford.edu/entries/pseudo-science/. A comprehensive, and recently updated, treatment of the science versus pseudo-science debate.

'McLean v. Arkansas', *Wikipedia*, http://en.wikipedia.org/wiki/McLean_v._Arkansas. A useful summary of the famous 1982 US court case involving Judge William Overton.

12

religious knowledge

- Is there any religious knowledge?
- The evidentialist challenge to religious knowledge
- Natural theology
- Fideism
- Reformed epistemology

IS THERE ANY RELIGIOUS KNOWLEDGE?

In the last chapter, we examined a kind of knowledge – scientific knowledge – which nearly everyone supposes we have (even if there is a lot of disagreement about what such knowledge involves and how it is acquired). In this chapter, in contrast, we will be exploring a type of knowledge which is widely contested: religious knowledge.

Religious knowledge is knowledge of religious truths, such as truths about the existence and nature of God. One reason why one might doubt whether there is any religious knowledge is because one holds that there are no religious truths. Knowledge, after all, is *factive*, in that if one knows that such-and-such is the case (that Paris is the capital of France, say), then what is known must be true (i.e. Paris must actually be the capital of France). Conversely, where there is no truth, there can be no knowledge. Thus, if there are no religious truths, then it follows that there cannot be any religious knowledge.

It should be straightforward to see why some think there cannot be religious truths. Not everyone, after all, believes that the subject matter of religion – God – exists, and if there is no God, then most religious statements will be false as they tend to make either explicit or implicit appeal to God's existence. So, for example, if someone believes a religious claim such as 'God is good', and there is no God, then this person cannot know what she believes since what she believes isn't true. (Any more than someone who believes that the entirely fictional Gotham City is the capital of France can know what she believes.)

One source of scepticism about religious knowledge thus comes from those who think that religious statements are false, and so not even in the market for knowledge.

DOI: 10.4324/9781003356110-15

Even if one thinks that there can be religious truths, however, it doesn't thereby follow that one can have knowledge of these truths. As we will see, there might reasons for holding that such truths are simply unknowable.

There are thus at least two ways in which the existence of religious knowledge could be challenged: in terms of whether there are any religious truths, and in terms of whether, even if there are religious truths, those truths can be known.

THE EVIDENTIALIST CHALLENGE TO RELIGIOUS KNOWLEDGE

Although one might dispute the possibility of religious knowledge by claiming that there are no religious truths, the most prominent form of scepticism about religious knowledge instead attacks the epistemic status of religious belief. In particular, it has been alleged that religious beliefs lack adequate supporting evidence, such that even if they are true they do not amount to knowledge. This is known as the *evidentialist challenge* to religious knowledge.

On the face of it, the evidentialist challenge might seem rather suspect, since isn't there quite a lot of evidence that religious believers can cite in favour of their beliefs? What about the evidence of scripture, or the testimony of church elders, for example? The evidentialist challenge to religious knowledge is, however, concerned with evidence of a very specific kind. What proponents of this challenge seek is *independent* evidence in support of religious belief, where this means evidence that even someone who didn't already have religious belief would regard as good evidence. So, for example, appealing to scripture as evidence in support of one's religious belief is no good, since if one did not already have religious belief, then one would not regard such scripture as offering evidential support in favour of religious belief.

Imagine, for example, that you don't believe in God and you are debating with someone who does, and who claims to know that God exists. If the only evidence your opponent could offer in support of their belief in God was that the Bible (or some other holy book – the details aren't important for our purposes) said so, would you find this at all persuasive? Surely not. The thinking behind the evidentialist challenge is that this evidential requirement on religious knowledge is one that is not only relevant to the debate between the believer and the non-believer, but also a standard that the believer should apply to their own religious belief, regardless of whether that belief is being challenged by someone without religious conviction.

Insofar as one grants the evidentialist challenge to religious knowledge, however, then religious knowledge will be hard to come by, since it is far from clear what independent evidence a religious believer could cite in support of their religious belief. The options facing the defender of religious knowledge are thus either to find a way of meeting this epistemically austere challenge or else to offer an argument for weakening this challenge (perhaps even to the point of abandoning it altogether).

• NATURAL THEOLOGY

One historically popular way of responding to the evidentialist challenge has been to grant the nature of the challenge and try to meet it head-on. In particular, some have tried to offer a defence of religious knowledge which does not make appeal to any kind of divine revelation, including that written down in scripture. This general way of answering theological questions is known as **natural theology**, in contrast to the alternative approach that appeals to divine revelation, which is known as *revealed theology*.

The reason why natural theologians restrict themselves to these sources of evidence is not because they do not believe in divine revelation, or do not endorse the word of scripture. It is rather because they hold that the appropriate epistemic standard by which to assess religious claims is in terms of the evidence that one can cite in support of them that does not appeal to these sources of religious belief. If this project is successful, it will supply a rational basis for religious belief which any rational agent could recognise as being sufficient, with true belief, for religious knowledge.

What kinds of epistemic support do proponents of natural theology offer for religious belief? Well, in its most heroic form, proponents of this view try to offer a priori proofs of God's existence. There are three main attempts at rationally proving the existence of God, and we will here briefly consider all three.

The first is the **ontological argument**, which is usually attributed to St Anselm of Canterbury (1033–1109), but which has subsequently been defended in various forms by a number of important philosophers, most notably René Descartes (1596–1650). The argument purports to show that it follows from the very concept of God that God must exist. The reasoning behind this argument goes as follows. God is, by definition, the greatest being that can be conceived of. If God didn't exist, then one could conceive of an even greater being (i.e. a being with all the attributes of God and which in addition existed). That would, however, be absurd, since God is by definition the greatest being that could be conceived. It follows that God must exist, since to suppose otherwise is to lead to absurdity.

The ontological argument is a highly abstract way of proving God's existence. The flaw in the argument, as Immanuel Kant (1724–1804) famously noted, is that it treats existence as being an attribute that something might have, like being red all over or being larger than the Empire State Building. But existence is not an attribute like other attributes. It's not as if a house that has been destroyed continues to be a house with all the attributes as before, except that it no longer has the attribute of existence. Or, if you prefer, take two houses, identical in every respect except that one exists and one doesn't. Is the non-existent house just lacking an attribute that the existent house possesses, as if we are comparing two existent houses, identical in every respect except that one of them is red and one of them is blue?

The moral to be drawn is that whether something exists is not a further attribute, like being red or blue. Rather, it concerns whether a description of something (i.e. a list of attributes) corresponds to something in the world. To take a further example for illustration: a unicorn that exists is not like a non-existent unicorn in every respect except that it in addition has the attribute of existence. Rather, both the existent and the non-existent unicorns are identical in terms of their attributes; it's just that the existent unicorn corresponds to something in the world in a way that the non-existent unicorn doesn't. If that's right, then something with all the attributes of God and who in addition exists is not superior to something with an identical list of attributes which doesn't exist. Rather, they are equivalent items; it is just that one of them exists and one of them doesn't.

A second popular proof of the existence of God is the **cosmological argument**. There are various versions of this argument, but in its most basic form, the cosmological argument contends that there must, by definition, be a creator of the universe, something that stands outside of the normal causal order of the world and who, as it were, sets alight the blue touch paper of creation. For imagine if there were no creator. What would then have to be the case? One option would be that the universe came into existence all by itself, but how could that be? That is, how could something arise out of nothing? Another option would that the universe has always been in existence. Is that even coherent? How could the universe stretch back infinitely without ever having been started by anything? But if the universe did not exist eternally, and did not come into existence all by itself, then how else could it have come into being without being created by a divine being like a God?

Of course, one way of responding to the cosmological argument is to dispute the key premise that the universe hasn't always been in existence. Is this really so unacceptable? Of course, we know that our particular universe came into being at a certain point in time (if the concept of time makes any sense independently of a particular existing universe), but it's consistent with this that *something* existed even prior to our particular universe coming into being. Perhaps our universe dies and in dying it brings itself into existence again, on an eternal loop. Is this possibility inherently incoherent? Put more pointedly, is this explanation of how our particular universe came into being any less coherent or less informative than the competing explanation that God created this universe from scratch?

Here we get to the nub of the problem with the cosmological argument. This is that none of the available explanations for the existence of the universe are very compelling, including the one offered by proponents of the cosmological argument. This is because it is a mystery that the universe exists. More precisely, it is a mystery that something exists rather than nothing at all, in the sense that nothing seems to be a good explanation of why there is a universe in the first place. That God exists is one possible explanation of why the universe exists, but it doesn't seem to be an inherently better explanation of why the universe exists than any one of a number of alternative explanations, such as that our particular universe keeps dying and coming back to life on a perpetual loop.

The third historically popular proof of God's existence is the so-called **design argument** (sometimes referred to as the *teleological argument*, in that it appeals to an apparent purpose, or *telos*, to nature). In a nutshell, the idea behind this argument is that the universe at least *appears* designed. Nature is highly complex, whether one considers the intricacies of the human eye or the minute detail found in insects.

Such complexity implies design, which in turn implies a designer, and who would be a better candidate for being the designer of nature than God?

'The God Wars' and the new atheists

'The God Wars' is a phrase that is used to characterise a specific upsurge in contemporary public debate regarding the existence of God, particularly in the USA, that occurred in the early 2000s. This debate attracted a number of high-profile intellectuals, including several philosophers. In the one camp, the detractors of religion – or the 'new atheists', as they were known – included the evolutionary biologist Richard Dawkins, the (late) journalist Christopher Hitchens, and the philosopher Daniel Dennett. In the opposing camp, one can find philosophers such as **Alvin Plantinga**.

There are several elements to the new atheism movement, over and above the claim that God does not exist. The new atheists typically claim, for example, that religion is not a force for moral good in the world but rather a force for ill. Relatedly, they also claim that religion has negative epistemological consequences, in that it turns people's attention away from rational ways of thinking, as embodied in science, and towards irrational and mystical ways of thinking. Finally, the new atheists often have a practical focus on what they see as the deleterious role of religion in public life.

This last point is very apparent in the public debate about whether creationism – the view that the world was created and designed by a divine being just a few thousand years ago – should be taught as a scientific alternative to evolutionary theory as part of science lessons in schools (this is an issue that we touched upon in the last chapter). This debate has a particularly sharp focus in the USA, where the constitutional division of religion and state means that religion ought not to be advocated within publicly funded schools. Thus, insofar as creationism is a religious doctrine rather than a scientific proposal, then it ought not to be taught as an alternative to evolutionary theory in publicly funded schools (indeed, perhaps it ought not to be taught in any schools, publicly funded or otherwise, but this is a further issue). Conversely, if it can be shown that it is a scientific theory, then there is nothing to stop it being taught as an alternative to evolutionary theory in publicly funded schools.

The new atheists have been keen to dismiss the putative scientific credentials of creationism, and to demonstrate the malign effects, particularly of an epistemic variety, that would accrue were it to be taught to schoolchildren as a scientific viewpoint alongside evolutionary theory. In contrast, the opponents of new atheism, while not necessarily willing to endorse creationism as a scientific theory, have tended to argue that such a view ought to be presented to schoolchildren as an alternative account of the origins of the universe and the complexity of the natural world around them.

In his 1802 book, *Natural Theology* (a book that was tremendously influential in the nineteenth century), the philosopher William Paley (1742–1805) offered a famous example to illustrate the design argument. Paley asked what one would suppose were one to find a watch on a heath. A watch is clearly a complex mechanism which has been designed to serve the particular purpose of telling the time. Finding such an item, wouldn't we suppose that there must be a watchmaker who created the watch? That much seems right, since it is not plausible that such a sophisticated entity should spring into existence by chance, in the way that a certain shape might by chance be over time carved out of a rock by the elements. Paley's idea, however, is that once we recognise the complexity inherent in nature, then what goes for the watch will go for nature itself, and hence we will be rationally led towards belief in a God who created nature.

The appeal of the design argument is in the idea that the best available explanation of the complexity of nature is the existence of a creator who designed nature to be this way. There are two key problems with this kind of strategy for defending the existence of God. The first is that even if we grant that the best explanation of the complexity of nature 200 years ago was a divine creator and designer, one would be hard pressed to argue that this is the best explanation available for the complexity of nature today. After all, we now have evolutionary theory, a theory which has been able to successfully explain many of the complexities found in nature without appealing to anything outside of normal natural mechanisms.

Note that this isn't to say that there is nothing that evolutionary theory struggles to explain. Indeed, as we noted in the last chapter, *all* scientific theories – even the ones that are most successful and enjoy very high levels of empirical support – face some 'recalcitrant' data which they struggle to accommodate, so it would be surprising if evolutionary theory were any different on this score. The point remains that even a theory which is sub-optimal in some minor respects can still offer a far more sophisticated explanation of a natural phenomenon – in this case the complexity inherent in nature – than rival proposals (such as the suggestion that nature was created and designed by a divine force).

This brings us to a second worry about the design argument, which is that it is far from clear whether appealing to the existence of a divine creator does offer very much by way of explanation of the complexity of nature. Think again about the watchmaker analogy that Paley offers. While it is surely reasonable to suppose that there must be a watchmaker who created the watch, isn't this because we know full well that there are watchmakers that construct such items? Given that what is in question is whether the complexity found in nature is attributable to divine agency, it is a big leap to conclude that this complexity in nature is relevantly akin to the complexity of a watch, which we independently know to be designed. Why couldn't the complexity in nature be entirely due to natural processes?

Moreover, insofar as we struggle to explain this natural complexity by appeal to purely natural processes, then how helpful is it to conclude that a divine being must have created and designed nature? To bring this point into sharp relief, consider the matter put this way: to what extent is this divine 'explanation' of the complexity of nature any less mysterious as conceding that one can offer no explanation at all? Remember, after all, that the design argument doesn't tell us anything at all about this divine creator, only that he (she? it?) must exist if we are to explain the complexity in nature. But isn't that just to trade one mystery (i.e. why is there complexity in nature?) with another (why did a divine being create nature in the particular manner in which we find it?)?

• FIDEISM

If any of the 'proofs' of God's existence offered by natural theology succeed, then this would go a long way towards meeting the evidentialist challenge to religious belief. If, however, one is sceptical that such proofs will succeed in their aim, then the defender of religious belief might opt instead to reject the evidentialist challenge itself. One way in which this challenge has been rejected is by arguing that religious belief should not be epistemically evaluated in the same way as other beliefs. Indeed, it has been argued that the proper way to assess religious beliefs is not to epistemically evaluate them at all. Thus, while the epistemic requirement laid down by the evidentialist challenge might be applicable to a wide range of beliefs, it simply doesn't have application to religious belief. This way of thinking about religious belief is known as **fideism**, and versions of this doctrine have been attributed to a diverse range of philosophers, most notably the Danish philosopher Søren Kierkegaard (1813–55) and the Austrian philosopher Ludwig Wittgenstein (1889–1951). A form of fideism is also often attributed to the French philosopher Blaise Pascal (1623–62) in virtue of the distinctive kind of argument, known as 'Pascal's wager', that he offered in support of belief in God's existence (see the box below to learn more about this argument).

Fideists highlight the differences between a religious and a non-religious way of life, and in particular emphasise that the religious life is fundamentally one of faith rather than reason. In this way, the religious life is held to offer a kind of understanding that is fundamentally different from, say, scientific theorising. Whereas the right way to evaluate scientific belief may well be to examine the evidence that the scientific believer has in support of her view, the same does not apply, according to the fideist, to religious belief. For religious belief is not meant to be a rational response to the world around one in the way that scientific belief is meant to be. Rather, it is a system of thinking about the world and one's place within it which answers to different standards to normal rational belief, standards which are internal to the religious life itself.

One important point to emphasise about fideism is that the claim is *not* that religious belief is irrational, but acceptable nonetheless. Instead, the idea is that religious belief, properly understood, is *neither* rational *nor* irrational, since it simply does not answer to a rational standard at all. Asking whether religious belief is appropriately grounded in evidence, as the evidentialist challenge does, is thus (according to fideism) to fundamentally misclassify what kind of belief religious belief is. Similarly, to worry whether one's religious beliefs amount to knowledge is to reveal a fundamental misunderstanding about the nature of religious belief, for by fideistic lights religious belief simply isn't in the market for knowledge in the first place.

Fideism is a radical response to the evidentialist challenge. Whereas the approach to this challenge offered by natural theology is epistemically heroic, in that it aims to deal with that challenge by rationally demonstrating that God must exist, fideism is epistemically heroic in a very different way by insisting that religious belief can be devoid of rational support and yet no less rightly held as a result. Is there not a middle way between these two heroic alternatives?

● REFORMED EPISTEMOLOGY

Just such a middle way has come to the fore in recent years, in the form of the **reformed epistemology** movement, as championed by such figures as the US philosopher Alvin Plantinga (1932–). Like fideists, reformed epistemologists reject the evidentialist challenge to religious belief, but not because they hold that religious belief isn't answerable to the kinds of epistemic standards applicable to normal beliefs. Instead, reformed epistemologists maintain that to hold religious belief to the requirements laid down by the evidentialist challenge is to submit religious belief to a *more* demanding epistemic standard than most other kinds of belief.

A key point that reformed epistemologists make in this respect is that perception is regarded by most epistemologists as a paradigmatic way of gaining knowledge about the world, in the sense that if we know anything about the world around us (which we might not, as we saw in Chapter 7 and will see again in Part VI), then we have at least some perceptual knowledge. Insofar as we do have perceptual knowledge, however, it does not seem that this is because perceptual belief satisfies the kind of epistemic requirement laid down by the evidentialist challenge.

Alvin Plantinga (1932–)

> The Christian philosopher has a perfect right to the point of view and pre-philosophical assumptions he brings to philosophic work; the fact that these are not widely shared outside the Christian or theistic community is interesting but fundamentally irrelevant.
>
> Plantinga, 'Advice to Christian Philosophers'

The US philosopher Alvin Plantinga has made distinctive contributions to a range of areas of philosophy, including epistemology, the philosophy of religion, and metaphysics. But he is most widely known for his work in religious epistemology, and in particular his defence of *reformed epistemology*, a view which, although it has a long historical precedent, he almost single-handedly introduced to contemporary epistemology in a series of important and influential journal articles.

(continued)

(continued)

Plantinga built on these early articles on reformed epistemology by producing an ambitious three-volume work covering both epistemology more generally and the epistemology of religious belief in particular. This is the so-called Warrant trilogy (*Warrant: The Contemporary Debate*, *Warrant and Proper Function*, and *Warranted Christian Belief*; all published by Oxford University Press, between 1993 and 2000). In the first volume, Plantinga offered a survey of the main proposals in contemporary epistemology in order to provide the philosophical basis for, in the second volume, his own distinctive account of epistemic warrant, a view that is known as *proper functionalism*. Note that the plausibility of this proposal is meant to be entirely independent of any religious commitment, and as such it is held to be a view that anyone in epistemology could (and, if Plantinga is right, should) endorse. What is particularly clever about Plantinga's appeal to proper functionalism is that only *after* demonstrating that the theory is a compelling alternative to competing contemporary epistemological proposals did he further go on to show that such an account was particularly amenable to a conception of religious belief which was in keeping with reformed epistemology.

In more recent work – in particular, his 2011 Oxford University Press book, *Where the Conflict Really Lies: Science, Religion, and Naturalism* – Plantinga has engaged with the public debate about religion that has come to be known as the 'God wars'. Here he has challenged the views of the so-called new atheists, which include the philosopher Daniel Dennett, the (late) journalist Christopher Hitchens, and the evolutionary biologist Richard Dawkins (see the box above for more details about this debate). In particular, he argues against a scientific naturalism which excludes the possibility of a divine creator, and has proposed instead that contemporary science, and evolutionary theory in particular, is compatible with the existence of God.

Plantinga has spent most of his academic career as a Professor of Philosophy at the University of Notre Dame, in Indiana. He is currently the John A. O'Brien Professor of Philosophy Emeritus at the University of Notre Dame and is the 2017 Templeton Prize Laureate.

Recall that the evidentialist challenge requires that the religious believer offers independent evidence in support of her belief, where this means evidence that is available even to the non-believer. But imagine that one were confronted by someone sceptical about the possibility of perceptual knowledge. Could one offer adequate evidence in support of one's perceptual beliefs that is independent in this way (i.e. which even the sceptic about perceptual knowledge would grant as being good evidence)? Clearly, the natural evidence that one might offer in this regard (i.e. the evidence of one's senses) is disallowed, since this is evidence that is gained via perception itself, the putative source of knowledge which is being called into question.

But what other evidence could one appeal to? It is not as if there are, by analogy with the tactic employed by natural theology, plausible 'proofs' readily available for the reliability of perceptual belief. But without having proofs to hand, what is one to appeal to in order to meet this challenge?

By parity of reasoning, proponents of reformed epistemology argue that rather than applying an austere epistemic test to religious belief in the form of the evidentialist challenge, we should instead apply whatever looser epistemic test we apply to perceptual belief. In particular, notice that we would ordinarily allow that perceptual belief could amount to knowledge and be rationally held just so long as it is formed in the right kind of way. That is, in normal conditions, if someone uses their reliable senses to form an appropriate belief about the environment – that it is raining, say, on the basis of seeing and feeling the falling rain – then this belief would be considered rationally held and, if it is true, could potentially amount to knowledge. Indeed, in normal conditions, note that we don't require people to be able to offer very much (if anything) by way of evidence in support of their perceptual beliefs; what counts is just that they gained their belief in an appropriate manner. In particular, we wouldn't normally require them to offer independent evidence in support of their perceptual beliefs before these beliefs counted as rationally held or as instances of knowledge. The ordinary epistemic standards for rational perceptual belief and perceptual knowledge thus tend to be quite loose indeed. Could one reasonably apply similar epistemic standards to religious belief?

First, let us ask whether religious belief could satisfy analogous epistemic standards to those applied to perceptual belief. The reason why we are happy to credit people with perceptual knowledge in normal conditions is because we are creatures who have innate sensory faculties that are generally good guides about the world around us, where these innate faculties have further been honed over time to make them even more reliable (e.g. we are aware that there are certain kinds of situations – when one is very tired, say, or when one's view is obscured by thick fog – where we should be more wary about relying on our senses). Can the religious believer claim that religious belief is the product of similar innate reliable faculties?

Well, there seems to be no inherent reason why not. Indeed, reformed epistemologists refer to a particular sense of divinity, or **sensus divinitatis** as it is called, through which they claim the religious believer can reliably gain religious belief, and thereby also gain rationally held religious belief and religious knowledge. Reformed epistemologists claim that if we can make sense of how our innate sensory faculties can, in the right conditions, lead us to rationally held perceptual belief and perceptual knowledge, then we ought to be able to make sense of how a corresponding story can be told about religious belief, such that the believer's innate religious faculty – her *sensus divinitatis* – can in the right conditions lead her to rationally held religious belief and (if the beliefs so formed are true) religious knowledge.

Of course, one who does not already believe in God may well be unpersuaded that such an innate faculty exists, but that's to miss the point. The reformed epistemologist is offering us an account of how rational religious belief/religious knowledge is acquired which is, they claim, just as good as the standard account offered by epistemologists about how we gain perceptual knowledge. The point is thus that insofar as we are happy for rational perceptual belief/perceptual knowledge to be acquired in this way, then there isn't a principled basis on which we can object to rational religious belief/religious knowledge being acquired in an analogous fashion.

Even if it is true that religious belief can satisfy the epistemic standards applicable to perceptual belief, however, one might nonetheless argue that religious belief is very different to perceptual belief, and hence that it should be subject to *different* epistemic standards. Here is one key difference between the two forms of belief: we all rely on our perceptual faculties in order to form beliefs about the world around us, but only some of us form religious beliefs. That we are all reliant on our perceptual faculties might give us cause to think that perception is a 'basic' source of knowledge and rational belief that is not subject to the same epistemic standards as other sources, on the grounds that we cannot do without it. In contrast, religious belief seems optional in a way that perceptual belief isn't, in that we can perfectly well do without such belief (indeed, many do). But if the *sensus divinitatis* is not a 'basic' source of knowledge/rational belief like perception, then perhaps religious belief should be subjected to a more demanding epistemic standard?

There is a deeper issue here, which is that, for large regions of the world anyway, religious believers exist in communities which are in large part *secular*. As a result, they regularly interact with people who do not believe the things that they do. The same is not true of perceptual belief, since it is not the case that many of us exist in communities of which large sections eschew this kind of belief. But note how it would change things if we did. Suppose, for example, that one were raised in a community where it was widely taught that perception was mostly unreliable, and so ought to be avoided as a source of belief as much as possible. Unless one had good reason to discount this advice, could one reasonably ignore it and form one's perceptual beliefs regardless? It's hard to see why this would be a rational way of forming one's beliefs. If that's right, however, then in such a scenario until one acquires a sound rational basis for discounting this advice one is unable to form perceptual beliefs that are rational and which could hence amount to knowledge.

What goes here for perceptual belief formed in these unusual (and non-actual) conditions ought to apply to religious belief as it is normally formed (i.e. in a largely secular context). That is, insofar as religious belief is epistemically analogous to perceptual belief, then one can gain religious knowledge/rationally held religious belief only insofar as one forms one's religious belief appropriately in conditions where there is no widespread scepticism about the source of one's belief. Since this is not the case for most religious believers, however (since they occupy secular communities), it follows that in order for them to gain religious knowledge/rationally held religious belief such believers need to do more than merely form their belief appropriately; rather, they need to also have some sound rational basis available to them for discounting the scepticism about rational belief that is all around them.

Whether this is a devastating problem for reformed epistemology depends largely on what one holds is required of a religious believer in terms of having a 'sound rational basis' for dismissing scepticism about the source of their belief. If, for example, one thinks that it is enough that one is aware that there are experts within one's religious community – philosophers such as Plantinga, say – who are fighting this intellectual battle on their behalf, then perhaps this problem might be easily resolved. If, on the other hand, one thinks that what is required is that the religious believers actually engage in this intellectual battle with the non-believers themselves, then this problem will be potentially hard to overcome.

This brings us to a final problem with reformed epistemology, which is that perhaps it is a proposal which proves too much. After all, if the religious believer can appeal to a *sensus divinitatis* to explain how they have rationally held religious belief and religious knowledge, then surely anyone can make a similar move to defend their unusual mystical beliefs, no matter how outlandish they might be. This is often known as the 'Great Pumpkin' problem. This is because in the popular comic strip *Peanuts*, there is a character called Linus who believes that there really exists a divine being known as the Great Pumpkin who visits every Halloween. The details of what Linus believes and why are not particularly important for our purposes. Rather, what is important is that on the face of it the very same epistemological proposal that the reformed epistemologist offers regarding normal religious belief could be equally applied to Linus and his beliefs about the Great Pumpkin. Perhaps Linus has a *sensus divinitatis* which enables him to gain knowledge that there is a Great Pumpkin?

In order to avoid this problem reformed epistemologists need to explain why their religious belief is different from Linus's Great Pumpkin belief. For example, they might appeal to the fact that their beliefs are grounded within a large religious community that has existed for many years, whereas Linus is a religious community of one with no history at all. But the challenge will be to explain why facts like this are epistemically important. If Linus's beliefs take hold with others around him, for example, then over time people who believe in the Great Pumpkin may well become part of a large religious community that has existed for many years. Do they thereby count as having rational religious belief, and thus potentially (i.e. if their beliefs are true) gaining religious knowledge?

• CHAPTER SUMMARY

- We explored the *evidentialist challenge* to religious knowledge, which is the challenge of showing that one has sufficient independent evidence in support of one's religious belief.
- We then looked at one way of dealing with the evidentialist challenge which has been put forward by proponents of what is known is *natural theology*. This approach to religious belief argues that there is a sound rational basis for believing in the existence of God, where this is a rational basis which can be recognised even by non-believers.
- We examined three historically prominent rational 'proofs' of the existence of God, and considered some problems that each of them faces. The first, the *ontological argument*, tries to demonstrate that God's existence follows from the very concept of God. The second, the *cosmological argument*, tries to demonstrate God's

existence by arguing that something must have brought about the existence of the universe, and that God is the only plausible candidate to play this 'creator' role. Finally, the third argument we looked at – the *design argument* – tries to demonstrate the existence of God by arguing that this is the only way to explain the complexity found in nature.

- Not everyone accepts the evidentialist challenge to religious knowledge. One proposal that we looked at in this regard, known as *fideism*, argues that religious belief ought not to be subject to normal epistemic standards. In particular, fideists argue that religious belief is neither rational nor irrational, since it is a kind of belief that should be evaluated in terms of its own standards rather than the normal rational standards that are applied to non-religious belief.
- A second kind of proposal that rejects the evidentialist challenge is *reformed epistemology*. This approach defends religious belief by arguing that it is akin to perceptual belief, and so should be answerable to the same kind of epistemic standard. Since perceptual belief is not subjected to an analogous evidentialist challenge, so religious belief can be rationally held and amount to knowledge even though it fails to satisfy the evidentialist challenge. We explored how this proposal makes appeal to an innate sense of divinity known as the *sensus divinitatis* – and considered some of the main objections that can be levelled against it.

● STUDY QUESTIONS

1 What is the evidentialist challenge, and what problem does it pose for religious knowledge?
2 In your own words, outline, and critically evaluate, one of the three 'proofs' for God's existence that we have looked at.
3 What is fideism? Can we make sense of the idea that there might be a type of belief which is not answerable to the normal rational standards?
4 Consider perceptual belief and religious belief. Try to list three ways in which they are alike, and three ways in which they are different. Evaluate whether – and, if so, to what extent – these similarities and differences are epistemically important.
5 What is the *sensus divinitatis*, and what role does it play in reformed epistemology?
6 Does it make an epistemic difference whether a religious believer has ever been exposed to challenges to their belief, such as from non-believers? Relatedly, does it matter from an epistemic point of view whether in forming one's religious beliefs one is manifesting one's participation in a widespread religious community with a long and rich history?

● INTRODUCTORY FURTHER READING

Nagasawa, Yujin (2011) *The Existence of God: A Philosophical Introduction* (London: Routledge). A very helpful introduction to the philosophy of religion, with particular focus on rational 'proofs' of God's existence.
Pritchard, Duncan (2017) 'Faith and Reason', *Philosophy*, 81, 101–18. This is a defence of a non-standard form of fideism, inspired by Wittgenstein's final

notebooks (which are published under the title *On Certainty*). Written for a general audience.

Zagzebski, Linda (2010) 'Religious Knowledge', *Routledge Companion to Epistemology*, S. Bernecker & D. H. Pritchard (eds), Ch. 36, pp. 393–9 (London: Routledge). A solid overview of the issues in religious epistemology, written by an expert in the field.

● ADVANCED FURTHER READING

Nielsen, Kai & Philips, Dewi Zephaniah (2005) *Wittgensteinian Fideism?* (Suffolk: SCM Press). This classic book brings together a series of exchanges by two prominent philosophers who explore the case for thinking that the Austrian philosopher Ludwig Wittgenstein endorses a distinctive form of fideism.

Plantinga, Alvin (2000) *Warranted Christian Belief* (Oxford: Oxford University Press). An important and highly influential book-length defence of a version of reformed epistemology by one its main instigators.

Zagzebski, Linda (2007) *The Philosophy of Religion: An Historical Introduction* (Oxford: Blackwell). An excellent textbook devoted to the philosophy of religion, written by a leading expert on this topic.

● FREE INTERNET RESOURCES

Amesbury, Richard (2022) 'Fideism', *Stanford Encyclopedia of Philosophy*, http://plato.stanford.edu/entries/fideism/. An accessible, and recently updated, overview of the main issues surrounding fideism.

Forrest, Peter (2021) 'The Epistemology of Religion', *Stanford Encyclopaedia of Philosophy*, http://plato.stanford.edu/entries/religion-epistemology/. A comprehensive, and recently updated, introduction to religious epistemology.

Oppy, Graham (2019) 'Ontological Arguments', *Stanford Encyclopedia of Philosophy*, http://plato.stanford.edu/entries/ontological-arguments/. A subtle survey of the main issues associated with the ontological argument. Quite demanding for the beginner.

Ratzch, Del & Koperski, Jeffrey (2019) 'Teleological Arguments for God's Existence', *Stanford Encyclopedia of Philosophy*, http://plato.stanford.edu/entries/teleological-arguments/. A helpful overview of design arguments for the existence of God. See also Himma (2009).

Reichenbach, Bruce (2022) 'Cosmological Argument', *Stanford Encyclopedia of Philosophy*, http://plato.stanford.edu/entries/cosmological-argument/. A sophisticated, and recently updated, survey of the main issues associated with the cosmological argument.

Taylor, James E. (2010) 'The New Atheists', *Internet Encyclopedia of Philosophy*, www.iep.utm.edu/n-atheis/. A useful, philosophically informed account of the 'new atheist' movement.

13
moral knowledge

- The problem of moral knowledge
- Scepticism about moral facts
- Scepticism about moral knowledge
- The nature of moral knowledge I: classical foundationalism
- The nature of moral knowledge II: alternative conceptions

THE PROBLEM OF MORAL KNOWLEDGE

Moral knowledge, if it exists, is knowledge of moral facts – i.e. true propositions that are concerned with moral claims. It is certainly common to suppose that we have an awful lot of moral knowledge. To take a hackneyed example in philosophical circles, don't we all know that kicking a small child for fun is wrong, and thus that what is known is a fact? But it is clearly a moral judgement that we are making here; hence if this is knowledge, then it is a paradigm case of moral knowledge. The problem though, as we will see, is that it is hard even to make sense of the idea of moral facts, let alone knowledge of these facts. In particular, even if there are moral facts, it is difficult to explain how one would come by such knowledge.

SCEPTICISM ABOUT MORAL FACTS

What is certainly true is that if there are moral facts, then they are not like other kinds of facts. In particular, moral facts, if they exist, seem to lack the sort of objectivity that most other facts are thought to have. Take, for example, a normal empirical fact such as that water boils at roughly 100°C. Admittedly, there is *something* subjective about this fact (so expressed anyway) in that it involves a system of measurement, and yet the system of measurement we employ is in a certain sense up to us. But subjectivity of this sort is both inevitable and also benign. After all, which other system of measurement are we to use, if not our own? Moreover, notice that if an alien were to come down and make this measurement with a different system of measurement, they would (wouldn't they?) gain the same result, albeit one expressed in a different manner. The point is that in the relevant sense empirical facts of this sort are *objective* in that they don't, in any essential fashion, depend on

DOI: 10.4324/9781003356110-16

our cognitive input, but are simply determined by the way things are. Put another way, what makes empirical facts true is the nature of the world and not us.

Compare a scientific discourse with a discourse where taste or opinion is what is important, such as one regarding what is funny. Here it doesn't seem so obvious to say that there is a genuine fact of the matter. Suppose, for example, that I think that the Woody Allen film *Bananas* is hilarious, while you think that it isn't remotely funny. Is it clear that one of us is right and one of us is wrong (i.e. that for one of us what is believed is a fact, whereas for the other what is believed is not a fact)? Of course, it is a fact that *I think* that *Bananas* is a funny film (just as it's a fact that you don't think this), but that's not what we're arguing about, which is whether it is a funny film *simpliciter*. In practice, we would probably just agree to disagree. But that in itself seems to suggest that this is not a dispute about 'objective' facts of the sort found in a scientific dispute. After all, we don't think it reasonable for two scientists with opposing views to simply agree to disagree!

This seems to suggest that there isn't a real disagreement here at all – that is, a disagreement over an 'objective' fact. For notice that if in saying that *Bananas* is funny, I am simply saying that *I think* it is funny, and in saying that *Bananas* is not funny, you are simply saying that *you think* it isn't funny, then we aren't really disagreeing at all, but just expressing our subjective opinions. If this is the right way to understand disputes over what is funny, however, then it is odd that we should argue about this kind of topic at all, since by definition there would be no way of ever resolving such a dispute as there is no objective fact at issue. But that is just to emphasise that disputes about what is funny are nothing like scientific disputes since there clearly is something objectively at issue in the latter case.

The foregoing seems to suggest that we should be careful about treating all statements as being on a par in terms of whether they are attempting to state that something is a fact. Plausibly, when a scientist states that a certain liquid boils at a certain temperature, she is expressing her conviction that it is an objective truth that this liquid boils at this temperature. In contrast, when it comes to other kinds of statements, such as regarding what we find funny or which films we like, we are not saying that what we believe is a fact, but rather just expressing personal views.

So what are we to make of moral statements? Are they like statements about what is (or what we find) funny, which arguably simply express subjective opinions rather than aiming to express objective facts? Or are they like scientific statements, which arguably do aim to express objective facts? Well, if there are such things as moral facts, it is hard to see why they would be objective in the same way as scientific facts. Let's take the clichéd example noted above that kicking a small child for fun is wrong. This truth – if it is a truth – is subjective in at least the sense that if creatures like us who cared about the things that we care about never existed, then this wouldn't obviously be true at all. Suppose, for example, that we humans had evolved in such a way that we don't feel pain. Would it still be true that kicking a small child for fun is wrong? Perhaps not. It depends very much on whether the putative wrongness of kicking a small child for fun relates to the potential pain felt by the small child who is being kicked. But if human beings don't feel pain, then this can't be a reason for thinking that kicking a small child for fun is wrong. Let's suppose for the sake of argument that the reason why we think kicking a small child for fun is wrong is indeed because this act would cause pain. It follows that there is a sense in which this statement expresses something subjective, in that its truth is at best relative to the kind of creatures we are (i.e. creatures who feel pain). In contrast, the fact that water boils at roughly 100°C is not subjective in this way, since it is something that intuitively would have been true regardless of whether any creatures like us existed.

But that moral statements are 'subjective' in this sense does not put them on a par with statements about what is funny, even if it does mean that they are not quite objective in the sense of a scientific statement. The simple fact is that we humans do indeed feel pain, and given this fact, and the putative moral relevance of pain, it follows that it is a truth that kicking a small child for fun is wrong. Put another way, although moral statements are subjective in the sense that they are contingent on the kind of creatures we have turned out to be, given that we are this kind of creature, they are objective; any creature that was like us in the relevant ways should have the same moral code.

If this is right, then there is a kind of objectivity that attaches to moral statements, in that they are not purely subjective like statements about what we find funny. After all, statements about what is funny are arguably *completely* subjective in that they are wholly dependent upon the tastes of the individual person concerned. In contrast, on this view moral statements don't purely express the opinions of the people who are involved, but rather express common human truths.

This line of defence against scepticism about moral truth might initially look attractive, but it is important to realise that its scope is severely limited. After all, while it might be a common truth about human beings that we feel pain, and feeling pain is at best unpleasant, arguably one can't account for the truth of the wide range of moral statements that we make by appeal to this fact alone. Take moral statements that appeal to notions like that of a human right, for example, such as the right to free speech. Suppose I claim that it is wrong to suppress free speech, even when the speech in question is offensive to most people. Lots of people think that something like this claim is true (i.e. that free speech is a universal human right), but it is hard to account for the truth of this by appealing only to our common aversion to pain. After all, the exercise of this free speech is, on the face of it, causing a great deal of pain, and hence should on this account be treated as immoral.

More generally, the crux of the matter is that while there may well be a basis in our common humanity to account for the 'objectivity' of some moral statements, the simple fact remains that there is an awful lot of disagreement about morality. Moreover – and this is the most worrying facet of this problem for the defender of moral truths – this disagreement often breaks down along familiar demographic lines (e.g. culture, race, gender). So, for example, some cultures think that obedience to recognised authority should take precedence over one's personal liberties, while for other cultures, the reverse is the case and one's personal liberties are regarded as sacrosanct. The concern, then, is that moral statements simply express our subjective tastes, where these are culturally determined. So, while it may seem as if moral statements express universal truths when we speak to people like us, once we start to speak to other people (who are different only in their cultural background) and discover that they have very different moral views, we realise that the 'objectivity' of moral statements is in fact just a locally shared subjectivity in disguise.

We are thus back where we started with the idea that moral statements don't express objective facts but rather subjective sentiments. Note, however, that if there are no moral facts, then there is nothing to be known in the first place, and hence moral knowledge is impossible. This philosophical position is known as **moral expressivism**, and it is quite a radical thesis to hold. The reason for this is that if you hold that there are no such things as moral facts, then you need to offer an explanation of what it is that we are doing when we confidently put forward moral claims. The explanation offered by the expressivist is that what we are doing is not asserting (something which we take to be) a fact – as one would do when one asserts that water boils at roughly 100°C – but rather merely expressing a sentiment. For example, to claim that kicking a small child for fun is wrong is to express one's own feeling that one shouldn't do such a thing. In effect, then, such a claim is equivalent to saying that one feels that one shouldn't kick babies for fun. Crucially, though, expressions of feelings are not normally thought of as assertions of fact at all.

A good analogy in this regard is with injunctions, such as 'Shut that door'. Although a statement of an injunction might superficially look like an assertion, no one would on reflection regard this statement as an assertion. One is, after all, clearly not trying to say something true, but rather simply trying to make something happen (i.e. to get the door to close). Some expressivists have thus argued that moral claims should be interpreted as injunctions rather than assertions. On this proposal, in saying that kicking small children for fun is wrong, one is in effect saying something like 'Don't kick small children for fun'. Rather than trying to say that something is the case (i.e. that kicking small children for fun is morally wrong), one is simply registering one's displeasure at this sort of thing and trying to ensure – by, in effect, issuing an order – that others do not act in a fashion that would generate this displeasure.

An advantage of thinking about moral claims in this way is that the expressivist can explain why we might initially suppose that we are committed to the existence of moral facts even though (according to the expressivist anyway) they don't exist. We have, as it were, been misled by language, in that we think we are making a factual assertion when we put forward moral claims, when in reality we are just expressing our feelings. If there are no moral facts, then one obviously doesn't need to engage with the above issue of explaining why moral facts, were they to exist, are so different to normal empirical facts. The challenge to those who believe in the existence of moral facts is thus to explain why we shouldn't think of moral statements along expressivist lines.

• SCEPTICISM ABOUT MORAL KNOWLEDGE

Suppose that we can resist the expressivist view and convincingly argue that there are moral facts. As noted above, this wouldn't suffice to show that moral knowledge is possible, since it could still be the case that these are facts that we are unable to know. One issue here is the diversity of moral opinion that we noted above. Some people think that abortion can sometimes be morally permissible, while others think that it is clearly immoral. Some think that animal experimentation can sometimes be morally permissible, while others think that it is always immoral. Some think that taxation is a form of theft and hence immoral, but many others disagree. And so on. Now of course one can find disagreements occurring in lots of different domains. Even among the best scientists, for example, there can be disagreements, and yet scientific inquiry (as conducted by the best scientists at any rate) is meant to be a paradigmatically good way of acquiring knowledge. But if the existence of such disagreements in science does not undermine our confidence that there is scientific knowledge, then why should the existence of disagreements about morality make us sceptical about moral knowledge?

A. J. Ayer (1910–89)

The propositions of philosophy are not factual, but linguistic in character – that is, they do not describe the behaviour of physical, or even mental, objects; they express definitions, or the formal consequences of definitions.

A. J. Ayer, *Language, Truth and Logic*

In his seminal book, *Language, Truth and Logic* (published in 1936, when he was only 26 years old), the British philosopher **A. J. Ayer** put forward a philosophical position that entails a robust form of scepticism about moral facts. Ayer was a *logical positivist*, and as such he argued that for a proposition to be meaningful, it had to be capable of being empirically verified. This meant that you needed to have some way of demonstrating, through experience, that the proposition was either true or false, at least in principle. Moral 'facts', however, do not meet this requirement, or so argued logical positivists like Ayer. For how would one go about empirically demonstrating that a moral statement was true or false? Accordingly, on this proposal moral statements are strictly speaking nonsense. Note, however, that it is not just moral facts that are under threat by the lights of this view. Think, for example, of the kinds of statements made in aesthetics (e.g. that Woody Allen has made some good films). Aren't these statements equally immune to empirical verification? In fact, much of philosophy gets called into question as well – logical positivists were particularly suspicious of metaphysical claims, for example. Indeed, embarrassingly for logical positivism, the very statement of the view fails to satisfy its own criteria, for how would one go about empirically verifying the statement that all meaningful statements are empirically verifiable? Hence the very statement of logical positivism is by its own lights nonsense too.

Notice, however, that the disagreements one finds in science are very different from those found with regard to morality. To begin with, the extent of the disagreement is not the same; there are far more moral disagreements than there are scientific disagreements. That this is so reflects two further differences between science and morality. First, morality is, as we noted above, very much culture-relative in that one's moral views tend to be shaped by the culture that one was raised in and yet different cultures can have strikingly different moral codes. In contrast, there is no analogue to this in science, which is arguably not at all culture-relative. To return to our example of the boiling point for water, for instance, while two distinct cultures might have a different system of measurement that they apply in this case, so long as they are carrying out their experiments properly, then they will reach equivalent conclusions.

Second, in the scientific case, it is usually clear to both parties what would resolve the dispute (e.g. what evidence would be required to settle the issue one way or the other). If a scientist were for some reason sceptical that water boils at 100°C, then we could convince her by doing the appropriate experiment to illustrate this fact. When it comes to morality, however, this is rarely the case. Indeed, both parties to a moral dispute might agree on all the relevant empirical facts yet still have opposing moral opinions. In the debate about the morality of abortion, for example, both parties might agree on such issues as the nature of conception, what the foetus is able to experience at different stages of development, and so on, yet still disagree about whether abortion can be morally permissible. If that's right, then it is very unclear how one could ever settle an entrenched moral dispute.

A natural way to respond to at least the first point is to argue that some cultures have better moral codes than others. We might regard some cultures as being morally inferior, for example, on account of how a greater number of their moral beliefs are false. Indeed, if there are moral facts, then on the face of it there seems no reason why there couldn't be moral progress (just as there is scientific progress). As we progress as a society, we shake off prejudices of old and become more enlightened, thereby enhancing our body of moral knowledge. Some cultures might thus simply have moral codes that are more developed down the road of moral progress than other societies.

The worry about this response, however, is how to defend it without slipping into a narrow moral parochialism. The problem is that every culture tends to suppose that its moral code is superior to all others, so how are we to be sure that our moral code really is the ascendant one that we take it to be? In short, how can we be sure that it isn't us who employ the 'primitive' moral code while the culture that we look down upon from a moral point of view is the one employing a progressive moral code?

This point highlights that the really important consideration that counts against moral knowledge is the second worry just raised regarding the difficulty of resolving moral disagreements. After all, if there were an objective way of resolving moral disagreements, then we wouldn't need to worry about the problem of moral parochialism. Like the scientist, we could just put our moral code to the objective test and find out whether it really is superior to the alternative moral codes offered by other cultures. That there is no objective test of this sort that we could subject our moral beliefs to means that we are cast adrift on this score, with no sure way to guide us through the moral challenges posed to us by alternative moral codes.

THE NATURE OF MORAL KNOWLEDGE I: CLASSICAL FOUNDATIONALISM

So far we have seen some pretty formidable obstacles to the idea that there is moral knowledge. Let us suppose, however – these concerns notwithstanding – that we do have moral knowledge. What would be the best epistemological account of this knowledge?

Perhaps the most natural model of moral knowledge treats such knowledge as involving a fairly complex inference which makes appeal to fundamental and universal moral truths – otherwise known as *moral principles* – and the concrete features of the case in hand. For example, that one should, all other things being equal, try to alleviate the suffering of others might be one such universal moral truth. That one should, all other things being equal, respect the sanctity of human life may be another possible universal moral truth. These universal moral truths wouldn't all by themselves tell us what we should do in any particular situation, however. For one thing, we would also need to bring our knowledge of the specifics of the case to bear. For another, these universal moral truths may well conflict with one another, prima facie anyway, and so one would need to consider how much weight to accord each truth (actually, they don't really conflict, as we explain below).

Let's look at how this might work in practice. Suppose that you see an attempted suicide take place, as a woman throws herself from a bridge into the cold driving water of a river. What should you do? Well, from a purely practical point of view (i.e. a point of view where one puts moral issues to one side), the answer would seem to be straightforward: you should walk on by, or at least do as little as possible to ensure that you are not subject to the practically troublesome censure of your fellow citizens – that is, you should phone the emergency services, say, and act suitably concerned about the fate of the woman, but nothing more. But the question we're interested in is what you should do from a specifically moral point of view. Here, the answer isn't so clear. For consider the moral 'truths' that you might appeal to in order to make a decision.

For example, as noted above, you might agree that there is a moral principle to the effect that you should try to alleviate suffering, all other things being equal (call this *principle 1*). So, that fact that this person will clearly suffer in the cold water of the river would seem to suggest that you should jump in to save her. Similarly, you might also agree that one should, all other things being equal, respect the sanctity of human life (call this *principle 2*). This may be another possible reason to take the plunge. But wait; before you strip off your expensive trousers and dive in, consider some other moral principles that you probably hold. One moral principle will surely be that – as ever, all other things being equal – one should respect the considered views of others (call this *principle 3*). Another will probably be that one has a duty to look after one's own wellbeing, all other things being equal (call this *principle 4*). The trouble is that, on the face of it at least, these four principles are in conflict with each other. After all, principles 1 and 2 seem to suggest that you should jump in, while principles 3 and 4 suggest that you should, respectively, (a) defer to (what seems to be) the considered view of the agent concerned and (b) value your own good self which would be put in danger by this act of heroism.

Of course, these principles are not actually in conflict because they all have this 'get-out' clause of 'all other things being equal'. Presumably, the kind of cases in which all things are not equal will include those cases where there is a prima facie tension between the applicable moral principles. In such cases, one needs to decide how to weigh the conflicting demands made by these principles. How would you do it? Well, for one thing you would first need to get a good sense of what the relevant facts are. Here are some (but by no means all) of the morally salient questions that one might ask:

- Did the person in question really choose to throw herself off the bridge?
- Was her decision to do this her considered view, made in a clear state of mind with due consideration for the consequences of her action?
- To what extent will this course of action cause her suffering? For example, will the fall kill her instantly?
- What are one's chances of saving her, were one to attempt to do so?
- What are one's chances of being harmed oneself, and to what extent, were one to try to save her?

In each case, the issue in question is straightforwardly factual in nature, but what answer one gives to these questions will affect on how one weighs up the conflicting demands of these moral principles. After all, if the person concerned is lost anyway (e.g. if she was killed on impact) then clearly principles 1, 2, and 3 are in effect inoperative here, since, respectively, (a) you're simply not in a position to alleviate this person's suffering, (b) you're not in a position anymore to respect her human life since it is no more, and (c) you're not in a position to respect (or disrespect, for that matter) her considered judgements about what is best for her. So with all that in mind, you are free, it seems, to follow principle 4 and make sure you are looking after your own wellbeing.

In practice, of course, one probably wouldn't be in a position to offer a confident answer to any of these questions, at least at that moment anyway. And yet, from a moral point of view, one would be required to act, and one would be morally judged on the basis of the choice that one made. Given that it is often the case that moral judgements involve such complex evaluations of the relative weight of moral principles in light of a range of facts about the nature of the situation, it is no wonder that making the right moral judgements is so darned hard.

With the foregoing in mind, we start to get a picture of how moral knowledge might come about. But what does this tell us about what the structure of moral knowledge is? Well, on the face of it at least, it would seem to suggest that a kind of *foundationalism* would be appropriate. After all, moral principles do seem to occupy a foundational role in this picture of moral knowledge. That is, knowledge of these principles appears to be epistemically basic in that one does not need to base one's belief in these principles on other beliefs that one holds. In particular, it seems that one can know these propositions a priori simply by reflecting on them, and a priori knowledge is often regarded as paradigmatically epistemically basic.

In contrast, our knowledge of particular moral truths (such as what the morally right action is on a specific occasion) seems to be essentially non-foundational. For to gain such knowledge, it appears that we need to undertake a complex inference which takes into account both one's non-moral knowledge, such as one's empirical knowledge of the relevant facts of the situation, and one's (putatively) foundational moral knowledge of the relevant moral principles. It thus seems that the right epistemology of moral knowledge is straightforwardly foundationalist. In particular, it seems that moral knowledge is either acquired through a priori reasoning (as when one gains moral knowledge of a foundational moral truth) or through a mix of a priori reasoning and empirical investigation (as when one gains moral knowledge of a non-foundational particular moral truth by considering the specific details of the case in light of the relevant moral principles). The form of foundationalism in play is thus classical foundationalism – of the sort that we considered in Chapter 4 – in that the foundations are *self-justifying*. That is, the thought is that the a priori knowledge one has of the foundational moral principles is a kind of knowledge which, in virtue of the manner in which it was acquired, does not require additional independent epistemic support.

● THE NATURE OF MORAL KNOWLEDGE II: ALTERNATIVE CONCEPTIONS

Although many are attracted to this classical foundationalist conception of moral knowledge, there is reason to think that it may not be the right way of thinking about moral knowledge. One challenge to this conception of moral knowledge comes from the *coherentist* who argues that while this view is right to treat our moral knowledge of particular moral truths as being essentially inferential, it is wrong in thinking that there is any foundational moral knowledge. In particular, they dispute that our knowledge of moral principles is a priori in the fashion that the foundationalist picture suggests.

But if a priori knowledge of moral principles is not possible, then on what basis does one acquire this knowledge? The coherentist answer is to say that knowledge of these principles is in effect gained by considering particular cases. That is, one has a body of relevant beliefs about moral matters, and one adjusts them in light of a range of relevant factors that one encounters. On this proposal, moral principles are just rather general moral beliefs that one holds with great conviction, but this doesn't mean that they are thereby epistemically basic, or that they are not gained through an inferential process involving one's empirical beliefs.

For the coherentist about moral knowledge, then, the (defeasible) starting point for moral knowledge might well be one's judgements about a range of cases that such-and-such action was either morally right or wrong. In light of such judgements, one might then formulate some general moral principle that one thinks captures what is common to the moral judgements that one is making, where this moral principle is itself regarded as provisional relative to what further moral judgements one makes about particular cases. In this way, or so the coherentist argues at any rate, one can capture how moral knowledge is in fact acquired. Rather than any particular moral belief being foundational, there is instead a constant interplay in terms of the moral beliefs that we hold, either regarding moral principles or more specific moral beliefs, such that no particular moral belief ever plays a foundational epistemic role in our system of moral belief. But provided that one in this way forms one's moral beliefs in a suitable fashion (and those beliefs are also true of course), then, argues the coherentist, one can gain moral knowledge.

Coherentism is not the only alternative to classical foundationalism when it comes to moral knowledge. In particular, there is also a non-classical foundationalism account available. The idea behind this proposal is that it is possible to know moral truths directly. Indeed, the claim made by proponents of this view is that moral knowledge, rather than being (at least for the most part anyway) inferential knowledge that is gained via reason (whether on the model that the classical foundationalist or the coherentist supposes), is better thought of as being (in paradigm cases anyway) more akin to a kind of perceptual knowledge, at least as such knowledge is conceived of by direct realism (see Chapter 7).

Before we start to ask how plausible this conception of moral knowledge is, it's important to first note that one key thing in favour of this proposal is that it seems to accord very well with how we *think* we gain moral knowledge. In particular, when one examines paradigm cases in which moral knowledge is acquired, it does not seem at all right to say that an inference was either actually involved or required. Rather, it seems that one is often able to simply 'see' that a certain act is morally right or wrong.

For example, when you see someone clearly doing something despicable, such as kicking a small child for fun, it seems odd to think that any kind of inference, even a very quick one, is required to form one's judgement that this act is wrong. Moreover, such spontaneous moral judgements often seem to count as knowledge even if one is unable to offer independent reasons in favour of this judgement, such as an appeal to a general moral principle that is applicable in this case. Indeed, if one's moral judgement were challenged, one would usually just reassert that the act in question is clearly morally wrong (probably with a degree of puzzlement, for, one might ask, what kind of person doesn't realise that hurting small children for fun is wrong?).

Interestingly, not only does it seem that we don't usually undertake inferences when acquiring moral knowledge, but that in a wide range of cases if one actually undertook such an inference then this would be a sign of some sort of moral corruption on one's part. That is, we expect decent people to respond instinctively to paradigm cases of morally good and morally bad acts, such that, for example, they are immediately in support of the former and immediately repulsed by the latter, and act accordingly. Indeed, the use of the emotive word 'repulsed' is entirely appropriate here, since our moral judgements – particularly about concrete cases – do often go hand in hand with an emotional response.

For example, if one sees someone hurting a small child for fun, one does not merely form the view that this act is wrong, but one actually feels angry that it is happening and (where feasible) one does what one can to stop it. More generally, I think we would be very worried about the moral character of someone who saw such a wicked act take place and formed her moral judgement in a cool, unemotional fashion (or, for that matter, who only formed an emotional response after considering the rational basis for her judgement). To see this, imagine the concrete case of witnessing a small child being hurt purely for someone's amusement. Now imagine that one is with someone who has no immediate moral or emotional response to this scene and only decides that what she is seeing is morally wrong, and hence acts (and feels?) accordingly, once she has reflected, say, on the fact that this cruel act contravenes what she takes to be a moral principle. Wouldn't one be at least puzzled by, if not more than a little concerned about, this person?

If this is the right way to think about moral knowledge, however, then it does seem that we should take the idea that we can (sometimes, at least) directly see that an act is morally right or wrong at face value. In one respect, then, moral knowledge, at least in paradigm cases, would be akin to perceptual knowledge in that it is acquired directly, without the need for further independent rational support, simply by observing the phenomenon in question. This would clearly be a very different way of thinking about moral knowledge than that offered by classical foundationalist and coherentist accounts. But what kind of epistemology of moral knowledge would it be?

A natural way of thinking about moral knowledge in this model would be along the kind of lines suggested by virtue epistemology. Recall that we noted in Chapter 6 that virtue epistemologists hold that knowledge is true belief that is acquired via the reliable epistemic virtues, and possibly also cognitive faculties, of the agent. Virtue epistemology offers an attractive account of perceptual knowledge because it can make sense of how our reliable cognitive faculties could be understood as able to directly enable us to gain knowledge even though one had no independent rational basis for the target belief (just as a chicken-sexer could conceivably gain knowledge while lacking a rational independent basis for her belief). Accordingly, one might opt to try to account for moral knowledge along the very same lines, and hence argue that moral knowledge can be directly gained via the employment of one's reliable epistemic virtues and cognitive faculties even though the agent concerned may lack any independent rational basis for this knowledge. That is, just as our perceptual virtues enable us to skilfully, but directly, gain perceptual knowledge, so our moral virtues–i.e. our cognitive abilities that help us navigate the moral realm–enable us to skilfully, but directly, gain moral knowledge.

The result would be a kind of epistemic externalism about moral knowledge. It would be a kind of foundationalism, in the minimal sense that some beliefs are appropriately epistemically supported even though they are not supported by further beliefs, but it would be very different from a classical foundationalism that treated the foundational beliefs as self-justifying. For what is in fact justifying these foundational beliefs by the lights of this alternative foundationalist account are 'external' facts (in particular, facts about how the belief was formed, about the reliability of the belief-forming process in play, and so on).

Notice that the strength of this account of moral knowledge is also what makes it problematic. For while this proposal has the advantage of allowing us to directly gain moral knowledge in certain cases even though we lack any independent rational support for our belief, one might by the same token argue that there is something troubling about the very idea of such directly gained moral knowledge. When it comes to knowledge gained by perceptual faculties, it is far more natural to think of this knowledge as potentially completely direct in this way, but this is because we are born with these capacities, and hence they predate our rational powers. If we do possess moral faculties, however, then it is hard to see how they could be innate. For one thing, if that were the case, then it would be very puzzling why one's moral code tends to vary with the culture in which one was raised. The problem, however, is that if one conceives of our moral faculties in such a way that one acquires, and then refines, these faculties over time as one matures as a person, then it is hard to see how one's moral knowledge, insofar as it really is moral knowledge, could possibly lack independent rational support. For wouldn't one over time acquire reasons to believe, for example, that one has a reliable ability to detect moral truths of the relevant kind?

So even if one can overcome the kind of problems that have made many think that moral knowledge is impossible, there is still a challenge remaining to explain what moral knowledge would be were it to be possible. In particular, one needs to tread a fine line between, on the one hand, avoiding the danger of over-intellectualising moral knowledge and, on the other hand, offering a sufficiently sophisticated story about moral knowledge such that we are willing to regard it as bona fide.

● CHAPTER SUMMARY

- We began by noting that it is far from obvious that there is any such thing as a moral fact, and that if there are no moral facts then it immediately follows that there can be no moral knowledge. Part of the worry about moral facts is that they don't seem to be objective in a way that 'real' facts are, such as scientific facts. For example, one's moral judgements seem to largely reflect one's cultural upbringing.
- If one holds that there are no moral facts, then one is endorsing *moral expressivism*. Moral expressivism holds that moral statements do not express facts but rather perform a very different role instead (e.g. expressing one's support for a certain action or one's desire to stop certain actions from taking place).
- Even if one rejects moral expressivism and argues that there are moral facts, it still doesn't follow that there is moral knowledge, since it could be that one is unable

to know these facts. The differences between a moral discourse and a scientific discourse might give one grounds for thinking that this is the case. For example, whereas scientific disagreements seem to be in their nature resolvable, moral disagreements are often completely intractable.

- Assuming that there is such a thing as moral knowledge, we then explored what the right epistemology of such knowledge might be. The first proposal we considered was a *classical foundationalism* that held that we had a priori knowledge of basic moral principles which, when coupled with our empirical knowledge of the particular circumstances of the case in hand, enabled us to appropriately form moral judgements about what to do in specific cases. One problem with this view was that it seemed to over-intellectualise what is required for moral knowledge.
- The second proposal that we considered was *coherentism*. This view held that there are no foundational moral beliefs, and thus that even one's beliefs in moral principles could be open to revision if suitable counter-evidence were to come to light.
- The final proposal we looked at was a type of *virtue epistemology* that allowed that one could, in certain cases, directly gain moral knowledge – even though one had no independent rational basis for one's belief – just so long as one appropriately employed one's epistemic virtues. We saw that such a view may be problematic in that moral knowledge – unlike, say, perceptual knowledge – does seem to essentially involve the possession of appropriate supporting reasons.

• STUDY QUESTIONS

1 Try to give a possible example of each of the following:
   - a scientific fact;
   - a moral fact; and
   - an aesthetic fact.
     Try to list some potential differences between the three kinds of facts, and explain why these differences might be thought to call the existence of moral facts into question.

2 What is moral expressivism? Do you find it compelling?
3 Explain, in your own words, why the existence of moral facts is compatible with scepticism about moral knowledge.
4 Describe, and critically evaluate, at least two grounds for scepticism about moral knowledge.
5 Describe the classical foundationalist account of moral knowledge. Is it plausible, do you think?
6 Describe the coherentist account of moral knowledge. How does it differ from the classical foundationalist account of moral knowledge? Is it preferable, do you think?
7 Describe the virtue epistemic account of moral knowledge. Critically evaluate whether this approach offers an account of moral knowledge which is most in keeping with our ordinary ways of thinking about moral knowledge.
8 Should we aim to offer an epistemology of moral belief that accords with our ordinary thinking about moral knowledge? If so, why? If not, why not?

INTRODUCTORY FURTHER READING

Audi, Robert (2010) 'Moral Knowledge', *Routledge Companion to Epistemology*, S. Bernecker & D. H. Pritchard (eds), Ch. 35, pp. 380–92 (London: Routledge). An excellent overview of the main issues regarding moral knowledge. To be read in conjunction with Sayre-McCord (2010).

Sayre-McCord, Geoffrey (2010) 'Moral Scepticism', *Routledge Companion to Epistemology*, S. Bernecker & D. H. Pritchard (eds), Ch. 43, pp. 464–73 (London: Routledge). An excellent summary of the main issues regarding moral scepticism. To be read in conjunction with Audi (2010).

Zimmerman, Aaron (2010) *Moral Epistemology* (London: Routledge). A readable overview of contemporary work on epistemological issues in ethics.

ADVANCED FURTHER READING

Audi, Robert (1999) 'Moral Knowledge and Ethical Pluralism', *Blackwell Guide to Epistemology*, J. Greco & E. Sosa (eds), pp. 271–302 (Oxford: Blackwell). A sophisticated and quite comprehensive overview of moral epistemology. Not for the beginner.

Lemos, Noah (2002) 'Epistemology and Ethics', *Oxford Handbook of Epistemology*, P. K. Moser (ed.), pp. 479–512 (Oxford: Oxford University Press). An excellent treatment of epistemological issues in ethics. Not for the beginner.

McGrath, Sarah (2019) *Moral Knowledge* (Oxford: Oxford University Press). A very recent, and comprehensive, treatment of moral epistemology.

Urban Walker, Margaret (2000) 'Moral Epistemology', *Companion to Feminist Philosophy*, A. M. Jaggar & I. M. Young (eds), pp. 363–71 (Oxford: Blackwell). A very useful discussion of the main issues in moral epistemology from the specific perspective of feminist theory.

FREE INTERNET RESOURCES

Campbell, Richmond (2019) 'Moral Epistemology', *Stanford Encyclopedia of Philosophy*, http://plato.stanford.edu/entries/moral-epistemology/. An excellent overview of the main issues regarding moral epistemology.

Sinnott-Armstrong, Walter (2019) 'Moral Skepticism', *Stanford Encyclopedia of Philosophy*, http://plato.stanford.edu/entries/skepticism-moral/. A very good, albeit quite sophisticated, discussion of the various types of moral scepticism.

Part IV

what are the
social dynamics
of knowledge?

14

disagreement

- Social epistemology
- The problem of disagreement
- Faultless disagreement
- Peer disagreement
- Peer disagreement and dogmatism
- Expert disagreement

SOCIAL EPISTEMOLOGY

In this part of the book, we will be looking at the social dynamics of knowledge, an area of epistemology known as **social epistemology**. A great deal of the history of epistemology has been largely individualistic in focus. For example, it asks question about what I, as an individual, can know, and explores such questions as what constitutes my evidence or my justification for believing what I do. But there is also an important social dynamic to epistemological questions, and this is what social epistemology explores. We have already encountered one core topic in social epistemology, which is that of testimony. Contemporary epistemology has witnessed a growth in interest in social epistemology, and in this part we will consider some of the other topics that contemporary social epistemologists discuss, beginning with disagreement.

THE PROBLEM OF DISAGREEMENT

One of the central ways in which social factors influence knowledge is via disagreement. This is because when people disagree, it can pose an epistemological problem. Where there is consensus about the answer to a question, this is at least some reason to think that what grounds this agreement is that we are getting to the truth of the matter. Of course, this reason is highly defeasible, as you may discover that everyone else is as ill-informed about the issue as you are, or that there are alternative explanations for this convergence which suggest that it does not indicate that we are getting to the truth (e.g. that we are all subject to same kind of cognitive bias). Nonetheless, agreement is usually epistemically comforting. In contrast, disagreement is usually epistemically disconcerting, as it suggests that our answer to the question in hand might be wrong.

DOI: 10.4324/9781003356110-18

As we will see in this chapter, disagreement comes in different forms, and the particular form that it takes can have a bearing on its epistemic significance. Before we get to these complexities, however, it is worth noting the contemporary significance of the problem of disagreement. For while disagreement has always been with us – there have always been disagreements of one sort or another about any significant question – the modern social media age has amplified disagreements to a remarkable extent. One reason for this is that we are more aware of opposing voices now than ever before. So while previously we could reasonably be oblivious to the fact that people disagree about certain issues, now that fact is completely evident. This might not be a bad thing, of course, in that sometimes these are voices that should have been heard and were illegitimately suppressed. (We will be talking about this issue in more detail in the next chapter when we cover the topic of epistemic injustice.) Moreover, if we want to get to the truth, then usually listening to multiple perspectives can be helpful, as it helps us sift through the different proposals on offer and subject them to proper scrutiny.

The problem, however, is that disagreements can prevent us from having knowledge that we might have otherwise possessed. After all, not everyone's opinion is on a par, and so insofar as we do take disagreements seriously, then we might be in danger of losing knowledge that was in fact perfectly in good order. One way this can happen is that the presence of disagreement can make us doubt ourselves, and thus no longer believe things that we really should believe. If that happens, then what we previously knew would no longer be knowledge (given that knowledge demands belief). For example, one might doubt that a highly effective vaccine works because one hears about there being disagreements over its effectiveness, even though the people who are disputing its effectiveness lack any kind of medical training. As a result, one no longer believes that the vaccine works, and so no longer knows this, even though that previously held belief was true and amounted to knowledge.

Another way that disagreement can destroy genuine knowledge is by being a **defeater** for that knowledge. A defeater is a consideration that prevents you from having knowledge either by indicating that the reasons for your belief don't sufficiently support the truth of that belief or else by providing you with independent reasons for thinking that the belief is false. So, for example, suppose you believe that your boss is in work today because you saw her walk past your office window. Imagine, however, that you are then told by someone reliable that your boss's twin sister, who looks just like your boss, is visiting the office today. If your only reason for believing that your boss is in work today is that you saw her earlier, then this new piece of information is a defeater in that it entails that your reasons for believing what you do don't sufficiently support the truth of your belief (for all you know the person you saw was the boss's twin sister).

Notice that a defeater needn't be true. For example, perhaps the person who told you that the boss's twin sister is in the office today was simply having a joke at your expense. Unless you find out that this is a joke, however, then it still acts as a defeater to your knowledge, given that your informant is normally reliable about this kind of thing. Relatedly, defeaters can be themselves defeated, in the sense that one can discover further information that enables one to discount them. That's exactly what happens when you find out that what you were told about the boss's twin sister visiting the office was just a joke. Now you are reunited with the knowledge that you had previously that the boss is in the office today, before you were presented with the defeater.

The relevance of this discussion of defeaters to our present concerns is that the presence of disagreement can act as a defeater. For example, suppose you believe that Riga is the capital of Latvia, because that's what you were told when you did geography at school. This is in fact true, and since you have good grounds for your belief (and the belief isn't Gettiered etc.), it is plausibly an instance of knowledge. Imagine now, however, that you discover that there is a live disagreement about whether Riga really is the capital of Latvia, with some people who you know claiming, quite plausibly as it turns out, that another city is the real capital of this country. Isn't your situation now rather like the person who was told that the boss's twin sister was visiting the office? That is, you now seem to have a defeater to your belief that Riga is the capital of Latvia and hence no longer know that this is the case. In particular, unless you are able to acquire further reasons that enable you to discount this defeater, such as grounds to think that the people who think that Riga isn't the capital of Latvia are making some kind of mistake, then this defeater undermines your knowledge, even though the defeater in question isn't true. Notice too that the defeater will undermine your knowledge even if you continue to believe that Riga is the capital of Latvia. What's important is that this belief, even though in fact true, wouldn't now amount to knowledge so long as the defeater remains undefeated.

• FAULTLESS DISAGREEMENT

Of course, not every disagreement counts as a defeater for one's knowledge. In particular, if the disagreeing party is clearly less knowledgeable than you are about the subject matter in question, then the fact that they disagree with you is easily discounted. For example, if you are a medical expert and someone with no medical training disagrees with you about a medical issue – on a purely anecdotical basis, say – then you would be quite right to disregard their opposing testimony.

Interestingly, it also seems to matter to whether a disagreement counts as a defeater what the disagreement is about. This is because some topics seem to allow for what is known as *faultless disagreement*, whereby the opposing parties are both entitled to maintain their positions. The obvious examples of this are topics that are entirely concerned with one's tastes or subjective preferences. For instance, if I say that I think Woody Allen films are fantastic and you say that you think that they are awful and self-indulgent, then we'd usually agree to disagree. That is, the mere fact that you disagree with me wouldn't seem to have any implication for whether I should change my mind (though it might lead me to reflect again on these films and their quality). In particular, it seems that both of us can retain our opinions regardless of the other person's opposing opinions and be perfectly within our epistemic rights to do so.

In contrast, when it comes to disagreements about matters of fact it seems that disagreement is never faultless in this way. For example, the medical expert is right to disagree with the layperson's opposing verdict about a medical matter because they have a better epistemic basis for their opinion – it is thus their opponent who is at fault. In general, if two people disagree about a matter of fact, then it seems that one of them must be wrong. In contrast, when it comes to matters of taste, this doesn't seem to apply. It is, after all, just my opinion that Woody Allen films are fantastic – what more is there to say?

One reason why we might allow faultless disagreement when it comes to matters of taste and subjective preference is that we don't think that there are any objective facts to disagree about. That might be one way of making sense of this situation, but notice that it comes at a very high cost. It means, for example, that there is nothing for one to know in this regard, as without there being a fact at issue, there is no fact to know. Of course, one can know what one's preferences are – for example, that one likes Woody Allen films – but one cannot know anything beyond that. In particular, one cannot know that Woody Allen films are fantastic (or, for that matter, that they are terrible), since on this view there is no fact of the matter as to whether they are. No wonder then that disagreements in this domain don't act as defeaters, as there is no knowledge for them to undermine.

We might initially think that this conclusion is harmless, at least if it only applies to aesthetic judgements. It is at least puzzling, however, in that we do think, for example, that one can improve one's aesthetic judgements. Relatedly, we also think that there are experts in this regard, who know more about aesthetic matters than we do. That's why, for example, we consult film critics. But if there is no knowledge in this domain, then there is nothing to improve upon with regard to our aesthetic judgements and there certainly can't be any aesthetic experts.

We might be able to live with this conclusion with regard to aesthetics, but it becomes even more disturbing once we start to reflect on other domains that might also seem to involve faultless disagreement. For example, we often treat ethical and political matters as open to faultless disagreement too. We might say, for example, that we should respect other people's different moral opinions and accordingly that we shouldn't try to change or otherwise influence them. But if that's right, then it suggests that ethics and politics are like aesthetics, in that they essentially involve subjective preferences.

We saw one way of making sense of this kind of view about ethics specifically in Chapter 13 where we considered moral expressivism. Recall that on this proposal there is no ethical knowledge because there are no facts to know – moral judgements instead just express one's personal preferences rather than stating facts. One could imagine a similar sort of position being applied to the political case. If that's right, then there really is no fundamental difference between aesthetics and domains like ethics and politics. If so, then we shouldn't worry about disagreement in these domains any more than we worry about them in aesthetics. In particular, there is no knowledge for disagreement to defeat.

Note, however, that this is a very radical position to draw in the case of ethics and politics. We certainly do believe in ethical and political progress, after all. Weren't the great civil rights movements of the twentieth century an indication of progress of this kind? Relatedly, we also think that some moral and political opinions are clearly wrong. We might be tolerant of certain kinds of difference of moral and political opinion, but it has limits. We don't, for example, think that fascism should be tolerated in public political debate (indeed, in many democratic countries it's illegal for there to be parties that stand on this kind of political platform). We also believe that there are moral and political experts, people who we can learn from. That's simply not possible if there are no facts in that domain to be known.

PEER DISAGREEMENT

Henceforth, let's put this issue to one side and focus on disagreements where there clearly is a fact of the matter that one is disagreeing about. One particular kind of disagreement that is of special interest to epistemologists is that of **peer disagreement**. This is a variety of disagreement that takes place between two agents who are *epistemic peers* – that is, people who have roughly the same levels of intelligence and are in possession of roughly the same evidence with regard to the issue at hand. Peer disagreement is an interesting case of disagreement because it's clearly not a form of disagreement that can be put down to one party being epistemically superior to the other (at least with respect this subject matter), as was the case, for example, in the scenario above involving the disagreement between the medical expert and the layperson about a medical issue.

Here is a familiar example of peer disagreement. You and a friend are at a restaurant and when the bill comes, you each calculate your share. Oddly, though, you come to different conclusions. This is thus an issue where you and the other party are roughly equally positioned to get a correct answer, but are disagreeing about what that correct answer should be. How should one respond to a peer disagreement of this kind?

One common response is that peer disagreement always defeats your knowledge, at least temporarily. That is, in response to such a disagreement you are rationally required to no longer think that you have knowledge of the issue in hand. Returning to our toy example, this would mean that while you would ordinarily think that you knew what your share of the bill would be, when faced with the defeater posed by this peer disagreement you should no longer think that you have this knowledge. Of course, you may subsequently discover some further evidence that will show that you were right all along – such as that your friend miscalculated – at which point you can return to treating yourself as having knowledge again (as the defeater is now defeated), but the point is that until that happens your knowledge is lost. This way of thinking about the epistemology of peer disagreement is sometimes called **conciliationism**, as you are effectively taking a conciliatory position with regard to your disputant by downgrading your confidence in the matter at hand.

One of the main motivations for conciliationism is that if you don't downgrade your confidence in this way, then that would seem to be a sign of *dogmatism* (i.e. a stubborn commitment to your own opinions, regardless of the reasons you have in support of these opinions). After all, on what basis could you hold that you are right and that your friend is wrong in such a scenario? It's not as if you have any reason to think that you are better positioned to know the fact in question than your friend is, as by hypothesis no party is better positioned than the other. Accordingly, the only reason for sticking to your judgement seems to be a blind commitment to your own opinions simply because they are *your* opinions, and that looks like dogmatism.

Conciliationism is not without its problems, however. One particular concern with this view is that it seems potentially self-refuting. This is because, as we'll see in a moment, epistemologists disagree about whether conciliationism is true. But isn't epistemological disagreement of this kind a form of peer disagreement? The disputing epistemologists might well be equally well-trained in philosophy and equally familiar with the details of the issue in hand. If that's right, however, then it seems that the conciliationist is obliged to downgrade their confidence in their own position, and hence no longer treat themselves as having knowledge of their own position! Moreover, while one can normally regain one's knowledge on this view by acquiring further evidence about the matter in hand (such as evidence that one's friend miscalculated the bill), it's not clear how this would work when it comes to an epistemological disagreement about conciliationism. What kind of evidence would come to light that would favour one's own commitment to conciliationism over one's adversary's opposition? It's not as if it's likely that those who reject conciliationism have made an obvious mistake (as might become apparent with regard to the calculation of the bill). It thus seems that when conciliationism is consistently applied, then it undermines itself, as it means that the inevitable philosophical disagreement about the status of conciliationism entails one is not then in a position to know that conciliationism is true.

● PEER DISAGREEMENT AND DOGMATISM

If one doesn't opt for conciliationism as a response to peer disagreement, then what is the alternative? We just noted that one core motivation for conciliationism is that it avoids the charge of dogmatism. Given the problem just noted with conciliationism, however, let's look a bit more at this motivation. Remember that conciliationism is insisting that we should *always* be conciliatory in the face of peer disagreement, and hence that we should always treat peer disagreement as a defeater of our knowledge. That it would be dogmatic to not be conciliatory certainly looks plausible in cases of peer disagreement like the split bill at the restaurant that we considered earlier. But if conciliationism is correct, then it should be dogmatic to not be conciliatory in *all* cases of peer disagreement. Is that plausible?

In order to see why it might not be, consider a different kind of peer disagreement where one has reflected on the matter in hand and come to a considered judgement about it. That's very different from the restaurant case, where one has simply formulated an answer to a new question for the first time. So, for example, imagine that one is an accountant, and one has carefully calculated a final tax figure for a client, a calculation that has been properly checked over. Now imagine that another accountant at your firm tells you that they have also been working on this client's account, and have come up with a different final tax figure. Finally, since this is a case of peer disagreement, we need to stipulate that you regard the other account-ant as roughly equally as competent as you are at their job, and that you've no reason to believe that they have been any less diligent as you've been in reaching this figure. How should one respond?

According to conciliationism, one is required to treat this case of peer disagreement as a defeater for one's knowledge, just like in the restaurant scenario. Notice, how-ever, that this case is rather different. Whereas in the restaurant case one quickly came up with that result, in this scenario the result in question has been arrived at very carefully indeed. Would it really be dogmatic in this case to stick to one's judgement?

A further point we need to make here is that sticking to one's judgement needn't mean that one is closed-minded, which is how dogmatism is usually understood. That is, in sticking to one's judgement, one could still be very interested in listening to how the other accountant arrived at their different figure, and in trying to work out how two equally competent and diligent accountants arrived at different results. Relatedly, in engaging with the other accountant in this way, you might well become convinced that you've made a mistake and hence change your mind. Sticking to one's judgement in the immediate aftermath of a peer disagreement doesn't pre-clude any of this. All it means is that one is satisfied that one has gained one's belief in this regard entirely properly, and hence that one is unwilling to simply abandon it just because there is now some dispute over its correctness.

This is a good juncture to return to the intellectual virtues that we encountered in Chapter 6 when we looked at virtue epistemology. Recall that we distinguished there between (mere) *cognitive abilities* and *epistemic virtues*, where the latter are also known as *intellectual virtues*. Cognitive abilities are simply skill-like traits that enable us to reliably form true beliefs. Some of these are innate, in the sense that they are naturally acquired as we biologically mature, in which case they are cogni-tive faculties. Think, for example, of how our innate memorial or perceptual skills enable us to regularly form true beliefs in the right kinds of environmental condi-tions. Some cognitive abilities, in contrast, are not innate but rather acquired via training. One might be trained to be able to differentiate between certain kinds of plants, for example, and in the process develop a more refined cognitive ability that draws on one's innate perceptual and memorial faculties. Or think, for example, of how one acquired one's arithmetical skills by learning them at school.

Intellectual virtues are also a kind of cognitive ability that one acquires through training, although they are of a particularly demanding type. Indeed, one needs to constantly cultivate one's intellectual virtues if one is to retain them, since other-wise they are easily lost. Intellectual virtues also involve a distinctive motivational state, in that to genuinely manifest an intellectual virtue one must actually desire the truth. In contrast, one doesn't need to care about the truth in order to manifest most cognitive abilities. For example, when you open your eyes in the morning, you come to know lots of facts about your environment, whether you desire the truth or are indifferent to it. These features of the intellectual virtues are central to why they are thought to be particularly admirable character traits to have.

Consider the intellectual virtue of being *intellectually conscientious*. The intellectually conscientious person is someone who appropriately attends to the evidence available to them in forming a judgement, often seeking out additional evidence when they realise that they have an insufficient evidential basis to form a view. The intellectually conscientious person doesn't simply rush to judgement, or believe what they want to believe, but is rather guided by the evidence available to them. This reflects the fact that they care about the truth, and so want to form the right judgement. Hence, it is important to them to attend to the evidence, since evidence is by its nature a guide to the truth. Notice too that no one is born intellectually conscientious. One must rather have this trait instilled in one, perhaps by one's parents or one's teachers. Moreover, unless one cultivates this trait in oneself, then it is easily lost, as one will end up taking the easier path of succumbing to wishful thinking and making snap judgements.

Or consider another intellectual virtue, that of being *observant*. Being observant is not the same as merely having reliable perceptual abilities (where the latter could well be an innate cognitive faculty). To take an extreme case, consider the contrast between Sherlock Holmes and his sidekick Watson. They both might perceive the same murder scene – i.e. their perceptual faculties are both working equally well. But Holmes will observe so much more about this scene than Watson does, and this will enable him to draw conclusions that are simply unavailable to Watson. Like the intellectual virtue of intellectual conscientiousness, being observant is not something that you are born with, or else Watson would be just as observant as Holmes. Rather, Holmes had to train his observational capacities to make them function in this way, and he needs to cultivate them in order to be sure that he retains them. Moreover, this intellectual virtue arises out of his desire for the truth. Holmes cares about the truth, and this is manifested in his observant take on the perceptual scene before him.

The significance of this discussion for our purposes is that dogmatism is usually thought of as an *intellectual vice* – i.e. the very opposite of an intellectual virtue. That is, while the intellectual virtues are acquired (and admirable) cognitive abilities that involve a desire for the truth, intellectual vices are acquired (and disreputable, rather than admirable) traits that manifest a lack of cognitive ability and/or a failure to care for the truth. For example, instead of having the intellectual virtue of being observant, one might have the intellectual vice of being *unobservant*, where one is simply incurious about aspects of one's environment that one ought to find significant. Similarly, dogmatism looks like a disreputable cognitive trait to have, the very opposite of intellectual virtue in this respect. In particular, dogmatism looks like the absence of the intellectual virtue of being *intellectually humble*. This is the admirable character trait of (amongst other things) being willing to listen to other people's viewpoints (and change one's mind if necessary) and generally being aware of one's own fallibility.

The key question for us is thus whether intellectual humility, as the intellectual virtue opposed to the intellectual vice of dogmatism, would insist that you should *always* adopt a conciliatory stance in response to peer disagreement. It's actually not clear that it does. For while adopting that stance seems generally appropriate in such cases, it's not obvious why it should be required in the specific kind of peer disagreement where the dispute is over your considered judgement (i.e. where you have reflected on the matter in hand, as in the tax calculation scenario described above). Since it is your considered judgement, it seems rather premature to downgrade your confidence in this regard at the first sign that an epistemic peer disagrees with you. Imagine, for example, that you respond to the tax calculation disagreement not by treating yourself as lacking knowledge but rather by simply engaging with your adversary and trying to find out more about how they calculated their different figure. Why wouldn't this suffice to show that you are not being dogmatic? You are willing to listen to another person's viewpoint, after all, and if it turns out that they say something convincing in support of their viewpoint, then you will change your mind, so it is not as if you're being closed-minded. The crux of the matter is that it seems that you can display the intellectual virtue of being intellectually humble without having to always take the conciliatory stance in response to peer disagreement.

This would thus be one way of motivating a response to peer disagreement that is importantly different to conciliationism. Whereas conciliationism claims that one should always treat peer disagreement as knowledge-undermining, this proposal maintains instead that this needn't always be the case. In particular, so long as the matter concerns one's considered judgement, and provided one goes about it in the right kind of way, then one can legitimately 'stick to one's guns' without thereby being dogmatic. As we've seen, a person who has the intellectual virtue of being intellectually humble – and hence who lacks the corresponding intellectual vice of being dogmatic – might respond to an epistemic peer disagreement about a considered judgement in just this fashion.

EXPERT DISAGREEMENT

A final issue that we will consider is what to do when the experts disagree. We've already noted that one should in general defer to experts when they disagree with you (about issues on which they are expert at least), as of course they know more about the topic in hand than you do. If you know nothing about medicine, then it would be bizarre to prefer your medical judgement over that offered by your doctor! This result shouldn't be surprising, as in general one should defer to experts over matters that fall within their field of expertise, as that's just what being an expert means – they know more about the subject matter at hand than do the non-experts. It's no wonder, then, that such deference should also extend to cases where the expert disagrees with you.

Generally deferring to the experts works well when the experts agree, as they usually do. But sometimes, of course, the experts disagree. What should one do then?

After all, if the experts disagree, then one cannot simply defer to the experts, as they are offering contradictory advice.

Some of these cases of expert disagreement are easier to deal with than others. To begin with, we need to recall our point from earlier that some topics allow for faultless disagreement. With that in mind, aesthetic expert disagreement is going to be very different from, say, scientific expert disagreement, as in the former case, but not the latter case, one can disagree about these matters without either party being at fault. Of course, as we noted earlier, this is one reason why one might be sceptical about whether there can be genuine experts regarding a subject matter like aesthetics. In any case, henceforth when we consider cases of expert disagreement, we will confine our attention to domains where there is a fact of the matter at issue, as is the case, for instance, in scientific disputes.

Experts and the COVID-19 Crisis

In 2020, a COVID-19 pandemic beset the whole world, leading to lockdowns in most countries, with heavy restrictions on travel and social interactions. Wholesale lockdowns of this kind bring with them extremely high costs, both of an economic and a personal nature. As regards the former, businesses close down for lack of trade, employees can no longer work and are dependent upon government support (which in turn increases state debt), and once vibrant markets become atrophied. The personal costs of lockdown, however, are even higher, with people unable to see their loved ones (in some cases unable to see them even on their death bed), sick people unable to get operations, children missing out on social interaction at a crucial stage in their development, and so on. What was especially interesting about this pandemic from an epistemological point of view was the role that experts, and would-be experts, played in this event. Although there was broad consensus among the experts about the seriousness of the pandemic, there was divergence among them about how best to deal with it. This meant that some countries had very different lockdown strategies (indeed, some countries hardly locked down at all). Relatedly, since the decision to lockdown a country is ultimately a political decision (the scientists merely advise the politicians what to do), there was divergence among politicians about how best to respond to the scientific conclusions being presented to them. Inevitably, there were also people who lacked the relevant expertise presenting themselves on social media as experts and giving advice, often in ways that were unhelpful to the ongoing public debate. The result of all these factors was that the public were often unsure who to trust, with many sceptical about the need for state interference in their day-to-day lives. Now that the lockdown is over, many countries are conducting inquiries about what happened, in order to better prepare for future crises of this kind. One key issue in this regard is to find improved ways to marshal expert opinion and communicate this to the public in a manner that sets it apart from the inevitable flurry of fake expert opinion.

A further point we need to remember when we discuss expert disagreement is that not everyone who presents themselves as an expert really is one. In this social media age, there are lots of people who present their opinions as expertise when in fact it is nothing of the kind. Clearly, however, if a non-expert who falsely presents themselves as an expert disagrees with an expert, then we should defer to the genuine expert. Relatedly, we should also remember that expertise is domain-specific. Accordingly, that someone is an expert in one domain doesn't mean that they are thereby an expert in a different domain. For example, that someone is a respected biologist means that their expertise in biology should be respected and given due epistemic weight. But if the biologist disagrees with a climate scientist about climate change, then only the latter is the expert with regard to the topic in hand. As a result, only the climate scientist is the expert in the relevant sense in this particular disagreement and hence they are the only expert that we should defer to in this regard.

Even with these points in mind, however, there clearly are genuine cases where *bona fide* experts within a factual domain disagree. So how should we, as non-experts, respond to these cases? There are two points to consider in this regard that can help one form a rational opinion in the light of this kind of expert disagreement.

The first is to be aware of the *scope* of the disagreement. Even though the experts in that domain are not in complete disagreement, it might nonetheless be the case that there is a broad consensus in play, with some experts adopting a stance that is an outlier relative to the other experts in that field. Clearly some of these experts are wrong, given that this is a factual matter that they are disagreeing about. Even so, science is not infallible – in fact, no discipline offers an infallible route to knowledge – and hence even first-rate scientists might end up forming different viewpoints about scientific questions. Put another way, that there is disagreement in this field needn't mean that there is something inherently problematic about this particular scientific domain (much less that science in general is inherently problematic), as there is no essential reason why well-conducted scientific inquiry should always lead to consensus. In any case, insofar as there is broad consensus in this regard, then one would be rational, as a non-expert, to defer to the consensus expert view over the non-consensus expert view.

The second point to bear in mind is the *depth* of the disagreement. This is often a tricky thing for a layperson to judge, so it can depend a great deal on the skill of the experts concerned to explain what really is at issue here. The crux of the matter is that even where the experts disagree, it could be that the disagreement is over details and not over broader issues. If that's right, then one can be rational in deferring to the experts over the main questions in that domain, even if one should remain agnostic about the details due to the expert disagreement.

We can illustrate both points by considering the contemporary debate about human-caused climate change. This is clearly a factual matter where some people such as climate scientists and those in related disciplines (geology, oceanography, meteorology, and so on) have genuine expertise to impart. There is clearly some expert disagreement in this domain. Notice, however, that there is also a broad consensus too, especially over the main points. For example, there is almost universal consensus that human-caused climate change is real. Indeed, where there is disagreement, it tends to be about details, such as the exact extent of the human-caused climate change, or the effectiveness of particular treatments of climate change. With these points in mind, the presence of expert disagreement doesn't prevent us from forming a rational viewpoint as a layperson about lots of core issues that might concern us, such as that human-caused climate change is real, that certain kinds of measures would be at least particularly effective at responding to this problem, and so on. Where we should be less confident in our opinions is where it comes to the detailed questions over which there is some dispute, such as which particular kind of measure would be the most effective at responding to specific aspects of climate change.

This is a good juncture to return to our discussion of conciliationism, since what is expert disagreement for us as non-experts is a case of peer disagreement for the experts themselves. Accordingly, if conciliationism were true, then the experts might be obliged to downgrade their confidence in their own expertise. As we have noted above, however, this seems too strong. In fact, it is not altogether surprising that there should be *some* expert disagreement even about a factual scientific matter like climate change. Moreover, since expert opinion is usually opinion that is formed in a careful and considered fashion, it seems that one could retain one's beliefs while nonetheless avoiding the charge of dogmatism by openly engaging with those other experts who disagree with you. Looking at actual cases of expert disagreement thus gives us further reasons to be suspicious of conciliationism.

● CHAPTER SUMMARY

- Our topic is the social dynamics of knowledge, an area of epistemology known as *social epistemology*. We explored one core topic in social epistemology, which is the epistemology of disagreement. This is concerned with how the presence of disagreements can have implications for what we know.
- One way in which the presence of disagreements can have implications for what we know is when our awareness that a (seemingly) reasonable person disagrees with us about something that we believe can lead us to no longer have this belief. Another way that disagreement can undermine our knowledge is by being a *defeater*. A defeater is a consideration that prevents you from having knowledge either by indicating that your reasons for your belief don't sufficiently support the truth of that belief or else by providing you with independent reasons for thinking that the belief is false.
- Not every disagreement is a defeater for our knowledge. For example, that someone who is clearly less knowledgeable about the topic at hand disagrees with us is not a reason to be less confident about what we believe. We also noted that some topics seem to allow for *faultless disagreement*, in the sense that both parties to the disagreement can legitimately stick to their positions. Domains where faultless disagreement seems plausible tend to involve expressions of taste or preference, such as aesthetics. In contrast, where a topic is concerned with a factual

matter concerning the world, such as a scientific domain, it seems that one of the disagreeing parties must be in the wrong. We noted that domains where faultless disagreement is allowed might be thought to be such that there is ultimately no fact of the matter to disagree about (and hence nothing to know either, much less be an expert about).

- One particularly interesting kind of disagreement from an epistemological point of view is *peer disagreement*. This is a variety of disagreement that takes place between two agents who are *epistemic peers* – that is, people who have roughly the same levels of intelligence and are in possession of roughly the same evidence with regard to the issue at hand.
- On the face of it, you are obliged to treat peer disagreement as a defeater for your knowledge. To do otherwise seems to be dogmatic in that it appears you are privileging your own opinion over your adversary's opposing viewpoint simply because it is your opinion.
- The view that one should always treat peer disagreement as a defeater for one's knowledge is called *conciliationism*, in that it entails adopting a conciliatory stance with regard to one's adversary. While this proposal avoids the charge of dogmatism, it does face a severe difficulty in that it appears to be self-undermining. This is because there is also peer disagreement among philosophers about whether conciliationism is true, and hence a consistent proponent of conciliationism shouldn't regard themselves as having knowledge of this proposal.
- An alternative to conciliationism is to argue that we are not always obliged to treat peer disagreement as a defeater. In particular, so long as the issue in hand is one that we have given proper thought and attention to, then one can legitimately retain one's conviction even in the presence of peer disagreement. We noted that this stance needn't lead to the intellectual vice of dogmatism. This is because the opposing intellectual virtue of intellectual humility is compatible with sticking to one's opinions in the right conditions. What is important to intellectual humility is that one is willing to openly engage with those who disagree with you, and be willing to change your mind if the evidence demands it. But one can do that while sticking to one's opinions.
- Finally, we looked at the topic of expert disagreement, which is what to do when the experts disagree. This is a problem because it is generally rational to defer to the experts, but if the experts disagree, then it isn't clear what such deferral would involve. We noted that it is important to expert disagreement that the subject matter is not one where there is faultless disagreement, and also that the experts who are disagreeing really are experts about that specific domain.
- Two further points that are relevant to expert disagreement are the scope and depth of the disagreement. As regards scope, if there is broad consensus among the experts, with only a minority disagreeing, then that is a reason to defer to the consensus expert opinion. As regards depth, if the experts tend to be in agreement about core claims, and only in dispute about the details, then this is a reason to defer to them about the core claims at least. We illustrated both points by considering the kind of expert disagreement that we find in climate change science.

● STUDY QUESTIONS

1 How might being aware that there is a disagreement about something that you believe lead you to stop believing it? Try to think of a concrete example for illustration.

2 What is a defeater? Give some examples that are independent of the problem of disagreement. How might the fact that there is a disagreement act as a defeater for your knowledge?

3 What is a faultless disagreement? Why might certain domains, like aesthetics, be compatible with faultless disagreements? Would this entail that such domains are not concerned with a genuine fact of the matter, such that there is ultimately nothing to know in these domains? If so, would that mean that, for example, there cannot be aesthetic experts?

4 What is a peer disagreement? (Make sure that you carefully explain what is involved in the notion of an epistemic peer.) Why are peer disagreements such plausible cases in which disagreement constitutes a defeater for our knowledge?

5 What is conciliationism? What are the main motivations for conciliationism?

6 Why might conciliationism be self-undermining?

7 How might one respond to a peer disagreement in a non-conciliatory fashion without thereby being dogmatic? How might the intellectual virtues be relevant in this respect? Why might it matter that the topic at hand is one that one has properly considered rather than something that one has formed a snap judgement about?

8 Why should we generally defer to experts? What is expert disagreement? Why does expert disagreement make such deferrals problematic?

9 Why does it matter to expert disagreement what the *scope* and *depth* of the expert disagreement is? Try to explain what is meant by both of these terms with reference to the kind of expert disagreement we find in climate change science.

● INTRODUCTORY FURTHER READING

Frances, Bryan (2010) 'Disagreement', *Routledge Companion to Epistemology*, S. Bernecker & D. H. Pritchard (eds), Ch. 7, pp. 68–74 (London: Routledge). A helpful overview of the contemporary debate about the epistemology of disagreement. See also this author's *Stanford Encyclopaedia of Philosophy* entry listed below.

Kusch, Martin (2010) 'Social Epistemology', *Routledge Companion to Epistemology*, S. Bernecker & D. H. Pritchard (eds), Ch. 77, pp. 873–84 (London: Routledge). Offers a distinctive account of social epistemology, reflecting the author's own specific (and highly interesting) take on these issues.

● ADVANCED FURTHER READING

Alfano, Mark, Klein, Colin & de Ridder, Jeroen (eds) (2022) *Social Virtue Epistemology* (London: Routledge). A very recent anthology of papers that explores the main topics of social epistemology through the lens of virtue epistemology.

Christensen, David & Lackey, Jennifer (eds) (2013) *The Epistemology of Disagreement: New Essays* (Oxford: Oxford University Press). An important recent collection that brings together many of the leading contemporary figures working on the epistemology of disagreement.

Pritchard, Duncan (2021) 'Intellectual Humility and the Epistemology of Disagreement', *Synthese*, 98, 1711–23. A recent discussion of how the intellectual virtues (and vices) are relevant to the epistemology of disagreement.

● FREE INTERNET RESOURCES

Frances, Bryan (2018) 'Disagreement', *Stanford Encyclopaedia of Philosophy*, https://plato.stanford.edu/entries/disagreement/. An encyclopedic discussion of the contemporary epistemology of disagreement.

Goldman, Alvin & O'Connor, Cailin (2019) 'Social Epistemology', *Stanford Encyclopaedia of Philosophy*, https://plato.stanford.edu/entries/epistemology-social/. A comprehensive overview of the subject, written by two leading figures working in the field.

15

ignorance and epistemic injustice

- Introduction
- Traditional views of ignorance
- Ignorance as a normative standing
- Vice epistemology
- Hermeneutical and epistemic injustice
- Ignorance and epistemic injustice

INTRODUCTION

Ignorance is clearly an important topic to epistemology. Whereas much of epistemology is focussed on *positive* epistemic standings, like knowledge, and how one might go about acquiring them, we can also ask about *negative* epistemic standings and how one might go about avoiding them. This is where ignorance comes into the picture, as this is the core negative epistemic standing that we want to avoid. Accordingly, understanding the nature of ignorance ought to be as important to us as understanding positive epistemic standings like knowledge. For just as an understanding of what knowledge is can help us to acquire it, so an understanding of what ignorance is can help us to avoid it.

While ignorance is undoubtedly of epistemological importance, one might nonetheless think that there is nothing essentially social about this notion. Accordingly, why are we discussing this in the part of the textbook devoted to the social dynamics of knowledge? It is certainly true that on traditional conceptions of ignorance, this notion is not essentially social in nature, but as we will see such asocial accounts of ignorance are inherently problematic. Moreover, once we start to conceive of ignorance along social lines, then this topic connects to two important concerns of contemporary social epistemology: vice epistemology and epistemic injustice.

DOI: 10.4324/9781003356110-19

• TRADITIONAL VIEWS OF IGNORANCE

The most common conception of ignorance in the literature is that it is simply a lack of knowledge. Such a view has the benefit of simplicity. It also fits neatly with a lot of our ways of talking about ignorance, where we use lack of knowledge and ignorance as interchangeable ways of describing people in lots of contexts. If this is the right way to think about ignorance, then it would also explain why there has tended to be relatively little discussion of the notion of ignorance by epistemologists. For if ignorance is just the absence of knowledge, then in understanding knowledge we thereby understand ignorance – there is thus no need for a separate account of ignorance over and above an account of knowledge.

Thinking about ignorance in this way is not without its problems, however. Think, for example, about the Gettier-style cases where the subject has a justified true belief and yet fails to have knowledge due to the presence of knowledge-undermining epistemic luck. Would we really want to say that the subject in this case is ignorant? Consider, for example, the 'sheep' case that we noted in Chapter 3. The farmer sees what looks like a sheep in the field, and so forms the belief that there is a sheep in the field. Unfortunately, what she is looking at is in fact a shaggy dog. Nonetheless, her belief is true regardless since hidden from view behind the shaggy dog is a gen-uine sheep. The farmer's belief is thus both true and justified, but not knowledge as it's just a matter of luck that her belief is true. Still, even though knowledge is lacking in this case, it's not obvious that our farmer is ignorant about whether there is a sheep in the field. After all, she truly and justifiably believes this proposition.

I think part of the explanation for our hesitation to ascribe ignorance in this case is that we naturally think of ignorance as reflecting a kind of failure of intellectual character. That is, we not only talk of people being ignorant with regard to par-ticular propositions that they fail to know but also talk of them as being *ignorant people*, where the latter is a judgement about their intellectual characters. We can express this distinction as being between *propositional ignorance* and *character igno-rance*. Clearly these two notions are not the same. That one is ignorant of a particular proposition needn't entail that one is character ignorant. Similarly, that one is char-acter ignorant needn't entail that one is ignorant of a particular proposition. Still, it seems there ought to be some correlation between these two notions. Indeed, isn't the notion of character ignorance the more fundamental notion here, in that we primarily ascribe ignorance to a person as a whole rather than to their relationship to specific propositions?

If that's right, then one ought to expect there to be some general sense in which propositional ignorance is related to character ignorance. For example, one natural way that this might go is that propositional ignorance is the kind of thing that some-one who is character ignorant is disposed to display. The problem, however, is that this kind of link between character ignorance and propositional ignorance seems to be incompatible with treating Gettier-style case as instances of ignorance. This is because the subject in a Gettier-style case is not displaying character ignorance at all, but rather believing exactly as they ought to, given the circumstances. This is why their belief is justified. Accordingly, this would explain why we might be reluctant to ascribe ignorance to subjects in Gettier-style cases, in that while they lack knowledge, this isn't because they are displaying character ignorance. As a result, if one wishes to hold that propositional ignorance is just lack of knowledge, then one is obliged to think that propositional ignorance can come quite radically apart from character ignorance, in that someone who is exhibiting no intellectual failings of character at all can nonetheless be propositionally ignorant.

Some commentators argue that the problems with the ignorance as lack of knowledge view go much further, in that it is never correct to treat a true belief as ignorance, regardless of how that belief is acquired. Ignorance on this proposal is thus a lack of a true belief. Accordingly, on this account of ignorance, even a completely unjustified true belief (such as a lucky guess) is not an instance of ignorance, even though it obviously is a case when the subject lacks knowledge. There is some intuitive support for this position, in that it does at least seem odd to ascribe ignorance to someone who truly believes the proposition in question. For example, suppose that someone on a gameshow guesses an answer to a question concerning the capital of Bulgaria, thereby coming to believe that it is the correct answer to the question, and ends up getting the answer right (Sofia). This is obviously not knowledge. But would we want to say that the person is *ignorant* of the answer to the question, given that they truly believe it? This isn't so clear.

If ignorance is not a lack of knowledge but rather simply a lack of true belief, then that would certainly explain why we are ambivalent about ascribing ignorance in Gettier-style cases. It would also explain why we feel somewhat conflicted about describing even an unjustified true belief as ignorance. This does seem like a highly permissive account of ignorance, however, as on this view, it takes very little to avoid a charge of ignorance – one just needs a true belief in the target proposition, regardless of the epistemic pedigree of that belief. It thus faces the opposite problem to that we saw for the lack of knowledge conception of ignorance. While on that proposal, one could form one's belief in an entirely appropriate way and yet count as ignorant, on the lack of true belief account one can form one's beliefs in an entirely inappropriate way and yet not count as ignorant. It thus seems that on either view the intuitively close connection between propositional and character ignorance is lost.

• IGNORANCE AS A NORMATIVE STANDING

What unites the two traditional views of ignorance that we have just looked at, whereby ignorance is defined in terms of lack of knowledge or true belief, is that they both hold that ignorance is nothing more than the absence of a positive epistemic standing. As we saw, one problem that both views face (albeit in different forms) is that they struggle to offer a plausible conception of how propositional ignorance is related to character ignorance. With this point in mind, one way of approaching the topic of understanding ignorance is to argue that there is more to ignorance than simply the lack of a positive epistemic standing, in that it also involves an intellectual failing on the part of the subject. So, for example, a simple version of this view might hold that ignorance involves a lack of knowledge which is due to an intellectual failing on the part of the subject.

Notice that this would immediately deal with Gettier-style cases, as they would no longer be cases of ignorance on this view, given that the subjects concerned do not exhibit any intellectual failing (as their lack of knowledge is entirely down to luck). We'd also now get a close connection between propositional and character ignorance. To call a person ignorant (character ignorance) is to claim that their intellectual character is deficient in some way. For example, that they are intellectually lazy, lacking in conscientiousness when dealing with evidence, incurious about topics about which they ought to have an interest, and so on. These are all kinds of intellectual failings. If character ignorance generates propositional ignorance, then it should be no surprise that propositional ignorance also involves an intellectual failing.

This kind of proposal also has a further advantage over traditional accounts of ignorance that treat ignorance as merely the absence of a positive epistemic standing. This is that there seem to be lots of kinds of cases where subjects lack knowledge or true belief but where we have no temptation to ascribe ignorance because the subject hasn't exhibited any intellectual failing. Consider, for example, the question of how many spoons there are in my kitchen cupboard. This is a question that I have never given any serious consideration, and so do not know the answer to, though I could easily find out this answer were I so inclined. Do I thereby count as ignorant in this regard? I don't think we would naturally say so. The crux of the matter is that when it comes to trivialities like this, one doesn't exhibit any intellectual failing in lacking knowledge of them. Indeed, it would be more likely that one would exhibit an intellectual failing in going to the trouble of knowing them, given that they are clearly not worth knowing.

This point is not confined to trivialities, since there are other kinds of case where a lack of knowledge doesn't seem to entail ignorance due to the fact that there is no intellectual failing involved. For example, we don't treat people as being ignorant of truths that there was no way for them to know. If your friends have gone to great lengths to keep your surprise birthday party under wraps, then while you don't know that it's going to happen, you aren't ignorant of it, as you have no way of knowing this. More generally, whether one counts as ignorant can depend to a large extent to whether one is in a position to know the target proposition. This is why, for instance, we don't tend to treat children as ignorant of complex claims that we would only expect adults to know.

This is where the social dimension to ignorance becomes most apparent, as what one is in a position to know can vary in terms of one's social position, as that can have a bearing on what one is in a position to know. The differential treatment of children and adults just noted is an instance of this, in that children are often not in a position to know some of the facts that adults are in a position to know. This is why it can be improper to charge them with ignorance even though an analogous charge to an adult would be appropriate. Or consider cases in which someone occupies a social role that involves specialist expertise. It can now be appropriate to charge that person with ignorance of truths where that wouldn't be appropriate for a layperson.

For example, if you are a consultant physician at a hospital, then you are expected to be abreast of recent developments in your field. If you fail to know these truths, then we would regard you as ignorant. But there is no such expectation for a layperson, which is why we wouldn't regard them as being ignorant of these sophisticated medical facts.

This way of thinking about ignorance is sometimes called the **normative account of ignorance**, in that it holds that ignorance involves, in addition to a lack of an epistemic standing, a further claim about how the subject has failed to satisfy a relevant norm. In particular, due to an intellectual failing on her part, she has failed know what she ought to have known, which is why her lack of knowledge amounts to ignorance. Crucially, however, what one ought to know can vary with one's social circumstances, as that can have a bearing on one's epistemic position in this regard.

• IGNORANCE AND VICE EPISTEMOLOGY

Since the normative account of ignorance allows for there to be a close connection between character and propositional ignorance, it can also make sense of ignorance in terms of intellectual vice. This leads us to the topic of *vice epistemology*. Whereas virtue epistemology is concerned with the intellectual virtues that generate knowledge (and other positive epistemic standings), vice epistemology (a sub-branch of virtue epistemology) is concerned with the intellectual vices that prevent us from having knowledge (and other positive epistemic standings). One natural way of thinking about character ignorance is that it involves intellectual vice. That is, to have an ignorant character is to have the intellectual character traits associated with intellectual vice rather than intellectual virtue, such as being incurious, dogmatic, unconscientious, and so forth. Moreover, if propositional ignorance is the expected result of being character ignorant, as is suggested by the normative account of ignorance, then it is also directly related to intellectual vice. Given that propositional ignorance on this account involves an intellectual failing on the part of the subject (reflecting the fact that character ignorance leads to propositional ignorance), that link between ignorance and intellectual vice shouldn't be surprising.

Thinking of ignorance in terms of vice epistemology also enables us to recast many of the issues considered by vice epistemologists in terms of ignorance. For example, take conspiracy theorists, such as people who believe that the earth is really flat and that we are being tricked by governments and the media into thinking otherwise. It is often noted by vice epistemologists that this kind of reasoning tends to be the result of intellectual vices, as the people concerned believe what they want to believe, ignoring all the evidence for the contrary. It thus involves a kind of dogmatic refusal to engage with the mounting evidence that counts against one's cherished beliefs in the conspiracy.

We can also think of conspiracy theorists in terms of ignorance. It is not just that they fail to know important truths, such as that the earth is not flat, but that this lack of knowledge reveals an intellectual failing on their parts, as it is the result of intellectual vice. It thus amounts to ignorance. Moreover, as their propositional ignorance is rooted in their intellectual viceful character, we capture the sense in which it is a manifestation of their character ignorance. It is this character ignorance that makes them prone to be susceptible to conspiracy theories in the first place, and which leads them to be propositionally ignorant about such matters as whether the earth is flat.

Understanding how people succumb to conspiracy theories is important to determining how best to respond to this phenomenon. In particular, notice that it would be a mistake to think that conspiracy theorists simply fail to know certain key facts, as if we could easily enlighten them by making them aware of the missing information. The problem is rather much deeper, in that it is rooted in patterns of intellectually viceful thought. This is why dealing with conspiracy theorists requires one to focus on helping the agent concerned develop their intellectual character rather than simply giving them information in the hope that this will suffice to change their minds. It also explains the importance of educating people in general to develop their virtuous intellectual character so that they don't end up succumbing to conspiracy theories in the first place.

The (intellectual) vice squad

Following on from the resurgence of interest in virtue epistemology in contemporary epistemology, in recent years, there has been a new focus on understanding intellectual vice. This is sometimes called *vice epistemology* (with the epistemologists devoted to working on this topic sometimes informally called the 'vice squad'). Whereas virtue epistemology in general tends to focus on how individuals can develop the admirable character traits that make up the intellectual virtues, vice epistemology (which is a sub-field of virtue epistemology) focusses on those deplorable character traits that make up the intellectual vices. The reason for this concern with intellectual vice is that it can help us explain some interesting contemporary phenomena such as the proliferation of conspiracy theories, science-denial (e.g. when people are sceptical about climate change science or vaccine science), and politically motivated reasoning (e.g. when people are willing to believe obviously false or groundless claims so long as it suits their political perspective). These phenomena are not new, of course, but they have become more acute as social problems due to the contemporary prevalence of social media. What seems to be core to all of these problems is that the people involved are displaying intellectual vices, such as being closed-minded and dogmatic, failing to conscientiously attend to evidence, and so on. It is thus important to understand the nature of these intellectual vices, both in their own right and in terms of the contemporary social mechanisms that facilitate them (such as when social media are designed in ways that prompt us to only think about our own perspectives and ignore contrary perspectives).

• EPISTEMIC INJUSTICE

There is a further social epistemic question that relates to our current concerns, though how it connects to the topic of ignorance requires some teasing out. This is the notion of **epistemic injustice** as identified by the British philosopher Miranda Fricker (1966–) in her seminal book, *Epistemic Injustice: Power and the Ethics of Knowing*. Fricker draws on a tradition of feminist epistemology to argue that there are social dynamics in play that prevent agents from fully participating in social epistemic practices.

Fricker argues that epistemic injustice comes in two forms: **hermeneutical injustice** and **testimonial injustice**. Hermeneutical injustice is concerned with how the existing social structures in place can prevent someone from being able to properly identify their situation, thereby epistemically disadvantaging them. A common example that is used to illustrate this kind of injustice is sexual harassment. You might be surprised to learn that this is a relatively recent concept, having been developed in the 1970s. Accordingly, someone who lived prior to this time and experiences unwanted sexual advances in the workplace might struggle to give expression to what they are experiencing, which would put them at a disadvantage when it comes to finding solutions to their predicament.

Significantly, the reason why a concept like sexual harassment wasn't developed earlier was almost certainly due to the fact that women were under-represented in many professions, particularly the kinds of professions where a concept like this would gain common currency, such as law, politics, academia, the civil service, journalism, and so forth. An earlier injustice in terms of representation is thus leading to a further injustice in terms of how people understand, and thereby deal with, their oppressed situation.

While hermeneutical injustice is not a specifically epistemic notion, it does have important implications for epistemology, especially social epistemology, as Fricker points out. For if people lack the conceptual resources to properly interpret their experiences, then this undermines their ability to have knowledge of what their situation is, and thereby communicate the knowledge to others. Hermeneutical injustice thus leads to people being unfairly prevented by social structures from having knowledge that it would be very beneficial for them to have.

The second kind of injustice that Fricker identifies, and which is more directly epistemic in nature, is what she terms **testimonial injustice**. This is when the credibility of someone's testimony is downgraded as a result of prejudice. For example, consider how in the workplace the contributions made by women are routinely downgraded. This puts them at an epistemic disadvantage, in that their testimony is unfairly not accorded the same status as their male colleagues. Worse, if people tend to automatically downgrade the credibility of what you say, then this can have the effect of leading you to downgrade your own confidence in your views. This can lead in turn to you not asserting things with the confidence that you ought, thereby giving others a reason to further downgrade your credibility. One is thus in a vicious cycle, with the result that one is severely epistemically impoverished as a result.

Testimonial injustice is important to social epistemology in at least two ways. First, it shows how social mechanisms can result in people being unfairly prevented from being treated as knowers. Notice too that the mechanisms that underlie testimonial injustice will also tend to unfairly treat people as knowers when they don't deserve to be. For instance, a society that unfairly tends to treat women's testimony as being less credible than it should be is also likely to be such that it unfairly treats men's testimony as more being credible than it should be. Either way, the crux of the matter is that there are problematic social mechanisms that entail that the people who are treated as knowers aren't always the people who actually have knowledge (and *vice versa*).

The second way in which testimonial injustice is important to social epistemology is that it describes a social mechanism that can lead people to unfairly downgrade their own confidence in their opinions, such that they are less likely to regard themselves as knowers than they ought to. This can lead to people lacking beliefs in propositions that they are in an excellent position to know. In this way, testimonial injustice can lead to subjects lacking knowledge.

● EPISTEMIC INJUSTICE AND IGNORANCE

Let's now consider how this notion of epistemic injustice intersects with our discussion of ignorance, starting with hermeneutical injustice. Going back to our previous discussion of ignorance, one question we might ask is whether someone who is experiencing hermeneutical injustice, and so lacks knowledge because they lack the conceptual resources to properly identify their experiences, is thereby ignorant. According to the traditional accounts of ignorance, they would be ignorant, but I think that this conclusion sounds very odd. In particular, it seems to fail to capture the particular nature of the subject's situation, given that their lack of knowledge is the result of social structures (usually themselves a product of previous injustice) that are generating an unjust epistemic outcome for our subject. In contrast, the normative account of ignorance seems on stronger ground in this regard, as it can explain why such subjects are not ignorant, even despite their lack of knowledge. This is because their lack of knowledge is not due to an intellectual failing on their part, but rather the result of wider social structures. In fact, the victim of hermeneutical injustice may exhibit no intellectual failing at all in their lacking knowledge.

The same applies to testimonial injustice. We noted that testimonial injustice can lead to people lacking confidence in their opinions, and hence lacking knowledge of propositions that they are in an excellent position to know. As with a lack of knowledge that is due to hermeneutical injustice, however, it would be odd to regard this lack of knowledge as ignorance, even though this is precisely what would be predicted by traditional accounts of ignorance. Moreover, the natural explanation of why this is so is that this is not a lack of knowledge that is the result of the subject's intellectual failings but rather reflects unfair social structures.

Epistemic injustice is clearly something that we should aim to rid ourselves of. We don't just want to live in a just society but also a society that is *epistemically* just, where everyone's word has the epistemic credibility that it warrants. Fricker's own solution to this problem is to argue that we need to help people develop the intellectual virtues so that they can avoid falling into this predicament. That will certainly help, as the intellectually virtuous subject will be such that they will be alert to how prejudices can infect one's judgements. Note, however, that our characterisation of how epistemic injustice relates to ignorance highlights something interesting about how the intellectual virtues are relevant here. As we have noted above, intellectual virtue helps us to avoid having an ignorant, and thus viceful, intellectual character, which in turn helps us to avoid being propositionally ignorant. One way of avoiding propositional ignorance is thus to develop one's intellectual virtue. In the cases of epistemic injustice that we have looked at, however, the subject who lacks knowledge is not ignorant. It is thus not they who need to develop their intellectual virtue in order to fix this problem, but rather the people who are involved in the unjust social structures that lead to epistemic injustice, such as the people who unfairly downgrade someone's testimony because of prejudice.

Fricker's focus in her book was on epistemic injustice as it applies to gender, but clearly the diagnosis she offers generalises to any marginalised group. Think, for example, about how people from certain underrepresented racial groups might be systematically treated as lacking in epistemic credibility, or how working class people can often be automatically regarded as less intelligent. Often this results from the prejudicial stereotypes that inform our society and which generate this kind of unfair differential treatment. Fricker's innovation is to show that the kind of thinking that underlies this form of bias also has important epistemic ramifications. We thus have a way of explaining how such factors as race or class (to give just two examples) can have a bearing on how, epistemically speaking, we are treated, and thus on how kinds of epistemic injustice can arise. Moreover, by embedding the notion of epistemic injustice within a normative account of ignorance, we are able to show that the burden of resolving this problem lies not with the victims of epistemic injustice, but rather with the perpetrators. While everyone can benefit from developing their intellectual virtue, in terms of correcting epistemic injustice, it is the perpetrators of the unfair social structures in play who need to work on their intellectual virtues in order to resolve this issue and make society epistemically more just.

● CHAPTER SUMMARY

- According to traditional views of ignorance, ignorance is to be understood as simply the absence of a positive epistemic standing. For example, one popular view is that ignorance is lack of knowledge. One problem that faces understanding ignorance as lack of knowledge is the Gettier-style cases, as they don't seem to involve ignorance, even though they do concern a lack of knowledge
- An alternative proposal along the same lines to the view that ignorance is lack of knowledge is that ignorance is lack of true belief. This proposal doesn't face the difficulty posed by Gettier-style cases, as on this view the subject, since she has a

true belief, isn't ignorant. The proposal does face the different problem, however, of making it seemingly too easy to avoid a charge of ignorance. Any true belief, no matter how it was formed, and even if it was formed in an epistemically inappropriate way, would thereby not be a case of ignorance.

- It was suggested that what is missing from the traditional accounts of ignorance is the idea that ignorance involves a normative dimension, in the sense that one's lack of knowledge (say) is the result of an intellectual failing. This is the *normative account of ignorance*. For example, one straightforward version of this view is that ignorance is a lack of knowledge that is the result of one's intellectual failing. In short, one fails to know what one ought to have known.

- The normative account of ignorance can explain why the subjects in Gettier-style cases are not ignorant, as they have not exhibited any intellectual failing. Moreover, it can also explain why there are lots of other cases where subjects lack knowledge where we wouldn't treat them as ignorant. For example, that one doesn't know a trivial claim, such as concerning how many spoons are in one's cupboard, doesn't amount to ignorance, as there is no intellectual failing involved in not knowing such trivialities.

- The normative account of ignorance can account for the close relationship between *character ignorance* and *propositional ignorance*. Character ignorance is when we charge a person with being ignorant – i.e. we are saying that they have an ignorant character. Propositional ignorance is concerned with a person's ignorance of a particular proposition. While these are two distinct notions, there does seem to be a close relationship between them, in that someone who is character ignorant is disposed to be propositionally ignorant. On the normative account of ignorance, character ignorance involves the failings of intellectual character that are manifestations of intellectual vice (as opposed to intellectual virtue). That's why someone who is character ignorant will be disposed to be propositionally ignorant, as they will tend to fail to have knowledge as a result of intellectual failings.

- The normative account of ignorance explains the social dimension to ignorance. In particular, whether one has exhibited an intellectual failing in not having knowledge can depend on what one was in a position to know. This is why children are not treated as ignorant of claims that their parents might be treated as ignorant of. It also explains why we might treat someone who has specialised expertise as being ignorant of claims that they really should know, in their position, even though we wouldn't consider a layperson to be ignorant of those same claims.

- The normative account of ignorance can be integrated within a branch of virtue epistemology known as *vice epistemology*, which focusses on the intellectual vices rather than the intellectual virtues. For example, vice epistemologists are very interested in how conspiracy theorists exhibit intellectual vices, such as by being dogmatic, uninterested in evidence that doesn't fit their views, and so on. On the normative account of ignorance, the problem with such people isn't just that they lack knowledge, but rather the intellectually viceful way in which they lack knowledge. It is this that makes them ignorant. Understanding why they are ignorant is important to knowing how to respond to this problem. For example, one is unlikely to persuade a conspiracy theorist to change their mind by offering them evidence against their view; one rather needs to help them to change their viceful intellectual character.

- *Epistemic injustice* is concerned with the social dynamics that unjustly prevent agents from fully participating in social epistemic practices. Epistemic injustice comes in two forms: *hermeneutical injustice* and *testimonial injustice*. Hermeneutical injustice is concerned with how social structures can prevent someone from being able to properly identify their situation, thereby epistemically disadvantaging them.

- Testimonial injustice is when the credibility of someone's testimony is downgraded as a result of prejudice. This can lead to some people not being treated as knowers even though they have knowledge (conversely, some people who don't deserve to be treated as knowers will be treated as knowers). Even worse, since one is systemically not treated as a knower, one tends to downgrade one's own confidence in one's opinions, which means that one (improperly) doesn't treat oneself as a knower either.

- Epistemic injustice can be understood in terms of the normative account of ignorance. For while the victims of epistemic injustice often lack knowledge, this is not because they are ignorant, as it doesn't involve an intellectual failing on their part. Instead, the cause of this lack of knowledge are unfair social structures. Relatedly, while everyone can benefit from developing their intellectual character, the responsibility for eliminating epistemic injustice lies with those who perpetrate epistemic injustice rather than its victims, as it is their intellectual vice that is playing an important part in generating the epistemic injustice.

• STUDY QUESTIONS

1 Why might one hold that ignorance is simply the lack of knowledge? How do Gettier-style cases pose a challenge for such a proposal?

2 Why might one hold that ignorance is simply the lack of a true belief? What do you think is the main objection to this proposal?

3 What is the difference between character ignorance and propositional ignorance? How are these two notions related to one another?

4 What is the normative account of ignorance, and how does it differ from the traditional accounts of ignorance in terms of a lack of knowledge or true belief? How does such a proposal deal with Gettier-style cases? What other kinds of case where lack of knowledge (/true belief) doesn't amount to ignorance does it claim to be able to capture?

5 What does the normative account of ignorance say about the distinction between character ignorance and propositional ignorance?

6 What is vice epistemology? How are the intellectual vices displayed by conspiracy theorists? How might it help our understanding of conspiracy theorists to categorise their propositional ignorance as arising out of their character ignorance?

7 What is epistemic injustice? What are hermeneutical injustice and testimonial injustice and how are they both forms of epistemic injustice?

8 Give an example of either hermeneutical or testimonial injustice and explain how this leads to the subjects concerned lacking knowledge (or being unfairly treated as if they lack knowledge).

9 Why might we hold that when a person lacks knowledge due to epistemic injustice that this isn't a case of ignorance? How might the intellectual virtues be relevant to eliminating epistemic injustice?

• INTRODUCTORY FURTHER READING

Cassam, Quassim (2019) *Vices of the Mind: From the Intellectual to the Political* (Oxford: Oxford University Press). Cassam is one of the pioneers of vice epistemology, and in this book, he makes an accessible case for using it to understand some important contemporary political issues.

Tanesini, Alessandra (2010) 'Feminist Epistemology', *Routledge Companion to Epistemology*, S. Bernecker & D. H. Pritchard (eds), Ch. 78, pp. 885–95 (London: Routledge). A helpful overview of contemporary work on feminist epistemology, written by a leading epistemologist.

• ADVANCED FURTHER READING

Fricker, Miranda (2009) *Epistemic Injustice: Power and the Ethics of Knowing* (Oxford: Oxford University Press). A seminal book in epistemology making the case for epistemic injustice.

Medina, Jose (2012) *The Epistemology of Resistance: Gender and Racial Oppression, Epistemic Injustice, and Resistant Imaginations* (Oxford, Oxford University Press). An important recent work that extends the notion of epistemic justice beyond its use in debates about gender to other areas, particularly race.

Mills, Charles (2017) 'White Ignorance', *Black Rights/White Wrongs*, Ch. 4 (Oxford, Oxford University Press). A classic treatment of the topic; highly influential. Note that this paper is reprinted in several other volumes, if you're struggling to get hold of it.

Pritchard, Duncan (2021) 'Ignorance and Normativity', *Philosophical Topics*, 49, 225–43. This recent paper offers a defence of the normative account of ignorance.

• FREE INTERNET RESOURCES

Grasswick, Heidi (2018) 'Feminist Social Epistemology', *Stanford Encyclopaedia of Philosophy*, https://plato.stanford.edu/entries/feminist-social-epistemology/. An excellent overview of contemporary work on feminist epistemology that includes a section devoted to epistemic injustice.

Janack, Marianne (2017) 'Feminist Epistemology', *Internet Encyclopaedia of Philosophy*, www.iep.utm.edu/fem-epis/. A useful overview of contemporary work on feminist epistemology.

Part V

how can the theory of knowledge be applied to particular domains?

16

technology

- Our increasing dependence on technology
- Extended knowledge?
- Intellectual virtue and extended knowledge

OUR INCREASING DEPENDENCE ON TECHNOLOGY

So far in the book we have asked lots of questions about knowledge, such as what is its nature, whether it is of special value, what kinds of knowledge there are, and so on. In this part of the book, we will aim to apply what we have learnt in particular domains, and thereby see what we have learnt about knowledge applied to practical questions and issues. We will be particularly interested in how some of these practical implications overlap.

We will begin by looking at an increasingly prevalent feature of our lives, which is our dependence on technology. Right now many of you reading this book will have immediate access to a wealth of information that far exceeds what would have been immediately available to people only a generation ago (indeed, you may even be reading this book on a tablet or computer). In all likelihood, for example, you will have access to a smartphone on which you can look up the internet and thereby extract information from vast knowledge resources, such as Wikipedia. Your phone will also contain an abundance of information that is particularly useful to you, such as details of your contacts, a maps function that will locate familiar addresses for you at the drop of a hat, a diary function that will remind you of upcoming commitments, social media apps that keep you informed of what everyone you know is up to, and so on.

As our dependence on technology increases, so this impacts on our daily lives, including our cognitive lives. As I write this, I am in my late forties, which means I'm just old enough to remember a time when most people would have a dozen or so (landline) phone numbers in their memory (e.g. one's home phone number, friends' phone numbers, a few work numbers). Now, however, it would be odd for anyone to memorise phone numbers in this way (except perhaps one's main mobile phone number), as of course this information is readily available on one's phone (and in one's laptop, and so forth). There is thus a sense in which our dependence on technology means that we don't need to know as much as we used to, and hence we lose some knowledge we previously had.

DOI: 10.4324/9781003356110-21

The Shallows

A number of recent authors have argued that our contemporary dependence on technology is making us dumber. In a bestselling book entitled *The Shallows: What the Internet Is Doing to Our Brains*, for example, Nicholas Carr argues that our reliance on the internet is degrading our cognitive development. Other prominent authors have made similar claims, including Baroness Susan Greenfield, a prominent neuroscientist, in a subsequent book entitled *Mind Change: How Digital Technologies Are Leaving their Mark on our Brains*.

It's not just phone numbers either. For lots of basic tasks, if one gets stuck then one knows that one can simply 'Google' one's query and thereby likely get a good explanation of how to fix the problem, perhaps even in the form of a YouTube video showing one what to do. There are, of course, epistemic advantages to this. Just like the availability of phone numbers in one's mobile phone, it means that there is information readily accessible that can help us in our day-to-day lives. But doesn't our awareness that this information is readily accessible also mean that we have less incentive to know lots of things that we previously might have known? For example, my parents, like many of their generation, are able to attend to a whole range of practical tasks around the house that I wouldn't have a clue how to fix. But then they needed to know this information, since it wasn't readily available to them otherwise. I, on the other hand, don't especially need to know this information, since I know that I can always look up what I need, or else easily access someone who can fix the problem for me.

There is thus a sense in which our dependence on technology means that we might end up knowing less, rather than more, even if it also means that we have greater access to a wider range of information. Is our dependence on technology making us dumb? As we will see, this is a complex issue, since it relates to exactly how we think about the nature of knowledge acquisition when one is embedded in highly technological contexts.

One thing that is certain, however, is that our epistemic dependence on technology might have potentially disastrous consequences if that technology were ever suddenly taken away. Clearly we would not find it easy to function in a world without technology, where we couldn't simply Google the answers we need, or look up the maps function on our phone to find the way to go, etc. Moreover, our contemporary dependence on technology means that we are worse off in this regard than our forebears. Since they didn't have the technological advantages that we have, they would not be so afflicted by the loss of technology.

For now, however, let's put the issue of what would happen if the technology we use were unavailable to one side, and focus instead on the broader issue of whether our dependence on technology is making us dumber. (We will also be putting aside some of the political issues associated with our contemporary reliance on technology, such as the extent to which we are potentially more susceptible to misinformation. This is an issue that we will be returning to when we look at politics and knowledge in its own right in a subsequent chapter.)

• EXTENDED KNOWLEDGE?

One reason why it is not a straightforward matter whether our dependence on technology is making us dumber comes from an influential research programme in the cognitive sciences known as **extended cognition**. According to proponents of extended cognition, we shouldn't think that every use of technology is simply a matter of a cognitive subject making use of an instrument. Rather, in the right conditions, the technology that one employs can be a genuine part of one's cognition. (Indeed, some proponents of extended cognition think that cognitive extension can also be *social* rather than just technological, in that other people can form part of a joint cognitive process. This is often known as *socially distributed cognition*, though we will be setting this to one side here and focusing instead on the simpler case of technologically extended cognition.)

The idea that the technology that we use can be a genuine part of one's cognitive processes may initially be surprising, since one might naturally think that cognition is the sort of thing that happens 'under the skin', as it were, in our brains (and possibly also in our central nervous systems). But defenders of extended cognition argue that it is arbitrary to think that cognitive processes can only take place within the skin and skull of the subject. In particular, they claim that if an extended cognitive process – i.e. one that employs technology – functions in just the same way as a normal (i.e. non-extended) cognitive process, then it should be treated as a genuine cognitive process, even despite the use of technology. In short, if the only reason one can offer for saying that an extended cognitive process is not a genuine cognitive process is that it is extended (i.e. it uses technology), then we should treat it as a genuine cognitive process. After all, why should it matter whether the cognitive process takes place exclusively within the skin and skull of the subject? Note that if there is such a thing as extended cognition, then it seems that there will also be such a thing as **extended knowledge** – i.e. knowledge that has been acquired via an extended cognitive process.

Of course, everything hangs here on whether the extended cognitive process really is akin to a non-extended cognitive process. Certainly, when we ordinarily use technology as an instrument – e.g. when we use a calculator to work out a sum – the cognitive processes involved are very different to the corresponding non-extended cognitive process (e.g. working out the sum in one's head). For one thing, when one uses an instrument in this way, there is an intellectual distance between you and the answer that is absent when you work out the answer by yourself. In the latter case, it is *your* answer, but in the former case, you are rather accepting the answer given to you by the calculator – the calculator is a kind of insentient 'testifier' on whose 'testimony' one is willing to rely. Relatedly, when you work out the answer yourself you are aware of how the answer was arrived at, in a way that might well be hidden if you are using the calculator (depending on how complex the calculation was anyway).

But all this shows is that not all uses of technology are cases of extended cognition, something that exponents of extended cognition readily grant. What they will claim, however, is that there are some genuine cases of extended cognition where one's relationship to the technology in question is not merely one of subject and instrument. Moreover, they often supplement this claim with the further thesis that we are increasingly engaging in extended cognition as we become more and more embedded within technologically enabled environments.

Consider, for example, someone who permanently wears a lens covering one of their eyes that is constantly feeding them information about their environment as they move around. The information might be of a kind that is supplied by one's smartphone, for instance, such as details about the amenities in the vicinity, directions to the appointment that's coming up, notifications about emails, messages, news items, and social media, and so on. (This scenario isn't science fiction either, as such lenses have already been developed by tech companies, though at the time of writing they are not yet commercially available.) One could imagine a subject, over time, becoming so au fait with the employment of this technology that it becomes a seamless part of their cognitive lives. That is, sometimes they are exclusively using their biological cognitive resources, sometimes they are exclusively using their non-biological extended cognitive resources, and sometimes they are using a mixture of both. Crucially, however, from the subject's point of view, it may not be obvious to them which cognitive resource they are relying on at any one time. That's not to say that they couldn't work this out if they wanted to. The point is just that, in the moment, they notice no difference between using the extended (or mixed) cognitive processes and using the non-extended cognitive processes. If this were to occur, then this is what the proponents of extended cognition would regard as a genuine case of extended cognition. Accordingly, it would also potentially be a route to extended knowledge.

The reason why this issue is important to our discussion of whether technology is making us dumber is that if extended cognition is a bona fide phenomenon, then there is a sense in which the technology constitutes a kind of *cognitive augmentation*. That is, far from it making us dumber, it is in fact dramatically enhancing our

Neuromedia

We have just looked at the putative phenomenon of extended cognition. **Neuromedia** is a special case of extended cognition that is particularly interesting. Whereas extended cognition is usually described as a cognitive process that employs technology that is outside of the skin and skull of the subject, neuromedia is a particular kind of extended cognition where the technological cognitive enhancement takes place *within* the skin and skull of the subject. Imagine, for example, that one is able to insert technology directly into the subject's brain and central nervous system to enable them to do cognitive tasks that they couldn't otherwise do with their natural cognitive resources (e.g. they can tell the time, track the temperature, have access to maps for navigation). Just like extended cognition, one could imagine that this cognitive augmentation becomes seamlessly integrated over time such that the subject is not even aware of when they are using their biological cognitive resources (their memory, say), or whether they are instead using the non-biological cognitive augmentation. Neuromedia is thus a kind of extended cognition where the extended cognition is in a sense 'internal' to the agent, albeit where there is still a technological (and thus in this sense 'external') cognitive augmentation of the agent taking place.

cognitive capacities. Whereas before we were limited in our cognitive tasks by the constraints of our biology, now we have the means to radically supplement our cognitive capacities by integrating this new technology into our cognitive lives.

INTELLECTUAL VIRTUE AND EXTENDED KNOWLEDGE

Even if extended cognition, and thus extended knowledge, is a real phenomenon, such that our dependence on technology can potentially, at least in a range of cases anyway, be regarded as a genuine extension of our cognitive powers, the point still remains that we are nonetheless now epistemically dependent on technology. In particular, were we to lose the technology, then we would lose a lot of our cognitive powers that depend upon that technology. If there were some sort of global catastrophe tomorrow, for example, such that there was no longer any electrical power available to support our technological devices, then of course we would be very much adrift. Lots of useful skills and knowledge that we might have hitherto developed and retained had we not had access to technology would be unavailable to us, just as we needed them most.

Note that this needn't be a point against ever relying on technology. Rather, it seems to instead count against the idea of being *completely* reliant on technology. The wise person will instead be wary of being too reliant on technology, and will also want to ensure that some fundamental skills and knowledge are retained. Relatedly, the wise person will also be wary of incorporating too many extended cognitive processes in their lives, as that can also lead to an over-reliance on technology.

This is a good juncture to reconsider the notion of an intellectual virtue that we have previously encountered (e.g. in Chapters 6 and 14). Recall that the intellectual virtues are a distinctive kind of cognitive ability that has a number of important properties, such as being motivated by a desire for the truth. The intellectual virtues are admirable character traits that are acquired and cultivated thought training and are thought to be an essential component, along with the other virtues (such as the moral virtues), of a good life of human flourishing (what the ancient Greeks called *eudemonia*). Very roughly, the good life, from a human perspective, is held to be a virtuous life. If that's right, then the virtues, including the intellectual virtues, have a special kind of value. (Going back to our discussion from Chapter 2, we can say that the ancient Greeks thought that the virtues were *non-instrumentally* valuable.) Examples of the intellectual virtues include intellectual humility, conscientiousness, and intellectual tenacity.

The crucial point for our current purposes is that while intellectual virtues are a type of cognitive ability, they are much more sophisticated than many of our other cognitive abilities. They require effort and motivation, for example. Relatedly, they are not the kind of trait that one can acquire and manifest passively as some other cognitive abilities can be (e.g. one's perceptual abilities), as one must consciously acquire them via training and then cultivate them thereafter. Their manifestation also essentially involves reflection, just as the intellectually conscientious person reflects on the available evidence, or the observant person reflects on what is significant about what they are looking at. The reason why all this is important for our purposes is that while we can make sense of offloading a lot of cognitive abilities either partially or fully onto technology, it is hard to see how the same could be true of our intellectual virtues.

In the world of the future, for example, one can imagine lots of cognitive tasks that we now undertake with our cognitive abilities being conducted instead by technology. What would be the point of memorising lots of information if one has the contents of Wikipedia and the World Wide Web instantly available to one? Sure, it might be impressive that someone can, say, name all the countries of Europe without technological assistance, but since having extended knowledge of this kind will be so common, it would be odd to train oneself up to perform such a memorial feat, as opposed to doing other, more worthwhile, activities. The same will go for lots of other skills that we presently possess. For example, what would be the point of learning languages if there is technology available that can make us instantly speak whatever language we want?

But the intellectual virtues are very different on this score. What would it even mean to cognitively offload one's intellectual virtues onto technology? As we noted above, it is in the nature of such traits that they involve characteristic motivations on one's part, that they are reflectively employed and cultivated. One could imagine using technology to encourage people to be intellectually virtuous – e.g. the technology reminding you to be intellectually conscientious – but whether you actually manifest the intellectual virtue will be ultimately down to you.

If that's right, then it means that there are inherent limits to extended cognition. Moreover, if intellectual virtues really are so important to a life of flourishing, then they are traits that a wise person will be sure to cultivate. We are thus able to capture a sense in which the wise person may be willing to depend on technology to a certain extent, but will also be keen to develop other kinds of traits that are not technologically dependent (or, at least, not technologically dependent in the same way or to the same degree).

Notice too that the intellectual virtues, even if they don't have the inherent (non-instrumental) value that the ancient Greeks thought they had, are nonetheless practically very valuable. Indeed, one can think of the intellectual virtues as akin to 'master' cognitive traits, in the sense that they afford the virtuous agent with the good sense to know what to do, including how best to employ their other cognitive traits. Having lots of cognitive abilities is not much use if you don't employ them to intellectually worthwhile ends, after all. For example, the utility of knowing lots of facts on account of being technologically hooked up to Wikipedia only takes you so far. If you are not intellectually conscientious, for example, then you still might find yourself forming the wrong judgement, perhaps because you ignore some information, or opt to focus on information that suits your preconceived views. Or consider the contrast between Watson and Holmes that we drew upon on Chapter 14. Watson might have access to the very same visual scene that Holmes does, but he observes so much less because he lacks the intellectual virtues that Holmes has.

Relatedly, in a world without technology, we may well be cognitively impoverished as a result, but if the absence of technology doesn't affect the intellectual virtues, then we would not be cognitively impoverished on this score. Moreover, it would surely be better to confront such a world armed with the intellectual virtues than without them. For one thing, one would be better placed to acquire the cognitive abilities and knowledge that one has lost. The upshot is that a wise person will want to cultivate her intellectual virtues regardless of the availability of epistemically useful technology.

• CHAPTER SUMMARY

- We are increasingly reliant on technology. On the one hand, this means that there is a wealth of information at our fingertips that was previously unavailable. But, on the other hand, this also means that we are now reliant on technology to do many cognitive tasks that we used to be able to do ourselves. Does the latter mean that our reliance on technology is making us dumber?

- We saw that one key issue in this respect is whether there is such a thing as *extended cognition*. Extended cognition is when a cognitive process extends beyond the skin and skull of the subject to involve 'external' factors, like technology. The claim is not that every use of technology is extended cognition, but only that extended cognition occurs when we are using technology in ways that is in every relevant respect analogous to how we employ our non-extended cognitive resources. We noted that some of the seamless ways in which we might integrate technology into our everyday lives would plausibly count as genuine instances of extended cognition.

- If there can be genuine cases of extended cognition, then there can be instances of *extended knowledge*, where one's knowledge is the result of an extended cognitive process.
- If extended cognition and extended knowledge are bona fide phenomena, then our contemporary reliance on technology might well be best thought of as a kind of augmentation of our biological cognitive capacities. In that case, it is not that this reliance on technology is degrading our cognitive capacities, but rather that it is enhancing them.
- We considered the distinction between mere cognitive abilities and the very specialised kind of cognitive abilities involved in the intellectual virtues. The distinctive properties of the intellectual virtues means that it is hard to see how they could be subject to extended cognition in the way that one's ordinary cognitive abilities can be. This means that developing one's intellectual virtues is something that a wise person would do regardless of the availability of epistemically useful technology.

● STUDY QUESTIONS

1 Is our dependence on technology making us dumber? If so, how exactly? If not, why not?
2 What is extended cognition, and how is it relevant to our dependence on technology?
3 What is extended knowledge? Do we have any? If so, explain why and give some examples to illustrate your point. If not, then why not?
4 Why might the existence of extended knowledge mean that our contemporary reliance on technology is less a degrading of our cognitive capacities than an augmentation of them?
5 What is neuromedia? In what ways is neuromedia a form of extended cognition, and in what ways, if any, is it different from normal forms of extended cognition?
6 What are the intellectual virtues, and how do they differ from (mere) cognitive abilities, such as our faculties? Give an example of at least one intellectual virtue to illustrate your points.
7 Can the intellectual virtues be subject to extended cognition in the way that many of our other cognitive abilities can be? If not, why not?

● INTRODUCTORY FURTHER READING

Carr, Nicholas (2011) *The Shallows: What the Internet Is Doing to Our Brains* (New York: W. W. Norton & Company). A popular text designed to make us worried about our epistemic dependence on technology. A fun read, but Lynch (2016) is much better, particularly for the epistemological implications of the new technology.

Lynch, Michael P. (2016) *The Internet of Us: Knowing More and Understanding Less in the Age of Big Data* (New York: Liveright). A philosophically oriented and enlightening discussion of our increasing epistemic dependence on technology, but no less accessible as a result.

● ADVANCED FURTHER READING

Clark, Andy (2008) *Supersizing the Mind: Embodiment, Action, and Cognitive Extension* (Oxford: Oxford University Press). In my view, the definitive contemporary work on extended cognition, written by its leading exponent.

Clark, Andy & Chalmers, David J. (1998) 'The Extended Mind', *Analysis*, 58, 7–19. This is the short, seminal paper that sparked the whole debate about extended cognition. Widely available online.

Pritchard, Duncan (2018) 'Extended Virtue Epistemology', *Inquiry*, 61, 632–47. Makes the case for thinking that while we can understand a lot of our knowledge and cognitive abilities as extended knowledge, we cannot make sense of the idea that the intellectual virtues can be extended in this way.

● FREE INTERNET RESOURCES

Cowart, Monica (2017) 'Embodied Cognition', *Internet Encyclopaedia of Philosophy*, www.iep.utm.edu/embodcog/. Not quite as good as the Shapiro and Spalding (2021) resource, but still a very useful overview of this topic. Note that embodied cognition is sometimes construed as a form of extended cognition, rather than identical to it, so do bear that in mind when reading this article.

Shapiro, Lawrence & Spalding, Sharon (2021) 'Embodied Cognition', *Stanford Encyclopaedia of Philosophy*, https://plato.stanford.edu/entries/embodied-cognition/. An excellent, and completely up-to-date, overview of the literature on this topic. Note that embodied cognition is sometimes construed as a form of extended cognition, rather than identical to it, so do bear that in mind when reading this article.

17

education

- The epistemic goals of education
- Intellectual virtue and education
- Technology and education

● THE EPISTEMIC GOALS OF EDUCATION

Education has many goals, and not all of them are epistemic. For example, it is often thought a requirement of a well-functioning democracy that one has an informed, and thus educated, electorate. If that's right, then education serves a *political* function. One might also think that access to education is a fundamental human right, such that to be denied such access – as many children in some parts of the world are – is to deny them their basic rights. If that's correct, then it follows that education serves an important *ethical* purpose. One might also plausibly argue that there is an *economic* case for education, in that society needs productive citizens who can fill the jobs that need doing. And so on.

But even if it is uncontroversial that education serves many non-epistemic purposes, it is also relatively uncontroversial that it surely serves an important *epistemic* goal as well. Isn't part of the role of education to give students useful knowledge, where this also includes the cognitive skills to gain further knowledge by themselves? Indeed, this is arguably a fundamental goal of education, in that one needs it for the other goals to be successful. For example, one can't educate people to be good democratic citizens without giving them the required knowledge (e.g. about how their democratic institutions function).

Before granting that there is an epistemic goal of education, however, we should at least register that there might be some scepticism about this claim. After all, if one thought that education was simply a form of *indoctrination* – as it surely is in certain political systems – then it might not be obvious that education serves any epistemic end at all. For example, suppose that one lives in a totalitarian state where one's education consists in learning only what serves the ruling regime (that the Leader is glorious, that all enemy nations and their citizens are amoral scoundrels who should be crushed, that the truth is what the Leader says it is and no more, etc.). In that case, the goal of education would merely be to serve an overarching political purpose of dubious pedigree, and no more. There certainly wouldn't be anything particularly epistemic about education of this kind.

DOI: 10.4324/9781003356110-22

I think we can set this kind of worry to one side, however. This is because even if an educational system of the kind just described is obviously possible (indeed, it is arguably *actual* in some parts of the world), education is not normally conducted in this way. In any case, our theoretical interest should be not in what educational practices look like when they are *done badly*, as they are in the scenario just described, but rather what they look like when they are *done well*. No one would think that indoctrination is a good way of educating one's citizens, after all. Moreover, when education is done well, it does serve clearly epistemic ends.

Granting that education serves epistemic ends doesn't in itself tell us which ones, however. There are competing proposals on this score. One conception of the epistemic ends of education, which is found more in newspaper columns than in the work of educational theorists, is what we might call the 'bucket' model. On this view, the overarching goal of education is simply to instil lots of useful true beliefs and basic cognitive skills into students, so that they can reproduce those true beliefs, or manifest those basic cognitive skills, when called upon to do so. For example, on this view, one might think it vital that students know lots of important facts – such as their multiplication tables, who won the Battle of Hastings, what the capital of France is, and so on. Relatedly, one might think that being able to manifest certain useful cognitive skills – such as a mastery of basic arithmetic – is also very important.

I say the bucket view is more often found in newspaper columns than in the work of educational theorists since one often hears of commentators bemoaning the fact that the 'children of today' haven't had certain facts and basic cognitive skills drilled into them in the way that was common for previous generations. This reflects an important change in how contemporary educational systems operate. Whereas previously the overarching educational model involved students learning lots of facts and basic skills by rote – i.e. by going over them over and again until they were second nature – contemporary educational systems are far less focused on learning of this kind. What has changed, and why?

In order to understand this shift in our educational practices, we need to first note what the epistemic focus of the bucket model is. On this view, the basic epistemic goal of education is to instil lots of true beliefs, and associated basic cognitive skills, into the student. True belief, and cognitive skill, are genuine epistemic goods, after all. But notice that they are also quite limited in their epistemic value. Being able to reproduce a true belief by rote does not entail that one has *knowledge*, for example. For instance, suppose one of the useful facts that one learns by rote is a complex scientific claim, such as a fundamental law of physics. That one can repeat this truth when called upon to do so doesn't mean that one has any grasp at all of what one is saying. If that's so, however, then one would hardly be thought to know what one asserts.

This is the reason why contemporary educational practices are less focused on rote learning, and more concerned to develop the wider intellectual capacities of the student (though there usually is some degree of rote learning for some of the most basic things that the student needs to know, such as the multiplication tables). The foregoing might suggest that we could model this shift in terms of changing the epistemic goal of education from the acquisition of true beliefs and basic cognitive skills to the promotion of knowledge. Would that be an accurate way of describing the change?

Perhaps. It is certainly a step in the right direction, in that I think we would naturally demand that students not merely be able to parrot the correct answer as a result of rote learning, but also that they have a sufficient grasp of the facts that they are reproducing to count as knowing them. But the reason why one might think that this can't be the whole story is that knowledge can often be had rather cheaply, and in ways that don't seem to be representative of what one would expect as the outcome of a good educational environment.

In order to see this, consider a statement of Pythagoras' theorem. This is a geometrical truth that states that the square of the hypotenuse of a right-angled triangle is equal to the sum of the squares of the other two sides. We can easily imagine someone learning this by rote who has no grasp at all of what it means, and hence who lacks knowledge of what they are repeating. But notice that there are ways of knowing this claim that aren't much better, from an epistemic point of view. Suppose, for example, that you know what the constituent terms mean (e.g. which side of the triangle is the hypotenuse, and so on), and you further know that your teacher is an expert on these matters, and hence that you can rely on her testimony. It would then surely follow that you know what you are repeating. But notice that this is nonetheless compatible with you lacking any real understanding of what you are repeating.

We can bring this point into sharp relief by imagining two students who know this geometrical claim. The first merely knows it – she understands the words involved, and is assured by her expert teacher that it is true, but that's all. The second doesn't just know this claim, but understands it, where this means that she grasps how this theorem works and can consequently apply this grasp to the world around her. Faced with right-angled triangles of various dimensions, and armed with the relevant information, she can draw the appropriate mathematical consequences. In contrast, her counterpart who merely knows this theorem, but doesn't (yet) understand it, will simply scratch her head when trying to work out how to apply it.

John Dewey (1859–1952)

One of the most important figures in the development of the philosophy of education was the American pragmatist philosopher John Dewey. In a famous book, entitled *Democracy and Education: An Introduction to the Philosophy of Education*, he argued for a more progressive, and less authoritarian (as was common at the time), approach to teaching in schools. For Dewey, the focus should be more on allowing the students to learn by doing than by simply instilling facts in them. Dewey also argued for the social importance of a good educational system, particularly in a democratic society. His ideas have had considerable impact on pedagogical practices throughout the world.

The point is that often having a genuine understanding of a subject matter involves more than having isolated pieces of knowledge. Rather, it involves having a deeper kind of grasp of how everything fits together and how to employ that grasp to the world around one, including perhaps in novel situations. In short, understanding seems at least sometimes to involve more than mere knowing. Wouldn't we think it remiss of an educator to stop the educational process at mere knowledge, and didn't continue to ensure that the student understood what she had learned (e.g. by making sure that she could apply her knowledge)? This would suggest that merely knowing is not the overarching epistemic goal of education, but rather understanding.

INTELLECTUAL VIRTUE AND EDUCATION

Before we conclude that it is understanding rather than knowledge that is the overarching goal of education, however, we need to first consider the role of the intellectual virtues in education. Recall that the intellectual virtues – such as being intellectually conscientious or observant – are very different from mere cognitive abilities, like being able to do basic arithmetic. For example, they involve distinctive motivational states, in that they arise out of a desire for intellectual goods like the truth. This sets them apart from mere cognitive abilities as they need not involve any motivational states at all (or else may involve motivational states that have nothing to do with intellectual goods, such as wanting to be famous, or rich). The intellectual virtues also arise in different ways, in that they are acquired, and subsequently maintained, by conscious effort on the part of the subject. In short, the intellectual virtues need to be *cultivated*. In contrast, one's mere cognitive skills can arise in purely unreflective ways. Indeed, some of them are innate, in the sense that they naturally arise as a result of continual exposure to specific stimuli (think about the chicken-sexer in this regard). The upshot is that one's intellectual virtues are essentially reflective in nature, in a way that one's mere cognitive skills are not.

The intellectual virtues are important to our current discussion precisely because it seems that the actual overarching epistemic goal of education is to develop one's intellectual virtues and, thereby, one's *intellectual character* (where this is one's integrated set of intellectual virtues and other cognitive abilities). To use the lingo that educationalists often employ, having a strong intellectual character, and thus possessing intellectual virtues, is a vital *transferable skill*. The intellectual virtues, after all, are tremendously useful in helping one to navigate the challenges that one faces – e.g. weighing up the evidence that one has on an important topic; evaluating conflicting testimony regarding an issue of note; working out what work item to prioritise. Having intellectual virtues – and, even better, having a strong intellectual character that involves lots of integrated intellectual virtues – means being able to navigate lots of significant challenges that one faces in one's daily life.

Relatedly, note that the intellectual virtues play a managerial role in one's intellectual activities, where this means that it helps one to direct one's other cognitive abilities. For example, it is no good being very accomplished in arithmetic (a mere cognitive skill) if one doesn't know how best to employ this cognitive skill to serve one's wider intellectual ends. But one needs intellectual virtue, and ideally a strong intellectual character that integrates several intellectual virtues, to do that.

The point is that it seems that what we really want from a good educational system, from a purely epistemic point of view, is ultimately a way of developing intellectual character and thus intellectual virtue. Note that this claim isn't in opposition to our previous point about how understanding seems to be educationally more important than mere knowledge. For notice that the goal of enhancing a subject's intellectual character goes hand in hand with the goal of ensuring that this subject genuinely understands the subject matter in front of them as opposed to possessing a lesser epistemic standing, such as mere knowledge. The shift to a focus on intellectual character rather concerns the fact that from the perspective of the epistemology of education, we are more interested with the development of character than with particular epistemic states, such as knowledge or understanding. If one can train up a student to think and learn for herself by cultivating her intellectual character, then she will have the capacity (at least when she is also appraised of the relevant factual information that she needs) to come to know, and thereby understand, the things that her curiosity seeks.

● TECHNOLOGY AND EDUCATION

In the previous chapter, we noted how we are increasingly dependent on technology. This is no less true of education. Think, for example, of how technology pervades the classroom, from the smart boards that the teacher uses, to laptops, iPads, calculators, and so forth that are all employed in an educational setting.

We also noted in the last chapter that there is at least a prima facie concern that our dependence on technology might be making us dumber, in that we are effectively offloading some of our cognitive abilities onto the technology (as when we use the calculator to do complex arithmetic rather than doing it in our heads). But we also noted that this might not be the full story, at least if there is such a thing as *extended cognition*. Recall that according to this proposal, one's cognitive abilities can be genuinely extended, where this means that items outside of the subject's skin and skull, such as technology, are constituent parts of the cognitive process. When an extended cognitive process gets us to truth, we are in a position to acquire *extended knowledge*. Is extended cognition manifested in educational contexts involving technology?

The short answer is 'probably not, at least at the moment'. This is because in order for there to be extended cognition one's use of the technology has to be a seamless part of one's cognitive processes (i.e. as seamless as our use of our 'on-board' cognitive processes, like memory). Otherwise, one's relationship to the technology is just of the more mundane subject-and-instrument variety. Right now, however, I take it that a lot of the technology we employ in educational settings is not employed in this seamless way just yet. But as the technology improves and becomes more embedded in our cognitive practices in educational settings, then there is the potential for one's cognitive processes to become extended.

If that happens, then it will have important implications for our educational practices. For example, is it wrong for students to be able to bring their technology into examination situations? Even if there isn't such a thing as extended cognition, the answer to this question might depend on what it is one is testing for. For example, if the purpose of the test is to see how students are able to use calculators to do complex mathematical sums, then it might make every sense to have them bring the calculators into the exam with them. This issue becomes more pointed once we bring in extended cognition, however. After all, if the technology is a genuine part of the subject's extended cognitive process, then we will need some way of evaluating that extended cognitive process, and that will obviously mean allowing the technology to be present, given that it is part of the cognitive process.

Of course, none of the foregoing means that we will abandon the idea of developing students' unextended cognitive processes too. It might still be important, for example, that students can do certain kinds of things (basic arithmetic, say) in their heads. There is also another important sense in which the emergence of extended cognition may have a limited bearing on our educational practices. We noted above that the overarching epistemic goal of education seems to be the development of the student's intellectual character, where this means her integrated set of intellectual virtues. Crucially, however, as we saw in the last chapter, it does not seem that the intellectual virtues are the kind of cognitive ability that can be cognitively extended. If that's right, then the educational goal of developing intellectual character will continue even in educational settings where extended cognitive processes are common.

● CHAPTER SUMMARY

- We began by noting that education has many goals, including political, social, and economic, but that one key goal is epistemic.
- On a very weak conception of this epistemic goal, education is about instilling students with useful information (i.e. true beliefs) and useful cognitive abilities (e.g. how to do arithmetic). We noted that this doesn't seem to capture what educationalists are aiming for, especially now that education is not generally done entirely in terms of passively learning by rote.
- A more sophisticated epistemic goal would be to instil students with knowledge rather than mere true belief. Even this seems to miss something important about our best educational practices, however, given that one can passively acquire lots of knowledge by rote too.
- We concluded that a more plausible epistemic goal is that of promoting understanding, where to understand something involves more than just passive knowledge. Instead, one needs to be able to grasp why something is true, rather than just know that it is true. Relatedly, when one genuinely understands something, as opposed to merely knowing it, then one is better placed to apply that understanding to novel situations.
- We compared this conception of the epistemic goal of education with the idea that this goal should be instead concerned with the development of the student's

intellectual virtues, and thus her intellectual character. As we saw, these are not two competing conceptions of the epistemic goal of education, but rather go hand in hand. This is because our intellectual virtues are cognitive traits that lead us to actively seek out understanding where possible, rather than being content to merely know. Plausibly, then, the overarching epistemic goal of education is the development of intellectual character, and thus intellectual virtue, and this is why we want students to understand and not merely know.

• Finally, we looked at the relationship between technology and education, and in particular the question of whether our increasing dependence on technology in educational settings is problematic from an epistemic point of view. This led us to reconsider the possibility of extended cognition, and thus extended knowledge, from the previous chapter. As we saw, if this is a genuine phenomenon, then it could be that the education of the future will be concerned to develop our extended cognitive abilities. Crucially, however, since the intellectual virtues are arguably not amenable to being cognitively extended in this way, it follows that the overarching epistemic goal of education will still be the same even if we become extended knowers in the classroom.

• STUDY QUESTIONS

1 Describe two non-epistemic goals of education, and why they are important.
2 Why is it important that our educational practices have epistemic goals? What would an education system look like that lacked any concern for epistemic goals?
3 What is problematic with the idea that the epistemic goal of education is simply to instil in students useful true beliefs and basic cognitive skills? Would such a proposal be less problematic if we insisted that the true beliefs in question must amount to knowledge?
4 Why might one think that the overarching epistemic goal of education is to promote understanding? How would this be different from thinking of the overarching epistemic goal of education in terms of the promotion of knowledge?
5 Why might one think that the overarching epistemic goal of education is to develop students' intellectual characters, and thus their intellectual virtues? How, if at all, is this conception of the overarching epistemic goal of education compatible with the idea that we want students to understand and not merely know?
6 Should we be worried about our increasing dependence on technology in educational settings? How might extended cognition be relevant to this issue?

• INTRODUCTORY FURTHER READING

Noddings, Nell (2016) *Philosophy of Education* (4th edn, Boulder, CO: Westview Press). An influential textbook on the philosophy of education. Very readable, and contains a helpful section on the epistemology of education.

Rocha, Samuel D. (2014). *A Primer for Philosophy of Education* (2nd edn, Eugene, OR: Cascade Books). A short and accessible book offering an overview of the philosophy of education, including some discussion of epistemological issues.

● ADVANCED FURTHER READING

Kotzee, Ben (ed.) (2013) *Education and the Growth of Knowledge: Perspectives from Social and Virtue Epistemology* (Oxford: Wiley-Blackwell). This recent volume brings together some of the leading epistemologists to discuss the specific topic of the epistemology of education.

Pritchard, Duncan Henry (2016) 'Intellectual Virtue, Extended Cognition, and the Epistemology of Education', *Intellectual Virtues and Education: Essays in Applied Virtue Epistemology*, J. Baehr (ed.), pp. 113–27 (London: Routledge). This article makes the case, in the context of the epistemology of education, that there are limits to the extent to which our cognitive abilities can be subject to extended cognition. In particular, it argues that the intellectual virtues cannot be cognitively extended.

● FREE INTERNET RESOURCES

Philips, Denis Charles, Siegel, Harvey, & Callan, Eamonn (2018) 'The Philosophy of Education', *Stanford Encyclopaedia of Philosophy*, https://plato.stanford.edu/entries/education-philosophy/. A comprehensive overview of the field, written by leading figures working in this area.

Pritchard, Michael (2022) 'Philosophy for Children', *Stanford Encyclopaedia of Philosophy*, https://plato.stanford.edu/entries/children/. Philosophy for children isn't quite the same thing as the philosophy of education of course, but is rather more about teaching children philosophical skills. There is nonetheless an interesting overlap with our concerns in this chapter, as much of the focus when it comes to teaching philosophy for children is about developing (what we have here termed) their intellectual character. (Incidentally, I'm not related to the author.)

18

˙law

- The epistemic goals of the law
- Adversarial versus investigatory trials
- Legal evidence

THE EPISTEMIC GOALS OF THE LAW

As with education, the legal process has many different goals, not all of them epistemic. For example, it is important that a well-functioning legal system is seen to be fair to all, regardless of who they are (e.g. their social standing, race, and gender). This is an important *social* good of the legal system. The legal system also serves a *political* purpose, at least in many countries, in that it enacts laws that have been created by elected officials. (In some countries, of course, the legal system reflects a more worrisome political purpose, in that it simply enacts the political will of the person or persons in charge. Here the political purpose of this particular legal system is running counter to the social good that a well-functioning legal system should serve.) And there are other non-epistemic purposes that a good legal system will serve (e.g. the social good of reducing crime).

As with education, however, there is also a clear epistemic goal of the legal system. Take the criminal trial, for example, which is probably what many of us think of when we consider the legal system (though in fact it is just a small part of it). We want a well-conducted criminal trial to get to the truth – to ensure that the right person is convicted and, where applicable, that the innocent person walks free. Many of the legal structures in play within the criminal trial are clearly meant to achieve this end. Think of perjury rules, for example. These rules ensure that people will tend to tell the truth under oath, since if they don't then they can be subject to legal penalties. That those testifying to a criminal trial tell the truth will clearly help ensure that the trial reaches its epistemic goal of determining whether the defendant is guilty or innocent. Or think of the various rules in place that limit what can count as **legal evidence**. In many legal systems, for example, one cannot cite mere hearsay (e.g. rumour) as evidence in a criminal trial, and the reason why is that such evidence is not a reliable way of determining guilt or innocence.

Interestingly, however, there are also some structures within the criminal trial that appear to actively militate against its epistemic aims. For example, it is a common feature of a lot of legal systems that there are strict restrictions in place on citing a

DOI: 10.4324/9781003356110-23

defendant's past convictions. And yet this is clearly epistemically relevant to determining that defendant's guilt, in that someone who, for example, has a history of stealing is surely more likely to be guilty of theft this time around. The rationale for this rule is that if the jurors were to know that the defendant had a criminal past, then they are likely to simply conclude that they must be guilty, regardless of what evidence the defence offers for their innocence. In effect, then, what is happening here is a kind of *epistemic paternalism*.

Paternalism is a kind of intervention whereby someone in authority acts in your best interests, rather than trusting you to make decisions yourself. We have laws insisting that motorcyclists wear helmets, for example, even though if you don't wear a helmet, the only person you are likely to harm is yourself. Even so, the authorities insist that you must wear a helmet, for your own benefit. In essence, the state isn't trusting individuals to make the right decision about their welfare, and so is effectively making this decision for them.

Something similar is happening in the criminal trial when we limit jurors' access to the defendant's past convictions. This evidence may well be epistemically relevant to whether the defendant is guilty, but the legal system has come to the conclusion that jurors cannot be trusted with this information, as they will rush too quickly to the judgement that the defendant is guilty. Accordingly, it decrees that this information be denied to the jurors. Effectively, as with the example of the motorcycle helmets, the jurors are not being trusted to make their own decisions in this matter.

Although evidence about past convictions is obviously epistemically relevant to whether the defendant is guilty, notice that this restriction on making this evidence available to jurors does seem to serve a broadly epistemic end. It is precisely because those in charge of the legal system think that jurors cannot be trusted to use this evidence wisely to determine guilt that they are prevented from having access to it. Accordingly, one could argue that restricting evidence in this case in fact reflects a concern on the part of those who run the legal system to ensure that it achieves its epistemic goals.

Normally, however, we wouldn't think epistemic paternalism of this kind is appropriate. We wouldn't think it appropriate for those in charge of the safety of our food, for example, to only allow us to see the evidence that we could 'handle appropriately'. Why is the criminal trial so different in this respect? There is one core reason for this, and it relates to the fact that the wrongful conviction of an innocent person would be a terrible injustice. Compare this with the case of food safety, where limiting our access to relevant evidence is likely to undermine our welfare. In contrast, imagine that you are an innocent person charged with a serious crime that you didn't commit, but where you have committed crimes of this kind in the past (this may be why you have been picked out by law enforcement as being the prime candidate for this crime). Wouldn't you want the evidence that's available to the jurors to be such that it wouldn't lead them to automatically conclude that you are guilty?

There is a general principle in play here, which is that we want a well-functioning legal system to err on the side of caution when it comes to generating convictions, given how awful it would be for an innocent person to be convicted of a crime that they didn't commit. This means that we want the system to in effect make it epistemically hard to deliver a conviction. Remember that a legal judgement in a criminal trial is not whether or not you committed the crime in question, but rather whether it has been shown, in accordance with the legal structures in place (such as the restrictions on legal evidence), whether you count as guilty.

Moreover, remember that the epistemic threshold for a judgement of guilt in a criminal trial is very high – it has to be *beyond a reasonable doubt*. This is a much higher constraint on forming a judgement than we normally apply. Ordinarily, after all, we form a view about whether something occurred by working out what is the most likely explanation. (Interestingly, this is, very roughly, the criterion of liability that tends to apply in civil court judgements.) In contrast, the constraint that one be sure beyond a reasonable doubt is very high. There is no hard and fast way of working out what this threshold involves, but I'm reliably told by someone senior in the Scottish legal profession that the practical advice they were offered on this score as part of their training was that the threshold was equivalent to what you'd demand for a life-changing decision, such as buying a house or making a large personal investment. That's a high threshold to clear.

Putting these points together, this means that it makes complete sense that a juror might decide that a defendant is *not* guilty even while being personally convinced that the defendant in fact committed the crime in question. There's no contradiction here, since the question of whether the defendant committed the crime and the question of whether they are guilty are distinct – the answer to the former could reasonably be 'yes' while the answer to the latter, where the epistemic thresholds are higher, could reasonably be 'no'. (It is for this reason that some jurisdictions, such as Scotland, have a third option of 'not proven', to accommodate cases where there is sufficient evidence to indicate that the defendant committed the crime, but not sufficient evidence to clear the 'beyond a reasonable doubt' threshold.)

The Blackstone formula

Sir William Blackstone (1723–80) was an English judge and politician who developed principles of law. The particular principle that he is famous for, which is designed to protect the innocent, is the so-called *Blackstone formula* that 'it is better that ten guilty persons escape than that one innocent suffer'. His idea is meant to encapsulate, in a simple principle, the thesis that a just legal system should have safeguards in place to ensure that the innocent are protected from conviction, even if that means that some guilty people walk free. How best to understand this principle – and, relatedly, how best to implement this principle within a legal system – is a vexed issue, however, with legal scholars disagreeing on the extent to which a just legal system should have safeguards of this kind in place.

● ADVERSARIAL VERSUS INVESTIGATORY TRIALS

Another point that we should note in this regard is that there are very different legal systems in the world (even when we set aside the problematic case of there being some demonstrably unjust legal systems, as when those politically in charge get to determine what is 'justice'). The legal system that many readers of this book will be familiar with is what is known as the *adversarial* system (which is the kind of legal system found in the UK and the USA, for example). This kind of legal system, at least when it comes to the criminal trial, is predicated on the idea that the best way to determine the guilt or innocence of the defendant is to have the prosecution put forward the strongest case that they can muster, and for the defence to put forward the strongest *opposing* case that they can muster. The idea is that this clash of viewpoints will provide the jurors with the best set of evidence to determine whether they should judge that the defendant is guilty, beyond a reasonable doubt.

But is this really the best way of determining guilt or innocence? In particular, doesn't this way of proceeding lead to situations whereby guilt or innocence is determined by whoever is the most effective advocate? Interestingly, note that this adversarial way of conducting the criminal trial is not universal. In some jurisdictions, for example, especially in continental Europe, it is common to accord the judge a more truth-seeking role, such that their aim is to determine the facts of the matter, rather than relying on the advocacy of those involved in prosecution and defence. This is sometimes referred to as an *investigatory* model of the criminal trial, in contrast to the adversarial model. Wouldn't this be a better way of determining the truth of the defendant's guilt/innocence than the adversarial model?

It would be nice if there were a clear answer to this question, but in practice, it simply isn't obvious which of these legal systems is better, from a purely epistemic point of view. While having the judge take a more investigatory role might make the criminal trial more effective at getting at the truth, there is also the danger that there might be some epistemic loss by abandoning the adversarial model. After all, if the prosecution and the defence are each charged with making the best case, they can for their respective side, then wouldn't one expect this to generate some epistemic benefits too? For example, when we are trying to work out which of two alternatives is better, it is common for someone to play 'devil's advocate' to see if they can make a good case for one of the options. We do this because we think that it's a good way of checking which alternative really is better, since it forces us to properly think through the options that we are considering. But isn't that just what the adversarial system is doing by pitting the prosecution and the defence against one another? If that's right, then it isn't straightforward that the investigatory model of the criminal trial really is epistemically better than the adversarial model.

● LEGAL EVIDENCE

We've already noted that not everything that counts as evidence thereby counts as legal evidence. The latter is a more specific notion, since it concerns evidence that is admissible in a legal context. That's why although evidence of your past convictions is undoubtedly bona fide evidence – all other things being equal, someone who has stolen before is more likely to steal again than someone who has never stolen – it is not normally counted as legal evidence, since it is deemed inadmissible in a legal context.

There are some puzzles about legal evidence. One issue concerns merely statistical evidence, an example of which we will look at in a moment. The concern is that merely statistical evidence, no matter how strong, doesn't seem enough to pass a legal judgement against someone. In this regard, let's start with legal judgements of liability, of a kind that are made in civil cases, rather than legal judgements of guilt that are made in criminal trials. The distinction is important because all that is usually demanded to determine liability is what is known as a *preponderance of evidence*, which roughly means that it's more likely, given the legal evidence cited, that the person is liable than not. This is a much lower epistemic threshold than that offered in criminal cases, where the defendant's guilt must be proved beyond a reasonable doubt. There is a good reason for this distinction, in that civil cases of liability will not normally result in someone being sent to prison, which is the serious consequence of a guilty verdict in a criminal trial that makes the epistemic standards so high. So our question is whether it is reasonable to treat someone as liable in a civil case merely on the basis of statistical evidence.

Here is an example often used to illustrate this point. Imagine that you know that nearly everyone who came to a concert – 80 per cent of the people there, say – did so using what they knew full well were counterfeit tickets. If statistical evidence is all that is required, then you could randomly pick people who you know were at the concert and sue them as being liable to give you compensation for using a counterfeit ticket, and thereby defrauding you out of the concert ticket revenue. After all, you have very strong evidence that most people at this concert were using the counterfeit tickets and that they were at the concert. But that doesn't seem right. After all, 20 per cent of the people at the concert paid for their ticket, and the merely statistical evidence on offer doesn't in any way discriminate between the ones with the counterfeit tickets and the honest concertgoers who paid for their ticket fair and square. (If you want, add to the case that those who honestly bought their concert ticket have no way of proving this – e.g. they paid cash and were given no receipt) The problem seems to be that the evidence being cited to establish liability is merely statistical, in that while it establishes a statistical connection between the person being sued and the harm in question, it does no more than that.

The reason this result is puzzling is that the mere statistical evidence on offer does meet the 'preponderance of evidence' requirement, as it surely is more likely than not that someone who was at the concert was knowingly using a counterfeit ticket. The upshot seems to be that merely having a preponderance of evidence is in fact not enough to establish liability. What we need, it seems, is evidence that goes beyond the mere statistical and actually establishes a connection between the person being sued and the harm at issue. In this case, for example, one could imagine the court demanding that the concert promoter be able to offer additional evidence that indicates liability, such as evidence that they used a counterfeit ticket (e.g. CCTV footage that links them with a particular counterfeit ticket being used).

But how far can one press this point? For example, what if the proportion of people at the concert using counterfeit tickets was 99 per cent rather than 80 per cent? Wouldn't this be enough to secure liability? There are two ways one might respond to this point. One possibility is to argue that statistical evidence is enough to secure liability, but only if it is very high. The thought might be that a mere preponderance of evidence is fine for liability when the evidence is not merely statistical, but it is not enough otherwise. This would mean that one could establish liability with merely statistical evidence, but the evidential threshold would be much higher than usual (and more than just a preponderance of evidence).

The alternative, however, would be to stick to one's guns and argue that merely statistical evidence is never enough to secure liability, no matter how strong. Rather one always needs to go beyond merely statistical evidence. There is a good rationale for this, as we saw above, but it can also have uncomfortable consequences in cases where the merely statistical evidence on offer is overwhelmingly strong.

What goes for civil cases applies with even more force in criminal trials, given that the evidential requirements are much stronger. If one thinks that merely statistical evidence can suffice to establish liability if the evidence is strong enough, then should one think that such evidence can also suffice to establish guilt? If one feels uncomfortable about establishing liability on merely statistical grounds, then one should feel even more discomfort with the thought of finding someone guilty in a criminal trial on this basis, given that their very liberty (and possibly, at least in some countries anyway, their life) is in jeopardy.

This brings us to a broader issue about legal evidence, which connects with the point we raised earlier about how criminal trials are effectively privileged towards the defendant, on account of the seriousness of the consequences of them being found guilty. Here is the broader point: is it ever right to convict in a criminal trial on the basis of a single piece of evidence, if that evidence is probabilistically strong enough? Remember that what we are looking for in a criminal trial situation is legal evidence that ensures that the person's guilt is beyond a reasonable doubt. Can a single piece of evidence ever establish that (a DNA sample at the crime scene, say)?

I think there are good reasons for caution on this point. Yes, a single piece of legal evidence could constitute an overwhelming amount of evidence for someone's guilt, but if that's all there is to go on, should a jury convict? Interestingly, in a number of jurisdictions – Scotland is one, as it happens – there is an explicit requirement that there should be *corroborating* evidence, which means that you would need two separate sources of evidence to establish guilt rather than just the one. The underlying rationale for this sort of requirement comes from the fact that we want to avoid there being cases where the innocent are wrongly convicted. A legal system is a human creation, which means that it is bound to be fallible. But we want this fallibility to be such that it avoids error of this kind as much as possible. This means that we want our legal system to be *safe*, where this entails that one couldn't easily be wrongfully convicted. What's interesting is that having one piece of evidence to convict, even if a very strong piece of evidence, doesn't seem to be enough to make the conviction safe. That is, it seems like one could very easily be wrongfully convicted on the basis of a single piece of evidence, in a way that one couldn't by having lots of independent evidence pointing towards one's guilt. That's why corroboration is important, since it helps to make the legal system safe.

Note that this point is separate from the issue about statistical evidence, though the problems are clearly related. The narrow issue is whether merely statistical evidence ever suffices (e.g. for establishing liability, where the evidential threshold is low). The broader issue is whether a single source of evidence can suffice for conviction in a criminal case, no matter how epistemically strong it is. As we have seen, there are grounds for scepticism not just about merely statistical evidence in civil cases but also whether single sources of evidence are sufficient to establish guilt in a criminal case.

Of course, any rule that is brought in to make a legal system safe in this sense will have the consequence that some criminals are wrongly acquitted of their crimes. This is why corroboration is controversial in some quarters, as there are certain kinds of criminal cases where it is often hard for the prosecution to secure corroborating evidence of this kind. An obvious example in this regard is sexual assaults, where the evidence might simply consist of the testimony of the victim (which is disputed by the accused). Having such a rule in place might thus entail that many crimes of this nature go unpunished, which is obviously highly undesirable. This reminds us of an important point about 'safe' legal systems that have these safeguards against wrongful conviction, which is that they also make it harder for victims of crime to get justice (and thus, ironically, a 'safer' legal system can entail that some citizens are not as safe as they ought to be). The challenge is to find the right balance so that we minimise convicting the innocent while also ensuring that victims of crime receive justice.

● CHAPTER SUMMARY

- Legal systems serve many ends, not all of them epistemic. But such systems do serve an important epistemic end, in that we want to be assured that our legal judgements – e.g. regarding whether someone is guilty or innocent of a crime – are epistemically well founded.
- Many of the rules regarding legal evidence restrict the use of evidence for epistemic reasons – i.e. to help ensure that jurors or judges reach the correct decision – but some rules actually work against the epistemic good. One example we looked at in this regard is the common rule that jurors are not made aware of a defendant's past convictions in a criminal trial. This clearly is evidentially relevant to their guilt, but it often does not meet the standards of counting as legal evidence.
- The rationale for limiting jurors' access to evidence of past convictions is that it is held that a criminal trial would be fairer with this restriction in play. This is a kind of *epistemic paternalism*, in the sense that the legal system is controlling what evidence the jurors have access to because it doesn't trust them to evaluate the evidence correctly (i.e. it expects them to jump straight to a verdict of guilt, and not properly evaluate the case in hand).
- There is a reason behind such epistemic paternalism, which is that we want our legal system to be such that it protects the rights of the innocent. This is why it puts safeguards in place like this to try to limit the potential for innocent people to be wrongfully found guilty of crimes.

- Relatedly, the question in a criminal trial is not whether the defendant committed the crime, but whether this fact has been established by the legal evidence provided beyond a reasonable doubt. This means that there need be no inconsistency in both thinking that the defendant committed the crime and also supporting a not guilty verdict.
- We looked at two different types of legal system. The first is the adversarial legal system that is found, for example, in the UK and the USA. This involves the prosecution and the defence each being charged to mount the strongest opposing case that they can. In contrast, there is also the investigatory legal system that is found, for example, in some countries in continental Europe. As we saw, there are potentially epistemic benefits and costs associated with each system, so it is hard to determine which of them is better from a purely epistemic point of view.
- Finally, we looked at the topic of legal evidence. We noted that it was problematic to base legal judgements on merely statistical evidence, even in the context of civil cases where we are trying to determine liability rather than guilt (and thus where the epistemic thresholds in play are lower). More generally, it is also problematic for a legal system to allow that someone could be convicted purely on the basis of a single piece of evidence, no matter how strong it is, as it would open up the prospect of there being an unduly high number of wrongful convictions. As we saw, however, ensuring that a legal system avoids wrongful convictions can also lead to some types of crime having very low conviction rates, and thus victims of crime not receiving the justice they deserve.

• STUDY QUESTIONS

1 What are the non-epistemic ends of the criminal trial? Try to describe at least two. What is the epistemic aim of the criminal trial?

2 Why are there restrictions on the evidence that one can adduce in a criminal trial? Are all the reasons for restricting such evidence epistemic ones (i.e. to ensure that the criminal trial process is more likely to achieve its epistemic ends)?

3 What is epistemic paternalism, and where might one see this in action in a legal setting?

4 Why need there be no inconsistency in a juror examining the legal evidence and coming to the conclusion that while the accused did commit the crime in question, they should be found not guilty of it?

5 How are civil cases different from criminal trials, from an epistemic point of view? In particular, why are the evidential standards that are set out to determine liability in a civil case much weaker than the corresponding standards to determine guilt in a criminal trial?

6 What is merely statistical evidence? Give an example to illustrate your point. Why might it be problematic to find someone guilty/liable purely on the basis of merely statistical evidence?

7 Can a single piece of evidence ever be so strong that one could find a defendant guilty purely on this basis?

• INTRODUCTORY FURTHER READING

Brand, Jeffrey (2014) *Philosophy of Law: Introducing Jurisprudence* (London: Bloomsbury). Good introductions to the epistemology of law are hard to come by, which I think reflects the fact that it is such a new field. This book is a very good recent introduction to the philosophy of law more generally, but alas there is very little here on the epistemological issues raised by the law.

Tebbit, Mark (2017) *Philosophy of Law: An Introduction* (3rd edn, London: Routledge). Another good introduction to the philosophy of law, though again very little on epistemological issues raised by the law – indeed, there is even less coverage of epistemological issues in this book than in Brand (2014).

• ADVANCED FURTHER READING

Gardiner, Georgi (2019) 'Legal Burdens of Proof and Statistical Evidence', *Routledge Handbook of Applied Epistemology*, D. Coady & J. Chase (eds), 179–95 (London: Routledge). This paper provides an excellent overview of the issues regarding the use of statistical evidence in legal contexts that we have covered in this chapter.

Pritchard, Duncan Henry (2018) 'Legal Risk, Legal Evidence, and the Arithmetic of Criminal Justice', *Jurisprudence*, 9, 108–19. DOI: 10.1080/20403313.2017.1352323. This is an academic journal article, so I'm afraid it isn't all that accessible, but it does offer an in-depth discussion of some of the issues that we have been exploring in this chapter.

• FREE INTERNET RESOURCES

Himma, Kenneth Einar (2017) 'Philosophy of Law', *Internet Encyclopaedia of Philosophy*, www.iep.utm.edu/law-phil/. An excellent general survey of the issues with regard to philosophy of law.

Ho, Hock Lai (2021) 'The Legal Concept of Evidence', *Stanford Encyclopaedia of Philosophy*, https://plato.stanford.edu/entries/evidence-legal/. A comprehensive, and recently updated, treatment of the nature of legal evidence.

19

politics

- Democratic politics and informed citizens
- Bullshit
- 'Post-fact' politics
- Fake news

DEMOCRATIC POLITICS AND INFORMED CITIZENS

It is often remarked that 'knowledge is power', and nowhere is that more true than when it comes to the political sphere. In democratic countries where the political leaders are elected, the electorate needs to be able to make informed decisions, and that has all kinds of consequences for how we think about how that society should be structured. It means that we want an educated electorate, for example, and this will probably entail some form of public education for all. It will entail a free press who are able to report on political issues without being in fear of retribution from those in charge. It also means that we need to be tolerant of a range of different viewpoints, since how else are we to determine which of them is the right one?

In democratic countries, we often take these features of the political landscape for granted, and yet there are many countries in the world that lack them (including some countries which, superficially at least, are democracies). Moreover, they are features that are continually under threat. Think, for example, of how propaganda can be used to mislead people and to play on their fears. Or think about how media ownership could be used to ensure that a certain misleading political narrative becomes the norm.

Indeed, even the idea that people should be free to express a range of different view-points – what is known as the *open society* – is also regularly threatened. The epistemic case for an open society is what the English philosopher J. S. Mill (1806–73) famously termed the 'marketplace of ideas'. The general thought is that a range of different viewpoints is required in order for citizens to properly develop their opinions. In particular, even considering faulty viewpoints can be useful as we can still learn something from engaging with them and understanding why they are false. Relatedly, even if our viewpoint is the right one, we still need to understand why it is correct, and that means developing arguments in its favour, and in opposition to

DOI: 10.4324/9781003356110-24

opposing perspectives. Accordingly, if we suppress the expression of a wide range of viewpoints, then we will all be epistemically worse off.

And yet there often are attempts to silence opposing opinions, even in well-established democratic societies. Interestingly, such attempts come from all political quarters. For example, political conservatives might try to silence the opinions offered by progressives by campaigning for them to not be represented in the media. But of course political progressives can also be found arguing that some viewpoints are so offensive that they simply mustn't be aired. What is especially tricky about this debate, however, is that clearly some viewpoints *are* too offensive to be given airtime – would we think it appropriate for neo-Nazis to be given airtime when political positions are being aired, for example?

Moreover, notice that silencing another viewpoint can happen in lots of different ways. We might all agree that the state shouldn't be interfering in silencing free expression of opinion, but what about in cases like the neo-Nazi where this expression of free speech is menacing minority citizens? This is why many democracies have some sort of restriction on *hate speech*, though it has proved very tricky to know how to delimit this notion so that it excludes only those things that we want to exclude (after all, most viewpoints will be highly offensive to *someone*).

Once we move beyond the state's interference in free speech, things get even trickier. Should a university be willing to allow all viewpoints to be aired on its campuses? (And does it matter whether the university is private or public?) How about privately owned media outlets? Why should they have to respect viewpoints that they don't agree with? Or do we oblige media owners to subscribe to certain principles in order to keep the idea of an open society alive?

Finally, what do we do about viewpoints that run contrary to the scientific consensus? There are many people who for religious reasons don't believe in evolution, for example, and yet the scientific consensus is firmly behind evolutionary theory. Or take human-caused climate change. Again there is an overwhelming scientific consensus behind this claim, and yet there are also prominent commentators (some of them with vested interests, but not all) who think that this is all a conspiracy. The problem posed by these particular viewpoints is that they are in opposition to an epistemic system – scientific inquiry – that is generally held to be our best way of finding out the truth about the world around us (and thus about issues such as whether there is human-caused climate change, or whether creatures evolve). Lots of political debate isn't like this. One can be a capitalist or a socialist and still be pro-science, but one can't reject evolutionary theory or human-caused climate change without being sceptical of the scientific method itself. But if science really is our best way of getting to the truth, then to be anti-science is thus to be anti-truth. But why should the viewpoints of those who don't care about the truth carry any weight in the public sphere?

One way of responding to this kind of challenge is to say that while we perhaps shouldn't be epistemically all that interested in those who reject science wholesale – in the sense that we shouldn't be willing to put anti-scientific claims on an epistemic par with scientific ones – that doesn't settle the issue of whether these viewpoints have a right to be aired. Living in a tolerant society where people are free to express their opinions may just simply be a good thing, even if it has some epistemic costs. Moreover, although a scientific consensus is a fairly good indicator of truth, we should also remember that scientific inquiry is nonetheless fallible, and so even claims that everyone agreed about now could be overturned in the future. If we are mistaken about a core scientific claim in this way, we will need the help of the 'sceptics' around us to see the error of our ways. So there can be some long-term epistemic benefits from having even anti-scientific beliefs expressed.

BULLSHIT

These issues about politics and epistemology have always been with us – don't forget that Socrates was himself tried and eventually killed by the state for his willingness to challenge prevailing opinions (his crime was the 'corruption of the youth'). But arguably these issues have become much more prominent in recent years, partly driven by the massive growth in technology that we have witnessed in the last few decades. To begin with this was propelled by the emergence of the 24-hour news cycle, which meant that politicians had to work even harder to control how their message was being presented to voters. This led to a level of political 'spin' that hadn't been witnessed before, with individuals paid large sums of money by political parties to ensure that the voters were 'fed' a strong party line, one that would help them to win elections.

This political focus on spin was viewed by many commentators as being epistemically problematic, since it often involved manipulating facts to suit their own ends. Indeed, it often verged closely on all-out lying, though a good media operator would usually be smart enough not to go that far. Spin may be politically effective, but once voters become aware of it, they also become jaded about politics, and that's not good for a well-functioning democracy.

In a provocatively titled (and bestselling) book, *On Bullshit*, the American philosopher Harry Frankfurt (1929–) argued that we needed a new epistemic category to capture what is going on here, which is *bullshitting*. The thing about the bullshitter, argued Frankfurt, is not that they are liars, but rather that they simply don't care about the truth. The 'truth' for them is just what is useful to assert to achieve their interests. If what they assert happens to be in addition true, then that's a bonus, but it's not a requirement. What's important to the bullshitter is just that you believe what she tells you.

We see this at work in the activities of the political spinners. The facts are for them helpful when they work for their interests, and an inconvenience to be worked around otherwise. But there is no real love of the truth at work in this job, and that's what's so disconcerting about their activities. One way of expressing this point, which draws on our earlier discussion of the intellectual virtues, is that the bullshitter lacks intellectual character. Recall that the intellectual virtues involve distinctive

Harry Frankfurt (1929–)

Harry Frankfurt is a prominent American philosopher, currently professor emeritus at Princeton University. He has made important contributions to a number of areas of philosophy, but especially the topic of free will, where he is known for the view that one can be free even if one couldn't have done otherwise. His book on the nature of bullshit became a surprise bestseller, and led to high-profile media appearances, including on some prime-time chat shows. Some commentators at the time speculated that part of the reason why he was invited onto these shows was because people loved to hear an esteemed academic say the word 'bullshit' live on air!

motivational states, such as a desire for the truth, and that having intellectual character is about having an integrated set of intellectual virtues. But the bullshitter doesn't care about the truth. Given the fact that the intellectual virtues are arguably core parts of a life of human flourishing, this is a very important lack on their part, and something that we should be trying to avoid ourselves. In short, the life of the bullshitter is not to be emulated!

● 'POST-FACT' POLITICS

One could plausibly contend that in more recent years, the political situation has in fact got even worse from an epistemic point of view. After all, we are now in the age of so-called post-fact politics, where those in charge of the political spin will flatly deny what is patently the case and argue that they are simply presenting 'alternative facts'. What has changed in the interim?

One key change has been the way that the internet has radically transformed how we access information. The 24-hour newsfeed noted earlier, which was initially just a TV phenomenon, has morphed into a 24-hour multimedia 'newsfeed' involving not just TV but the internet and associated social media. This means that the people who create the news that we consume are a highly disparate group of people, from official news outlets to individuals who have high-profile social media accounts that are followed by millions. This means that it is particularly difficult to determine whether any particular news story is credible.

Consider, for example, stories that are fabricated purely in order to generate attention ('clicks') on social media. Such stories are usually designed to make people interested (and usually enraged!) as that's the best way to generate attention. So designed, the story could trend on social media and be attracting millions of hits within hours, before anyone has the chance to demonstrate that it is false. But once it's out, then it can change people's opinions, even though its lack of epistemic credibility means that it shouldn't be having this effect. Moreover, it can be very difficult to tell false reports apart from the real deal, as some of it is so well constructed as to be very plausible. (Indeed, these fabricated stories increasingly employ 'deepfake' videos that look just like the real thing, such as a video of a political candidate saying something truly outrageous.) Trickery of this kind is, alas, a reality, and it's transforming the political landscape, but with false stories like this now common currency in our online lives is it any surprise that we also have people advocating post-fact politics?

One response to this new trend might be that it doesn't matter all that much, in that everyone is so savvy when it comes to the new political reality and hence won't be taken in by this new kind of misinformation. But is that really plausible? For many democratic countries, elections can be won or lost based on the swing votes in just a small number of constituencies. Someone with the relevant demographic know-how and ability to marshal the resources of social media could be well placed to introduce just enough false stories into people's newsfeeds just prior to an election to swing that election in their favour. Indeed, there is evidence to suggest that this might have already happened, in which case this threat is not potential but actual.

In any case, even if voters are not regularly taken in by false reporting (something I very much doubt), the phenomenon of post-truth politics would still be very worrying. This is because once reason is abandoned in the public realm, then what will replace it? The danger is that into the vacuum will come the closely connected phenomena of **relativism** and dogmatism. We are going to talk about relativism in its own right in the last chapter, but for now let us just say that it is the view that there is no such thing as an 'objective' truth (or objectively good reasons for that matter), as 'the truth' is just relative. Often we aren't told by the relativist what truth is relative to, but the usual candidate would be to particular viewpoints, so that what's true for you needn't be what's true for me. Of course, to say this is just to say that there is no truth, since truth is *defined* by being objective – it is not just a matter of

Post-fact politics

Post-fact politics, or post-truth politics as it is sometimes termed, is very much a feature of the contemporary political landscape. Very roughly, it refers to how truth seems to be of secondary importance to political life, if it is important at all. Whereas previously politicians and their representatives (e.g. spin doctors) would be worried about asserting a falsehood, now we find that they often brazenly assert false claims. A good example of this in recent years is the claim made by 'Brexit' supporters that the UK leaving the EU would result in £350 million a week of additional funding for the National Health Service. Although experts immediately pointed out that this claim could not possibly be true, it was nonetheless regularly repeated, and is still repeated by some leading politicians to this day. Another famous example is the claim by then US President Donald Trump and his representatives that more people attended his inauguration ceremony than Barack Obama's, even though the photo evidence of the ceremony clearly demonstrated that this is not the case.

subjective opinion. So 'relativism about truth' is in fact a bit of a misnomer, in that to be a relativist about truth is not to have a particular view about the nature of truth, but rather just to deny that there is any. (And what about the relativist's statement expounding relativism about truth? Is that objectively true, or just a matter of subjective opinion? If the former, then the view is objectively false. If the latter, then why should we believe it anyway?)

The reason why a post-fact world, and the politics that go with it, can lead to relativism is that it can make people think that the truth simply doesn't matter, in which case why not be a relativist about truth? I noted earlier that relativism and dogmatism tend to go hand in hand. This may seem surprising, as dogmatists are very different from relativists, in that they insist that there is only one objective truth – i.e. *their own* – and will not listen to anyone else's viewpoint. When you think about why a post-truth world can lead to relativism, however, it becomes clear that it is equally susceptible to generating dogmatism.

What a post-truth world really undermines is the idea of there being good reasons to believe something, reasons which indicate that one viewpoint is epistemically better (i.e. more likely to be true) than another viewpoint. If you give up on truth, then you also give up on reasons, but in that case rather than opting for relativism (though this is one option as we just saw), why not instead just shout your preferred view at the top of your voice and ignore what anyone says to the contrary? After all, reasons, like truth, don't matter, remember. Interestingly, you might even find traces of relativism and dogmatism in the same person, which is unsurprising given that they have a common source. The relativist might say that there is no objective truth, that it is all relative, but they may also be very keen for you to take on board 'their' truth while completely ignoring 'your' truth.

How should we guard against these new epistemic challenges? One response that has been spearheaded by social media companies themselves is to find ways of signalling that a trending story might be fabricated before it gains traction. If that could work, then it might counteract some of the problematic aspects of how the new technology is functioning. But there is a worry inherent here, which is that an issue of global public concern is now in the hands of private companies, who might not have our best interests at heart (including our best epistemic interests). In recent times, for example, we have witnessed privately owned companies like Twitter closing down the accounts of prominent democratically elected politicians because they are deemed to be spreading falsehoods. Even if one grants that this is what these accounts are doing (which is, of course, contentious in itself), it is still discomforting that private companies could have this kind of power to influence democratic institutions and processes.

As we noted in an earlier chapter, our reliance on technology increases year by year, and this brings with it new ways in which we can be manipulated and deceived. The recent problems with fabricated stories should make us wary of buying into the new technology wholesale. Think about how much worse the phenomenon of false reporting could be if it is combined with the extended cognition that we have looked at previously. What assurances do we have that there are suitable bodies in place to prevent us from being hooked up to devices which, far from enhancing our cognitive lives, in fact radically diminish them, such as by exposing us to greater levels of propaganda and spreading lots of false information? This will be a crucial issue for societies to address in the coming years.

• FAKE NEWS

I want to close by examining a particular feature of contemporary social media that is especially epistemically troubling. This is what is known as *fake news*. What's interesting about this notion is that it's not immediately obvious what it refers to. For example, one might claim that it is concerned with any news item that is factually incorrect, but a moment's reflection reveals that this can't be correct. Respectable news outlets sometimes make mistakes, after all, and when they do they are hardly engaged in putting out fake news. Indeed, it's not even clear that fake news needs to be false. Remember that the thing about bullshit is not that it's false, necessarily, but rather that the bullshitter doesn't care whether what they say is true. The same seems to be true of fake news. If someone puts out fake news that happens to be correct – they release a completely fabricated story as clickbait that, incredibly, ends up being true – then it wouldn't cease to be fake news.

Indeed, the situation is even more complicated once one starts to consider fake news in detail. For notice that one could present a story that one knows to be literally true and it be nonetheless fake news, if one is presenting it in such a way as to mislead the audience. This relates to an important fact that we need to remember in the social media age, which is that the literal truth can be just as misleading as a falsehood (sometimes even more so). The reason for this is that a literal truth, divorced from any context, might give the audience completely the wrong impression. For example, one might plant a story about the police turning up at a politician's house while neglecting to mention that they were there as part of a planned event rather than to arrest or investigate anyone. The story, while literally true, would then be nonetheless highly misleading. This looks a lot like fake news, even though there is no falsehood involved in the report at all.

With the foregoing in mind, let's take a step back and try to think about how we should approach the question of understanding fake news. I think the best approach is to initially focus not on fake news itself, but on genuine news and work back to fake news from there. So just as we might understand what constitutes counterfeit currency by working out how it differs from genuine currency, so we will understand what fake news is by comparing it with the genuine article.

So what then is genuine news? We've already noted that genuine news can be false, as even the best news agencies can make mistakes, and when that happens, it doesn't automatically make what they report fake news. What seems to be important to genuine news is that it comes from a source that is aiming to convey accurate information so as to inform people. That's why if the BBC or the *New York Times* accidentally reports a falsehood it doesn't thereby become fake news, as they are in the business of trying to accurately report information so as to inform people. Moreover, notice that the desire to *inform* – i.e. telling people what they don't know—is important to news too. Simply going around telling people what they know already is not giving them news.

If that's the right way to think about genuine news, then it gives us a handle on what fake news might be. What this account of genuine news suggests is that fake news involves deliberately conveying misleading information with an intent to mislead. Notice that this account of fake news is compatible with the idea that fake news can as it happens be true, as one can deliberately convey misleading information with an intent to mislead and yet, by chance, report something true. Indeed, it is also compatible with the idea that fake news can sometimes involve releasing highly misleading information that one knows to be literally true. What's important about fake news is thus ultimately not whether or not it is true (though obviously it will usually be false), but rather the motivations behind it.

On this way of thinking about fake news it isn't merely an epistemically deficient version of genuine news, any more than a counterfeit coin is merely a damaged or worn-down version of a genuine coin. Consider, for example, a fledgling news agency that has been recently established, and which is regularly making lots of errors in its reporting. This would be an epistemically poor kind of news source, but the news it reports wouldn't thereby be fake news. This is because the agency is aiming to accurately report information so as to inform people. Fake news is thus different in kind from genuine news, and not merely a low-grade version of it.

Our account of fake news can also explain why some other kinds of media that aren't news aren't fake news either. For example, there are satirical news magazines like *The Onion* and *Private Eye*. To the untrained eye, they might seem like genuine news magazines (though a closer look would surely disabuse most people of that notion). Even so, they are not fake news, for while they might mislead some people, they are not designed to mislead – it would just be unlucky that some people are taken in by their satirical 'reporting'.

Now you might think that all of this focus on trying to understand what constitutes fake news is beside the point, in that what we really need to be doing is finding way to combat it. But the point is that in order to combat fake news, we need to first know what it is. On the view that we just presented, for example, fake news is different in kind from genuine news, rather than being an epistemically deficient version of it. This is important to how one detects fake news. This is because the kinds of cognitive skills needed to tell epistemically good sources of genuine news apart from epistemically deficient sources of genuine news are likely not to be the same kinds of cognitive skills needed to tell genuine news from fake news.

In order to see why this might be the case, consider again the case of genuine currency versus counterfeit currency. We can imagine someone who works at the mint where currency is made whose job it is to ensure the quality of the currency produced. This person will thus be an expert at spotting when the currency produced is deficient in some way. We can also imagine another person who works at this mint whose job it is to spot counterfeit currency that is in circulation and which is brought to them for examination. Crucially, these two people are likely to be employing very different skills. After all, the deficient currency has not been designed to mislead anyone, which makes it very different from the counterfeit currency. The person on the look out for counterfeit coins might thus have to be alert to subtle features of the currency that simply aren't relevant when it comes to the quality control of genuine currency. Moreover, it is likely to also be important to their job to know something about where the potentially fake currency that is presented to them came from, as this will provide evidence about whether it is likely to be counterfeit. The crux of the matter is that spotting fake currency can involve very different skills to spotting low-quality currency.

What goes for currency also applies to genuine news and fake news. That one is proficient at spotting whether genuine news has a good epistemic pedigree might not ensure that one is proficient at spotting when one is being presented with fake news. With this in mind, we need to make sure that we are developing the right kinds of cognitive skills in people that enable them to differentiate fake news from the genuine article.

● CHAPTER SUMMARY

- We began by looking at the importance to well-functioning democracies of having informed citizens, and how this places epistemic demands on one's society, such as ensuring that there is a free press, that a range of differing viewpoints can be aired (i.e. a right to free speech), and that there is a good education system.
- We noted, however, that such epistemic conditions on a well-functioning democracy are often under threat. For example, there can be attempts to silence differing viewpoints, either because they are perceived to cause harm to some social group or because they are contrary to the interests of those who control the media outlets. This issue is particularly difficult because clearly some viewpoints are offensive and shouldn't be allowed to prosper, but it is hard to determine how to limit freedom of speech in ways that don't undermine the epistemic ideal of a 'marketplace of ideas' whereby citizens are exposed to a range of viewpoints that they can engage with.
- One particularly challenging aspect of this debate concerns how to treat opposing viewpoints that challenge the scientific consensus, such as those who deny evolutionary theory on religious grounds or those who reject human-caused climate change. As we saw, one can have politically divergent views without thereby being in conflict with the scientific consensus, but there are some viewpoints that are explicitly opposed to the scientific method, even though it is widely regarded as our best way of determining the truth about the world around us. The challenge posed by such debates is to find a way that we can accord scientific inquiry its epistemically privileged status while at the same time acknowledging that it is a fallible enterprise, and thus that the epistemic benefits of the marketplace of ideas might mean that even proposals that go against the scientific consensus should be tolerated.

- We examined the notion of *bullshit*, where this is understood as a philosophical concept. The thing about the bullshitter is not that she is lying but that she doesn't care about the truth. We looked at this notion through the lens of the modern phenomenon of spin, particularly political spin, and considered how such a disposition to bullshit is contrary to the intellectual virtues.
- We also looked at the contemporary notion of a 'post-fact' politics, and what this means in terms of our political climate. In particular, we saw how this is driven by new technological changes, and how the development of this technology may make us increasingly susceptible to propaganda, with serious epistemic consequences.
- We described how a post-fact world could generate the (superficially very different) twin epistemic challenges of relativism and dogmatism. The former is the idea that there is no objective truth since truth is relative. As we saw, this is tantamount to simply saying there is no truth. The latter is a certain kind of dialectical stance, whereby one strongly asserts one's own viewpoint and is unwilling to listen to opposing viewpoints. As we saw, although these positions are (superficially at least) very different, they both gain support from a post-fact world. If truth is unimportant, then it doesn't matter if there isn't such a thing. Relatedly, if truth isn't important then neither are reasons – our guides to truth – important either, in which case why listen to other people's viewpoints at all?
- Finally, we looked at fake news. We noted that it doesn't suffice for something being fake news that it involves a false report, as sometimes even genuine news can involve mistakes. Indeed, fake news doesn't have to be false anyway, as it could be true by chance. It could even be known to be true by the person who presents it, as even literally true reports can be highly misleading, and hence amount to fake news.
- In order to get a handle on what fake news is, we turned our attention to the question of what constitutes genuine news. We argued that genuine news comes from a source that is aiming to convey accurate information so as to inform people. That account of genuine news allows that sometimes even genuine news sources get it wrong. It also captures the idea that genuine news does not involve telling people what they already know, but rather providing them with new knowledge by informing them about it.
- Just as a counterfeit coin is not a genuine coin that has become damaged in some way, so fake news is not an epistemically deficient form of genuine news, but rather a different thing entirely. What makes something fake news is that it involves deliberately conveying misleading information with an intent to mislead. That's compatible with fake news sometimes being true. It also explains why, for example, satirical news magazines are not fake news even if they sometimes mislead people, as they are not designed to mislead.
- Understanding what constitutes fake news is important to combatting this phenomenon. In particular, the cognitive skills involved in differentiating fake news from genuine news needn't be the same cognitive skills that would be involved in differentiating epistemically good quality genuine news from epistemically low-quality genuine news.

● STUDY QUESTIONS

1 What are the epistemic aims of a well-functioning democracy? Why might we have a specifically epistemic interest in structuring our democratic societies?

2 What is the 'marketplace of ideas', and why is it thought to be epistemically beneficial to a democratic society? Is it?

3 If one believes in an open society, then is one committed to allowing freedom of speech even for those with offensive views? If one limits freedom of speech, then how does one square this with the epistemic demands of the open society?

4 What is the particular challenge posed by differing viewpoints that oppose the scientific consensus? How should we respond to such challenges, compared with dealing with differing viewpoints that don't oppose the scientific consensus?

5 What is bullshit, and why is it different from simply lying? Why might the bullshitter be lacking in intellectual virtue?

6 Why can't we just say that fake news is simply any report that's false? Try to explain both how fake news could be true by chance and also how fake news might even be known to be true by the person presenting it.

7 What constitutes genuine news? What constitutes fake news and how does it relate to genuine news? Is fake news just an epistemically deficient version of genuine news?

8 Why might understanding what fake news is have a bearing on how we would go about combatting this phenomenon?

● INTRODUCTORY FURTHER READING

Aikin, Scott F. & Talisse, Robert B. (2020) *Political Argument in a Polarized Age: Reason and Democratic Life* (Oxford: Wiley). This is a wonderfully absorbing treatment of how we should argue with one another in a well-functioning, albeit inevitably polarised, democratic society.

Frankfurt, Harry G. (2005) *On Bullshit* (Princeton, NJ: Princeton University Press). A punchy, short book arguing that we need to take the phenomenon of bullshitting seriously, and contending that it is distinct from lying.

Lynch, Michael P. (2014) *In Praise of Reason: Why Rationality Matters for Democracy* (Cambridge, MA: MIT Press). A clever and engaging book making the case for the importance of reason for well-functioning democratic societies.

● ADVANCED FURTHER READING

de Ridder, Jeroen & Hannon, Michael (eds) (2021) *The Routledge Handbook of Political Epistemology* (London: Routledge). This excellent new anthology captures the state-of-play with regard to the kinds of topics that we have covered in this chapter, and many more besides.

Pritchard, Duncan (2021) 'Good News, Bad News, Fake News', *Epistemology of Fake News*, S. Bernecker, A. Flowerre & T. Grundman (eds), pp. 46–67 (Oxford: Oxford University Press). This offers a critical survey of some of the recent accounts of fake news while developing the proposal offered in this chapter in more detail.

● FREE INTERNET RESOURCES

Goldman, Alvin & O'Connor, Cailin (2019) 'Social Epistemology', *Stanford Encyclopaedia of Philosophy*, https://plato.stanford.edu/entries/epistemology-social/. This comprehensive survey of contemporary work on social epistemology contains several sub-sections of special interest to this chapter, such as concerning the role of truth and reason in a democracy and the proliferation of misinformation on social media.

Mahon, James Edwin (2015) 'The Definition of Lying and Deception', *Stanford Encyclopaedia of Philosophy*, https://plato.stanford.edu/entries/lying-definition/. One of the central features of contemporary political epistemology concerns the extent to which deception and misinformation are common in the information age. This survey article on lying and deception will thus be useful to understanding what constitutes deception.

Part VI

do we have any knowledge?

20

scepticism about other minds

- The problem of other minds
- The argument from analogy
- A problem for the argument from analogy
- Two versions of the problem of other minds
- Perceiving someone else's mind

THE PROBLEM OF OTHER MINDS

We take it for granted in our everyday lives that we are not alone in the universe; that there are other people who inhabit this place with us. As we will see, however, once one starts to reflect on the matter, it isn't entirely obvious what entitles us to this belief. Why are we so sure that there are other people out there, people who have minds like our own?

The problem confronting our knowledge of other minds is that, on the face of it at least, we don't actually observe other minds in the way that we observe objects like trees and cars. One's mind seems to be something that *underlies* one's body such that, although one's bodily behaviour manifests one's mind, simply observing an agent's behaviour is not the same as observing their mind. Accordingly, the thought runs, in order to know that someone has a mind we have to do more than merely observe their behaviour; we also have to infer that there is something underlying that behaviour and giving rise to it – namely, a mind.

If this picture of how we come to know that there are other minds is correct, then scepticism about the existence of such minds is just around the corner (i.e. the view that knowledge that other minds exist is impossible). After all, if we have to *infer* the existence of other minds from observed behaviour, then the question naturally arises as to whether that observed behaviour could be manifested even though there is no mind underlying the behaviour. Perhaps the 'people' that one interacts with on a daily basis are nothing more than unminded automata or zombies who have no thoughts and feelings at all. How would we tell the difference? (This is particularly

DOI: 10.4324/9781003356110-26

troubling in the case of zombies, where there is no obvious underlying physical difference.) This difficulty concerning how we know that there are other people who have minds like we do is called the **problem of other minds**.

• THE ARGUMENT FROM ANALOGY

So how might one respond to the problem of other minds? Perhaps the most famous line of response – a version of which is usually credited to **John Stuart Mill** (1806–73) – makes use of a form of inductive reasoning known as an **argument from analogy**. Essentially, the idea behind this approach to the problem of other minds is to maintain that we can come to know that there are other minds by observing how the behaviour of others mirrors that of our own (where we know that we have minds). The thought is that since we know that we have minds, it follows that the behaviour of others which is similar to our own shows that these others have minds too.

The starting point for this argument is our knowledge both of the existence and nature of our own minds. After all, we cannot seriously doubt that we have a mind, since who then would be doing the doubting? (This is the point of Descartes' famous '*cogito ergo sum*': 'I think, therefore I am'.) Moreover, it is also held that there cannot be any troubling sceptical argument concerning our access to what is going on in our own minds because this access is *privileged*. That is, we have immediate non-inferential access to what is going on in our own minds – what we are thinking and feeling – and this means that our knowledge in this regard is entirely secure (at least if any knowledge is). It seems to follow that we can put our knowledge of our

---

John Stuart Mill (1806–73)

> If all mankind minus one were of one opinion, and only one person were of the contrary opinion, mankind would be no more justified in silencing that one person, than he, if he had the power, would be justified in silencing mankind.

Mill, *On Liberty*

The English philosopher and economist, John Stuart Mill, was one of the most influential men of his day. Like his father, James Mill (1773–1836), Mill was a prominent liberal reformer committed to *utilitarianism* – the view that actions are morally right to the extent to which they promote the greatest happiness in the greatest number of people. As a liberal, he was very interested in articulating what liberty amounts to, and working out what the reasonable limits of an individual's liberty should be. Mill was a member of the British parliament and was one of the first parliamentarians to argue for the rights of women, such as the right to vote.

own minds together with our knowledge of how we, as minded creatures, behave, to determine what sort of behaviour a minded creature should have.

For example, we might notice that when we are in pain, as when we accidentally burn ourselves on a match, we respond in certain ways (e.g. by calling out). Suppose we notice a number of these correlations between external stimuli (e.g. the burning of a match, the tickle of a feather), external response (e.g. calling out, giggling), and the associated mental state (e.g. pain, pleasure). Suppose further that we observe other apparently minded people behaving in the same ways in response to the same stimuli (i.e. they call out when burnt by matches and giggle when tickled with feathers). Wouldn't we then be entitled to inductively infer that there are other minds just like our own?

Here is the form of the inductive argument that is being used here:

A1 There are patterns in my behaviour in response to external stimuli which reveal that I am having mental states of a certain sort (e.g. my crying out in response to being burnt by a match indicates that I am in pain).
A2 This same behaviour in response to external stimuli is exhibited by others.
AC These others experience the same mental states that I do, and so are minded, just like me.

On the face of it at least, this looks like a good way of responding to the problem of other minds.

A PROBLEM FOR THE ARGUMENT FROM ANALOGY

Although initially persuasive, the argument from analogy runs into problems on closer inspection. For one thing, the style of argument being employed here is not a good one, even if we set aside the more general worries, one might have about inductive arguments that we looked at in Chapter 10. Compare the argument given above with the following inductive argument:

1 Box A is brown and it contains a book.
2 Boxes B, C, and D are brown.
C Boxes B, C, and D contain a book.

Clearly, this is a very bad style of argument in that the mere fact that one brown box contains a certain item does not give us any reason to believe that any other brown box contains that sort of item. The problem with this argument is that it only considers a particular instance of a brown box, an instance that we have no reason to think is representative of brown boxes in general. As we noted in Chapter 10, however, good inductive arguments are always ones that reason from *representative* premises to conclusions. Accordingly, we cannot reason from this instance to a more general conclusion that applies to any brown box we care to pick.

Notice that the following argument would be OK:

1* Lots of brown boxes have been observed over many years and in a wide range of environments and they have all contained books.
2 Boxes B, C, and D are brown.
C Boxes B, C, and D contain a book.`

If it is indeed true that we have observed a representative range of brown boxes and found them all to have a book in them, then there is no problem in justifiably concluding that any other brown box we find will also have a book in it. The problem, however, is that the argument from analogy is more akin to the first of these 'brown box' arguments than the second. The reason for this is that it begins with the observation of a correlation in a single case (between my behaviour and my mindedness) and draws conclusions about the relationship between behaviour and mindedness in general. But that is a very bad way of reasoning, as the first 'brown box' argument shows.

If we were entitled to suppose that our case is somehow representative of minds in general, so that what holds for my mind would hold for others, then we could properly use an argument from analogy to draw conclusions about the existence of other minds. But how would we come by such a supposition without in the process simply assuming that which is to be shown (i.e. that there are other minds out there which are like my own)?

This is not the only problem facing the argument from analogy, but it is the most decisive one. One simply cannot legitimately infer that there are other minds on the basis of one's own case.

• TWO VERSIONS OF THE PROBLEM OF OTHER MINDS

As if the problem of other minds as it is presented above weren't bad enough, there is a second difficulty lurking here. This is that even if we could come to know that there exist other minds, it isn't at all clear how we could come to know that these other minds are like our own. There are thus two problems here which can easily be run together if one isn't careful. The first is whether any other minds exist, regardless of what those minds are like. The second is whether, given that other minds exist, those minds are like our own.

Clearly, one could answer the first problem without having any answer to the second. In order to see this point, take it for granted for a moment that there are indeed other minds. Now ask yourself how you can be sure that other people's minds are like your own. A standard motif of science fiction movies, for example, is that of the alien taking over someone's mind. In such a case, we have someone who may well nearly always behave as she used to, but who no longer thinks and feels like a human but like an alien. How would we tell the difference if there was nothing in the alien's appearance or behaviour to give the game away?

> ### Invasion of the Body Snatchers
>
> The main premise of the seminal 1956 film *Invasion of the Body Snatchers* is that people are being quietly replaced by alien duplicates. In many ways, though not in all ways, these aliens act just like the people they have replaced, which is what makes it so difficult to tell the alien duplicates apart from the 'real' people. Presumably, while these aliens look and act like real people, they do not experience the world as we do. This raises the question, central to this section of the chapter, of how we can be sure that others are minded in the specific way that we suppose them to be. How do we know that they feel pain like we do, for example? After all, the alien duplicates act just like we act, so it seems that we cannot tell what their minds are like just by observing their behaviour. But if we can't do it in this way, then how can we do it?

Indeed, we don't need to consider science fiction movies in order to get an example of this sort of 'deviant' mindedness. After all, some people are colour-blind, for example, and so see colours very differently to 'normal' people. Others have unusual senses of taste and hearing, perhaps being unable to taste/hear things that others can taste/hear, or tasting/hearing them differently. Often we can tell that this is happening because it has an impact on someone's behaviour. For example, if a certain fruit that tastes sweet to others tastes very sour to them, then they will respond with disgust upon tasting it. We can easily imagine cases, however, in which another person experiences the world very differently and yet this difference does not manifest itself in experience. For instance, suppose that someone sees red as blue and vice versa. Accordingly, they would grow up calling what they experience as blue 'red', and vice versa. Would this difference ever come to light? It might in that it might affect how they respond to other colours on the spectrum, for example. Equally, however, it might not in that this person might just go through life systematically mistaking red for blue and blue for red. If this is possible, however, then it raises the question of how certain we can be that we are all experiencing the world in the same way. Perhaps we have just learned to categorise the world in a standard way, even though the subjective natures of our experiences are in fact very different from case to case?

• PERCEIVING SOMEONE ELSE'S MIND

One way in which one might respond to the problem of other minds – in both its forms – is to question its guiding premise that our knowledge of other minds is by its nature inferential. After all, common sense would seem to suggest otherwise on this score. Suppose I see someone writhing in agony on the ground before me. Do I really need to make an *inference* in order to know that he is in pain? Can't I just see, directly, that he is in pain?

The thought is thus that perhaps, at least when it comes to some very clear-cut cases, I could know that someone is having a certain experience – of being in pain, say – simply by observing them. And if I can know what kind of experience someone is having in this direct way, then presumably I can also come to know that this person is a creature with a mind that is capable of experiences in the first place. That is, I can come to know, without inference, both that there is someone else with a mind and that the experiences that this person has are at least in certain respects like mine. If this is right, then the worry that the inference involved in the argument from analogy is unsound does not get a grip, at least not on these select cases of direct knowledge of other people's minds, as there is no inference taking place.

At first pass, this proposal might look like mere dogmatism: how could we be sure that what we are observing really is the case? Notice, however, that this sort of view is structurally very similar to the direct realism as regards perceptual knowledge that we looked at in Chapter 7. One of the key motivations for direct realism was the thought that we should resist the inference from the fact that our perceptual experience could be undetectably misleading to the conclusion that what we are directly aware of in perceptual experience is only the way the world seems to us rather than the way the world is. Although it is true that in deceived cases, such as the scenario in which I am visually presented with a mirage of an oasis, I am not directly aware of the world but only with the way the world appears, this should not be thought, says the direct realist, to entail that in non-deceived cases, such as that in which I am actually looking at an oasis right in front of me, I am not directly acquainted with objects in the world.

One might apply the same line of reasoning here. There clearly are cases in which one might make a judgement about what someone is experiencing and be wrong. Moreover, we can certainly conceive of cases in which one makes a judgement that something has a mind – a robot, say – when in fact it doesn't. Conceding this much, however, doesn't by itself ensure that you can never know what someone else is experiencing – or, indeed, that they have a mind – just by observing them. Why should the cases in which one's judgements go wrong dictate whether one has knowledge in cases where one's judgements go right? Of course, such knowledge, if it is possessed, is bound to be fallible – we could be wrong. But then we are usually happy to grant knowledge in the absence of **infallibility**, so why not here?

• CHAPTER SUMMARY

- The problem of other minds concerns the fact that it seems that we are unable to observe another person's mind in the same way that we can observe physical objects like tables and chairs. So how, then, do we know that there are other minds in the first place?
- One way to try to resolve this problem is to make use of the argument from analogy, which notes correlations between our behaviour and our mental states, and thereby inductively draws conclusions about the mental states of others who behave in ways that are similar to how we behave.

- The style of reasoning employed in the argument from analogy is defective, however, since one cannot legitimately reason from a correlation that holds in a single (and apparently unrepresentative) case to a general conclusion that applies to many cases.
- We then distinguished two closely related problems that are involved in the problem of other minds. The first (noted above) is whether other minds exist. The second is whether, given that other minds exist, these minds are like our own. As we noted, it could be that we are able to know that there are other minds, but are nevertheless unable to know that these minds are like our own. This is because it seems possible that other people might experience the world very differently from how I experience it, but in such a way that these differences in subjective experience are undetectable to others.
- Finally, we looked at one way in which one might respond to the problem of other minds (in both its forms), which is to hold that we can, at least sometimes, have direct knowledge of another person's mind. For example, if I see someone writhing around on the ground before me, I could come to know, without needing to make any inference, that this person is in pain. We noted that such a view is very controversial.

• STUDY QUESTIONS

1 Why might it be thought problematic to suppose that one can know that there are other minds? What is it about our beliefs in the existence of other minds that makes them suspect?
2 What is the argument from analogy, and how is it supposed to resolve the problem of other minds? What difficulties does this argument face? Does this argument succeed in showing that we can have knowledge of other minds?
3 Explain, in your own words, why there is a difference between doubt about the existence of other minds, and doubt that others have minds like one's own. What special reasons might there be to doubt the latter?
4 Is it plausible to suppose that one can directly observe someone else's pain, and thereby come to know, without inference, that they are in pain? If one could, then how would this help us resolve the problem of other minds?

• INTRODUCTORY FURTHER READING

Avramides, Anita (2010) 'Skepticism about Knowledge of Other Minds', *Routledge Companion to Epistemology*, S. Bernecker & D. H. Pritchard (eds), Ch. 40, pp. 433–44 (London: Routledge). An authoritative introduction to the problem of other minds, written by an expert in the field. Essential reading. (Note too that Avramides has an excellent online resource available on this topic too – see below.)

Claeys, Gregory (2022) *John Stuart Mill: A Very Short Introduction* (Oxford: Oxford University Press). A good source of introductory material for those who wish to learn more about the philosophy of John Stuart Mill.

● ADVANCED FURTHER READING

Avramides, Anita (2001) *Other Minds* (London: Routledge). An excellent book-length treatment of the problem of other minds.

Dilulio, John Peter (2022) *Completely Free: The Moral and Political Vision of John Stuart Mill* (Princeton, NJ: Princeton University Press). An accessible overview of the main themes of John Stuart Mill's thought.

● FREE INTERNET RESOURCES

Avrimades, Anita (2019) 'Other Minds', *Stanford Encyclopedia of Philosophy*, http://plato.stanford.edu/entries/other-minds/. An excellent overview of the problem of other minds.

Macleod, Christopher (2016) 'John Stuart Mill', *Stanford Encyclopedia of Philosophy*, http://plato.stanford.edu/entries/mill/. A helpful overview of the life and work of John Stuart Mill.

Thornton, Stephen P. (2004) 'Solipsism and the Problem of Other Minds', *Internet Encyclopedia of Philosophy*, www.iep.utm.edu/s/solipsis.htm. A good overview of the problem of other minds.

21

radical
scepticism

- The radical sceptical paradox
- Scepticism and closure
- Mooreanism
- Contextualism

THE RADICAL SCEPTICAL PARADOX

In Chapter 20, we looked at scepticism about other minds, which is the view that we know very little, if anything, about other minds (both about whether there are other minds and also about what their minds are like given that they do exist). This chapter is also devoted to scepticism, but of an even more dramatic form. Whereas scepticism about other minds is restricted to a certain domain, the kind of scepticism that we will be looking at here holds that it is impossible to know anything much at all about the world around you, or at least anything of any consequence. Because it is so dramatic and general in scope, this type of scepticism is known as **radical scepticism**.

As it is usually understood in the contemporary debate, radical scepticism is not supposed to be thought of as a philosophical position as such (i.e. as a stance that someone adopts), but rather as a challenge that any theorist of knowledge must overcome. That is, radical scepticism is meant to serve a *methodological* function. The goal is to show that one's theory of knowledge is scepticism-proof, since if it isn't – if it allows that most knowledge is impossible – then there must be something seriously wrong with the view. Accordingly, we are not to think of the 'sceptic' as a person necessarily – i.e. as someone who is trying to convince us of anything – but rather as our intellectual conscience that is posing a specific kind of problem for our epistemological position in order to tease out what our view really involves and whether it is a plausible stance to take.

There are two main components to sceptical arguments as they are usually understood in the contemporary discussion of this topic. The first component concerns what is known as a **sceptical hypothesis**. A sceptical hypothesis is a scenario in which

DOI: 10.4324/9781003356110-27

you are radically deceived about the world and yet your experience of the world is exactly as it would be if you were not radically deceived. Consider, for example, the fate of the protagonist in the film *The Matrix*, who comes to realise that his previous experiences of the world were in fact being 'fed' into his brain while his body was confined to a large vat. Accordingly, while he seemed to be experiencing a world rich with interaction between himself and other people, in fact he was not interacting with anybody or any *thing* at all (at least over and above the tubes in the vat that were 'feeding' him his experiences), but was instead simply floating motionlessly.

The problem posed by sceptical hypotheses is that we seem unable to know that they are false. After all, if our experience of the world could be exactly as it is and yet we are the victims of a sceptical hypothesis, then on what basis could we ever hope to distinguish a genuine experience of the world from an illusory one? The first key claim of the sceptical argument is thus that we are unable to know that we are not the victims of sceptical hypotheses.

The second component of the sceptical argument involves the claim that if we are unable to know the denials of sceptical hypotheses, then it follows that we are unable to know very much at all. Right now, for example, I think that I know that I am sitting here at my desk writing this chapter. Given that I do not know that I am not the victim of a sceptical hypothesis, however, and given that if I were the victim of a sceptical hypothesis the world would appear exactly the same as it is just now even though I am *not* presently sitting at my desk, then how can I possibly know that I am sitting at my desk? The problem is that, so long as I cannot rule out sceptical hypotheses, I don't seem able to know very much at all.

We can roughly express this sceptical argument in the following way:

1 We are unable to know the denials of sceptical hypotheses.
2 If we are unable to know the denials of sceptical hypotheses, then we are unable to know anything of substance about the world.
C We are unable to know anything of substance about the world.

Two very plausible claims about our knowledge can thus be used to generate a valid argument that produces this rather devastating radically sceptical conclusion.

The Matrix

The Matrix, a 1999 movie starring Keanu Reeves, is the first part of a famous series of films. The movie follows the story of a computer hacker called Neo, played by Reeves, who discovers that his experiences of the world are in fact entirely artificial, and that he is instead floating in a vat of nutrients and being 'fed' his experiences. In this nightmarish scenario, supercomputers have enslaved the human race and now use the 'essences' of humans as a power source. Neo escapes from the vat in which he has been floating and leads a rebellion against the supercomputers.

In this sense, the sceptical argument is a **paradox**. That is, from a series of apparently intuitive premises, we are able to validly infer an absurd, and thus highly counter-intuitive, conclusion.

One might think that the weakest link in this argument is the second premise, on the grounds that it is far too much to ask of a knower that they are able to rule out radical sceptical hypotheses. Why should it be, for example, that in order to be properly said to know that I am sitting at my desk right now I must first be able to rule out the possibility that I am being 'fed' my experiences by futuristic supercomputers that are out to deceive me? Surely all that I need to do in order to have knowledge in this case is to form my belief in the right kind of way and for that belief to be supported by the appropriate evidence (e.g. that I can see my desk before me)? To demand more than this seems perverse, and if scepticism merely reflects unduly restrictive epistemic standards, then it isn't nearly as problematic as it might at first seem. We can reject *perverse* epistemic standards with impunity – it is only the *intuitively correct* ones that we need to pay serious attention to.

Nevertheless, there is an additional way of motivating premise 2, one that makes its truth seem entirely uncontentious. Consider the **closure principle** for knowledge:

The closure principle

If an agent knows one proposition, and knows that this proposition entails a second proposition, then the agent knows the second proposition as well.

For example, if I know that I'm sitting here in my office right now, and I also know that if I'm sitting in my office right now then I'm not standing up next door, then it seems that I must also know that I'm not standing up next door. So expressed, the principle seems entirely unremarkable.

Notice, however, that it follows from the fact that I am seated at my desk in my office that I am not encased in a large vat being 'fed' the experiences as if I were sitting at my desk (aside from anything else, if I were in the vat then I wouldn't be *seated* at all, but *floating* in the nutrients contained therein). Accordingly, given the closure principle, it follows that if I know that I am currently seated in my office, then I also know that I am not encased in a large vat being 'fed' experiences that are designed to deceive me. However, as the sceptic points out in premise 1 of their argument, that seems precisely the kind of thing that I could never know. As a result, concludes the sceptic, it must be that I don't know that I am presently seated in my office either.

In effect, what the sceptic's use of the closure principle does is make knowledge of normal 'everyday' propositions (i.e. the sort of propositions which we would usually regard ourselves as unproblematically knowing) contingent upon knowledge of the denials of sceptical hypotheses. Moreover, since the principle is so plausible, it makes this connection seem entirely intuitive. That is, the demand that I should know the denials of sceptical hypotheses seems now to be the product of entirely reasonable epistemic standards, not perverse ones. The trouble is, of course, that with this demand in place, the sceptical conclusion appears irresistible.

● SCEPTICISM AND CLOSURE

What is one to do about this sceptical argument? One possibility might be to respond by rejecting the closure principle, although this is easier said than done. After all, how could such a plausible principle be false? How could it be that I could know one proposition, know that it entails a second proposition, and yet fail to know that entailed proposition? Indeed, the only instances where this kind of principle seems at all problematic is when it is employed in sceptical arguments, and this suggests that perhaps the reason why we find the closure principle problematic here is simply that it is helpful to the sceptic. If this is right, then the move to deny this principle smacks of desperation.

Nevertheless, there are motivations that can be offered in defence of rejecting this principle, at least as the sceptic employs it. One way in which some philosophers have gone about rejecting the closure principle is by appeal to the fallibilist intuition that in knowing something I only need to be able to rule out all *relevant* possibilities of error, and don't have to rule out *all* possibilities of error. Taking 'rule out' here to mean 'know to be false', this means that in order to know something I only need to know that a restricted range of error possibilities are false, not that all of them are (that would be **infallibilism**). The complaint raised by fallibilists against the closure principle, however, is that it demands that we know the falsity of even far-fetched – and thus, intuitively, *irrelevant* – error possibilities, such as sceptical hypotheses, and hence that there is something deeply suspect about it.

Although superficially appealing, this line of argument is not that persuasive on closer inspection. Notice that the closure principle is entirely compatible with **fallibilism**. This principle does not demand that you know that *all* error possibilities are false, but only those error possibilities which are known to be incompatible with what you know, which is a much weaker claim. One cannot therefore reject the closure principle solely on fallibilist grounds.

Everything thus rests on the further claim being made here about relevance: that sceptical hypotheses are far-fetched and therefore of their nature irrelevant. The problem with this suggestion is that it is hard to see just what, besides a blank statement of intuition, could justify the thought that sceptical hypotheses are irrelevant. Indeed, why doesn't the fact that we know that they are inconsistent with our everyday beliefs, such that those beliefs cannot be true if the sceptical hypotheses obtain, make them relevant?

A different tack taken by fallibilists in order to attack the closure principle has been to suggest that the following **sensitivity principle** applies, such that knowledge entails that one has a true belief which is *sensitive* to the truth:

The sensitivity principle

If an agent knows a proposition, then that agent's true belief in that proposition must be sensitive in the sense that, had that proposition been false, she would not have believed it.

For example, consider a case in which no one thinks that the agent has knowledge, such as a Gettier case like the 'stopped clock' example we looked at early on in this book. In this case, we have an agent who forms a true belief about what the time is by looking at a stopped clock, one that just happens to be showing the right time. The agent in this case clearly doesn't know what the time is, even if her belief is justified, since it's just a matter of luck that her belief is true. One way of fleshing out this idea that the belief in this case is just too luckily true to count as knowledge is to notice that it is a belief which is insensitive. After all, had what the agent believed been false – if the time had been a minute earlier or later, for example, but everything else had stayed the same – then she would have carried on believing what she does regardless, even though it is no longer true. In contrast, someone who finds out what the time is by looking at a working clock will form a sensitive belief about what the time is, since were the time to have been different (but everything else had stayed the same), then the clock would have displayed a different time and the agent would therefore have formed a different (and likewise true) belief about what the time is. In short, a sensitive belief is one that changes as the facts change so that one does not end up with a false belief, while an insensitive belief is one that doesn't so change.

What is interesting about the sensitivity principle is that while most of our everyday beliefs are sensitive to the truth, our anti-sceptical beliefs, such as our belief that we are not brains in vats, are not sensitive. My belief that I am presently sitting at my computer writing this, for example, is sensitive since, were this to be false, but everything else the same – such as if I were standing up next to my computer, for example – then I wouldn't any longer believe that I was sitting; I'd believe that I was standing instead. In contrast, think of my belief that I am not a brain in a vat. Were this belief to be false – so that I was indeed a brain in a vat – then I would carry on believing that I am not a brain in a vat regardless. Indeed, it is explicitly part of how we characterise sceptical hypotheses that our beliefs in their falsehood are insensitive in this way.

If the sensitivity principle captures something essential about knowledge, therefore, then we can account for why we feel that we can know an awful lot of propositions which we think we know even while failing to know the denials of sceptical hypotheses. Of course, this would necessitate denying the closure principle, and that's a high price for any theory of knowledge to pay – perhaps *too* high – but notice that we would at least have *motivated* the denial of this principle in terms of how it conflicts with another epistemological principle (i.e. the sensitivity principle) which we have also seen is quite intuitive.

• MOOREANISM

A very different sort of response to this argument might be to try to use the closure principle to your own anti-sceptical advantage. The general idea is that one can employ the closure principle in order to show that we do know the denials of sceptical hypotheses after all, because we know lots of mundane claims that entail the falsity of these hypotheses.

For example, I seem to be sitting at my desk right now and everything appears to be entirely normal. In these circumstances, we would typically grant, provided that what I believe is true of course, that I do know that I am seated at my desk. As noted above, however, if we grant knowledge in this case, then it seems to follow, given that I know that I cannot be both sitting at my desk and floating in a vat of nutrients, that I must know that I am not floating in a vat somewhere being 'fed' misleading impressions of the world. The anti-sceptical thought that might arise at this point is thus to contend that, despite first impressions, we *do* know that we are not the victims of sceptical hypotheses after all and, moreover, we know this precisely *because* of our knowledge of rather mundane things (such as that we are seated) and the truth of the closure principle. Something like an anti-sceptical argument of this form is often associated with the remarks made about scepticism by **G. E. Moore**, and thus this approach to scepticism is often referred to as **Mooreanism**.

This way of trying to turn the closure principle back against the sceptic is really quite dubious, however. For one thing, what is at issue is whether we do know anything of substance, and thus it seems somewhat question-begging to make use of an instance of everyday knowledge in order to show that we can know the denials of sceptical hypotheses, especially since we have already seen that the sceptical claim that we cannot have such knowledge is very plausible.

Moreover, given the plausibility of the sceptical premise regarding our inability to know the denials of sceptical hypotheses, the current state of play seems to be less

---

G. E. Moore (1873–1958)

I can prove . . . that two human hands exist. How? By holding up my two hands, and saying, as I make a certain gesture with the right hand, 'Here is one hand', and adding, as I make a certain gesture with the left, 'and here is another'.

G. E. Moore, 'Proof of an External World'

G. E. Moore was a distinguished British philosopher – he spent his entire academic career at Cambridge University – who was very influential on twentieth-century philosophy. His work influenced both Ludwig Wittgenstein and Bertrand Russell, but unlike Wittgenstein and Russell, Moore's philosophical approach was very much to defend common sense rather than advance any grand philosophical theses. In epistemology, this manifested itself with Moore's astonishingly direct response to the problem of scepticism. In ethics, another area of philosophy where his work has had long-lasting impact, his common-sense approach led him to claim that goodness could not be defined, contrary to the many definitions of goodness offered by ethicists.

a victory to Mooreanism as merely a further problem for one's theory of knowledge that needs to be resolved. How could it be that we can know the denials of sceptical hypotheses given that there appears to be nothing in our experiences which could possibly indicate to us that we are not in such a scenario? The Moorean cannot simply assert that we have such knowledge without also explaining how such knowledge could come to be possessed – but that is far more difficult than it might at first seem.

Nevertheless, there are ways of giving Mooreanism some further motivation in this regard. One way of doing this is by allying the view to some form of direct realism, of the kind we saw in Chapter 7. Recall that the direct realist claimed that we directly experience the world, and thus argued that we should not conclude from the fact we are unable to tell the difference between cases where we are not deceived and counterpart deceived cases (i.e. cases where everything seems the same, such as the brain in a vat case) that we do not directly experience the world in non-deceived cases. On this picture, then, the thought is that our experiences in the non-deceived cases are not the same as in deceived cases, even though we cannot tell the difference between them. If this is right, it could go some way to supporting Mooreanism since it undermines the sceptical claim that we can't possibly know the denials of sceptical hypotheses given that our experiences would be exactly the same even if such hypotheses obtained.

That said, the support offered Mooreanism by this move is limited. After all, the chief worry that the sceptic raises is not that our experiences are the same in counterpart deceived and non-deceived cases, but rather that we cannot tell the difference between such cases, and there is nothing in direct realism (at least as we have just described the view) which undermines *that* claim.

With this in mind, Mooreans often take a different tack and try to show how we can know the denials of sceptical hypotheses even though we are unable to tell such cases apart from counterpart non-deceived cases. To do this, they often propose the following **safety principle**:

The safety principle

If an agent knows a proposition, then that agent's true belief in that proposition must be *safe* in the sense that it couldn't have easily been false (alternatively: were the agent to continue believing that proposition in similar circumstances, then the belief would almost always still be true).

Informally, the idea behind the safety principle is to capture the intuition that knowledge cannot be lucky. Think of the skilled archer that we looked at in Chapter 1. What constitutes such a skill is that the archer can usually hit the target in a wide range of relevant conditions, and that's what sets a skilled archer apart from someone who only just happens to hit the target by luck. We noted in Chapter 1 that we can think of knowledge in terms of this metaphor, where the arrow is belief and the target is truth. The idea is that knowledge arises when our beliefs hit the target of truth through skill and not through luck.

The safety principle offers a way of cashing out this archery analogy. After all, one way of expressing the difference between the skilled archer who hits the target and the clumsy archer who hits the target is that the clumsy archer (but not the skilled archer) could very easily have missed. (Alternatively, there are lots of similar circumstances in which the clumsy archer misses the target, while only very few in which the skilled archer misses the target.) Similarly, someone who genuinely knows, rather than someone who merely happens to truly believe, has a belief that could not have easily been false (i.e. were that belief to be formed in similar circumstances, then it would usually still be true).

In order to see this, contrast someone who finds out what the time is by looking at a reliable working clock with someone who finds out what the time is by looking at a broken clock, albeit one which, as it happens, is showing the right time. In the first case, the true belief is safe in that a belief about the time formed in similar circumstances (e.g. where the time was slightly different) would continue to be true. In contrast, the true belief in the second case is unsafe, since there are lots of similar conditions in which the agent forms a belief about the time and yet her belief is false (e.g. situations in which the time is slightly different).

What is interesting about the safety principle for our current purposes is that it lends some support to the Moorean claim that we are able to know the denials of sceptical hypotheses. Even though I may lack any good reason for thinking that I'm not a brain in a vat – I wouldn't be able to tell the difference between being a brain in a vat and not being a brain in a vat, after all – just so long as circumstances are pretty much as I take them to be, then my true belief that I'm not a brain in a vat will be safe. This is because there won't be any similar circumstances in which I form this belief and my belief is false for the simple reason that if the world is pretty much as I take it to be then there are no similar circumstances in which I am a brain in a vat – this sort of thing only happens in circumstances that are very different from the ones I'm in. If this line of thought is granted, then it might be possible to allow that we can know the denials of sceptical hypotheses, even though we lack good grounds for these beliefs, and if we can grant *that* then the motivation to deny the closure principle as a way of dealing with the sceptical problem subsides. (Notice that, so construed, Mooreanism is clearly committed to some form of epistemic externalism, since it is allowing that we can have knowledge of the denials of sceptical hypotheses even while lacking good grounds in favour of our beliefs in the denials of sceptical hypotheses.)

One might want to object to this line of thought by saying that we can't simply presuppose that the world is pretty much as we take it to be, since once we presuppose that then we've already sidestepped the sceptical problem. This presupposition is not nearly as contentious as it might at first seem, however. To begin with, notice that no one disputes that if we are victims of sceptical hypotheses then we don't know very much. The interesting question is whether, *even if we're not so deceived*, we are able to know very much, and to this question, the sceptic replies negatively. The sceptic is therefore claiming that *whatever* circumstances we find ourselves in, we are unable to know very much (including that we are not the victim of a sceptical hypothesis). If this is right, then it follows that we can assume anything we like about what circumstances we are in without dodging the sceptical challenge.

Even if this objection is not fatal, however, one might still worry about the idea that we can possess knowledge of the denials of sceptical hypotheses in this way. After all, the analogy with the skilled archer suggests that we gain knowledge in virtue of forming beliefs in a way which involves being responsive to how the world is, and yet on this view our knowledge of the denials of sceptical hypotheses seems to be gained even though there is no responsiveness to the world at all. (Remember that the Moorean grants that we can't tell the difference between everyday life and a sceptical hypothesis.) In short, the worry one might have regarding such knowledge is that it involves no skill at all, and thus is in this sense only luckily true, even though it may well involve a safe true belief.

CONTEXTUALISM

One final anti-sceptical theory that we will look at is **contextualism**. This view holds that the key to resolving the sceptical problem lies in recognising that 'knowledge' is a highly context-sensitive term. Think for a moment about other terms that we use that might plausibly be thought to be context-sensitive, such as 'flat' or 'empty'. For example, if, in normal circumstances, I tell you that the fridge is empty, then you will understand me as saying that it's empty of food, and not that it's empty of *anything* – it contains *air*, after all. Similarly, if, in normal circumstances, I tell you that the table is flat, I mean that it's not especially bumpy, and not that there are no imperfections *whatsoever* on the surface of the table (I'm not suggesting that the table is a perfectly frictionless plane). In different contexts, however, what is meant by calling something 'flat' or 'empty' could change. When a scientist requests a 'flat' table to put their highly sensitive instrument on, for example, they probably have in mind something an awful lot flatter than the sort of table that we would normally classify as 'flat'.

Suppose for a moment that 'knows' is also context-sensitive in this way. One way in which this might have import for the sceptical problem could be if the sceptic was using the term in a more demanding way than we usually use it, just as the scientist is using a more demanding conception of what counts as a 'flat' surface in the example just offered. In this way, just as we can consistently grant that a table is 'flat' by our everyday standards even though it might not meet the scientist's more exacting standards, so we can, it seems, grant that we 'know' an awful lot relative to our everyday standards even though we may not count as knowing very much relative to the sceptic's more exacting standards.

More specifically, the contextualist thought is that whereas in normal contexts we count an agent as having knowledge just so long as she is able to rule out mundane non-sceptical possibilities of error, what the sceptic does is raise the standards for knowledge such that in order to count as having knowledge, that agent must in addition be able to rule out far-fetched sceptical possibilities of error. Accordingly, the contextualist claims that while we have lots of knowledge relative to everyday standards, this claim is entirely compatible with the sceptical claim that we lack knowledge relative to more demanding sceptical standards.

On the face of it, this is a neat resolution of the problem. For one thing, we don't have to deny the closure principle on this view, since provided we stick within a single context – whether every day or sceptical – we'll either have knowledge both of everyday propositions and the denials of sceptical hypotheses or we'll lack knowledge both of everyday propositions and the denials of sceptical hypotheses (i.e. there will be no context in which one knows the former without also knowing the latter). Moreover, we can respond to the sceptical problem while conceding that there is *something* right about scepticism – the sceptic is, after all, perfectly correct if her argument is understood relative to more exacting sceptical standards.

On closer inspection, however, the contextualist response to scepticism is not nearly so compelling. For one thing, consider again the analogy with terms like 'flat' and 'empty'. Hasn't science shown us that, strictly speaking, *nothing* is ever really flat or empty (because every surface has *some* imperfections, no matter how small, and there are no vacuums in nature)? Of course, we talk as if there are flat surfaces and empty containers, but in fact when we think about it we realise that nothing really corresponds to these ascriptions of flatness and emptiness – we are just talking loosely. Accordingly, if we follow through the analogy with 'knows', then the natural conclusion to draw is that we don't really know anything – because no one could rule out *all* possibilities of error, including sceptical error possibilities – even though we often talk, loosely, as if we do know a great deal.

At the very least, then, it seems that contextualists must be careful about what analogy they draw when they say that 'knowledge' is highly context-sensitive. But even if there are context-sensitive terms which better fit the contextualist picture, there will still be other problems remaining. In particular, perhaps the most pressing difficulty is that it just isn't clear that the sceptical problem does trade on high standards. After all, the sceptical claim is that we have no good grounds *at all* for thinking that we're not the victims of sceptical hypotheses, not that we have good grounds but the grounds we have aren't good enough. If this is right, then it is hard to see how appealing to different epistemic standards will help since it seems to follow, *relative to any epistemic standards that you care to choose*, that we lack knowledge of the denials of sceptical hypotheses, and this will mean, given the closure principle, that we lack everyday knowledge as well, again relative to any epistemic standards that you care to choose.

Relatedly, if we really can make sense of the idea that we can know the denials of sceptical hypotheses, relative to *any* normal epistemic standard, then it's not clear what the motivation for contextualism would be. Why not simply opt for a form of Mooreanism that maintains that we know the denials of sceptical hypotheses and leave the matter at that? That is, why not stop with Mooreanism rather than going further and opting for contextualism which holds *both* that we can know the denials of sceptical hypotheses *and* that knowledge is a highly context-sensitive notion?

So while superficially appealing, the contextualist response to scepticism, like the other responses that we have looked at, is far from being unproblematic.

• CHAPTER SUMMARY

- Radical scepticism is the view that it is impossible to know very much. We are not interested in the view because anyone positively defends it as a serious position, but rather because examining the sorts of considerations that can be put forward in favour of radical scepticism helps us to think about what knowledge is.

- One dominant type of sceptical argument appeals to what is known as a *sceptical hypothesis*. This is a scenario that is indistinguishable from normal life but in which one is radically deceived (e.g. the possibility that one is a disembodied brain floating in a vat of nutrients being 'fed' one's experiences by supercomputers).

- Using sceptical hypotheses, the sceptic can reason in the following way. I'm unable to know that I'm not the victim of a sceptical hypothesis (since such a scenario is indistinguishable from normal life), and thus it follows that I can't know any of the propositions that I think I know which are inconsistent with sceptical hypotheses (e.g. that I'm presently writing this chapter).

- We noted that this argument seems to rest on the *closure principle*, which roughly holds that if you know one proposition (e.g. that you are sitting at a computer typing), and know that it entails a second proposition (e.g. that you are not a brain in a vat), then you also know that second proposition. One way of responding to the sceptical argument is thus to deny this principle, and therefore hold that one can know 'everyday' propositions (e.g. that you are sitting at a computer) even while being unable to know the denials of sceptical hypotheses (e.g. that you are not a brain in a vat).

- Given the plausibility of the closure principle, we saw that denying it is easier said than done. One way in which epistemologists have tried to motivate this claim is by arguing that knowledge is essentially concerned with having *sensitive* true beliefs (i.e. true beliefs which, had what is believed been false, the agent would not have held). This is known as the *sensitivity principle*. Most of our 'everyday' beliefs are sensitive, but our anti-sceptical beliefs are not.

- If one wishes to retain the closure principle, then one possibility is to opt for *Mooreanism* and hold that we can know the denials of sceptical hypotheses. One way of doing this is by appealing to a form of direct realism, though we saw that this sort of motivation for Mooreanism is not all that helpful on closer inspection. A more promising way of supporting the idea that we can know the denials of sceptical hypotheses is by saying that knowledge is essentially concerned with having *safe* true beliefs (i.e. true beliefs which could not have easily been false). This is known as the *safety principle*. It is possible for our beliefs in the denials of sceptical hypotheses to be safe; thus, if knowledge is essentially concerned with safety, we might be able to know such propositions.

- Finally, we looked at the response to the sceptical problem offered by *contextualism*. This held that 'knowledge' is a radically context-sensitive term. On this view, while the sceptic is right to contend, relative to her very demanding epistemic standards, that we are unable to know very much, this claim is consistent with our possessing lots of knowledge relative to the more relaxed standards in operation in normal contexts. One problem that we noted for this proposal is that it's not obvious that the sceptical argument does trade on high epistemic standards in this way. Indeed, it seems that the sceptical argument goes through relative to *all* epistemic standards, not just very austere ones.

● STUDY QUESTIONS

1 What is a sceptical hypothesis, and what role does it play in sceptical arguments? Try to formulate a sceptical hypothesis of your own and use it as part of a radical sceptical argument.
2 What is the closure principle, and what role does it play in sceptical arguments? Give an example of your own of an inference that is an instance of this principle.
3 What is the sensitivity principle? Why do proponents of this principle hold that we need to reject the closure principle?
4 What is the safety principle, and what role does it play as part of a Moorean anti-sceptical argument? In light of this principle, critically assess the Moorean claim that we are able to know the denials of sceptical hypotheses.
5 What is the contextualist response to scepticism? Do you find it persuasive? If so, try to think of some reasons why others might not be persuaded. If not, then try to state clearly why you think the view is problematic.

● INTRODUCTORY FURTHER READING

Greco, John (2007) 'External World Skepticism', *Philosophy Compass*, https://doi. org/10.1111/j.1747-9991.2007.00090.x. A sophisticated, yet still accessible, survey of the main issues as regards scepticism of the variety that concerns us in this chapter.

Luper, Steven (2010) 'Cartesian Skepticism', *Routledge Companion to Epistemology*, S. Bernecker & D. H. Pritchard (eds), Ch. 38, pp. 414–24 (London: Routledge). An authoritative survey of the kind of scepticism that is of interest to us in this chapter.

Pritchard, Duncan (2019) *Scepticism: A Very Short Introduction* (Oxford: Oxford University Press). A short, but comprehensive nonetheless, treatment of the problem of radical scepticism and its relevance to everyday life, written for the general reader.

Steup, Matthias, Turri, John & Sosa, Ernest (eds) (2013) *Contemporary Debates in Epistemology* (2nd edn, Oxford: Blackwell). This volume contains a number of sections that are relevant to the topics covered in this chapter. See especially the exchange between Fred Dretske and John Hawthorne on the closure principle; the exchange between Earl Conee and Stewart Cohen on contextualism; the exchange between Jonathan Vogel and Richard Fumerton on scepticism; and finally the exchange between Duncan Pritchard and Stephen Hetherington on whether there can be lucky knowledge.

● ADVANCED FURTHER READING

Coliva, Annalisa & Pritchard, Duncan (2022) *Skepticism* (London: Routledge). A systematic overview of the contemporary literature on radical scepticism.

DeRose, Keith & Warfield, Ted (eds) (1999) *Skepticism* (Oxford: Oxford University Press). A useful collection of some classic papers discussing scepticism.

Greco, John (ed.) (2008) *The Oxford Handbook of Skepticism* (Oxford: Oxford University Press). A comprehensive collection of contemporary articles on the topic of scepticism.

Pritchard, Duncan (2015) *Epistemic Angst: Radical Skepticism and the Groundlessness of Our Believing* (Princeton, NJ: Princeton University Press). I've been working on the problem of radical scepticism all my professional life – it's what got me interested in philosophy in the first place in fact. So if you want to know what my personal take on the problem is, this is the book to read.

● FREE INTERNET RESOURCES

Baldwin, Tom (2004) 'George Edward Moore', *Stanford Encyclopedia of Philosophy*, http://plato.stanford.edu/entries/moore/. A comprehensive overview of G. E. Moore's philosophy.

Black, Tim (2006) 'Contextualism in Epistemology', *Internet Encyclopedia of Philosophy*, www.iep.utm.edu/c/contextu.htm. An excellent survey of the issues relating to contextualism.

Comesaña, Juan & Klein, Peter (2019) 'Skepticism', *Stanford Encyclopedia of Philosophy*, http://plato.stanford.edu/entries/skepticism/. A detailed discussion of the literature on scepticism.

Pritchard, Duncan (2002) 'Contemporary Skepticism', *Internet Encyclopedia of Philosophy*, www.iep.utm.edu/s/skepcont.htm. An accessible introduction to the literature on scepticism.

22

truth and objectivity

- Objectivity, anti-realism, and scepticism
- Truth as the goal of inquiry
- Authenticity and the value of truth
- Relativism

● OBJECTIVITY, ANTI-REALISM, AND SCEPTICISM

Right back at the beginning of this book, in Chapter 1, I noted that I was going to take it as given that truth is *objective* in the following sense: for at least most of the propositions about the world that you believe, your thinking that they are true does not make them true. As I said there, whether or not the world is round has nothing to do with whether or not we think that it is, but simply depends upon the shape of the earth.

Objectivism of this ilk goes hand in hand with a kind of fallibilism, such that no matter how good your reasons are for believing that the world is a certain way, it could still be that it isn't that way; you could be wrong. Objectivism about truth thus goes together with what we might term 'epistemic modesty'. Notice, though, that epistemic modesty is not the same as scepticism, even though the two can often be confused. After all, that there is always the possibility of error does not by itself mean that you are unable to know very much – the latter only follows from the former if one advances a form of infallibilism about knowledge, the view that knowledge requires that one can eliminate *all* possibilities of error. But why would anyone hold such an austere thesis? Provided that we are fallibilists about knowledge, then there is no direct entailment from epistemic modesty to scepticism. (In any case, as we saw in the last chapter, you don't need infallibilism to generate the sceptical problem, since fallibilism faces that problem too.)

Even though objectivism about truth does not directly license scepticism, one might think that the root cause of scepticism lies in a strong version of this thesis. Take a *strong* version of objectivism to hold that it is *always* possible that what you believe about the world could be false. In contrast, take a *weak* version of objectivism to

DOI: 10.4324/9781003356110-28

hold simply that what we believe about the world right now could be false. Weak objectivism, but not strong objectivism, is consistent with the thought that the truth of the matter as regards what the world is like cannot *ultimately* outstrip our best formed judgement in this respect. That is, it may be that right now it is possible that most of our beliefs are false, but once we have got the best grounds available for believing what we do, it cannot any longer be possible that what we believe is false. This thesis is known as **anti-realism** about truth. It is often characterised as holding that the truth is ultimately just our best opinion, and therefore cannot be different from it. For example, one way in which some anti-realists often express this point is by saying that the truth is what we discover at the *end of inquiry* (i.e. when all the relevant evidence has been assembled) – whatever we think is the case when we reach this point *is* the case, and that's the end of the matter. In contrast, **realism** about truth embraces the strong objectivism that we just noted, whereby the truth can always potentially outstrip our powers to know it.

Although superficially it may appear as if anti-realism will help us with the sceptical problem, it isn't at all clear on closer inspection just how it is supposed to help. We are right now, I take it, not at the end of inquiry, and so it is certainly possible that our beliefs can be radically in error and thus that we do not know very much. Scepticism is still a live possibility for us, then, and so we need to deal with it. But even when we do reach the end of inquiry, such that there is then no difference between best opinion and the truth, how would we know this point has been reached such that we can be confident that the possibility of massive error has now passed? After all, new evidence can always come along that could call our previous best opinion into doubt, so how could we be sure that such evidence is not around the corner? Without any decisive indication that the end of inquiry has been reached, however, it is of no comfort at all to be told that there is no gap between the truth and best opinion for the sceptic to exploit once we reach this stage.

● TRUTH AS THE GOAL OF INQUIRY

The motivation for anti-realism about truth thus does not obviously come from any inherent ability it might have to help us resolve the sceptical problem. Where proponents of anti-realism are on stronger ground is when they claim that the realist notion of truth inherent in a commitment to strong objectivism – one that can always outstrip best opinion, such that it is always possible that best opinion is wrong – is in some sense an 'idle cog' when it comes to our inquiries. Suppose that all the relevant evidence really is available as regards a particular subject matter, such as evolution, and that this evidence points towards a certain class of propositions as being true. According to the realist, our beliefs in these propositions could still be wrong, and so our best opinion could come apart from the truth of the matter. But, claims the anti-realist, why should we care about this possibility? That is, if all the evidence points towards one proposition, and will never point towards any other proposition, then why not just treat the target proposition as true and leave the matter at that?

In short, the thought is that a notion of truth which extends beyond our best opinion is *necessarily* irrelevant to our inquiries. It certainly cannot be something, the anti-realist claims, that we aspire to in inquiry, since inquiry will always fall short of truth in this sense. What we aspire to in inquiry must thus be best opinion, but since the difference between truth and best opinion cannot possibly make any difference to us, why not just treat best opinion as the truth and forget about this idle cog, the realist conception of truth? As the anti-realist sometimes puts it, if there is no difference to tell, then why think that there is a difference at all?

It's not altogether clear how best to understand this argument. One way of understanding it might be as follows: if the truth is indistinguishable from best opinion, then the truth can't be something that we should value over best opinion. Although this inference has a superficial appeal, it is not all that compelling once you start to think about it. Imagine that we're all being systematically deceived by a demon who is continually frustrating our efforts at finding out how the world is – preventing us from gaining the evidence we need in order to form our beliefs properly, for example. In such a case, wouldn't we want to say that best opinion was just wrong, even though it was indeed best opinion such that it could never be improved upon? And doesn't it *matter* that our beliefs would be wrong in this case, even though we can never tell that they're wrong?

In general, the fact that two things are indistinguishable does not mean that they are of the same value. Imagine two books: one the first ever produced on the first ever printing press; and the other an exact replica constructed in recent times by lasers. It could be that these two books got mixed up a long time ago and no one can now tell – nor will ever be able to tell – which is which. Still, wouldn't we want to say that the book produced on the first ever printing press is of more value, even though we'll never know which it is? If you share this intuition then I think you should resist the inference from the fact that we can't tell truth and best opinion apart to the conclusion that best opinion and truth are just as valuable (such that we might as well just treat best opinion as the truth and leave the matter at that).

Another way of understanding the anti-realist's argument could be as follows: the fact that we can't tell truth and best opinion apart means that the goal of inquiry must in fact be the latter rather than the former. But why should best opinion have any precedence over truth in this regard? I take it that the underlying thought here is that where two goals are indistinguishable, we should regard ourselves as aspiring for the easier of the two to achieve, which in this case is best opinion rather than truth. Since we can't tell the difference between truth (as the realist conceives of it) and best opinion, and since we know that we can in principle attain best opinion, we should regard ourselves as aiming for best opinion rather than truth.

Now this sort of inference might be acceptable in lots of cases, but it's not clear that it applies here. After all, we only care about best opinion because best opinion is a reliable guide as to what the truth is. Accordingly, if we shift our aim to best opinion, then what could be our reason for desiring it now? And note that it is no good saying here that on the anti-realist view best opinion *is* the truth, since if that's the case then that we value the truth can't offer any *independent* reason for why we care about best opinion. Moreover, if best opinion *is* the truth then how do we go about determining that it is best opinion, for don't we determine best opinion in terms of whether it is likely to be true? For example, don't we judge the expert opinion of an astronomer about the position of Pluto in the night sky as better than my untutored opinion on the grounds that her opinion has a greater likelihood of being true? But if that's right – if we assess and value best opinion in terms of its propensity to lead us to the truth – then how can best opinion just be the truth?

None of this suffices to show that anti-realism is wrong, of course, since we are only considering some of the most basic considerations that can be advanced in its favour. But it does indicate that we should be wary of drawing any quick conclusions about truth on the basis of the kinds of considerations that most immediately seem to favour anti-realism. In fact, I think that anti-realism is an important philosophical thesis because it poses a standing challenge to realism that the latter must deal with if it is to be accepted. This is to explain why we value, or at least should value, a realist conception of truth. It is this issue that I want to explore in its own right in the next section.

● AUTHENTICITY AND THE VALUE OF TRUTH

Think again about the two indistinguishable books mentioned above: the one that was the first book produced on the first-ever printing press and an exact replica. We clearly value the former book over the latter, and value it because of how it was produced – but why? I think the answer lies in how in many areas of life – indeed, I would suggest, in the most important areas of life – we value what is *authentic*.

In order to see this, think again of the kind of life lived by the brain in a vat that we looked at in the previous chapter. This scenario is explicitly set up so that we can't tell the difference between being a brain in a vat and not being a brain in a vat who has similar experiences. Presumably, the anti-realist will say that since you can't tell the difference between the two cases, then it really shouldn't matter to you whether you are a brain in a vat. Crucially, however, it *does* matter! You might initially be suspicious of this claim, but if so, imagine for a moment that you're given a choice between living your life inside a vat and living a 'real' life outside of the vat. Indeed, imagine in addition if you like that the envatted life will be more enjoyable – you will never come to harm and all your dreams will seem to come true, for instance. Even so, would you really *choose* the envatted life? After all, remember that such a life is entirely fake – the relationships that you form in this envatted world are not real, after all, but fake, and none of your apparent achievements are real either. Wouldn't such a life be pretty pointless, even if undetectably so?

What I'm suggesting is that the kind of life that we want to lead is an authentic life – one that is in touch with the world – where the relationships that we form are genuine and the achievements we strive for are real. This means, of course, that we have to face the hardship of having relationships that go awry and have to sometimes see our goals go unrealised; but an authentic life, even one full of hardship, is still of more value than a fake life of empty pleasure. Indeed, I would go so far as to suggest that the underlying reason why we care about resolving the sceptical problem is because we recognise that a good life is a life in which one is not radically deceived and in fact knows a great deal. It is thus imperative that one has some assurance that one is not the victim of a sceptical hypothesis.

In short, I'm claiming that it is because we value authenticity that we value truth, and value it over mere best opinion, even when we cannot tell the difference.

• RELATIVISM

With this last point in mind, we will close by considering a view about truth which is radically non-objective. Recall that relativism about truth – a view that we briefly encountered in Chapter 19 when we were exploring politics and epistemology – holds that *whatever* you think is true is true. Relativism is a much more radical position than anti-realism – which holds that truth is best opinion – since on the relativist picture, truth just *is* opinion, best or otherwise. Notice that on this view, two opposing propositions can both be true at the same time. You may think that the earth is flat while I think that it is round. According to the relativist, we are *both* right. (This won't happen on the anti-realist view because although the end of inquiry may not produce a verdict on every proposition, it certainly wouldn't generate two conflicting verdicts.)

Relativism is clearly false because it is self-undermining. For example, if relativism is true, then it follows that the opinions of the realist about truth are just as true as the opinions of the relativist. But it is part of the very essence of realism to deny relativism since on this view merely thinking that something is the case does not make it the case (in contrast to what the relativist holds). It therefore follows that they can't both be right, and thus the fact that the relativist is forced to concede the truth of the realist's opinions about truth means that they are driven down a logical cul-de-sac. If relativism is true, then so is realism. But if realism is true, then relativism is false. So relativism must be false.

People can sometimes be led into relativism because they confuse it with either scepticism or anti-realism. They confuse it with the latter because both anti-realism and relativism reject the strong form of objectivism advanced by the realist. Notice, however, that while anti-realism is a problematic thesis, it is not obviously false in the way that relativism is. It is thus important to keep the two views well apart.

In contrast, people often confuse relativism with scepticism because the worry about whether we are able to know anything of substance gets illicitly converted into the thought that in terms of truth, anything goes. But that there is a problem about how we gain knowledge of the truth does not mean that there is no gap at all between what you think is true and what is true. In any case, the sceptical problem cannot possibly be thought to be a motivation for relativism, since there could be no sceptical problem for the relativist as on this view there is no gap between truth and belief for the sceptic to trade on.

Moreover, it is not as if we can make sense of the idea of relativism being a *response* to the sceptical problem since so construed it is more like a complete capitulation rather than a counter-attack. Even if we can make sense of the idea that your belief that the earth is flat is just as true as my belief that the earth is round (and I don't think we can), we surely can't make sense of the idea that we can both have *knowledge* of these inconsistent propositions. As we've noted at various junctures in this book, knowledge is non-lucky true belief, analogous to the success at hitting the target exhibited by the skilled archer. If one gets to the truth just by believing it, then there is no sense any more to belief aiming at the truth, and thus no sense to the idea that knowledge results when one gets to the truth in a non-lucky fashion – where one's aim is skilfully achieved. It would be like living in a world in which every arrow that gets fired hits its target, no matter where it is fired. In such a world, there could be no skill of archery. Similarly, if the relativist is right, there is no knowledge.

We care about getting things right, and that's why we care about the truth, and thus about knowing the truth. According to relativism, however, there just is no sense to the idea of 'getting things right', since what you think is so *is* so, and thus there is nothing to care about. I'm not sure that anyone actually is a relativist (although some claim to be), because anyone who puts a modicum of thought into what the view is about will surely realise that it is self-defeating. But if there is such a person, then it ought to be clear that endorsing such a view cuts that person off from some of the most important values that make life worthwhile. In particular, if one does not care about the truth, then one does not care about authenticity either since the two go hand in hand, and yet the good life is clearly an authentic life.

We began this book by considering the value of knowledge, and we end it on a similar note. We care about knowledge because knowledge is crucial to a worthwhile, valuable life. The questions of epistemology may be abstract, but their importance to our lives is vital.

● CHAPTER SUMMARY

- To say that truth is objective is to say that merely thinking that the world is a certain way does not entail that it is that way. We noted that such objectivism goes hand in hand with fallibilism, since the key idea behind objectivism is that our beliefs can be wrong.
- We distinguished between a strong form of objectivism, which holds that it is always possible for our beliefs to be wrong, and a weak form of objectivism, which merely holds that what we believe right now could be wrong. The former view we called *realism* about truth, and it holds that the truth can in principle outstrip our best inquiries – no matter what reasons we have for thinking that the world is a certain way, it is always possible that it is not that way. In contrast, weak objectivism is consistent with *anti-realism*, the view that truth cannot ultimately outstrip best opinion.
- One motivation for anti-realism comes from the thought that a realist conception of truth is in some sense an idle cog in inquiry. As we saw, it is not clear how we

are to make sense of this sort of argument for anti-realism. For one thing, even when two things are indistinguishable, it can still be the case that we care about the difference, and so that we can't distinguish between truth and best opinion needn't mean that we shouldn't value the former over the latter. Moreover, unless we distinguish between truth and best opinion, it isn't at all clear why we should value best opinion in the first place, since the value of best opinion seems to derive from the fact that it is a reliable guide to the truth.

• Still, the anti-realist does pose an important challenge to the realist, which is to explain why we value truth given that it can on this view undetectably outstrip best opinion. I argued that the answer to this question lies in the fact that we value *authenticity*, even when such authenticity is undetectable. (A fake life as a brain in a vat is of less value than a real life outside of the vat, even if it would be impossible to tell the two lives apart.)

• Finally, we looked at *relativism*, the view that truth is just what you think it is. Such a view is self-defeating since it follows on this proposal that what the realist thinks about truth is also true, which is just to say that relativism is false. We also noted that the relativist can neither make any sense of our ever possessing knowledge, nor of why we should care about truth if it is understood in this way.

• STUDY QUESTIONS

1 What does it mean to say that truth is objective? Give two examples of propositions which everyone once thought were true but later found out to be false. Why does objectivism about truth go hand in hand with fallibilism?

2 Describe, in your own words, the realism/anti-realism distinction concerning truth. Offer two arguments for each position.

3 Think about the brain in a vat. Is a life lived in this way any less valuable than a life (with essentially the same experiences) lived outside the vat? Defend your answer.

4 What is relativism about truth? Why is this view self-defeating?

• INTRODUCTORY FURTHER READING

Blackburn, Simon (2005) *Truth: A Guide for the Perplexed* (Harmondsworth: Allen Lane). A very readable introduction to the issues as regards the philosophy of truth. Arguably the best place to start for the interested reader.

Boghossian, Paul (2010) 'Epistemic Relativism', *Routledge Companion to Epistemology*, S. Bernecker & D. H. Pritchard (eds), Ch. 8, pp. 75–83 (London: Routledge). A sophisticated introduction to the epistemological issues raised by relativism.

Lynch, Michael (2010) 'Truth', *Routledge Companion to Epistemology*, S. Bernecker & D. H. Pritchard (eds), Ch. 1, pp. 3–13 (London: Routledge). An accessible survey of the main issues as regards the philosophy of truth.

● ADVANCED FURTHER READING

Baghramian, Maria & Coliva, Annalisa (2019) *Relativism* (London: Routledge). A detailed recent account of the main arguments regarding relativism.

Lynch, Michael (2005) *True to Life: Why Truth Matters* (Cambridge, MA: MIT Press). A very readable introduction to the issues as regards the philosophy of truth.

● FREE INTERNET RESOURCES

Baghramian, Maria & Carter, Adam J. (2020) 'Relativism', *Stanford Encyclopedia of Philosophy*, http://plato.stanford.edu/entries/relativism/. A very sophisticated, and recently updated, survey of the issues as regards relativism, which also offers a neat taxonomy of the kinds of relativist position that are available.

Glanzberg, Michael (2018) 'Truth', *Stanford Encyclopedia of Philosophy*, http://plato.stanford.edu/entries/truth/. A comprehensive overview of the issues as regards truth, though quite technical in places. Not for the beginner.

Miller, Alexander (2019) 'Realism', *Stanford Encyclopedia of Philosophy*, http://plato.stanford.edu/entries/realism/. An excellent overview of the philosophical literature on realism, taking in not just realism about truth but realist views in philosophy more generally.

˙further reading

● REFERENCE WORKS

Bernecker, Sven & Pritchard, Duncan (eds) (2010) *The Routledge Companion to Epistemology* (London: Routledge). A mammoth collection of articles on all the key areas of epistemology.

Blaauw, Martijn & Pritchard, Duncan (2005) *Epistemology A–Z* (Edinburgh: Edinburgh University Press). A short and inexpensive dictionary of epistemology.

Dancy, Jonathan, Sosa, Ernest & Steup, Matthias (eds) (2010) *A Companion to Epistemology* (2nd edn, Oxford: Blackwell). A very full list of entries. The second edition also includes twenty self-profiles from prominent epistemologists and ten new review essays on central topics in epistemology. Very useful to have to hand.

Greco, John & Sosa, Ernest (eds) (1999) *The Blackwell Guide to Epistemology* (Oxford: Blackwell). A series of introductory articles on the main topics in epistemology. A very good collection of papers.

Hetherington, Stephen (2012) *Epistemology: The Key Thinkers* (London: Continuum). Helpful profiles of some of the main figures in epistemology, going right back to the ancients and extending up to the present day.

Moser, Paul K. (ed.) (2002) *The Oxford Handbook of Epistemology* (Oxford: Oxford University Press). Contains lots of essays on the main topics in the area, written by the key figures involved.

Steup, Matthias, Turri, John & Sosa, Ernest (eds) (2013) *Contemporary Debates in Epistemology* (2nd edn, Oxford: Blackwell). An excellent idea: the main figures in the literature offer alternative perspectives on a key issue, and then respond to each other's articles. The second edition includes several newly commissioned exchanges and covers all the core topics in contemporary epistemology. (NB. I understand that a third edition is presently in the works.)

● TEXTBOOKS

Audi, Robert (2010) *Epistemology: A Contemporary Introduction to the Theory of Knowledge* (3rd edn, London: Routledge). An excellent textbook, though perhaps a little advanced in places.

Bonjour, Laurence (2009) *Epistemology: Classic Problems and Contemporary Responses* (2nd edn, Totowa, NJ: Rowman & Littlefield). A sophisticated textbook on epistemology, distinctive by being quite historically orientated in its approach to the subject.

Bonjour, Laurence & Sosa, Ernest (2003) *Epistemic Justification: Internalism vs. Externalism, Foundations vs. Virtues* (Oxford: Blackwell). It is not quite true to say that this is a textbook, since it in fact features two opposing essays from the main contributors, along with a critique and response from each contributor to the other. Nevertheless, an excellent way of getting an overview of some of the key issues in the contemporary literature.

Carter, J. Adam & Littlejohn, Clayton (2021) *This Is Epistemology* (Oxford: Blackwell). A great new textbook that has recently hit the market. Very nicely done, though note that it is quite demanding in places.

Chisholm, Roderick (1989) *Theory of Knowledge* (Englewood Cliffs, NJ: Prentice Hall). This is an old classic (the original edition of which dates back to 1966), and is perhaps the most influential book in epistemology of the last fifty years. While inevitably a little dated now in terms of its scope, it is a model of clarity and still well worth working through today.

Craig, Edward (1990) *Knowledge and the State of Nature: An Essay in Conceptual Synthesis* (Oxford: Clarendon Press). A rather idiosyncratic approach to epistemology, though very interesting, even if missing many of the key issues central to contemporary epistemology.

Dancy, Jonathan (1985) *Introduction to Contemporary Epistemology* (Oxford: Blackwell). For a long time one of the best epistemology textbooks around, though now a little dated, and quite difficult in places.

Dew, James K. & Foreman, Mark (2020) *How Do We Know? An Introduction to Epistemology* (2nd edn, Downers Grove, IL: InterVarsity Press). A contemporary introduction to epistemology written from a specifically Christian perspective.

Feldman, Richard (2003) *Epistemology* (Englewood Cliffs, NJ: Prentice Hall). An accessible introduction to epistemology.

Fumerton, Richard (2006) *Epistemology* (Oxford: Blackwell). A very readable overview of the area, though misses out on some of the main trends in contemporary epistemology.

Goldman, Alvin & McGrath, Matthew (2014) *Epistemology: A Contemporary Introduction* (Oxford: Oxford University Press). A very useful textbook, written by two leading epistemologists. Note that the terrain covered rather reflects the particular epistemological interests of the authors, but in my view that's not a count against it (indeed, this is also true of my own advanced textbook on epistemology).

Hetherington, Stephen (1996) *Knowledge Puzzles: An Introduction to Epistemology* (Boulder, CO: Westview Press).

Landesman, Charles (1997) *An Introduction to Epistemology* (Oxford: Blackwell).

Lehrer, Keith (1990) *Theory of Knowledge* (Boulder, CO: Westview Press). A classic textbook, written by a leading epistemologist, though quite dated now.

Lemos, Noah (2020) *An Introduction to the Theory of Knowledge* (2nd edn, Cambridge: Cambridge University Press). This textbook offers a detailed overview of the traditional questions of epistemology. Recently updated.

Morton, Adam (2002) *A Guide through the Theory of Knowledge* (3rd edn, Oxford: Blackwell). Very readable, and pitched at a very accessible level. Misses out some key features of the contemporary literature, though.

Nagel, Jennifer (2014) *Knowledge: A Very Short Introduction* (Oxford: Oxford University Press). A very readable and accessible introduction to some key issues in epistemology, pitched at the general reader.

Pojman, Louis P. (2000) *What Can We Know? An Introduction to the Theory of Knowledge* (Belmont, CA: Wadsworth).

Pollock, John & Cruz, Joseph (1999) *Contemporary Theories of Knowledge* (Totowa, NJ: Rowman & Littlefield). This textbook was quite influential for a period after it came out, but it is now starting to look a little dated.

Pritchard, Duncan (2016) *Epistemology* (London: Palgrave Macmillan). This book is written for advanced undergraduates and aims to offer an opinionated overview of some of the main themes in contemporary epistemology. (NB: This book is the retitled second edition of the earlier Palgrave Macmillan textbook, *Knowledge*.)

Sosa, Ernest (2017) *Epistemology* (Princeton, NJ: Princeton University Press). A superb book, written by the world's leading epistemologist – arguably the best advanced epistemology textbook available. (Note that it pains me to say this, as I'm also an author of an advanced epistemology textbook.)

Steup, Matthias (1996) *An Introduction to Contemporary Epistemology* (Englewood Cliffs, NJ: Prentice Hall).

Turri, John (2013) *Epistemology: A Guide* (Oxford: Blackwell). This is cleverly designed to accompany an anthology edited by Ernest Sosa, Jaegwon Kim, Jeremy Fantl & Matthew McGrath *Epistemology – A Guide* (2008). Having the original papers and this textbook side by side is a great way of working through the main themes of epistemology.

Welbourne, Michael (2002) *Knowledge* (Chesham: Acumen). Short and readable, though sticks quite closely to the author's own epistemological theory.

Williams, Michael (2001) *Problems of Knowledge: A Critical Introduction to Epistemology* (Oxford: Oxford University Press). A very readable introduction to epistemology that traces a somewhat different path to many other textbooks in that it is more focused on the history of epistemology and on related debates in the philosophy of science.

● ANTHOLOGIES

Alcoff, Linda (ed.) (1998) *Epistemology: The Big Questions* (Oxford: Blackwell). A good selection of articles, with more breadth than most collections, but as a consequence not quite so much depth.

Bernecker, Sven (ed.) (2006) *Reading Epistemology* (Oxford: Blackwell). A nice collection of articles, each of which is accompanied by a very useful commentary from the editor.

Bernecker, Sven & Dretske, Fred (eds) (2000) *Knowledge: Readings in Contemporary Epistemology* (Oxford: Oxford University Press). An excellent and well-priced anthology of articles.

Gendler, Tamar Szabo & Hawthorne, John (eds) (2015) *Oxford Studies in Epistemology* (Oxford: Oxford University Press). This is a new series of anthologies in epistemology containing cutting-edge work in the area. Not for the beginner.

Huemer, Michael (ed.) (2002) *Epistemology: Contemporary Readings* (London: Routledge).

Moser, Paul K. & Vander Nat, Arnold (eds) (2003) *Human Knowledge: Classical and Contemporary Approaches* (Oxford: Oxford University Press). Very comprehensive, with good coverage of some of the relevant historical texts.

Neta, Ram & Pritchard, Duncan (eds) (2009) *Arguing about Knowledge* (London: Routledge). This collection aims to cover the main themes in epistemology by offering a selection of articles which present a 'for and against' treatment of the relevant positions.

Pojman, Louis P. (ed.) (2003) *The Theory of Knowledge: Classical and Contemporary Readings* (Belmont, CA: Wadsworth). Very comprehensive, with good coverage of some of the relevant historical texts. Expensive though.

Sosa, Ernest (ed.) (1994) *The International Research Library of Philosophy, Vol. 9: Knowledge and Justification* (2 vols, Aldershot: Dartmouth Publishing Company). Very comprehensive, though not the sort of book to purchase – look out for it in your nearest library.

Sosa, Ernest & Villanueva, Enrique (eds) (2004) *Philosophical Issues 14: Epistemology* (Oxford: Blackwell). Good selection of papers, though a little tricky to get hold of – look out for it in your nearest library.

Sosa, Ernest, Kim, Jaegwon, Fantl, Jeremy & McGrath, Matthew (eds) (2008) *Epistemology – An Anthology* (2nd edn, Oxford: Blackwell). An excellent and well-priced anthology of articles which has recently been updated to include a number of new articles on recent developments in the epistemological literature. Note that John Turri has now produced a textbook that accompanies this anthology.

Tomberlin, James (ed.) (1988) *Philosophical Perspectives 2: Epistemology* (Oxford: Blackwell). Good selection of papers, though difficult to get hold of – look out for it in your nearest library.

Tomberlin, James (ed.) (1999) *Philosophical Perspectives 13: Epistemology* (Oxford: Blackwell). Good selection of papers, though again a little tricky to get hold of – look out for it in your nearest library.

• INTERNET RESOURCES

Routledge Encyclopedia of Philosophy, www.rep.routledge.com. This is the internet version of the main encyclopedia of philosophy currently available. You'll need a subscription to access it, though most universities subscribe to this service, so if you belong to a university library then you should be able to get access to it this way. An excellent resource, fully searchable, and with lots of good entries on epistemology. (Incidentally, the epistemology entries in this resource are edited by yours truly.)

Internet Encyclopedia of Philosophy, www.iep.utm.edu/. The second best completely free internet encyclopedia of philosophy available. It's not quite as comprehensive or authoritative as the *Stanford Encyclopedia of Philosophy* (see below), but still contains some good entries on epistemology.

PhilPapers, https://philpapers.org. This free site collates the wide range of publications on philosophy, so you will find lots of useful information on there. See especially the sub-section on epistemology, edited by Matthew McGrath (https://philpapers.org/browse/epistemology).

Stanford Encyclopedia of Philosophy, http://plato.stanford.edu/. The best completely free internet encyclopedia of philosophy available. It's continually being updated, and has many great articles on epistemology.

glossary of terms

Abduction
Consider the following inference, an instance of abductive reasoning: There are feet exposed under the curtain in the hall. Therefore: There is someone hiding behind the curtain. This seems like a perfectly legitimate form of inductive reasoning, which proceeds from a premise which supports, but which does not entail, the conclusion. Unlike most other inductive reasoning, however, this abductive inference does not make appeal to a large and representative set of observations. Instead, it simply proceeds from a single observed phenomenon to the best explanation of that phenomenon. This is why abduction is sometimes called 'inference to the best explanation'. *See also* **induction**.

Ability knowledge
This is often referred to as 'know-how', since it involves knowing how to do something, such as ride a bike or swim. It is usually contrasted with propositional knowledge, which is knowledge of a proposition. The two types of knowledge are treated differently because, intuitively at least, one might know how to do something (e.g. swim) without having any relevant propositional knowledge (e.g. without knowing that you can swim, perhaps because you forgot that you could until you fell in the water). *See also* **propositional knowledge**.

Agrippa (*c.*100)
See p. 33.

Agrippa's trilemma
According to Agrippa's trilemma, there are only three options available to us when it comes to responding to the challenge to show how our beliefs are supported: say that our beliefs are unsupported; or say that our beliefs are supported by an infinite chain of justification (i.e. one in which no supporting ground appears more than once); or say that our beliefs are supported by a circular chain of justification (i.e. one in which a supporting ground appears more than once). None of these options is particularly appealing, however, and this is why this challenge is posed as a *trilemma* (i.e. as presenting us with a choice between three unpalatable options, one of which we must choose). *See also* **coherentism; foundationalism; infinitism**.

Anti-realism/realism
The anti-realism/realism distinction as it is used in this book concerns truth. (Philosophers sometimes use these terms to refer to debates about other philosophical

topics.) The realist about truth holds that truth can, in principle, outstrip our capacity to know it, such that even one's best opinion of what the truth is (e.g. the kind of opinion formed at the end of inquiry) could nevertheless be false. Anti-realists deny this claim, holding that there can be no distinction between the truth and best opinion.

A posteriori knowledge
See **a priori/empirical knowledge**.

A priori/empirical knowledge
The distinction between a priori and empirical knowledge – note that the latter is sometimes known as *a posteriori* knowledge – relates to whether the knowledge in question was gained independently of an investigation of the world (what is known as an *empirical* inquiry). If it was, then it is a priori knowledge; if it wasn't, then it is empirical knowledge. For example, my knowledge that Minsk is the capital of Belarus is empirical knowledge because I gained it by making an investigation of the world (e.g. I looked it up in an atlas). In contrast, my knowledge that all bachelors are unmarried is a priori knowledge, because I gained it by reflecting on what the words mean and so no investigation of the world was required (though note that I could have gained this knowledge empirically, by asking someone, for example).

Argument from analogy
The argument from analogy is a famous response to the problem of other minds that is often attributed to John Stuart Mill (1806–73). The problem of other minds arises because it seems that we are unable to directly observe that others are minded in the way that we are. Essentially, the idea behind this approach to the problem of other minds is to maintain that we can come to know that there are other minds by observing how the behaviour of others mirrors that of our own (where we know that we are minded). The thought is that since we know that we have minds, it follows that the behaviour of others which is similar to our own shows that these others have minds too. The argument from analogy is thus an inductive argument which proceeds from observations regarding our own minds and our own behaviour to draw conclusions about what is giving rise to similar behaviour in others. *See also* **other minds, problem of**.

Argument from illusion
Consider the visual impression caused by a genuine sighting of an oasis on the horizon and contrast it with the corresponding visual impression of an illusory sighting of an oasis on the horizon formed by one who is hallucinating. Here is the crux: *these two visual impressions could be exactly the same*. The problem, however, is that it seems that if this is the case then what we experience in perception is not the world itself, but something that falls short of the world, something that is common to both the 'good' case in which one's senses are not being deceived (and one is actually looking at an oasis) and the 'bad' case in which one's senses are being deceived (and one is the victim of a hallucination). This line of reasoning, which makes use of undetectable error in perception in order to highlight the indirectness of perceptual experience, is known as the argument from illusion. It suggests an 'indirect' model

of perceptual knowledge, such that what we are immediately aware of when we gain such knowledge is a sensory impression – a *seeming* – on the basis of which we then make an inference regarding how the world is. *See also* **indirect realism**.

Aristotle (384–322 BC)
See p. 59.

Ayer, A. J. (1910–89)
See p. 142.

Berkeley, George (1685–1753)
See p. 74.

Chicken-sexer
A chicken-sexer is, so the story goes at any rate, someone who, by being raised around chickens, has acquired a highly reliable trait which enables them to distinguish between male and female chicks. Crucially, however, chicken-sexers tend to have false beliefs about how they are doing what they do because they tend to suppose that they are distinguishing the chicks on the basis of what they can see and touch. It turns out, however, that there is nothing distinctive for them to see and touch in this regard, and that they are actually discriminating between the chicks on the basis of their smell. Note that there may not actually be any chicken-sexers. The point of the example is merely to test our intuitions about what we should say about these cases – in particular, whether we should allow that the beliefs that the chicken-sexer is forming amount to knowledge. If one holds that reliability is all important – as reliabilism, a version of epistemic externalism, claims – then one ought to regard the chicken-sexer as having knowledge. In contrast, if you think that mere reliability by itself isn't enough for knowledge – because, for example, one needs to have some reason for thinking that one is reliable, which is what epistemic internalists typically demand – then one should regard the chicken-sexers as lacking knowledge. *See also* **epistemic externalism/internalism; reliabilism**.

Chisholm, Roderick (1916–99)
See p. 20.

Classical account of knowledge
Otherwise known as the *tripartite* (or three-part) account of knowledge, the classical account of knowledge maintains that knowledge of a proposition, *p*, consists of three components: one must believe that *p*; one's belief must be true; and one must have good reasons in support of one's belief (i.e. one's belief must be justified).

Classical foundationalism
Classical foundationalism is a form of foundationalism which holds that some beliefs – the foundational beliefs – do not require further justification because they are *self-justifying*. For example, if a belief was found to be completely immune to rational doubt, and therefore certain and self-evidently true, then it might plausibly be regarded as self-justifying and so a foundational belief by the lights of classical foundationalism. *See also* **foundationalism**.

Closure principle

This principle states that if an agent knows one proposition, and knows that this proposition entails a second proposition, then the agent knows the second proposition as well. So, for example, if I know that Paris is the capital of France, and I know that if Paris is the capital of France, then it is not the capital of Germany, then I also know that Paris is not the capital of Germany.

Cognitive faculties

One's perceptual faculties, such as one's eyesight, are cognitive faculties, in that, when working properly in an environment for which they are suited at least, they enable you to reliably gain true beliefs, in this case about your environment. In general, a cognitive faculty is a natural and innate faculty which enables you to gain true beliefs reliably. *See also* **epistemic virtues**.

Coherentism

Coherentists respond to Agrippa's trilemma by arguing that a circular chain of supporting grounds *can* justify a belief, at least provided that the chain is large enough. *See also* **Agrippa's trilemma**.

Conciliationism

Conciliationism is a popular response to the problem of *peer disagreement*. According to this proposal, the only rational way to respond to a disagreement of this sort is to downgrade one's confidence in one's belief in the proposition under dispute. *See also* **peer disagreement**.

Contextualism

Contextualism is the view that 'knowledge' is a highly context-sensitive term, and that this can help us resolve certain fundamental problems in epistemology, such as the problem of radical scepticism. Consider other terms that we use that might plausibly be thought to be context-sensitive, such as 'empty'. For example, if, in normal circumstances, I tell you that the fridge is empty, then you will understand me as saying that it's empty of food, and not that it's empty of *anything* (it contains *air*, after all). If 'knows' is also context-sensitive in this way, then it could then be that in one context 'knows' means one thing, while in another context, it means another. More specifically, it could be that 'knows' picks out quite demanding epistemic standards in one context, but quite weak epistemic standards in another. It is this last suggestion that is particularly relevant to the problem of radical scepticism, since the thought is that the sceptic is using the term in a more demanding way than we usually use it. Accordingly, we can, it seems, grant that we know an awful lot relative to our everyday standards even while simultaneously granting that we may not count as knowing very much relative to the sceptic's more exacting standards. More precisely, the contextualist thought is that whereas in normal contexts we count an agent as having knowledge just so long as she is able to rule out mundane non-sceptical possibilities of error, what the sceptic does is raise the standards for 'knowledge' such that in order to count as having knowledge the agent must be able to in addition rule out far-fetched sceptical possibilities of error (i.e. rule out sceptical hypotheses). Accordingly, the contextualist claims that while we have lots of knowledge relative to everyday standards, this claim is entirely compatible with the sceptical claim that we lack knowledge relative to more demanding sceptical standards. *See also* **scepticism**.

Cosmological argument

The cosmological argument is meant to be a rational proof of God's existence. It argues that since it is not coherent that the universe should have existed eternally, it follows that it must have been brought into existence at some point, and that only God could have brought this about. Hence, God must exist.

Credulism

Credulism is primarily a thesis as regards the epistemology of testimony that is usually attributed to Thomas Reid (1710–96). In this regard, credulism holds, in contrast to *reductionism*, that one can be justified in holding a testimony-based belief even though one lacks any independent grounds in support of that belief. Credulism has also been applied to other types of belief, such as belief formed via memory. Here credulists argue that one can be justified in holding a memory-based belief even though one lacks any independent grounds in support of that belief. *See also* **reductionism**; **testimony**.

Criterion, problem of the

Suppose I want to offer a definition of knowledge. One way I might do this is by first gathering together lots of instances of knowledge (i.e. cases in which an agent has knowledge) and working out what all these cases have in common. The problem with this strategy, however, is that if I don't already know what the distinguishing marks – or *criteria* – of knowledge are, then how am I supposed to identify cases of knowledge in the first place? Accordingly, one might think that the right thing to do is *first* identify what the criteria for knowledge are and then use this knowledge to identify instances of knowledge. The problem now, however, is that unless I'm already able to identify instances of knowledge, then it's not clear how I would go about determining what the criteria for knowledge are. We are thus stuck, it seems, in a very small circle, and this is the problem of the criterion. In order to identify cases of knowledge, one needs to know what the criteria for knowledge are; but in order to identify the criteria for knowledge, one needs to be able to identify cases of knowledge. It seems, then, that in order to offer a definition of knowledge, one must either groundlessly assume that one can identify cases of knowledge, or else groundlessly assume that one knows what the criteria for knowledge are. Neither option seems particularly appealing. *See also* **methodism**; **particularism**.

Deduction

A deductive argument is an argument where the premises *entail* the conclusion (i.e. where, if the premises are true, the conclusion must be true also). *See also* **induction**.

Defeater

A defeater is a consideration that prevents one from having knowledge by either indicating that one's reasons for one's belief don't sufficiently support the truth of that belief or by giving one an independent reason for thinking that one's belief is false.

Deontic epistemic rationality
According to this conception of epistemic rationality, you are epistemically rational if you form your beliefs responsibly by your own lights. This means that if you blamelessly use the wrong epistemic norms – for example, if you blamelessly think that coin-tossing is a good way of deciding a defendant's guilt, and employ this method – then your belief is still epistemically rational. A non-deontic epistemic rationality, in contrast, would insist that the epistemically rational agent uses the right epistemic norms. *See also* **epistemic norm**; **epistemic rationality**.

Descartes, René (1596–1650)
See pp. 35–36.

Design argument
The design argument – sometimes known as the *teleological argument* – is meant to be a rational proof of God's existence. It argues that the best explanation of the complexity found in nature is existence of a God who created and designed the world.

Direct realism
Direct realism is a thesis about perceptual experience that has ramifications for perceptual knowledge. It holds that, at least in non-deceived cases, what we are aware of in perceptual experience are aspects of the external world itself. That is, if I am genuinely looking at a cup right now, then I am directly aware of the cup itself, and thus I can have perceptual knowledge that there is a cup before me without needing to make an inference from the way the world seems to how it is. *See also* **argument from illusion**; **indirect realism**.

Empirical knowledge
See **a priori/empirical knowledge**.

Empiricism
In its strongest guise, empiricism is the view that all knowledge – or, at least, all knowledge of any substance – should be traced back to sensory experience. Proponents of this view – *empiricists* – are thus suspicious of any knowledge which does not seem to depend on knowledge of the world, such as logical knowledge. Accordingly, they either deny that such knowledge exists, or else deny that it is knowledge of substance and so claim that it is in a certain sense trivial. Proponents of (some form of) empiricism include John Locke (1632–1704), George Berkeley (1685–1753), and David Hume (1711–76); collectively, these three philosophers are known as the *British empiricists*.

Epistemic externalism/internalism
In essence, the distinctive demand made by epistemic internalism is that when an agent has justified belief/knowledge, that agent must be able to offer good grounds in favour of what she believes. Epistemic externalism, in contrast, resists this demand and thus allows, at least in some cases, that an agent can have justified belief/knowledge and yet be unable to offer good grounds in favour of what she believes. *See also* **chicken-sexer**.

Epistemic injustice

Epistemic injustice is concerned with the social dynamics that unjustly prevent agents from fully participating in social epistemic practices, such as when someone's testimony is not given sufficient credibility due to prejudice. *See also* **hermeneutical injustice; testimonial injustice**.

Epistemic internalism

See **epistemic externalism/internalism**.

Epistemic norm

An epistemic norm is a rule that one follows in order to gain true beliefs. That one should take care when weighing up evidence, and be as impartial as possible as one does so, is an example of an epistemic norm, since following this rule enables one to have a better chance of getting to the truth.

Epistemic rationality

This is a form of rationality that is aimed at gaining true belief. For example, a person who weighs up the evidence carefully in forming a belief about whether she can jump a ravine is being epistemically rational since she is trying to find out what the truth of the matter is, and is employing a good method in this regard. In contrast, someone who knows that she can't comfortably jump the ravine, but who, despite this, manages to convince herself that she can because she knows that only a committed jump will stand any chance of success – she has to jump this ravine, say, and she doesn't want to die trying – is not being epistemically rational (though she may be being rational in other regards).

Epistemic virtues

An epistemic virtue (sometimes called an *intellectual virtue*) is a character trait which makes you better suited to gaining the truth. An example of such a trait might be *conscientiousness*. An agent who is conscientious in the way in which she forms her beliefs (i.e. she is careful to avoid error and takes all available evidence into account) will be more likely to form true beliefs than someone who is unconscientious. *See also* **virtue epistemology**.

Epistemology

This is the name given for the theory of knowledge. Those who study epistemology – known as *epistemologists* – are also interested in those notions closely associated with knowledge, such as truth, justification and rationality.

Extended cognition

Extended cognition involves cognitive processes that do not take place completely within the skin and skull of the subject, but rather involve external factors, such as technology and sometimes other agents. Note that these external factors are not mere instruments if this is genuine extended cognition, but rather bona fide constituents of the (extended) cognitive process itself. *See also* **extended knowledge; neuromedia**.

Extended knowledge
Extended knowledge is knowledge that results from an extended cognitive process, where this in turn is a cognitive process the constituents of which extend beyond the skin and skull of the subject. *See also* **extended cognition**; **neuromedia**.

External world, problem of the
According to the argument from illusion, all that I am directly aware of in perceptual experience is how the world appears, not how it is independently of how it appears. If all that I am directly aware of in perceptual experience is the way the world appears, however, then this opens up the possibility that the way the world appears might be no guide at all to how the world is. (There is, after all, nothing about my experiences that would indicate that this is not the case.) This is the problem of the external world (i.e. a world that is 'external' to our experience of it). *See also* **argument from illusion**; **indirect realism**.

Fallibilism
Fallibilism is the view that one can have knowledge even while having a belief in what one knows which is fallible. *See also* **fallible**; **infallibilism**.

Fallible
If one's belief is fallible, then it could be in error (though it might not be). *See also* **fallibilism**; **infallibility**.

Falsification
This is a rather radical response to the problem of induction, put forward by Karl Popper (1902–94). Popper claimed that good scientific reasoning did not make use of induction at all, as most assume, but rather employs a process he called falsification. This is where the scientist puts forward a bold hypothesis and then seeks to refute that hypothesis definitively by discovering a counter-example. For example, the scientist might propose that all emus are flightless (because no flying emu has yet been observed), and then set about trying to find a flying emu. If such an emu were found, then the hypothesis would be shown to be false. Notice, however, that the inference that would then be made would be deductive rather than inductive, since if a flying emu does exist then this *entails* that the hypothesis that all emus are flightless is false. *See also* **induction, problem of**.

Fideism
Fideism is the view that religious belief should not be judged by the same epistemic standards as other beliefs. In particular, religious belief is neither rational nor irrational, since it should be judged relative to its own internal standards, and not according to the rational standards that are applicable to most other forms of belief.

Foundationalism
Foundationalists respond to Agrippa's trilemma by arguing that some beliefs can be justified without being supported by any further beliefs. In this way, the chain of justification can come to an end with beliefs that serve the special role of providing a foundation for other beliefs. One version of foundationalism, *classical foundationalism*, holds that these foundational beliefs are able to play this role because they are *self-justifying*. *See also* **Agrippa's trilemma**; **classical foundationalism**.

Frankfurt, Harry (1929–)
See p. 214.

Gettier cases
Gettier cases are scenarios in which an agent has a justified true belief and yet lacks knowledge because it is substantially due to luck that the belief in question is true. A good instance of a Gettier case is the 'stopped clock' example. In this scenario, we are asked to imagine an agent who forms her belief about what the time is by looking at a stopped clock that she has every reason for thinking is working. Crucially, however, she happens to look at the clock at the one time in the day when it is showing the right time, and so forms a true belief as a result. Her belief is thus both true and justified, yet it isn't a case of knowledge since it is just luck that her belief is true given that the clock is not working. Gettier cases show that the three-part, or *tripartite*, account of knowledge that analyses knowledge into justified true belief is unsustainable.

Hermeneutical injustice
Hermeneutical injustice is a variety of epistemic injustice. It is concerned with how social structures can prevent someone from being able to properly identify their situation, thereby epistemically disadvantaging them. *See also* **epistemic injustice**; **testimonial injustice**.

Hume, David (1711–76)
See p. 82.

Idealism
Idealism is the view that there is no external world (i.e. no world that is independent of our experience). In its simplest form, the view is not very appealing since it entails that the world ceases to exist when it is not being experienced. (For example, in order for a tree to fall in a forest, it is essential that there be someone present to perceive it fall.) In order to make the view more appealing, philosophers have supplemented the view in various ways. For example, George Berkeley (1685–1753) gets around some of the more counter-intuitive aspects of the view by arguing that God is always present and perceives everything, and thus the world does not cease to exist when it is not being experienced. Some other ways of modifying idealism transform it into a very different thesis. For example, the form of idealism – called *transcendental idealism* – that is proposed by Immanuel Kant (1724–1804) maintains that while it is impossible to ever experience the external world, nevertheless we can know, through reason, that such a world must exist. In this sense, then, the view is not strictly speaking an idealist view at all.

Incommensurability
Two scientific theories are incommensurable when there is no basis that is common to both theories on which they may be assessed. It follows that there is no theory-neutral way in which proponents of one of these two theories might defend their theory over the competing theory.

Indirect realism
According to the argument from illusion, one's experiences when one is perceiving normally could be exactly the same as the experiences one would have were one to

be deceived in some way (e.g. if one were having a hallucination). Indirect realists embrace the conclusion of this argument by claiming, in opposition to direct realists, that one never directly experiences the world in perception. Instead, one experiences only how the world seems to one, and on this basis, one must make inferences regarding how the world is independently of how it appears. *See also* **argument from illusion; direct realism.**

Induction
An inductive argument is any argument where the premises, while offering support for the conclusion, do not *entail* the conclusion. Lots of scientific knowledge is gained inductively – the scientist makes a series of observations (say, regarding how every emu she comes across is a flightless bird) and on this basis draws a conclusion that goes beyond what she has observed (that all emus are flightless). The premise in this inference, however (that all observed emus are flightless), is entirely consistent with the falsity of the conclusion (i.e. it is consistent with the possibility of there being an unobserved flying emu). *See also* **deduction.**

Induction, problem of
This problem, the discovery of which is usually credited to David Hume (1711–76), concerns the fact that it seems impossible to gain a non-circular justification for induction. This is because inductive inferences are only legitimate provided that we are already entitled to suppose that observed regularities provide good grounds for the generalisations we inductively infer from those regularities. The difficulty is that our grounds for this supposition themselves depend upon further inductive inferences (i.e. that we have found the connection between observed regularities and the relevant generalisations to hold in the past). But if this is right, then our justification for making any particular inductive inference will be itself at least partly inductive, and this means that there can be no non-circular justification for induction. *See also* **induction.**

Infallibilism
Infallibilism is the view that in order to have knowledge one must have a belief which is infallible. *See also* **fallibilism; infallibility.**

Infallibility
If one's belief is infallible, then it could not be in error. *See also* **fallibility; infallibilism.**

Inference to the best explanation
See **abduction.**

Infinitism
Infinitists respond to Agrippa's trilemma by holding that an infinite chain of justification can justify a belief. *See also* **Agrippa's trilemma.**

Instrumental value
This is a kind of value that accrues to something in virtue of the fact that it serves some valuable goal. A thermometer is instrumentally valuable, for example, because it helps us to find out something of importance to us (i.e. what the temperature is). *See also* **non-instrumental value.**

Introspection

Introspection is a kind of 'inner' observation where we try to find out something by examining our own psychological states. For example, one might introspect one's own psychological states in order to try to determine whether one prefers the taste of one wine over another.

Kant, Immanuel (1724–1804)
See p. 75.

Legal evidence

Legal evidence is evidence that is admissible within a specifically legal context, such as a criminal trial. Not everything that would ordinarily count as good evidence is admissible within a legal context (e.g. evidence relating to past convictions on the part of the defendant is often disallowed).

Locke, John (1632–1704)
See p. 72.

Methodism

A term coined by Roderick Chisholm (1916–99) to describe one historically popular way of responding to the *problem of the criterion*. According to this problem, if we try to understand what knowledge is, we immediately face a dilemma. Either we must assume that we can independently come to know what the criteria for knowledge are in order to identify instances of knowledge, or else we must assume that we can identify instances of knowledge in order to determine what the criteria for knowledge are. Methodists opt for the first assumption over the second, claiming that we can, through philosophical reflection, determine what the criteria of knowledge are without needing to refer to any particular instances of knowledge. *See also* **particularism; criterion, problem of the**.

Mill, John Stuart (1806–73)
See p. 226.

Moore, G. E. (1873–1958)
See p. 238.

Mooreanism

Mooreanism is the name given to the strikingly direct response to the problem of radical scepticism, often attributed to G. E. Moore (1873–1958). This response involves arguing that since we do indeed know a great deal about the world, it follows that we must also know the denials of sceptical hypotheses as well, since such hypotheses are known to be inconsistent with most of our knowledge of the world. So, for example, since I know that I have two hands, and I know that if I have two hands then I am not a (handless) brain in a vat, it follows that I must also know that I am not a brain in a vat. So construed, Mooreanism seems to be making use of the principle of closure. What is problematic about the view, however, is that many find it highly intuitive to suppose that we *can't* know the denials of sceptical hypotheses. It is thus incumbent on the proponent of Mooreanism to explain how this could be possible after all. To this end, recent defences of Mooreanism have appealed to the *safety principle* as a way of explaining how we could know the denials of sceptical hypotheses. *See also* **safety principle**; **scepticism**.

Moral expressivism

Moral expressivists hold that moral statements do not express facts but rather perform a very different role instead, such as expressing one's support for a certain action, or one's desire to stop certain actions from taking place.

Natural theology

Natural theology is the attempt to provide a rational defence of religious belief which appeals only to facts which are common to all. As such, natural theology does not try to defend religious belief by appeal to divine revelation, whether of an individual variety, or in written form (e.g. in the form of scripture).

Neuromedia

Neuromedia is a particular kind of cognitive augmentation, whereby one's cognitive processes are technologically upgraded, albeit in ways that the technology is (for the most part anyway) hidden under the skin of the subject and is employed so seamlessly that the subject is often not aware they are using it. Neuromedia is similar to extended cognition, in that one's on-board biological cognitive processes are intertwined with non-biological cognitive resources. It is unlike normal cases of extended cognition, however, in that the non-biological cognitive resources are (at least for the most part) within the skin and skull of the subject. *See also* **extended cognition**; **extended knowledge**.

Non-instrumental value

To say that something is non-instrumentally valuable (also known as *finally valuable*) is to say that it is valuable for its own sake, and not merely for the sake of something else. A plausible example of non-instrumental value is friendship. We don't value our friends because they are useful to us (though having friends is undoubtedly useful), but simply because they are our friends; that is, we value our friends for their own sake, and not merely because they serve some further purpose (such as making us happy). *See also* **instrumental value**.

Normative account of ignorance

According to the normative account of ignorance, there is more to ignorance than simply the lack of a positive epistemic standing, like knowledge. In addition, to be ignorant means that one has exhibited an intellectual failing. For example, one might hold that ignorance involves not just the lack of knowledge but also that this lack of knowledge is due to an intellectual failing. In essence, in being ignorant, one lacks knowledge that one ought to have.

Ontological argument

The ontological argument is meant to be a rational proof of God's existence. It argues that since the very concept of God involves the idea that no being can be conceived which is greater than God, so God must exist. For if God didn't exist, then there would be a being of which we could conceive which was even greater than the (non-existent) God of which we were conceiving. As this possibility is ruled out by the very concept of God, hence God must exist.

Other minds, problem of
The problem of other minds concerns the fact that it seems as if we don't actually observe other minds in the way that we observe objects in the world like trees and cars. After all, one's mind seems to be something that *underlies* one's body and one's bodily behaviour such that, although one's behaviour manifests one's mind, simply observing an agent's behaviour is not the same as observing their mind. Accordingly, the thought runs, in order to know that someone has a mind we have to do more than merely observe their behaviour; we also have to infer that there is something underlying that behaviour and giving rise to it – namely, a mind. The reason why this is a problem is that it is not obvious what entitles us to this inference. *See also* **argument from analogy**.

Paradox
A paradox is an apparently valid argument that proceeds from premises which seem entirely intuitive, but which generates an absurd conclusion.

Particularism
A term coined by Roderick Chisholm (1916–99) to describe one historically popular way of responding to the *problem of the criterion*. According to this problem, if we try to understand what knowledge is, we immediately face a dilemma. Either we must assume that we can independently come to know what the criteria for knowledge are in order to identify instances of knowledge, or else we must assume that we can identify instances of knowledge in order to determine what the criteria for knowledge are. Particularists opt for the second assumption over the first, claiming that we can identify instances of knowledge without first having a grasp of what the criteria for knowledge are. *See also* **methodism**; **criterion, problem of the**.

Pascal's wager
See p. 43.

Peer disagreement
Peer disagreements concern disagreements between parties who are roughly equal in terms of their background knowledge and their cognitive abilities, at least as regards the topic under dispute. (These are known as *epistemic peers*.) This kind of disagreement is particularly epistemically interesting, as it seems to entail that one should downgrade one's confidence in one's opinions. *See also* **conciliationism**.

Plantinga, Alvin (1932–)
See pp. 131–32.

Plato (*c.*427–*c.* 347 BC)
See p. 13.

Popper, Karl (1902–94)
See p. 102.

Primary/secondary qualities
This is a distinction that was drawn (in modern times) by the philosopher John Locke (1632–1704). A primary quality is a feature of an object that the object has independently of anyone perceiving the object, while an object's secondary qualities

are dependent upon the perception of an agent. A good example of a primary quality is shape, in that the shape of an object is not in any way dependent upon anyone perceiving that object. Compare shape in this respect with colour. The colour of an object is a secondary quality in that it depends upon a perceiver. If human beings were kitted out with different perceptual faculties, then colours would be discriminated very differently (as they are, for example, for many animals).

Problem of other minds
See other minds, problem of.

Problem of the criterion
See criterion, problem of the.

Problem of the external world
See external world, problem of the.

Proposition
A proposition is what is stated by a declarative sentence. For example, the sentence 'The cat is on the mat' states that something is the case; namely, that the cat is on the mat, and this is the proposition expressed by this sentence. Notice that the same proposition will be expressed by an analogue declarative sentence which is in a different language, such as French, just so long as what is stated by that sentence is the same.

Propositional knowledge
This is *knowledge that* something (i.e. a proposition) is the case. It is typically contrasted with ability knowledge, or *know-how*. The two types of knowledge are treated differently because, intuitively at least, one might know how to do something (e.g. swim) without having any relevant propositional knowledge (e.g. without knowing that you can swim, perhaps because you forgot that you could until you fell in the water). *See also* ability knowledge.

Quine, W. V. O. (1908–2000)
See p. 34.

Radical scepticism
See scepticism.

Realism
See anti-realism/realism.

Reductionism
Reductionism is primarily a thesis as regards the epistemology of testimony that is usually attributed to David Hume (1711–76). Reductionism holds, in contrast to *credulism*, that in order for a testimony-based belief to be justified, it is essential that the agent concerned is able to offer independent grounds in favour of that belief – that is, grounds which are not themselves further testimony-based beliefs. A similar position is also available as regards the epistemology of memory. Such a view holds that in order for a memory-based belief to be justified, it is essential that the agent concerned is able to offer independent grounds in favour of that belief – that is, grounds that are not themselves further memory-based beliefs. *See also* credulism; testimony.

Reformed epistemology

Reformed epistemologists argue that so long as religious belief is subjected to the same epistemic standards that are usually applicable to beliefs which paradigmatically count as knowledge, such as perceptual beliefs, then there is no inherent bar to religious belief being both rationally held and, if true, amounting to knowledge. A key element of one popular version of reformed epistemology is the appeal to an innate 'sense of divinity', or *sensus divinitatis*, through which agents are held to be able to reliably gain religious knowledge in an analogous fashion to how agents gain perceptual knowledge of the world around them via their innate sensory faculties. See also ***sensus divinitatis***.

Reid, Thomas (1710–96)
See p. 84.

Relativism
The kind of relativism that we have discussed in this book – there are other varieties that come under this name – concerns truth. This type of relativist holds that what you think is true is true. Thus, if I think that Paris is the capital of France, and you think that Paris is not the capital of France, on this view, we are both right.

Reliabilism
A reliable belief-forming process is any process which tends to produce true beliefs rather than false beliefs. For example, in normal conditions, our perceptual faculties (e.g. our eyesight) are reliable belief-forming processes, enabling us reliably to form true beliefs about our immediate environment. According to a simple form of reliabilism, knowledge is just reliably formed true belief. More complex forms of reliabilism, such as certain types of virtue epistemology, hold that knowledge is true belief that arises out of the operation of one's reliable epistemic virtues or cognitive faculties. Both simple and complex forms of reliabilism are species of epistemic externalism, in that they hold that an agent can sometimes have knowledge even while lacking good grounds in support of her belief, just so long as certain other 'external' conditions hold (e.g. that her belief was in fact formed reliably). *See also* **epistemic externalism/internalism**; **virtue epistemology**.

Safety principle
The safety principle holds that if an agent knows a proposition, then that agent's true belief in that proposition must be *safe* in the sense that it couldn't have easily been false. For example, provided circumstances are normal, your belief right now that you are reading this book is safe, since it is a belief that couldn't have easily been false (since if, in normal circumstances, you believe that you are reading a book, then you are reading a book). That is, it is not just that you happen to have a true belief in the particular circumstances in which you find yourself; instead, you would tend to form true beliefs about this subject matter across a range of relevantly similar circumstances. What is striking about the safety principle is that our beliefs in the denials of sceptical hypotheses may well be safe, and so if safety is (at least sometimes) all there is to knowing, it follows that it might be possible to know the denials of sceptical hypotheses after all, contrary to intuition. For example, my belief, in normal circumstances, that I am not a brain in a vat seems to be safe, since there is

no relevantly similar situation to this one in which I believe this proposition and yet what I believe is false. *See also* **Mooreanism**.

Sceptical hypotheses

A sceptical hypothesis is a scenario in which you are radically deceived about the world and yet your experience of the world is exactly as it would be had you not been deceived. Consider, for example, the fate of the protagonist in the film *The Matrix*, who comes to realise that his previous experiences of the world were in fact being 'fed' into his brain while his body was confined to a large vat. Accordingly, while he seemed to be experiencing a world rich with interaction between himself and other people, in fact he was not interacting with anybody or any *thing* at all (at least over and above the tubes in the vat that were 'feeding' him his experiences), but was instead simply floating motionlessly. The problem posed by sceptical hypotheses is that we seem unable to know that they are false. After all, if our experience of the world could be exactly as it is and yet we are the victims of a sceptical hypothesis, then on what basis could we ever hope to distinguish a genuine experience of the world from an illusory one? Sceptical hypotheses are thus used to motivate scepticism. *See also* **scepticism**.

Scepticism

To advance scepticism about a certain subject matter is to argue that it is impossible to have any knowledge of that subject matter. For example, scepticism about the existence of other minds would be the view that it is impossible to know that there exist other minds. Radical scepticism is a form of scepticism which targets a very broad subject matter. For example, one form of radical scepticism argues that we are unable to know anything at all about the external world (i.e. a world that is 'external' to our experience of it). Although it is natural to speak of radical scepticism as being a philosophical position, it is not usually advanced in this way but is rather put forward as a challenge to existing theories of knowledge to show why they don't generate the type of radical scepticism in question.

Secondary qualities

See **primary/secondary qualities**.

Sensitivity principle

The sensitivity principle states that if an agent knows a proposition, then that agent's true belief in that proposition must be *sensitive* in the sense that, had that proposition been false, she would not have believed it. For example, provided circumstances are normal, your belief that you are reading this book right now is sensitive since, had this not been true (but everything else remained the same), then you wouldn't believe that you were reading this book, but would believe that you were doing something else instead (e.g. reading another book or taking a nap). Some beliefs, in contrast, seem to be by their nature insensitive. Consider my beliefs in the denials of sceptical hypotheses, for example, such as my belief that I am not a brain in a vat. Were this belief to be false (i.e. were I to be a brain in a vat), I would be in a situation in which I would be deceived about whether I was a brain in a vat, and so would continue to believe that I wasn't a brain in a vat regardless. Thus, if sensitivity is a prerequisite of knowledge, it follows that we are unable to know the denials of **sceptical hypotheses**.

Sensus divinitatis

The *sensus divinitatis*, or 'sense of divinity', is a key component of *reformed epistemology*. It is held to be an innate belief-forming faculty which can in the right conditions generate religious knowledge. It is held to function much like our innate sensory faculties which can, in the right circumstances, lead us to perceptual knowledge. See also **reformed epistemology**.

Social epistemology

Social epistemology studies epistemological topics that have a specifically social dimension, such as testimony, disagreement, and epistemic injustice. It is also concerned with understanding social phenomena that have an epistemological dimension, like fake news or conspiracy theories.

Soundness

A sound argument is a valid argument that has true premises. *See also* **validity**.

Testimonial injustice

Testimonial injustice is a variety of epistemic injustice. It occurs when the credibility of someone's testimony is downgraded as a result of prejudice. *See also* **epistemic injustice; hermeneutical injustice**.

Testimony

In this book we have understood the notion of testimony quite broadly to include not just the formal verbal transmission of information that one finds taking place in, say, a courtroom, but also the intentional transmission of information in general – whether verbally or through books, pictures, videos, and so on.

Transcendental idealism

Transcendental idealism is a version of idealism proposed by Immanuel Kant (1724–1804). Kant agrees with the simple idealist that it is impossible to ever experience the external world (i.e. a world that is independent of our experience of it). Nevertheless, unlike the idealist, he argues that we are required to suppose that there is an external world that gives rise to this experience since, without this supposition, we would not be able to make any sense of such experience. On the face of it, such a view might look like a version of indirect realism since, like indirect realism, it appears to make our knowledge of the external world inferential. What is key to the view, however, is that we cannot gain knowledge of a world that is independent of experience through experience *at all*, directly or otherwise. It is in this sense that transcendental idealism is a form of idealism. *See also* **idealism**.

Validity

A valid argument is an argument where the premises *entail* the conclusion (i.e. where it is not possible for the premises to be true and the conclusion false). All good deductive arguments are valid. If a valid argument has true premises, then it is sound. *See also* **deduction; soundness**.

Virtue epistemology

A virtue epistemology is any theory of knowledge which holds that knowledge is true belief that is gained as a result of the operation of reliable epistemic virtues or cognitive faculties. One version of this thesis is simply a refinement of a simple form of *reliabilism*. Whereas reliabilism in its most basic form holds that one can gain knowledge through *any* reliable belief-forming process, the virtue epistemologist of this sort claims that only certain reliable belief-forming processes are knowledge-conducive (i.e. those which are epistemic virtues or cognitive faculties of the agent). In common with reliabilism, this form of virtue epistemology is a form of epistemic externalism, in that it holds that an agent can have knowledge simply by forming a true belief via one of her reliable cognitive faculties, even if she lacks good grounds to back up that belief. In contrast, there are versions of virtue epistemology that are allied to epistemic internalism rather than epistemic externalism, and so claim that it is essential that a knowing agent is able to offer good grounds in favour of what she believes. This form of virtue epistemology holds that it is essential that one gains one's true belief via one's epistemic virtues, the thinking being that one cannot correctly employ one's epistemic virtues without thereby acquiring good grounds in favour of what one believes. *See also* **cognitive faculties**; **epistemic virtues**; **reliabilism**.

GLOSSARY OF KEY EXAMPLES

Lucky punter (Ch. 1): Harry forms his belief that the horse Lucky Lass will win the next race purely on the basis that the name of the horse appeals to him. Luckily for Harry, his belief is true, in that Lucky Lass does win the next race.

The moral: Harry has a true belief, but he lacks knowledge; one can't gain knowledge that a horse will win a race by forming one's belief on this aesthetic basis. Hence, true belief is not sufficient for knowledge.

Broken clock (Ch. 3): John comes downstairs one morning and sees that the time on the grandfather clock in the hall says '8.20'. On this basis, John comes to believe that it is 8.20 a.m. This belief is true, since it is 8.20 a.m. Moreover, John's belief is justified in that it is based on excellent grounds. For example, John usually comes downstairs in the morning about this time, so he knows that what the grandfather clock says is roughly correct. Furthermore, this clock has been very reliable at telling the time for many years and John has no reason to think that it is faulty now. He thus has good reasons for thinking that the time on the clock is correct. Crucially, though, the clock is broken; it stopped 24 hours earlier at 8.20 a.m.

The moral: John has a justified true belief, but he lacks knowledge; one can't come to know what the time is by looking at a broken clock. Hence, justified true belief is not sufficient for knowledge. This is thus a Gettier case.

Hidden sheep (Ch. 3): Gayle, a farmer, forms her belief that there is a sheep in the field by looking at a shaggy dog which just happens to look very like a sheep. As it turns out, there is a sheep in the field, hidden from view behind the dog, and hence Gayle's belief is true. Moreover, her belief is justified too, since she has very good grounds for believing that there is a sheep in the field (the shaggy dog does look very like a sheep, after all).

The moral: Gayle has a justified belief, but she lacks knowledge, and so justified true belief is not sufficient for knowledge. This is thus a Gettier case. What is interesting about this Gettier case, however, is that Gayle doesn't seem to be making a false presupposition in gaining her true belief (as often happens in Gettier cases); rather, she just spontaneously forms the true belief that there is a sheep in the field.

Mr Phone Book (Ch. 5): Telly spends his days memorising as many phone numbers as he can from the phone book. In this way, he gains an awful lot of true beliefs. But Telly neither owns a phone (and has no intention of getting one), nor does he know anyone who has a phone. These true beliefs are thus completely useless to him.

The moral: Telly's passion for forming lots of true beliefs in this way seems irrational, and that seems to suggest that rationality is not merely a matter of maximising one's true beliefs.

Conscientious stooge (Ch. 5): Nell forms her belief with great care, and follows the epistemic norms of her community very closely. She has no reason to think that these norms are in any way epistemically faulty. Unfortunately, she has been taught the wrong epistemic norms (e.g. that one can determine a defendant's guilt by tossing a coin).

The moral: Nell's beliefs are (in one sense at least) responsibly formed, since she is doing the best she can by her lights, but given that she is following the wrong norms it is not clear that they are rational. *See* **deontic epistemic rationality**.

Trusting child (Ch. 5): Ethan is a small child who forms a belief that there is a toy in front of him because that is what he sees. He does see a toy, and so his belief is true, and circumstances are normal.

The moral: Arguably, Ethan knows that a toy is before him. If that's right, however, then it would seem to follow that knowledge does not require responsible, and thus rational, belief since Ethan merely believes what he sees and exercises no rational control over his believing. One could thus argue that this case shows that knowledge does not require even **deontic epistemic rationality**. Given that Ethan is unable to offer reasons in favour of his belief, this case also seems to lend support to **epistemic externalism**.

Chicken-sexer (Ch. 6): Chucky has an unusual natural trait in that by virtue of being raised around chickens, he is able to reliably distinguish between male and female chicks. But he doesn't have any good grounds that he can offer in favour of his beliefs. He doesn't, for example, know how he can distinguish between the chicks, nor does he know that he is reliable in this regard (though it is).

The moral: If you think that Chucky knows that, say, the chicks before him are of a different sex, then one will be very tempted to endorse epistemic externalism and so claim that knowledge does not require that the agent in question is able to offer good grounds in favour of his belief. In contrast, you might think that Chucky does not have knowledge in this case. If so, then you will be very tempted by the opposing proposal, epistemic internalism. In particular, you will probably think that the reason why Chucky lacks knowledge is because he is unable to offer good grounds in favour of his belief, where this is necessary for knowledge. *See* **epistemic externalism/internalism**.

Lost in the desert (Ch. 7): Beau is lost in the desert, and in his dehydrated state, he hallucinates that there is an oasis in front of him. Since this is just a mirage, Beau's experiences are not a good guide to the way the world is. But if Beau really had seen an oasis, his experiences would have been completely subjectively indistinguishable.

The moral: Cases like this seem to suggest that experiences fall short of the world in an important respect: whether one's experiences are a good guide to the world is not something that one can 'read' off the experiences themselves. Some philosophers conclude from this point that we should be indirect realists about perceptual knowledge and so treat such knowledge as essentially inferential. *See* **argument from illusion**; **direct realism**; **indirect realism**.

Restaurant bill (Ch. 14): You and your friend are both calculating your share of the restaurant bill. You each know that the other is an *epistemic peer*, which means that you are both equally knowledgeable about the matter in hand and have similar levels of relevant cognitive skills (e.g. at arithmetic). Nonetheless, you each reach a different conclusion about what your respective share of the bill is.

The moral: Cases like this seem to suggest that the mere presence of disagreement with an epistemic peer should lead you to downgrade your confidence in your opinions, to the point where you no longer regard yourself as having knowledge. Peer disagreement thus amounts to a defeater for your knowledge. *See* **conciliationism**; **defeater**; **peer disagreement**.

Brain in a vat (Ch. 21): Neo has been abducted, without him being aware of it. His brain has been removed from his body and is now floating in a vat hooked up to supercomputers. The supercomputers are 'feeding' him experiences which are, as far as he knows, an authentic guide to the external world. So, for example, he has experiences which seem to be about trips to see his friends, experiences which are completely illusory given that he is in fact floating in a vat.

The moral: Cases like this are often thought to lend support to radical scepticism. The reason for this is that there seems no way in which we could exclude the possibility that we are not being deceived in this way, yet if we were the victim of such a deception most of what we believe would not amount to knowledge. So what is our basis for supposing that we know a great deal about the external world right now? *See* **sceptical hypotheses**; **scepticism**.

index

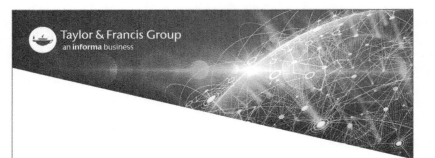